Practical Perforce

Laura Wingerd

O'REILLY®

Beijing · Cambridge · Farnham · Köln · Paris · Sebastopol · Taipei · Tokyo

Practical Perforce
by Laura Wingerd

Published by O'Reilly Media, Inc., 1005 Gravenstein Highway North, Sebastopol, CA 95472.

O'Reilly books may be purchased for educational, business, or sales promotional use. Online editions are also available for most titles (*safari.oreilly.com*). For more information, contact our corporate/institutional sales department: (800) 998-9938 or *corporate@oreilly.com*.

Editor:	Jonathan Gennick
Production Editor:	Adam Witwer
Cover Designer:	Karen Montgomery
Interior Designer:	David Futato

Printing History:

November 2005:	First Edition.

 This book uses RepKover™, a durable and flexible lay-flat binding.

ISBN: 0-596-10185-6
ISBN13: 978-0-596-10185-5
[M]   [02/07]

Table of Contents

Preface . . . . **vii**

1. Files in the Depot **1**
The Perforce Filespec Syntax   1
Browsing Depot Files   7
File Types at a Glance   15

2. Working with Files **17**
An Overview   17
Creating a Workspace   20
Synchronizing a Workspace   26
Local Syntax, Wildcard Expansion, and Special Characters   29
Working with Local Files   31
Working with Pending Changelists and Submitting Files   39
Removing and Restoring Files   44
Useful Recipes   46

3. Resolving and Merging Files **49**
Resolving: When, What, and How   49
How Perforce Merges Text Files   62
Reconciling Structural Changes   66
Tips for Smoother Collaboration   74
The Arcana of Merging   78

4. Branching and Integration **87**
The Classic Case for a Branch   88
Creating Branches   89
Integrating Changes from Branch to Branch   96

Reconciling Structural Changes 112
The Arcana of Integration 118

5. **Labels and Jobs** **127**
Saving Important Configurations 127
Using Labels 129
Using Jobs 137
Jobs as Changelist Markers 142

6. **Controlling and Automating Activity** **144**
Depot and File Access 144
Accessing Files in Other Domains 146
Saving and Restoring Specs 150
Change Notification and Change Monitoring 152
Scripting Tips 157
Behind-the-Scenes Version Control 163

7. **How Software Evolves** **167**
The Story of Ace Engineering 167
The Mainline Model 169
Ace Engineering Revisited 183
Containerizing 186

8. **Basic Codeline Management** **189**
Organizing Your Depot 189
General Care and Feeding of Codelines 199
Nightly Builds 205
Is Bug X Fixed in Codeline Y? 208

9. **Release Codelines** **216**
Creating a Release Codeline 216
Working in a Release Codeline 222
Integrating Changes into the Mainline 227
Making a Release 231
Distributing Releases 235
Breaking the Rules 237
Retiring a Release Codeline 240
Task Branches and Patch Branches 242

10. **Development Codelines** **249**
   Creating a Development Codeline   249
   Working in a Development Codeline   255
   Keeping a Development Codeline Up to Date   258
   Working with Third-Party Software   263
   Delivering Completed Development Work   267
   The Soft Codelines   275

11. **Staging Streams and Web Content** **282**
   Staging Web Content   282
   Visual Content Development   288
   Bug Fixes and Staging Streams   297
   Major Web Development   302

  A. **Setting Up a Perforce Test Environment** **305**

  B. **Perforce Terminology and P4 Commands** **311**

Bibliography **315**

Glossary **317**

Index **321**

Preface

What Is Perforce?

If you've picked up this book simply because of its riveting title, you may be wondering what Perforce is. Perforce is a *software configuration management* (SCM) system. SCM systems are used by software developers to keep track of all the software they build and all the components that go into it.

A good SCM system can explain the mysteries of software development and head off its disasters—mysteries like lost bug fixes, and disasters like botched file merges. In large-scale and commercial environments, good SCM is absolutely essential to producing good software.

It's All Software and We're All Software Developers

SCM was once concerned with files that computer programmers produced. Now it is concerned with files of all types that a business produces. Software, when viewed from the perspective of SCM, is any endeavor that calls a computer home. Documention, web content, spreadsheets, schematics, graphics, sound—it's *all* software. If it's stored in computer files and gets built, embedded, or packaged into a deliverable result, it's software. The term *software developer* may not sound like it applies to web content authors, graphic artists, test engineers, and technical writers, but for the purpose of this book, anyone whose work involves creating computer files from intellectual thought is a software developer.

Perforce, like all SCM systems, keeps track of changes as people do concurrent, parallel work on files. It logs activity; reports who did what; compares, merges, and branches files; and stores files and file configurations. Some of Perforce's most salient features are:

The depot

> Perforce stores files in a protected repository known as the *depot*. The depot is a centrally located, permanent archive of all file content submitted by users.[*]

Workspaces

> Perforce users work on files in *workspaces*, private disk areas of their own that contain copies of depot files. In this book we'll describe effective ways that developers can use workspaces, and we'll also discuss how workspaces can be used to automate nightly builds, release packaging, web staging, and other software production tasks.

Changelists

> Perforce *changelists* tie files changed together into single units of work. Every change to the depot can be traced to a changelist, and every changelist marks a known, reproducible state of the depot; the depot evolves as changelists are submitted. In the Perforce view of SCM, it is the changelist—not the file revision, nor the delta—that is the atomic transaction of software development. This book will discuss a variety of ways changelists can be used, including treating them as snapshots and using them to identify file dependencies.

Filespecs and views

> The Perforce *filespec* syntax, and the *views* that use it, allow selection of files for Perforce operations. Filespecs can define not only the common file collections, like directories, but arbitrary collections of files that constitute codelines, modules, delivery streams, and other containers. They are the key to treating collections of files as versioned objects that can be inspected, rolled back, branched, labeled, compared, and merged at any version.

Jobs

> In Perforce you can record externally defined tasks and states—bug reports, feature requests, and project milestones, for example—in objects it calls *jobs*. Jobs can be linked to changelists to provide a record of software changes related to tasks. Jobs are also the linchpin of any integration between Perforce and external systems, as we'll see in later chapters.

Branching

> Perforce uses *Inter-File Branching* to model file variants. In the traditional version tree branching model used by most SCM systems, a file can be branched and merged only into revisions of itself. In Perforce, any two files can have a branching relationship; branched files are peers, not offshoots, of their originals. A number of chapters in this book are dedicated to describing Perforce branching and its unexpectedly useful applications.

---

[*] The data format of the Perforce depot is not proprietary; it is, in fact, consistent with the RCS archive format. Because of this, there is a common misperception that Perforce is an RCS wrapper. It's not.

Integration history

In Perforce, branching and merging are referred to as *integration*. Perforce records a history of integration events and uses it to direct merges and prevent unnecessary remerging. In this book you'll see how Perforce does that and learn how to anticipate the effect of merges you perform.

Change tracking

Perforce combines filespecs, changelists, jobs, and integration history to track changes as they are merged from branch to branch. In this book you'll learn how these objects can be used to determine whether a change—a bug fix, for example—made in one branch has been merged to another, no matter how distantly related.

In addition to these features, which could be considered the interesting capabilities of Perforce, there are also the standard housekeeping and productivity features you're likely to find in any SCM system, including labels, triggers, change notification, graphical merge tools, file histories, and so forth.

The Perforce System in a Nutshell

Perforce is a client/server system (see Figure P-1). The domain of a Perforce system encompasses a master file repository (the depot), a database, and a constellation of users running client programs. One Perforce Server typically serves an entire Perforce domain. Its job is to communicate with Perforce client programs, analyze and execute user commands, archive and serve up file content, run event triggers, and record system activity in the Perforce database. It also performs a variety of database housekeeping tasks, some on demand and some automatically.

The client component of Perforce, shown in Figure P-2, manages workspace files and communicates with the server. It's implemented in a variety of tools designed for users at almost every technical level.

Perforce client tools can be divided roughly into three categories:

Graphical user interfaces

The Perforce GUIs are the point-and-click client applications. This category includes P4V, P4Win, and P4Web. (The latter is actually more of a plug-in, but because it turns your browser into a Perforce GUI it is marketed as a GUI itself.) Although they don't support every possible Perforce command, the GUIs do support the day-to-day operations of the typical software developer, and they are easy on the eyes. They also provide a variety of data-mining features, including some very nice visualizations of branching and file evolution. For these reasons, even die-hard command-line adherents find them useful. P4V, P4Win, and P4Web can be used interchangeably, although there are some variations in the range of operations they support. All three come with embedded help files that provide rudimentary coaching in how to use Perforce.

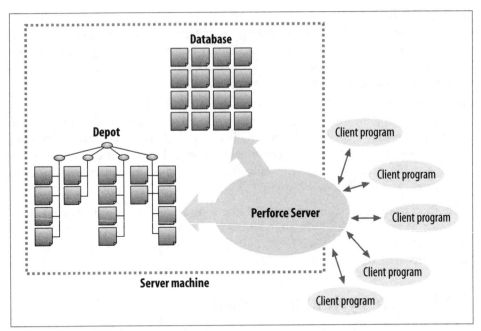

Figure P-1. The Perforce client/server system

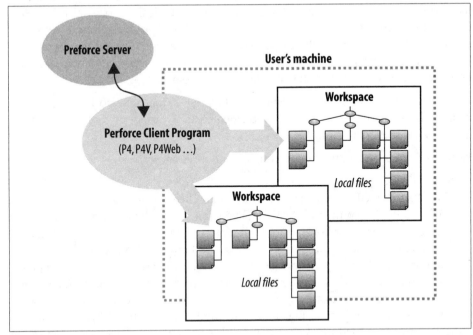

Figure P-2. The Perforce client component

Plug-ins

The Perforce plug-ins category consists of client programs that run behind the scenes, usually on the user's machine, to enable other applications to work with Perforce. The most widely used is the Perforce SCC Plug-in, which integrates Perforce with Visual Studio .NET. (That's SCC as in Microsoft Source Code Control API; any Windows application that supports the Microsoft SCC API is likely to work just fine with the Perforce SCC Plug-in.)

As Perforce's popularity grows, plug-ins are emerging that wed less technical applications to Perforce. P4FTP, for example, makes Perforce transparent to people using applications that rely on FTP, and P4Report turns the Perforce database into an ODBC data source for Windows spreadsheet and database tools.

Programmable clients

The programmable interfaces to Perforce are P4 and P4API. P4, the Perforce Command-Line Client, can be used in interactive shells and in scripts. It's the canonical client program—if you can't do it with P4, it can't be done. P4API, the Perforce C/C++ API, is available to embed the client component in applications, scripting languages, and other software. P4 and P4API run on all the operating system platforms Perforce supports—and there are a lot of them—and they support all Perforce operations, including administrative and privileged operations.

Why Perforce?

The features and capabilities of an SCM system are important, but equally so is its ability to meet expectations and thrive in its habitat. Perforce runs as a self-reliant, self-contained system, and you don't need other software or hardware components installed to use it. Unlike many other SCM systems, Perforce fits into almost any computing environment, thanks to the following features:

Speed

Perforce is fast. It doesn't make developers wait to check out, check in, compare, or update files, and it doesn't add a processing burden to developers' machines.

Centralized repository

In the Perforce system, there is one centralized repository per domain for files and SCM data. Very large companies may have several Perforce domains, but that's typically an organizational choice, not a limitation of domain size. (Perforce domains at some large companies are known to encompass over 1,000 users each.) While it may be argued that a centralized repository puts your SCM system at risk of a single point of failure, that risk is vastly outweighed by several advantages. First, you have only one machine per domain to take care of to protect your assets. Second, you don't have to worry about where your assets are. Office moves and machine upgrades don't perturb your central SCM repository. And third, as long as your central SCM server is running, all your users have access to it. The failure of one machine doesn't impede SCM access for users elsewhere in your system.

No external database required

Some SCM systems require you to configure and administer an external database system like SQL Server or MySQL. Perforce provides its own database. When you install Perforce, you're installing a reliable, self-contained database, customized for Perforce SCM.

Because the Perforce database can't be accessed by any other means than the Perforce Server, there's not much that can go wrong. It does require that the system administrator schedule regular checkpoints and backups, but other than that, very little hands-on administration is required. Database recovery performed after a disk failure or other misfortune can be done manually by the system administrator or through automated tools. Perforce provides tools for checkpointing, for recovery, and for automatically upgrading the database when a new release is installed.

No reliance on networked file sharing

Some SCM tools rely on networked file sharing (NFS) of one kind or another. NFS is not an ideal solution for SCM; network file sharing can be slow, and make it difficult for the SCM tool to handle file format differences. (Have you ever opened up a file in Notebook only to see all its lines running together? Or opened up a file in vi and seen ^M characters at the end of every line?) NFS is also very machine-dependent; clock synchronization and other interoperability issues make version control difficult.

Perforce does not use NFS. Instead, it does its own file transport using TCP/IP. This approach gives it control over the files it cares about and, because TCP/IP is so universally supported, makes it capable of running on more operating system platforms.

No HTTP server required

Some SCM systems require you to configure an HTTP server, like Apache or IIS, to perform the duties of an SCM server. Perforce provides its own server and runs independently of your web servers.

Traditionally, software development organizations were formed of developers working together at the same company, at the same location. Most SCM systems, including Perforce, are suited for that kind of organization. But Perforce has built-in features that make it suitable for nontraditional teams, including teams formed of developers who work outside of the office, developers who work in separate divisions, and even developers who work for completely different companies:

Process impartiality

Perforce imposes almost no built-in workflow or process rules. It's designed with certain software development activities in mind (all of which will be discussed in later chapters), but it can accommodate almost any procedure or methodology. Any workflow or process you have established (or that you would like to establish) can be automated with Perforce.

File types

While some SCM systems have restrictions on handling certain file types, Perforce can store and manage text files, binary files, Unicode files, native Apple files on the Macintosh, Mac resource forks, and Unix symlinks in its repository.

Product distribution and vendor drops

The Perforce Server can access file repositories in other Perforce domains. This makes a seamless, Perforce-to-Perforce distribution of software products possible. In other words, you can distribute your product directly from your Perforce repository to other organizations, as long as they have Perforce, too. And you can receive vendor drops from other organizations directly from their Perforce repositories. In fact, you can even branch or merge files from their repositories directly into yours. All the while, a history of what you've released and received is being collected and recorded in your SCM database.

Firewalls and tunnels

As mentioned, Perforce uses TCP/IP to communicate between its components. The firewall that prevents external access to machines inside your network also prevents access to your Perforce repository. However, that doesn't mean that all your developers have to be inside your firewall. Perforce can be used in a Virtual Private Network (VPN), when one has been created, and authorized users can use Secure Shell (SSH) to tunnel through a firewall with Perforce commands. The advantage here is that you can extend your SCM—and hence your software development projects—to participants all over the world without having to give them direct access to your machines or intranet.

For a commercial product, Perforce is unusually accessible. Many new users are lured to Perforce simply because it's so much easier to get started with it than it is with any other SCM system:

Easy to install

Unlike open source software, which generally has to be configured and built, Perforce tools are executable out of the box. By comparison, CVS and Subversion may be free, but they aren't free of the problems of building open source software. If you've ever been down the rabbit hole of trying to find, configure, compile, and install all the components in the dependency chain of an open source tool, you'll appreciate the simplicity of getting Perforce up and running. It's literally a 10-minute job: you download a couple of binary files, run one to start up a server, and run the other as your client-side interface to it.

Runs everywhere

Perforce runs on a huge variety of operating system platforms. Your laptop, the fully loaded machine at your office, the discount PC in your child's room, the old VAX you found on the sidewalk on trash collection day, even the ground-breaking new operating system you're developing—chances are very good that there's a version of Perforce that runs on it.* Since its inception, Perforce Software has made a point of porting its tools to as many platforms as possible. That's been relatively easy to do, because the core components of Perforce are small, standalone programs. And to this day, every version of Perforce ever released can be downloaded for free—in prebuilt, executable form, no less—from the Perforce FTP site.

Costs nothing to try

You can download all Perforce software and documentation for free, without having to talk to a sales rep or even fill out a form on the Web. The software you download is fully functional; it's the vendor's intent that you try Perforce and really see whether it meets your needs before you commit to buying it. If you want to test-drive Perforce in an environment with more than two users, Perforce Software will give you a limited-term license for as many users as you need. So instead of spending time in meetings arguing with everyone else about whether Perforce will meet your needs, you and your colleagues can spend time actually trying it out.

Easy budget planning

It's easy to plan a budget for Perforce. How many developers will you have? That's what you'll be paying for. Perforce is priced per user, regardless of what they're doing and the environments in which they're working.

All-inclusive pricing

Once you've paid for Perforce, you can download and run as many server programs as you need, on as many operating systems as you have, as long as you don't exceed the number of users you've paid for. You can run your servers anywhere in the world, and any of your users can use any of your servers (if you allow them to). The price you pay includes all of the Perforce client programs, plug-ins, and tools.

Free to students, hermits, and saints

In fact, if you're going to use Perforce for educational purposes—you're teaching a programming class, or developing software for a school project, for example—the vendor will provide you with a free license to cover as many users as are involved. Just contact Perforce Software and let them know about your project.

---

* The Perforce web site used to boast that "if the client program doesn't run on your platform, we'll port it there." Paradoxically, while compatibility with exotic, leading-edge platforms gave Perforce a foot up in the SCM market, the market itself has become more homogeneous. Today, established Windows and Linux operating systems seem to be the preferred platforms for even the newest software technology projects.

You need a license, by the way, only if you have more than two users accessing your Perforce repository. That means that if you're working on a software development project all on your own, or with just one other person, you can use Perforce for free, forever. And if you are one of the saints developing open source software for no remuneration, you can get a free Perforce license to cover you and everyone else working on your project.

About This Book

This book is written with a particular reader in mind. The reader is familiar with SCM in general, and is most likely a programmer, a project manager, or a build engineer involved with software development. This book is written especially for the reader who wears more than one of those hats on the job and is responsible for some or all of the interconnection between the roles they represent. If you're pursuing better ways to keep it all connected, and are interested in seeing how Perforce fits in, this book is for you.

One purpose of this book is to present Perforce's potential as a software configuration management tool. This is a strictly academic purpose—you need not be a Perforce user to gain insight from it. Anyone interested in comparative SCM will find worthwhile material in this book.

The second purpose of this book is to help Perforce users understand *why* Perforce works the way it does. Most users come to this level of understanding on their own eventually; it is the level of understanding that prompts them to post "Aha!" messages to online Perforce discussions. This level of understanding also makes the difference between simply using Perforce to do what any SCM system can do and exploiting Perforce to accomplish what other systems can't. This book will get you to that level sooner.

There are two parts to this book:

- Part I (Chapters 1–6) describes Perforce commands and concepts. It's not a tutorial, nor is it a reference—it's more of a whirlwind technical tour. It will provide you with a baseline knowledge about fundamental Perforce operations.
- Part II (Chapters 7–11) describes the big picture, using Perforce in a collaborative software development environment. It outlines recommended best practices and shows how to implement them with the Perforce operations you were introduced to in Part I.

 The examples in this book are based on Perforce 2005.1, although some features new to Release 2005.2 are covered as well.

What's Not in This Book

This book contains no tutorials, no hands-on exercises, and no getting-started guides. Although it does contain numerous examples of basic and advanced commands, this book is not meant to be a primary source of instruction for new Perforce users. The role of this book is to complement the existing product manuals with tips and ideas for using Perforce to its full advantage.

This book doesn't document actual case studies. It's almost impossible to describe actual case studies without detail-laden examples that put a reader right to sleep. So we've foresaken realism on the principle that simple, readable examples can be extrapolated to complicated, real-world solutions more easily than simple solutions can be inferred from painstakingly realistic examples.

This book won't address industry standards, benchmarks, or certification models, although it will surely be of use to practioners of such standards. Perforce's strength is in its versatility and accessibility. It makes a robust foundation for a compliance process, but it does not itself enforce compliance.

This book is rather light on system administration issues. Perforce is a tool you can use to great effect without knowing anything about installation, security, backups, upgrades, migration, or performance. When you do need to know about these things, you'll find the Perforce manuals and other materials that are readily available at the Perforce Software web site to be a rich resource.

This book doesn't start with a chapter explaining SCM. There was a time when SCM was arcane and indistinct, but those days are gone, and the world now abounds with books and web sites designed to bring novices up to speed.

Additional Reading

Software configuration management, as a topic, is finally conquering measurable shelf space in the computer section of bookstores. A number of SCM issues and challenges have been fully explored by other writers, and this book won't retread that ground. If you're a complete SCM novice, you might want to take a look at some of the introductory or complementary titles available, including:

Real World Software Configuration Management, by Sean Kenefick (APress)
> If software configuration management is in your job description, this book is for you. It's a no-nonsense explanation of SCM best practices with down-to-earth advice about getting going and sticking with them.

Software Configuration Management Patterns: Effective Teamwork, Practical Integration, by Steve Berczuk with Brad Appleton (Addison Wesley)
> This is a concept book that manages to be quite practical nevertheless. Its detailed analyses of SCM problems and solutions are for the most part

independent of any particular SCM system. It also offers a comprehensive comparison of the terminology used by contemporary SCM systems.

Configuration Management: The Missing Link in Web Engineering, by Susan Dart (Artech)
This wide-ranging survey of risk management and return on investment includes brief case studies of a variety of SCM systems in use.

Open Source Development with CVS, by Karl Fogel and Moshe Bar (Paraglyph)
This very readable book combines a detailed guide to using CVS with an interesting discussion of its history and its application in open source projects. It's a good source of insight into how today's SCM terminology and usage conventions have evolved from their earliest progenitors.

Software Configuration Management Strategies and Rational ClearCase, by Brian A. White (Addison Wesley)
With its in-depth coverage of the ClearCase view of problems and solutions, this book presents an interesting contrast to SCM with Perforce.

The Pragmatic Programmer, by Andrew Hunt and David Thomas (Addison Wesley)
Not about SCM per se, this book touches on many software development practices that harmonize with good SCM.

Finally, while this book will teach you about Perforce, it won't teach you about all the Perforce commands, command forms, and command options available to you. For that level of detail, go to the Perforce web site and check out the following product manuals:

The Perforce Command Reference
An A-to-Z reference to P4 commands. You may wish to bookmark this manual and refer to it to find out more about—or alternatives to—the command forms and options shown in *Practical Perforce*.

The P4 User's Guide
A detailed guide to using Perforce for working with files. This manual is geared toward end users and uses P4 commands in its examples. Consult this manual for in-depth information about the Perforce user environment and a variety of typical developer tasks.

The Perforce System Administrator's Guide
A detailed guide to setting up a Perforce Server and managing a Perforce system. Consult this manual for in-depth information on backups, security, triggers, scripting, job customization, review daemons, performance, and OS-specific issues.

The online versions of these and other Perforce product manuals are available free at *http://www.perforce.com/perforce/technical.html*. You can also buy bound, hard copy versions of the same manuals; check the web site for details.

Conventions Used in This Book

This book uses the following typographic conventions:

- `Constant width` is used for names of commands, command fragments, and command options.
- *Italic* is used for filenames and for characters used in the context of file identifiers.
- Button labels in graphical application windows are shown in regular text, and are often intercapped.
- Menu → Item → Item represents sequential selections in graphical application menus.
- Examples that show commands as they are typed, but that do not show command output, look like this:

    ```
    type this command
    ```

- Examples that show commands as they are typed, and that show command output as well, look like this:

    ```
    type this command
    and you will see
    output that looks like this
    ```

- Examples that show the contents of files and scripts look like this:

    ```
    these are lines
    that appear in
    a file
    ```

- Examples of Perforce *spec forms* look like this:

    ```
    Field1          value1
    Field2          value2
    ```

In addition, the following formats are used to grab your attention and relieve the tedium of what could otherwise be monotonous reading:

  Indicates a tip, suggestion, or general advice.

  Indicates a warning or caution.

Using Code Examples

This book is here to help you get your job done. In general, you may use the code in this book in your programs and documentation. You do not need to contact us for permission unless you're reproducing a significant portion of the code. For example, writing a program that uses several chunks of code from this book does not require permission. Selling or distributing a CD-ROM of examples from O'Reilly books *does* require permission. Answering a question by citing this book and quoting example code does not require permission. Incorporating a significant amount of example code from this book into your product's documentation *does* require permission.

We appreciate, but do not require, attribution. An attribution usually includes the title, author, publisher, and ISBN. For example: *"Practical Perforce,* by Laura Wingerd. Copyright © 2006 O'Reilly Media, Inc., 0-596-10185-6."

If you feel that your use of code examples falls outside fair use or the permission given here, feel free to contact us at *permissions@oreilly.com.*

Safari® Enabled

 When you see a Safari® Enabled icon on the cover of your favorite technology book, that means the book is available online through the O'Reilly Network Safari Bookshelf.

Safari offers a solution that's better than e-books. It's a virtual library that lets you easily search thousands of top tech books, cut and paste code samples, download chapters, and find quick answers when you need the most accurate, current information. Try it for free at *http://safari.oreilly.com.*

How to Contact Us

We have tested and verified the information in this book to the best of our ability, but you may find that features have changed or that we have made mistakes. If so, please notify us by writing to:

O'Reilly Media, Inc.
1005 Gravenstein Highway North
Sebastopol, CA 95472
(800) 998-9938 (in the United States or Canada)
(707) 829-0515 (international or local)
(707) 829-0104 (FAX)

You can also send messages electronically. To be put on the mailing list or request a catalog, send email to:

info@oreilly.com

To ask technical questions or comment on the book, send email to:

bookquestions@oreilly.com

We have a web site for this book, where you can find examples and errata (previously reported errors and corrections are available for public view there). You can access this page at:

http://www.oreilly.com/catalog/practicalperforce

Acknowledgments

Practical Perforce couldn't have been written without the participation and encouragement of many people. I thank Christopher Seiwald, creator of Perforce the product and Perforce the company, for seeing the value in this project from its outset. I thank Kathy Baldanza for coaxing early drafts out of me and asking painful questions like "How's that book coming?" I thank everyone who reviewed the drafts (especially Jason Kao!) for catching so many of my dumb mistakes. I thank Jonathan Gennick at O'Reilly for making the endgame painless. And I thank Chris Comparini for making many hours spent sitting with a laptop a pleasant and companionable experience.

Above all, I thank the many people—users, customers, consultants, colleagues, and friends—who have indulged my compulsion to talk—at trade shows, at conferences, at the office, and at parties—about how SCM works in general and how Perforce pays off in particular. Their stories, their diagrams, and their sharp insights have shaped my ideas. They are the "we" in this book, the voice that narrates the knowledge I've tried to impart.

CHAPTER 1

Files in the Depot

This chapter describes how Perforce stores files and directories in its repository, the depot. It starts by introducing the syntax that allows you to work with depot files and follows with examples of how to browse the depot and get information. Finally, it touches on file properties and their effect on how Perforce handles file content internally.

 You may be happiest using a GUI (graphical user interface) for your day-to-day work. This book, however, bases most of its examples on P4, the Perforce Command-Line Client. One reason we stick with P4 is simply that it's easier to create and write about text examples than it is to create and write about screenshots. So don't take our bias toward P4 as a snub of the Perforce GUI programs. In fact, we'll point out some P4V features that show you at a glance what P4 would take thousands of lines of output to tell you. On the other hand, the GUIs are somewhat limited—only P4 offers the complete lexicon of Perforce commands. So, while you are encouraged to use a GUI, expect to use the command line from time to time to do the things the GUIs don't do.

The Perforce Filespec Syntax

Perforce is widely used partly because it is so portable, and part of that portability comes from the platform-independent file syntax it provides. While native platform syntax can be used to refer to workspace files, Perforce provides its own uniform syntax for referring to workspace and depot contents. This syntax is known as a *file specifier*, or "filespec." A filespec can refer to a single file or a collection of files, to a specific revision or a range of revisions, and to depot files or workspace files. More importantly, the filespec syntax applies to all operating systems; Perforce converts filespecs to native file references for local operations.

The depot hierarchy

Depots, where Perforce keeps master file content, and workspaces, where users work on files, are hierarchical structures of directories and files. A filespec uses "//" to indicate the root of the hierarchy, and "/" as a directory path and filename separator. For example:

```
//depot/projectA/doc/index.html
```

Although we often refer to an entire repository as "the depot," there can be multiple depots in a Perforce repository. The filespec root identifies the name of the depot. The filespec *//depot/projectA/doc/index.html* refers to a depot named "depot" (see Figure 1-1).

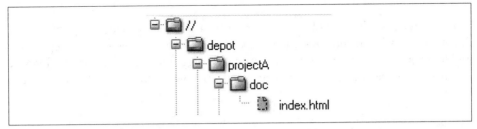

Figure 1-1. Filespecs and the depot hierarchy

A filespec can express a relative path as well as an absolute path. An unrooted filespec is a relative reference to the current directory (if you're using a command shell) or the current folder (if you're using a GUI). Depending on the context, *doc/ index.html* or even just *index.html* could indicate the same file. In the Chapter 2 section "Local Syntax, Wildcard Expansion, and Special Characters," you'll find out how to use relative references to files and directories.

Wildcards and file collections

When filespecs contain wildcards, they define entire collections of files instead of single files. For example, the "*" wildcard matches characters in filenames at a directory level. Depending what files are actually present, a filespec like *projectA/d*/*. html*, for example, can define a collection of files like:

```
projectA/dev/index.html
projectA/doc/diagnostics.html
projectA/doc/index.html
```

The "..." wildcard (pronounced "dot-dot-dot") matches filename characters at or below a directory level. A filespec that ends in /..., in other words, is a succinct reference to the complete collection of files in a directory hierarchy. For example, *projectA/...* refers to the files in the *projectA* directory. Depending on what's in the directory, the filespec *projectA/...* might represent the following files:

```
projectA/bin/win32/app.exe
projectA/bin/win32/app.dll
projectA/dev/index.html
projectA/dev/main.cpp
projectA/doc/app/index.html
projectA/doc/app/reference.html
projectA/doc/diagnostics.html
projectA/doc/index.html
```

Views and mappings

A filespec is a special case of the Perforce construct called a *view*. The Perforce database stores views for a variety of uses, including access permissions, labels, branching, triggers, and change reviews. The scope of every Perforce operation is constrained by the views that affect it.

Some of the views involved—filespec views, or workspace views, for example—are evident to users. Some views, however, like those that define access permissions, are not. For example, consider the P4 command that shows the history of changes to HTML files in the *//depot* path:

```
p4 changes //depot/.../*.html
Change 1386 on 2005/06/10 ... 'New page for promo...'
Change 1375 on 2005/06/05 ... 'Fix links on sign-up...'
Change 1369 on 2005/05/29 ... 'Add press releases...'
```

This command is affected by two views. The first is the filespec you see on the command line. The second is a view you don't see: the set of depot files you have permission to access. If, for instance, the access permission view is

```
//depot/projectA/...
//depot/projectB/...
```

the net effect is that you will see the history of the files in the *intersection* of the two views. In other words, you will see the history of the set of files defined by this view:

```
//depot/projectA/.../*.html
//depot/projectB/.../*.html
```

Views are also used to map files to each other. Client workspace views, for example, map depot files to workspace files, as you'll see in Chapter 2. In Chapter 4 you'll see how view mapping comes into play to relate branches to one another.

File and directory revisions

Perforce stores file versions in a sequence of numbered revisions. Figure 1-2 illustrates the revisions of *//depot/projectA/doc/index.html*. A filespec can refer to an absolute, numbered file revision, prefixed with "#". For example, *index.html#10* is the tenth revision of *index.html*.

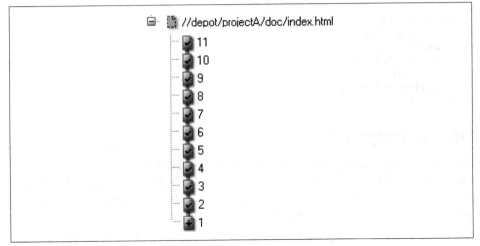

Figure 1-2. Revisions of a single file

Filespecs can also refer to dates and labels, prefixed with @. For example, *index. html@2004/11/21* is the revision of *index.html* as of November 21, 2004.

You can refer to directories by date as well. The filespec *//depot/projectA/...@2004/11/21* refers to the collection of files that made up the *//depot/projectA* directory as of November 21, 2004.

Two kinds of revision specifiers can be used in Perforce. One kind is the absolute revision. For instance, in this filespec

    doc/index.html#14

the *#14* is a an absolute revision. It refers to the fourteenth revision of the file named *doc/index.html*.

Absolute revisions can't be used with directories. (A filespec like *doc/...#14* refers to the fourteenth revision of each and every file in the *doc* directory, not to the fourteenth revision of the directory.) However, you can use any of the symbolic revisions with both files and directories. For example, *#head* is a symbolic revision that refers to the newest, most up-to-date revision of a file or directory. For example:

    doc/...#head

Perforce's reserved-word symbolic revisions are delimited by the character "#". Other symbolic revisions are delimited by "@." Dates, as you saw previously, are an example of the latter:

    doc/...@2004/01/04

Labels can also be used as symbolic revisions. (You'll see how to create labels in Chapter 5.) A label can be used to refer to file revisions to which it has been applied:

    doc/...@Good2Go

There are also symbolic revisions you can use to refer to files in a workspace, as you'll see in Chapter 2.

Dates, Times, and Perforce

In a filespec, the date 2004/11/21 is actually shorthand for 2004/11/21:00:00:00. Saying *index.html@2004/11/21* refers to the revision of *index.html as of* November 21 is slightly misleading. It refers to the latest revision of the file as of *the commencement* of November 21, 2004.

Dates and times in Perforce are always relative to the Perforce Server. The revision *2004/11/21:12:00:00*, for example, specifies 12 noon on 21 November 2004 *in the server's time zone.* (See Appendix A.)

Changes and changelists

Perforce uses *changelists* to track changes submitted to the depot. Changelists are numbered; when a changelist number is used as a symbolic revision, it refers to revisions that were newest at the moment the change occured. For example,

```
doc/...@3405
```

refers to the head revisions of the *doc* directory files at the moment changelist 3405 was submitted.

You'll notice in the preceding examples that the rightmost element of the filespec—exclusive of the revision specifier—is a filename, or a wildcard that matches a set of filenames. Perforce's filespecs always refer to files, not directories. In fact, there are no Perforce commands that operate on directories. This is not to say you can't organize your files into directories, or restore older versions of directories, or get the history of a directory. After all, when a Perforce command operates on the collection of files in a directory, it is in fact updating a directory. But in Perforce you don't explicitly create or version directories; it just happens automatically.*

In Perforce, a directory's revision (and its very existence, in fact) is construed from the file revisions it contains. You saw how file revisions can be identified by dates and changelists as well as by absolute revision numbers. Actually, you can refer to *any* file in the depot with *any* changelist number. Changelists represent points in time at which users submitted files. If you plot file changes over time, left to right, you'll see that changelist numbers slice file collections vertically—every changelist number is associated with a unique state of the collection.

---

* Yes, this *is* a bit of a challenge to the Perforce plug-ins. They bend over backward to support applications that think repository directories have to be created before new files can be added.

Consider the collection of files shown in Figure 1-3, for example. Here we see that in changelist @100, *foo.c* was added, creating *foo.c#1*. In changelist @114, *foo.c* was updated, creating *@foo.c#2*, and *bar.c* was deleted, creating *bar.c#2* (a deleted revision). *ola.c*, which was created in changelist @105, was unaffected by changelist @114. Therefore, revision @114 refers to this collection of files:

```
foo.c#2
bar.c#2
ola.c#1
```

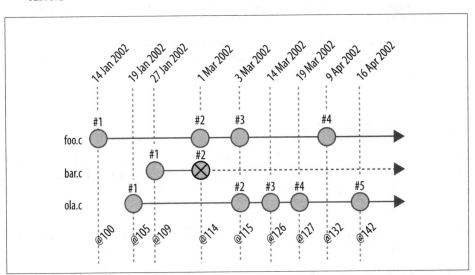

Figure 1-3. A collection of files changing over time

Note that labeling the time axis in a diagram like this with both dates and changelist numbers is redundant. Because changelists can't overlap—each marks a unique point in time—the sequence of Perforce changelists *is* a representation of time. It often makes just as much sense (and less clutter) to chart file evolution along the changelist axis, as we see in Figure 1-4.

The sequence of changelists associated with file revisions in a collection is, in fact, a history of the collection. And when a collection is a directory, the sequence of changelists associated with it is the history of the directory. If the *projectA* directory contains only the files shown in Figure 1-3, for example, collapsing the diagram into a single timeline would show the history of *projectA*. We see this in Figure 1-5.

In the next section you'll see how to list and compare directory revisions. Later chapters will show how directory revisions can be used for populating workspaces and in branching and merging operations.

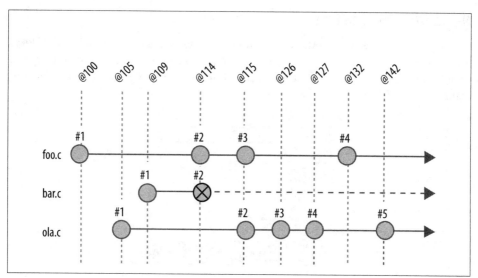

Figure 1-4. The changelist axis

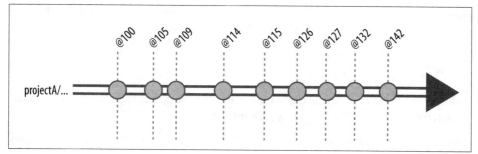

Figure 1-5. The history of a directory

Browsing Depot Files

You can do extensive browsing in a Perforce depot without having to set up a work-space of your own. In fact, there is very little reason to reproduce depot files locally just to see their contents. You can explore the depot hierarchy, peruse file history, read change descriptions, examine file content, and compare depot files, without going to the trouble of setting up a workspace.

Many of the examples that follow are from the Perforce Public Depot. You, too, can browse the Public Depot by connecting to *public.perforce.com:1666* (see Appendix A). However, some of the outputs shown here have been somewhat abridged to shorten line lengths and reduce clutter. If you connect to the Public Depot and try these com-mands for yourself, you'll get more verbose results.

Navigating the file tree

The depot is a file tree, and the easiest way to navigate it is with a GUI. With P4V, for example, all you have to do is point and click to step down the tree and expand its subdirectories (or folders, as they're called in P4V). A P4V depot tree is shown in Figure 1-6.

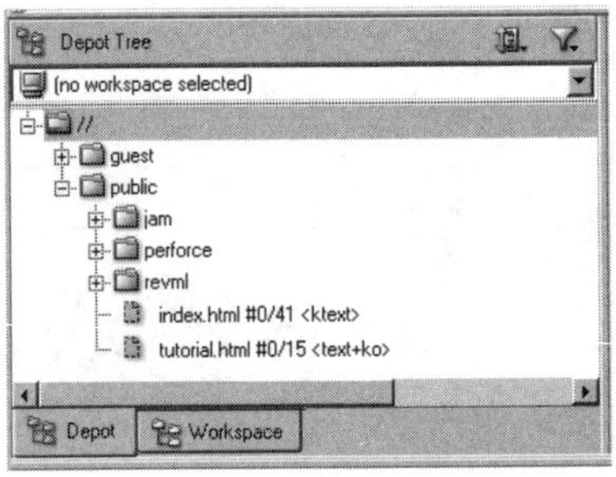

Figure 1-6. Navigating the depot tree in P4V

However, you can also navigate from the command line, using P4. To list the top-most levels of the tree, for example, use this dirs command:

```
p4 dirs "//*"
//guest
//public
```

Notice that the dirs argument is quoted—that's so the command shell won't expand the asterisk before passing it to the p4 command.

Another way to show the top level of the depot hierarchy is with the depots command:

```
p4 depots
Depot guest  'Depot for guest users. '
Depot public 'Perforce's open source depot. '
```

Listing directories

The dirs command can be used at any level of the depot tree to list the subdirectories at that level. For example:

```
p4 dirs "//public/*"
//public/jam
//public/perforce
//public/revml
```

Listing directory history

The changes command shows the history of a directory, listing the most recent changes first:

```
p4 changes -m5 //public/revml/...
Change 4971 on 2005/05/21 ... '- Added test to make sure big_r'
Change 4970 on 2005/05/21 ... '- Allow sdbm files to handle la'
Change 4969 on 2005/05/21 ... '- Added a special command line '
Change 4968 on 2005/05/21 ... '- Use module name instead of lo'
Change 4967 on 2005/05/21 ... '- Removed "-d", leaving only "-'
```

(The -m5 flag restricts the output to the five most recent changes. Each change is identified with a changelist number and the first 30-odd characters of a description. If you want to see entire descriptions, use changes -l.)

In P4V you can use Folder History to see the history of a directory, as Figure 1-7 shows.

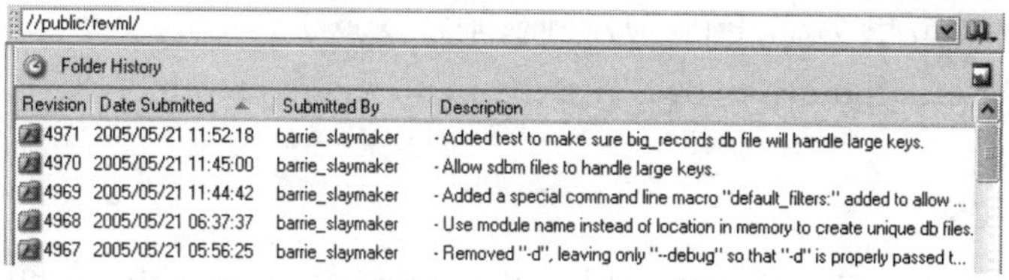

Figure 1-7. Using P4V to browse the history of a directory

What's in a changelist?

In addition to marking points in time, changelists also record the files that were changed and the user who changed them. You can show the details of a changelist with the describe command:

```
p4 describe -s 4417
Change 4417 by barrie on 2004/08/19 20:11:50
  - Adapt to "estimated values" messages
  - Adapt to more accurate test suite
Affected files ...
... //public/revml/bin/gentrevml#56 edit
... //public/revml/lib/VCP/TestUtils.pm#65 edit
... //public/revml/t/91cvs2revml.t#16 edit
... //public/revml/t/91vss2revml.t#7 edit
... //public/revml/t/95cvs2p4.t#30 edit
```

(The -s flag suppresses diff output. If you use describe without it, you'll get a diff of every file in the changelist!)

Listing files and file information

You can list the files in a directory with the `files` command:

```
p4 files "//public/revml/*"
//public/revml/CHANGES#81 - edit change 3640 (text)
//public/revml/MANIFEST#45 - edit change 4234 (text)
//public/revml/ui.png#1 - add change 3671 (binary)
//public/revml/ui.ps#1 - add change 3671 (text)
```

Each line of output gives a bit of information about the file revision shown. For example, *//public/revml/CHANGES#81* is a text file, last edited in change 3640.

You can list files in subdirectories recursively, using "..." with the `files` command:

```
p4 files //public/revml/...
//public/revml/CHANGES#81 - edit change 3640 (text)
//public/revml/MANIFEST#45 - edit change 4234 (text)
//public/revml/bin/analyze_profile#2 - edit change 2679 (xtext)
//public/revml/bin/compile_dtd#1 - add change 2454 (xtext)
//public/revml/dist/vcp.exe#10 - edit change 4233 (xbinary)
//public/revml/dist/vcp.pl#4 - add change 4235 (xtext)
```

(Note that the `dirs` command, by contrast, has no recursive form.)

Finding files

As you can see, the `files` command has the potential to yield thousands of lines of output. If you're looking for a particular file, you can use wildcards to pare down the results. For example, here we're looking for files named *index.html*:

```
p4 files "//public/revml/.../index.html"
//public/revml/docs/html/index.html#2 - edit change 2307 (text)
//public/revml/product/release/0.90/html/index.html#1 - add change 4344 (text)
//public/revml/product/release/1.0.0/html/index.html#1 - add change 4311 (text)
```

Perusing file history and file origins

You can use either `changes` or `filelog` to see a file's history. The output of `changes` is the same for a file as for a directory:

```
p4 changes //public/revml/dist/vcp.pl
Change 4235 on 2004/03/18 by barrie '- experimental dist/vcp.pl'
Change 4023 on 2003/12/11 by barrie '- Remove outdated "fat"'
Change 1859 on 2002/05/24 by barrie 'fat script version '
Change 1738 on 2002/04/30 by barrie 'Add "fat" script '
```

The `filelog` output, by comparison, shows file revision numbers and the action (add, delete, and so on) that took place at each revision:

```
p4 filelog //public/revml/dist/vcp.pl
//public/revml/dist/vcp.pl
... #4 change 4235 add    'experimental dist/vcp.pl'
... #3 change 4023 delete 'Remove outdated "fat" '
```

```
... #2 change 1859 edit    'fat script version '
... #1 change 1738 add     'Add "fat" script '
```

(You'll also see date, user, and file type information in `filelog` output. They've been removed here to make lines fit on the page.)

Normally `changes` and `filelog` limit their scope to the file you specify. However, files that have been renamed, cloned, or branched from other files inherit the history of their ancestors. You can use the -i flag with `changes` and `filelog` to show inherited[*] history:

```
p4 filelog -i //public/revml/lib/VCP/Dest/texttable.pm
//public/revml/lib/VCP/Dest/texttable.pm
... #5 change 4506 edit    '- testtable handled undef field'
... #4 change 4496 edit    '- minor POD cleanups to prevent'
... #3 change 4488 edit    '- BFD and Text::Table no longer'
... #2 change 4037 edit    '- VCP::Dest::texttable function'
... ... branch into //guest/timothee_besset/lib/VCP/Dest/texttable.pm#1
... #1 change 4036 branch '- VCP::Dest::texttable created.'
... ... branch from //public/revml/lib/VCP/Dest/csv.pm#1,#4
//public/revml/lib/VCP/Dest/csv.pm
... #4 change 4021 edit    '- Remove all phashes and all ba'
... ... branch into //guest/timothee_besset/lib/VCP/Dest/csv.pm#1
... ... branch into //public/revml/lib/VCP/Dest/texttable.pm#1
... #3 change 4012 edit    '- Remove dependance on pseudoha'
... #2 change 3946 edit    '- VCP::Source::vss now parses h'
... #1 change 3828 add     '- VCP::Dest::csv dumps rev meta'
```

P4V's `Revision Graph` gives you a bird's-eye view of a file's inherited history, as you can see in Figure 1-8.

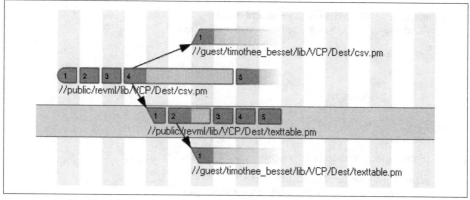

Figure 1-8. A bird's-eye view of inherited file history

---

[*] It's only coincidence that -i is the flag that makes `changes` and `filelog` show inherited history. The "i" really stands for "integration"; you'll see why later in the book.

Perusing file content

P4V offers a nice content browsing tool for files. If you select a text file in P4V and click Time-lapse View you'll see the file's current content, along with a sliding control that changes the display to its content at any previous point in time. Other controls can be used to highlight the age of lines in the file, users who changed the lines, and the diffs for each revision. The black-and-white screenshot you see in Figure 1-9 doesn't begin to do justice to the usefulness of this tool.

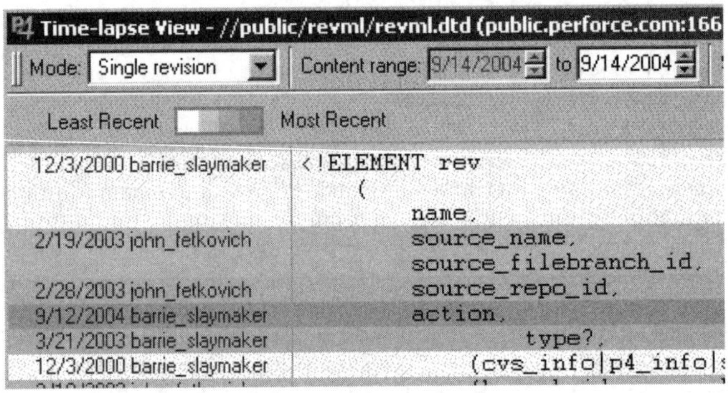

Figure 1-9. P4V's Time-lapse View

P4V's Time-lapse View is generated from the output of the annotate command, among others. You can get annotated file content in text form as well. For example, to see each line of a file annotated with a changelist number, you would use:

```
p4 annotate -c //public/revml/revml.dtd | more
//public/revml/revml.dtd#19 - edit change 4514 (text)
...
467: <!ELEMENT rev
467:     (
467:         name,
2743:         source_name,
2743:         source_filebranch_id,
2802:         source_repo_id,
...
```

To see plain, unadulterated file content, use the print command:

```
p4 print //public/revml/revml.dtd | more
//public/revml/revml.dtd#19 - edit change 4514 (text)
...
<!ELEMENT rev
    (
        name,
        source_name,
        source_filebranch_id,
        source_repo_id,
...
```

Saving informal copies of files

The print command is also useful for saving informal copies of files. Simply redirect its output to a local file:

```
p4 print -q //public/revml/revml.dtd > revml.dtd
```

(The -q option suppresses the one-line header that print normally outputs.)

Comparing depot files

To compare any two depot files, use the diff2 command. For example:

```
p4 diff2 //public/jam/README //guest/dick_dunbar/jam/README
==== //public/jam/README#2 (text) -
    //guest/dick_dunbar/jam/README#1 (text) ==== identical
```

(This output has been edited to fit on the page.)

The same command can be used to compare any two revisions of a depot file:

```
p4 diff2 //public/revml/README#2 //public/revml/README#3
==== //public/revml/README#2 (text) -
    //public/revml/README#3 (text) ==== content
...
45,47c45,46
<    make
<    make test
<    make install
---
>    $ perl -MCPAN -eshell
>    cpan> install VCP
...
```

In P4V the Tools → Diff files command can be used to diff any two files or revisions. Figure 1-10 shows an example of a graphical diff in P4V.

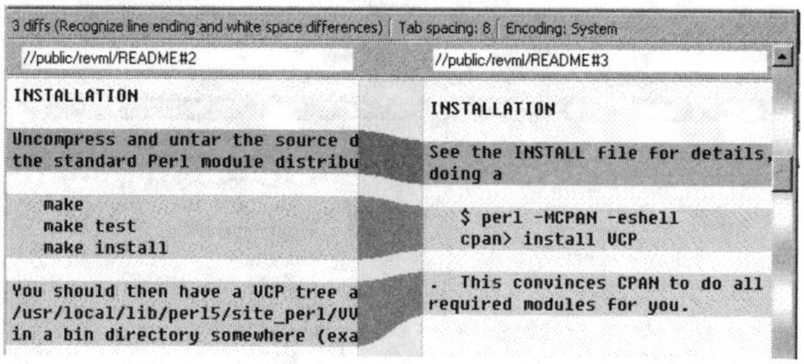

Figure 1-10. Graphical diff in P4V

Comparing depot directories

You can also compare any two directories in the depot. For example, to compare //public/revml to //guest/timothee_besset:

```
p4 diff2 -q //public/revml/... //guest/timothee_besset/...
==== ... bin/gentrevml#56 - ... bin/gentrevml#1 ==== content
==== ... lib/VCP.pm#19 - ... lib/VCP.pm#1 ==== content
==== <none> - lib/VCP/Dest/ab.pm#1 ====
```

This shows us that there's a revision of *bin/gentrevml* in both directories, but their contents do not match. Same with *lib/VCP.pm*. And the *lib/VCP/Dest/ab.pm* file appears in the *//guest/timothee_besset* directory but not the *//public/revml* directory. (The -q flag is used on the diff2 command to suppress line-by-line text diffs. Note that the output shown here has been drastically edited to fit the page.)

The same command can be used to compare any two revisions of a directory. For example:

```
p4 diff2 -q //public/revml/...@3660 //public/revml/...@4498
==== .../dist/packages.mball#1 - <none> ====
==== <none> - .../dist/vcp-rh8#4 ====
==== <none> - .../dist/vcp.exe#10 ====
==== .../dist/vcp.pl#2 - .../dist/vcp.pl#4 ==== content
```

This shows us that between revisions @3660 and @4498 of the *//public/revml* directory, the *dist/packages.mball* file has been deleted, *dist/vcp-rh8* and *dist/vcp.exe* have been added, and *dist/vcp.pl* has been modified.

P4V gives you the same directory comparisons in a much nicer display, as you can see in Figure 1-11. You can use Tools → Diff files to launch it, or just select Folder History on a folder and drag one folder revision to another.

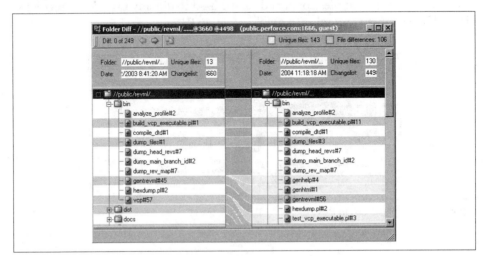

Figure 1-11. Comparing directory revisions in P4V

File Types at a Glance

Perforce does most of the hard work for you when it comes to storing and managing file content. However, there are some aspects of file storage and behavior that you can control. These aspects are a factor of a file's type; in this section we'll take a brief look at the common file types and their properties. In the next chapter we'll show examples of how to set and change file types.

Perforce supports several types of file content, text and binary being the most common. A file's content type dictates how Perforce will handle it in future operations:

Text files

Text files are stored in the depot as *deltas*. That is, a revision of a file is not stored in its entirety; only the lines that have changed are stored. Consequently, umpteen revisions of a very large text file don't take much depot space if only a small part of the file changes at each revision. Delta storage is completely transparent to the user, of course—the server takes care of constructing a specific file revision from deltas when you synchronize your workspace.

As it transfers text files to and from workspaces, Perforce translates them so that their line-end delimiters match the local filesystem's format. If your workspace is on Unix, for example, Perforce makes sure lines in text files end with the *LF* character. If you workspace is on Windows, Perforce makes sure lines end with the *CR/LF* character pair.

Binary files

Binary files are stored in the depot in their entirety. Each revision is stored as a compressed copy of the file. The Perforce client program gets the file revision you need and uncompresses it when you synchronize your workspace. Other than compression, no modification is made to binary files when they are transferred between workspace and server.

 Perforce can compare and merge text files. It can't do that with binary files, beyond simply pointing out that the files are different and letting you choose one or the other. (If you have programs that *can* compare and merge binary files, however, Perforce can invoke them for you. In Chapter 3 we'll take a closer look at this.)

Unicode files

Perforce assumes your text files are ASCII. However, there's another text file type Perforce supports, called "unicode." If your Perforce Server is configured as an internationalized server, unicode files will be translated to your local character set when they're copied to your workspace. And when you submit unicode files, they'll be translated from your local character set to UTF8. To find out about internationalizing your server, see Tech Note 66, *Internationalization Support in Perforce*, on the Perforce Software web site.

Although you can use the unicode file type to store files as UTF8 even with a non-internationalized Perforce Server, your local editor and other tools are more likely to corrupt these files than not. Moreover, unicode files can't be mixed with text files in Perforce commands that compare and merge files.

Perforce also supports OS-specific file types, including Unix symbolic links and Macintosh files and resource forks. To find out more about these file types, run:

```
p4 help filetypes
```

Type modifiers

The content type of a file—text or binary, for example—is considered its base type. In addition to a base type, files in Perforce can have type modifiers that specify how they will behave in workspaces and in the depot. When you list files with Perforce, you may see file types like text+k and binary+lw—these are the modified file types. Some of the most commonly used file type modifiers are:

Modifier	Behavior
+x	The workspace file is executable. (On Unix, the file's execute bit is set.)
+w	The file is writable as soon as it's copied to the workspace. (Normally you have to open files to make them writable.)
+k	RCS-like keywords in the file are expanded when the file is copied to the workspace.
+l	The file is exclusively locked when opened so that only one person can have it open at a time.
+m	The file's modification time is propagated with the file so that it shows up in the timestamp of synchronized copies.
+S	Only one revision (the head revision) of the file is stored in the depot. (This is useful for files generated and submitted by nightly builds, for example.)

To see the complete inventory of file type modifiers, run the help filetypes command.

What kind of file is this?

In P4, you can list a file's content type with a number of commands, including files, opened, and filelog. For example:

```
p4 files *
//depot/projectA/www/index.html ... (text)
//depot/projectA/www/logo.gif ... (binary+l)
```

P4V shows file content types in its navigation trees; you saw an example of this in Figure 1-6.

CHAPTER 2

Working with Files

In this chapter, we'll survey the Perforce commands you're most likely to use for basic software development. We'll discuss creating and managing a workspace, working on files, and finding out who did what when. If you're already using Perforce, this chapter will be a review. You can skim through it—maybe you'll find something here you didn't know about—or skip it now and come back to it later if you care to.

If you're new to Perforce, this chapter will introduce you to a variety of useful commands. What's more, this chapter will serve as a quick reference to many common tasks. There's more to each of the commands introduced here, of course. You'll find the complete inventory of commands and command options in the *P4 Command Reference*.

You may wish to experiment with these commands as you read along. See Appendix A if you don't already have Perforce installed.

Whether you're a Perforce user or not, you'll need at least a glancing familiarity with the basic commands described in this chapter so that you can make sense of them as they appear throughout the book.

An Overview

In Perforce, working on files involves setting up and synchronizing a workspace, adding and working on files, resolving parallel changes (if necessary), and submitting changes to the depot:

Setting up a workspace

The first thing you do before you can work on files is define a *client workspace* for yourself. A client workspace specification, or *client spec*, tells Perforce where in your local filesystem you want your workspace to be rooted. It has a *view* that defines the areas of the depot you want access to, and maps them to directories beneath the workspace root. Once you've set up your workspace, you can work on files.

Adding new files

If you have files in your workspace already—files that you created or moved there yourself—you can add them to the depot. In Perforce, any change you make—adding files, for example—involves two Perforce operations. First you *open* your workspace files, indicating whether you want to add, change, or delete them. Then, after making changes locally, you *submit* files to the depot.

> Don't confuse Perforce's idea of "open" with the idea of opening files in applications. In Perforce, an *open file* is a file that you intend to change. Opening a file with Perforce does not launch an application. And an application—Word or Vim, for example—can open a workspace file whether or not Perforce considers it open.

Synchronizing your workspace

To work on files that are already in the depot, you must first *synchronize* your workspace (see Figure 2-1). This step gets local copies of the latest depot files. Your workspace is considered to be "in sync" when all the files in it match their depot counterparts.

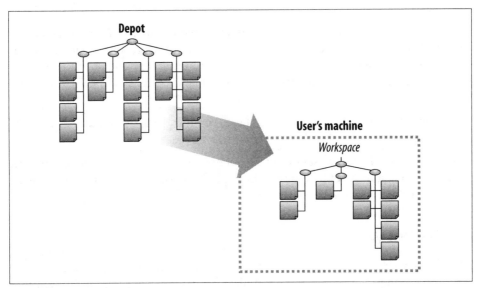

Figure 2-1. Synchronizing a workspace

Working on files

By default, Perforce creates nonwritable files in your workspace. This is meant as a gentle reminder to you that these files are under its control. Although you're free to do what you want in your workspace, including changing file permissions, the preferred method is to let Perforce know what you're up to by opening files first. You open files with commands that indicate what you plan to do—add, edit, or delete, for example. Perforce updates the workspace per your intent: files you open for editing are made writable, for example, and files you open for deletion are removed from the workspace.

Files in the depot are not affected when you open workspace files. Perforce doesn't automatically lock depot files, but you have the option of locking them explicitly. Also, while opening files first is the preferred method, you can modify files first and open them after the fact. Thus you don't have to be on the network, connected to Perforce, to modify your workspace files.

As you work, you always have the option of *reverting* opened files to their unmodified state. Perforce reverts workspace files by replacing them with fresh copies from the depot, effectively discarding any changes you made.

Resolving parallel changes

You can, and should, resynchronize your workspace every now and then to update your local files. Synchronizing replaces stale files with the newest depot versions. It does not, however, affect the files you're working on, except to mark them *unresolved*. When you're ready, you can *resolve* them to reconcile parallel changes.

Resolving files is a Perforce operation in which you choose whether you want to merge, copy, or ignore the newer depot versions. If you choose to resolve files by merging them, Perforce will do as much automatic merging as it can. It can't automatically merge files with conflicting changes, however—those you'll have to do individually. You can use one Perforce's merge tools, or a merge tool of your own choosing, to merge files individually.

Submitting changes to the depot

As you open files, Perforce builds up what's called a *pending changelist*. This is the set of files you plan to submit as a single unit of work. Although we speak of submitting files, you really submit the pending changelist. At your option, you can have more than one pending changelist in your workspace. By juggling opened files between them you can control which files will be submitted together.

You can't submit files if there are newer versions of them in the depot. In other words, Perforce won't let you inadvertently overwrite other people's changes. Instead, you'll have to resolve them and try submitting them again.

Files successfully submitted are sent from your workspace to the depot and stored as new revisions (see Figure 2-2). Your submitted changelist becomes an event in the evolution of the depot, recorded for eternity.

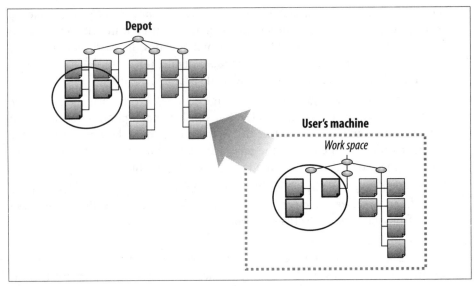

Figure 2-2. Submitting a changelist

 A *changelist* is an object in the Perforce database that records file revisions involved in a specific change to the depot. As far as the Perforce Server is concerned, there is no difference between a "change" and a "changelist." In fact, P4 command outputs and error messages use the more succinct "change" instead of "changelist." (See Appendix B, "Perforce Terminology and P4 Commands.") In this book we'll use either "change" or "changelist" depending on the context.

Creating a Workspace

A Perforce workspace has a physical part and a conceptual part. The physical part is the area on your local disk where Perforce will read and write files. The conceptual part of your workspace is the client object that represents it in the Perforce database.* The client object has to exist before you can do any work on files. You create it by editing a client spec.

Specs and spec forms

The Perforce database models many non-file objects, including workspaces, users, user groups, depots, and so forth. The interface to these non-file objects is what

---

* Although we—this book, much of the Perforce documentation, and some of the Perforce client programs—talk about *workspaces*, the Perforce Server doesn't. It refers to workspaces as *clients*. If you find yourself confused by warnings or error messages that contain the word "client," try mentally substituting "workspace."

Perforce calls a *spec form*. Perforce gives you a spec form to edit when you run commands like:

```
p4 client
```

To command-line users, the spec form will be simply a text file that looks something like this:

```
Client: testws
Owner:  bill
Root:   c:\workspace\test
View:
    //depot/proj/...  //testws/proj/...
    //depot/utils/... //testws/utils/...
```

Fields in the form start in the left-hand column. (In this example, the fields are Client, Owner, Root, and View.) The value in each field follows the field name. Single-line values can be placed on the same line as the field name. Multiline values start on the line following the field name; each line in the value is indented by tabs or spaces.

The Perforce GUI programs (P4V and the rest) give you an actual form to fill out, so you don't have to worry about field names and indentation.

There will be plenty of references to spec forms in this book. We'll use a format for them that looks like this:

Client	testws
Owner	ron
Root	c:\workspace\test
View	//depot/proj/... //testws/proj/... //depot/utils/... //testws/utils/...

This format is not what you'll see either in the GUI programs or in your editor. It's the same information, however; it's simply formatted for easy reading.

In this book, we'll often preface the spec form by the P4 command that launches it in your editor. If you're using a GUI, look for the equivalent command in the application menus. (In P4V, for example, a command that lets you edit a workspace client spec is Connection → Edit Current Workspace.)

Editing a client spec

The `client` command brings up a *client spec* form in an editor. In the form, you specify—among other things—a view. The view identifies the areas of the depot you want access to and maps them to directories on your local filesystem.

For example, say you want to configure a workspace named Bill-WS. First, you open up a client form in the editor:

```
p4 client Bill-WS
```

In the editor, you modify the template that appears there and save the file. That, in effect, configures the workspace. For example, say you saved a form that looks like this:

```
Client        Bill-WS
Root          c:\ws
View          //depot/dev/www/...    //Bill-WS/dev/www/...
              //depot/main/www/...   //Bill-WS/main/www/...
```

By saving this client spec, you have just configured a workspace as follows:

- The name of this workspace is Bill-WS.

- This workspace is rooted in the directory *c:\ws* on your local disk. (You must create this directory yourself. Perforce will create its subdirectories for you, but it won't create the root directory.)

- This workspace has a view of two depot directories, *//depot/dev/www* and *//depot/main/www*. They are mapped to the local filesystem's *c:\ws\dev\www* and *c:\ws\main\www* directories, respectively. For example, the *c:\ws\dev\www\index.html* file will be mapped to *//depot/dev/www/index.html*.

  (Do you recognize the filespec syntax? Workspace views are defined by pairs of filespecs. On the left of each pair is a depot filespec, and on the right is a filespec that shows a workspace location relative to the root. Where you see *//Bill-WS* on the right, mentally substitute the workspace root, *c:\ws*, to understand where files will be located.)

- The files you'll be working on are either in *c:\ws\dev\www* or in *c:\ws\main\www*. Files outside of these paths are outside of the workspace view (even if they happen to be beneath the workspace root directory).

Customizing a workspace view

If a simple workspace view won't suffice, there are a number of ways you can customize it:

- You can use as many mapping lines as you need in order to limit your view to specific areas of the depot. For example:

```
View          //depot/dev/www/products/...    //Bill-WS/dev/www/products/...
              //depot/dev/www/training/...     //Bill-WS/dev/www/training/...
              //depot/dev/www/manuals/...      //Bill-WS/dev/www/manuals/...
              //depot/main/www/products/...    //Bill-WS/main/www/products/...
              //depot/main/www/training/...    //Bill-WS/main/www/training/...
              //depot/main/www/manuals/...     //Bill-WS/main/www/manuals/...
```

- You can use wildcards. For example:

```
Root          c:\ws
View          //depot/dev/www*/...    //Bill-WS/dev/www*/...
```

This extends the view to include subdirectories of *//depot/dev* whose names begin with www. For example, files like *//depot/dev/www-qa/index.html* and *//depot/dev/www/eguide/schedule.html* would fall within this view.

- You can refer to filenames or pathnames that have spaces in them, as long as you put quotes around the filespecs that contain them. For example:

```
View            //depot/dev/www/...         //Bill-WS/dev/www/...
                "//depot/Our Web Site/..."  "//Bill-WS/Our Web Site/..."
```

- You can prefix mapping lines with a hyphen (-) to exclude specific subdirectories or files. For example:

```
View            //depot/dev/www/...         //Bill-WS/dev/www/...
                -//depot/dev/www/prices/... //Bill-WS/dev/www/prices/...
```

This view encompasses all the files in the *//depot/dev/www* path except for the ones in its *prices* subdirectory.

- You can prefix mapping lines with a plus (+) to overlay more than one depot area to a single workspace area. For example:

```
Root            c:\ws
View            //depot/main/www/...  //Bill-WS/www/...
                +//depot/dev/www/...  //Bill-WS/www/...
```

This view maps the *//depot/main/www* files to the local *c:\ws\www* directory. It also maps the *//depot/dev/www* files to the same local directory. When the same local filename matches a file in both depot areas, precedence is given to the *//depot/dev/www* path.

You can combine mappings like the ones shown in the preceding examples to configure the workspace view you need. However, just because you *can* create very complicated workspace views doesn't mean it's a good idea. Complicated views are complicated to work with—your mappings can confuse you, and the more complicated your client spec gets, the harder it is to change it without making a mistake.

On the other hand, don't make your workspace view so simple that it encompasses a very large depot in its entirety. While an all-encompassing view might be easier for you to maintain, it may require hard work on the Perforce Server's part when you run commands. For best server performance, limit your workspace view to the areas of the depot you'll actually be using.

In Part II of this book we'll look at using filespecs to define *codelines* and *modules*, the two essential file containers for parallel software development. Once you've defined codelines and modules, you can base your workspace views on them rather than on ad hoc filespecs.

Identifying the current workspace

When you run Perforce commands, there is a current client workspace in effect, whether you know about it or not. The same info command that tells you which server you're connected to tells you the name of the current workspace:

```
p4 info
Client name: spirit
Client unknown.
```

This shows that the current client workspace is named "spirit," and that it has not been configured yet. (That is, there is no entry for it in the Perforce database.)

If the current client workspace isn't the one you want to use, you'll have to choose the one you want and make it your current client workspace.

Listing workspaces

You can use the clients command to list client workspaces that have already been configured:

```
p4 clients
Client AndyB_Home root Sources:Home:Perforce 'Created by andyb'
Client RM-Build4  root c:\Perforce          'Build4/nightly'
Client jh_WS1     root /Users/jh/perforce    'Created by jh'
Client lw-play    root /usr/team/laura/play   'Created by Laura'
Client lw-win     root c:\clients\lw-win      'Laura's example '
Client pete       root c:\DevTools            'Created by pete'
```

Each line represents a named, configured client workspace. From the clients output, you can make a guess as to which workspaces are yours and which is appropriate for your current environment. If the succinct clients output doesn't give you enough information, you can use the client command to display the details of a workspace:

```
p4 client -o lw-win
Client:       lw-win
Owner:        Laura
Access:       2004/09/01 10:09:06
Host:         spirit
Root:         c:\clients\lw-win
Description:
        Laura's example workspace on Windows.
```

(The -o flag on the client command is used to dump the details to output rather than open up an editor.) From the output of this command, we can see that the client workspace called "lw-win" is owned by Laura, and was last accessed on September 1. It is associated with a host machine called "spirit" and its root directory is *c:\ clients\lw-win*.

Setting the current workspace

The P4 program uses the P4CLIENT environment variable to determine the current client workspace name. If P4CLIENT is not set, the name of your host machine will be used as the current workspace name. Setting the current workspace is a matter of setting P4CLIENT. As with P4PORT, you can set P4CLIENT in your environment. On Unix, for example:

```
export P4CLIENT=lw-play
```

Or on Windows:

```
p4 set P4CLIENT=lw-win
```

P4V offers you a list of workspaces to choose from when you launch it. The P4CLIENT setting in your environment doesn't affect P4V.

Switching between workspaces

It's not unusual for a developer involved with several tasks to have two or three workspaces. One way to switch between workspaces is by opening a command window for each, setting each window's P4CLIENT variable to a different workspace name, and switching between windows.

> If you have more than one workspace on one machine, make sure each has its own distinct root directory. That's the easiest way to keep yourself from inadvertently mixing up files in workspaces.

You can also use what are known as P4CONFIG files to switch between workspaces. First, set the P4CONFIG variable in your environment to a filename like *p4.config*. On Windows, for example:

```
p4 set P4CONFIG=p4.config
```

Next, create files named *p4.config* in each of your workspace root directories. In each file, set the value of P4CLIENT. For example, the *p4.config* file in the root directory of the Bill-WS workspace will contain:

```
P4CLIENT=Bill-WS
```

Now, when you run a P4 command, Perforce will look in your current directory and all its parent directories until it finds a file named *p4.config*. It will use the P4CLIENT setting it finds in that file.

Note that P4CONFIG files are of very little use with P4V. You can switch current workspaces in P4V with the Connection → Open Connection command.

P4V limits you to one open workspace window per Perforce Server connection. So, while it's easy to switch between workspaces, there's no way to have two workspace windows open at the same time. You can get around this limitation by starting up a second instance of the P4V application and connecting it to your second workspace.

Synchronizing a Workspace

The next step after configuring a workspace and making it the current workspace is to synchronize it. When you synchronize your workspace. Perforce does two things. First, it copies files from the depot to your local disk. Second, it makes an internal record of the file revisions you have on disk.

Listing unsynchronized files

If you want a preview of the files you need to synchronize, or if you're simply interested in seeing which depot files have been updated since the last time you synchronized, use the sync command with the -n option:

```
p4 sync -n
```

Synchronizing the entire workspace

Use the sync command to synchronize* your workspace:

```
p4 sync
```

Without arguments, the sync command synchronizes your entire workspace. It copies the latest versions of depot files to their corresponding locations on your local disk. (Assuming there are files in the depot, of course. If you're using a virgin Perforce installation, there won't be anything to synchronize with yet.)

If you're synchronizing for the first time, be sure to preview the operation first! In other words, run the following command first:

```
p4 sync -n
```

A common mistake is to start synchronizing before realizing that your workspace view is too large. This is not an irreparable situation, of course, but you can save yourself some grief by making sure you know what's going to be synchronized before Perforce starts filling up your disk.

---

* Because the P4 command to synchronize files is sync, the Perforce product documentation uses *sync* as a verb. In this book, we use *synchronize* instead, because *sync* just doesn't conjugate very well. But outside of this book, be prepared to see wording like "the file was synced" and "as you are syncing."

You can run sync as often as you like—it refreshes only the files that have changed. Perforce is smart enough not to recopy files that are already present in your workspace.

Synchronizing in bits and pieces

Normally, commands like sync operate on your entire workspace. But you can also synchronize your workspace in bits and pieces. Just supply a filespec to the sync command. For example, this command effectively synchronizes the *//depot/dev/www* directory:

```
p4 sync //depot/dev/www/...
```

Another useful way to limit the scope of synchronization is with wildcards that match to only certain files:

```
p4 sync "//.../*.png"
```

This command synchronizes only the *.png* files, rather than the entire workspace. (The *//...* prefix roots the filespec in the root of the workspace and matches *.png* files in all subdirectories. Without a root, the *.png* would apply to the current directory. The filespec argument is quoted so that the asterisk doesn't get expanded by the command shell before p4 sees it.)

When did I last synchronize?

Perforce can't actually tell you when you last ran the sync command, but it can give you a clue. For example:

```
p4 changes -m1 "#have"
Change 4462 on 2004/09/03 ...
```

This tells you that your workspace was probably last synchronized with depot revision @4462 on September 3, 2004. (The -m1 flag on the changes command limits output to the single most recent change. The *#have* filespec is shorthand for all the files in the workspace; it's in quotes so that the shell doesn't interpret it as a comment.) We say "probably" last synchronized because all changes is really telling us is that September 3 is the date of the latest revision of the files in your workspace. If you've been in the habit of keeping your entire workspace synchronized, that is most likely the date you last ran sync.

What's new in the depot?

You can also use changes to get an idea of the changes that have occured in the depot since you last synchronized:

```
p4 changes "@>4462"
```

(The @>4462 is undocumented syntax that means revisions after @4462. You have to quote the string in which it appears to keep the command shell from tripping on the > character.) Again, this yields an approximately correct result. The more fastidious you are about keeping your entire workspace synchronized to the same point in the depot, the more correct the output is.

You can also apply this changes command to a particular path to see a list of changes that have occured in it since you last synchronized:

```
p4 changes "//depot/dev/www/...@>4462"
```

 Perforce, curiously enough, offers a handful of nominally undocumented features. The @> revision syntax, for example, is one them. To find out more about it, run:

```
p4 help undoc
```

Perforce's undocumented features are not so much undocumented as unsupported. Some are backwardly compatible artifacts of previous releases and some are harbingers of upcoming new functionality. You can use the undocumented features, but you can't count on them to behave the same in future releases.

Synchronizing with older revisions

Normally Perforce copies the head revisions of files to your workspace. To synchronize with older revisions, supply a revision identifier. Here, for example, the August 10, 2004 revision of the *//depot/dev/www* directory tree will be copied to the workspace:

```
p4 sync //depot/dev/www/...@2004/08/10
```

(When you do this, of course, you can no longer assume that p4 changes -m1 "#have" shows you when you last synchronized.)

Listing files in your workspace

You can list the files Perforce *thinks* you have with the have command:

```
p4 have //.../index.html
```

Detecting missing workspace files

In the Perforce vernacular, the list of files you have in your workspace is called the *have list*. The have list is really the inventory of files that have been synchronized. It's not the inventory of files *actually* in your workspace, because it may include files that have since gone missing, and it doesn't include files that didn't come from the depot.

To list synchronized files that are now missing, use diff with the -sd flag:

```
p4 diff -sd
```

Replacing missing files

Your workspace files are under your control and there's nothing to stop you or the programs you run from erasing files Perforce put there. But because Perforce thinks you have them already, you won't be able to replace them with a simple `sync`. To force Perforce to recopy files it thinks you already have, use `sync -f`. For example:

```
p4 sync -f //depot/dev/www/index.html
```

A nice trick of P4 is that you can pipe the output of `diff -sd` to `sync -f` to resynchronize files missing from your workspace:

```
p4 diff -sd | p4 -x- sync -f
```

(The `-x-` flag says to operate on files listed in the standard input stream as opposed to filespec arguments on the command. The `-f` flag says to copy files to your workspace even though Perforce thinks you already have them.)

Detecting files that didn't come from the depot

You can't use Perforce commands to list files Perforce doesn't know about. Thus, it's a little trickier to detect the files in your workspace that didn't come from the depot. You have to use your OS to list the files under your workspace root, pipe that list to the `have` command, and look for error messages. If the root of your Windows workspace is *c:\ws*, for example, you could run:

```
dir /s/b/a-d c:\ws | p4 -x- have >have.txt 2>havenot.txt
```

Here, `dir` is a Windows command whose output is piped to `have`. The `have` output, in turn, is split into standard output and standard error streams, each of which is redirected to a file. The *havenot.txt* file will now contain error messages about files that didn't come from the depot:

```
more havenot.txt
C:\ws\www\.index.html.swp - file(s) not on client
C:\ws\www\junk.txt - file(s) not on client
C:\ws\www\img\icon1.gif - file(s) not on client
```

(*Files not on client* is Perforce's way of saying that the database object—the client—associated with your workspace contains no reference to the files in question.)

Local Syntax, Wildcard Expansion, and Special Characters

Once you have files in your workspace, refering to them with Perforce filespec syntax may be a bit confusing. However, you can also use the syntax native to your local machine to refer to workspace files. If your workspace is on Windows, for example, you can refer to a file with local syntax like:

```
c:\ws\projectA\www\index.html
```

For its internal operations, Perforce translates that to a depot filespec like:

```
//depot/projectA/www/index.html
```

(The actual location of the file in the depot is determined by the workspace view.)

If your current directory is beneath your workspace root, you can also use relative filenames. For example, if you're in the workspace directory mapped to the depot's *//depot/projectA/www* directory, you can use a command like:

p4 have index.html

to refer to the *//depot/projectA/www/index.html* file.

You can mix and match local syntax with filespec syntax. Usually you do this when you want to use Perforce revisions or wildcards with local filenames. For example:

p4 sync c:\ws\projectA\...@Rel2.4

This hybrid of local syntax and filespec is acceptable. In this example, it identifies the collection of depot files that is mapped to the *c:\ws\projectA* path. The sync command shown here will copy the depot file revisions labeled *@Rel2.4* to the workspace.

As you saw earlier, spaces in filenames and pathnames have to be quoted when they are referenced in views. The same goes for commands. Anywhere you enter a filespec—on a command line, or in a spec form—a space in a file or pathname is likely to be misunderstood. To prevent this, put quotes around the filespec. For example:

p4 have "My Dog.jpg"

With quotes as shown, P4 assumes there is one file argument, as you intended. Without quotes, P4 assumes you mean two files, *My* and *Dog.jpg*.

When you use P4 commands in a command shell, by the way, you should be aware that the shell is likely to expand special characters *it* recognizes before passing your file arguments to the P4 program. When you type

p4 sync *.html

for example, the command shell may actually be invoking:

p4 sync index.html contacts.html

Thus, Perforce never sees your wildcard character and never gets a chance to expand it to the depot files it matches. To slip Perforce wildcard characters past the command shell, use quotes. For example:

p4 sync "*.html"

Regardless of whether you use quotes, local syntax, or filespec syntax, Perforce always treats wildcard and revision delimiter characters as meaningful. Consequently, you can't use local syntax to refer to filenames or pathnames that contain these special characters. Instead, you must use URL-style encodings for them (that is, two-digit hexadecimal ASCII codes prefixed with %). A file whose local name is *Me@Age6.JPG*, for example, must be refered to as *Me%40Age6.JPG* in Perforce commands:

```
p4 have Me%40Age6.JPG
```

This is the only way to refer to the file without confusing Perforce. It's also the name Perforce uses to refer to the file internally.

There's one exception to the rule about encoding special characters. The P4 add command (which will be given more attention in the next section) has an option, -f, that forces it to treat special characters as names, not revision syntax. For example:

```
p4 add -f Me@Age6.JPG
```

 The nuances of local syntax, wildcard expansion, and special characters are a significant factor only if you're typing P4 commands in a command shell or invoking them from a script. If you're using Perforce through a GUI or a plug-in, the client program will generally construct file arguments appropriate to the command you are executing.

Working with Local Files

When you synchronize your workspace with depot files, Perforce normally puts read-only files on your local disk. To make files writable, you have to open them. You also have to open files you plan to add to or delete from the depot.

 Remember, in Perforce, an "open" file is a file you plan to submit to the depot. Don't confuse Perforce's meaning of "open" with the idea of opening files in an application.

The basic flow of work in Perforce is that you open files as you work, then submit all your opened files at once when you have completed a unit of work. In this section we'll concentrate on ways to open files. In the next section we'll look at various ways to submit them.

Opening files for editing

Use the edit command to open files for editing. For example:

```
p4 edit index.html locations.html
```

Opening files for editing makes them writable so that you can edit them or otherwise modify them locally. None of your local changes are visible to other users, of course, until you submit your files to the depot:

```
p4 submit
```

Which files am I working on?

Files you haven't submitted yet can be listed with the opened command:

```
p4 opened
//depot/dev/www/index.html#1  - add default change (text)
//depot/dev/www/prices.html#1 - add default change (text)
```

Each line of opened output shows a file revision, the reason it was opened (add), the pending changelist it belongs to (default change), and the file's type (text).

Who's working on these files?

You can check to see who's working on any files at any time with opened -a:

```
p4 opened -a contacts.html
//depot/dev/www/contacts.html#3 - edit by tina
```

Also, you'll notice that as you open files, Perforce informs you if anyone else is working on them as well:

```
p4 edit contacts.html
//depot/dev/www/contacts.html#3 - opened for edit
... - also opened by tina@tina-web-prep
```

Which files did I change?

Just because you've opened files for editing doesn't mean you've gotten around to changing them. To list the opened files you've really changed, use:

```
p4 diff -sa
```

If you want to see the actual text diffs, use diff with no flags:

```
p4 diff
```

Because the diff command can produce a lot of output, you may prefer using it with specific file arguments. For example:

```
p4 diff www/index.html
```

Adding new files to the depot

You also have to open files you plan to add to the depot. Use the add command to do that. Here, for example, three local files are added to the depot:

```
p4 add img/hat1.gif img/hat2.gif img/bag4.gif
p4 submit
```

You can open files only if they're in your workspace view. If the files you want to add are outside your workspace view, move them to a location within the workspace first, then run the add command.

Note that when you're opening new files to be added, Perforce won't expand wildcard characters, even if you do slip them past the command shell. Why not? Because the files you're referring to are not in the depot yet—Perforce has nothing to match wildcards to. So with the add command, you *do* want to use syntax that will be expanded by the shell. For example:

```
p4 add www/*.html
```

Adding an entire directory tree of files

Typically you'll want to add an entire directory tree full of files at once. If you're using P4V, opening a tree of files for adding is simply a matter of navigating to the directory and right-clicking Mark for Add.

It's a little trickier with P4 because no command shell can expand Perforce's handy ... wildcard. That's why *this command will not work*:

```
p4 add img/...    Won't work!
```

Do not despair. You've already seen how the -x- flag can be used with the p4 command to make it read a list of file arguments from standard input. You can let your OS find the files in the directory you are adding and pipe the result to p4 -x- add. On Unix, for example, you'd use:

```
find img -type f -print | p4 -x- add -f
```

The Windows equivalent is:

```
dir /s/b/a-d img | p4 -x- add -f
```

The Unix find and the Windows dir commands output filenames in local syntax. The -f flag is used on the add command to force it to accept filenames with special characters, should there happen to be any. It's not a problem if the list of files piped to add contains files already opened or already in the depot—add will simply emit warnings about them.

You don't have to do anything special to create directories in the depot. Perforce creates directories automatically to accommodate the files you're adding.

Deleting depot files

Even files you want to delete have to be opened first:

```
p4 delete products/betatest.html
p4 submit
```

The `delete` command opens files to be deleted; it also removes them from your workspace. They're deleted from the depot when you run `submit`.

Deleting is only one of several ways of removing files, as you'll see later in the chapter in "Removing and Restoring Files."

Cloning depot files and directories

You can create depot files that are copies of other depot files. (We'll call this "cloning" files for now, to distinguish it from local file copying.) To clone files, use the `integrate` command. For example:

```
p4 integrate products/logo.gif training/logo.gif
```

creates a new file, *training/logo.gif*, in your workspace that is an exact copy of the depot file *products/logo.gif*. It also opens the file (for branching). You still have to submit the new file, of course:

```
p4 submit
```

When you submit it, the *training/logo.gif* file will be created in the depot.

You can use the usual Perforce wildcards with `integrate` to clone entire directory trees. For example:

```
p4 integrate projectA/... projectB/...
edp4 submit
```

clones all the files in the *projectA* directory into the *projectB* directory, in the same way the previous single file was cloned.

When you clone files, bear in mind that:

- The files you create by cloning must fall within your workspace view. Surprisingly, the originals they are cloned *from* do not have to be in your view! (That's because you're not modifying the originals.)

- Even if the originals are synchronized in your workspace, they will not be used by `integrate`. The `integrate` command always clones from *depot* originals.

 A less effective way to clone files is to synchronize them in your workspace, copy them to another location in your workspace, then use add to open them for adding, as if they were new files. The trouble with this approach is that the new files won't have any history. By contrast, files created with the `integrate` command will inherit the history of their originals.*

---

* If you think cloning looks like branching, you're right. This is merely the tip of the `integrate` iceberg. You'll get the whole story in Chapter 4.

Modifying files as you clone them

As you just read, cloned files are copied into your workspace first. In your work-space, they'll appear as read-only files. To modify the clones before submitting them, reopen them with the add command. This makes them writable—at least until you submit them—and tells Perforce to clone from your workspace files instead of from the depot originals. For example:

```
p4 integrate products/logo.gif products/logosmall.gif
p4 add products/logosmall.gif
```

At this point, *products/logosmall.gif* is writable and can be modified. To send your modified file to the depot, submit it:

```
p4 submit
```

Renaming files and directories

Renaming files is just like cloning files except that you delete the originating files. For example, to rename a file from *hat1.gif* to *hat001.gif*:

```
p4 integrate hat1.gif hat001.gif
p4 delete hat1.gif
p4 submit
```

Here, the integrate command cloned *hat1.gif* into *hat001.gif*, leaving the latter in your workspace, opened for branching. Then *hat1.gif* was opened for deleting. When these opened files are submitted, *hat001.gif* replaces *hat1.gif* in the depot.

As with cloning, integrate can be used with wildcards to rename entire directories. For example, this pair of commands renames the *prod* subdirectory to *products*:

```
p4 integrate www/prod/... www/products/...
p4 delete www/prod/...
p4 submit
```

Moving files and directories works exactly the same way. For example, to move the *www/onsale.html* file into the *www/products* directory:

```
p4 integrate www/onsale.html www/products/onsale.html
p4 delete www/onsale.html
p4 submit
```

Note that both the originating *and* the destination files have to be in your workspace for renames and moves.

 Remember that files created by the integrate command inherit the history of their ancestors. See Chapter 1 for ways to display inherited history.

Replacing and swapping file content

Replacing file content is similar to renaming files, but because the target file exists, a little extra work is required. For example, to replace the contents of *misc.txt* with content from *readme.txt*:

```
p4 integrate -i readme.txt misc.txt
p4 resolve -at
p4 submit
```

(The combination of integrate -i and resolve -at effectively does the content replacement. Don't worry just yet about how it does it—you'll find out in Chapter 4.)

In the same vein, you can swap the contents of a pair of files. Here we swap the contents of *misc.txt* and *readme.txt*:

```
p4 integrate -i readme.txt misc.txt
p4 integrate -i misc.txt readme.txt
p4 resolve -at
p4 submit
```

Locking files

Opening files before you submit them is a way of politely earmarking them for your upcoming changes. Once you've opened files, Perforce will warn other users if they open the same files in their workspaces. It won't prevent people from opening them, however, and it won't stop them from submitting their changes before you submit yours. (In Chapter 3 you'll read all about what happens if they do submit their changes first.)

To prevent other users from submitting changes first, you can use lock on your opened files:

```
p4 lock
```

No one can submit changes to files you have locked. If you lock files you've opened for adding, no one can add files with the same names. A lock persists until you've submitted or reverted your files. (We'll get to reverting in a moment.)

Designating file types

When you open a file to be added, the Perforce client program can determine its type to some extent. It peeks at the file's first 1,024 bytes to make the determination. It can tell whether a file is text or binary, for example, and on Unix, it can tell if you're adding a symlink.

If the base file type chosen by Perforce is suitable to you, you don't have to do anything. As you read in Chapter 1, however, special file type modifiers—+l for exclusive locking, for example, and +w for always writable—can be used to control file behavior. Modified file types have to be designated explicitly.

You can designate a file's type as you add it to the depot. You can also change its type once you've already added it. File type changes, like all other changes to depot files, can be made only to open files, and like all other changes to open files, they don't affect depot files until they are submitted.

 Remember, you can get a complete inventory of base types and type modifiers from:

```
p4 help filetypes
```

For example, say you're adding new PDF files. Normally, Perforce would designate binary as the type for PDF files, and this may suit your needs as is. But you may decide to designate these files as binary+l (binary files with exclusive locking). You can do this with the add command:

```
p4 add -t +l *.pdf
```

(The -t flag designates the type. In this case, only the +l type modifier was designated; the base type was left to be determined by Perforce.)

You can use opened to see which types were assigned to your opened files:

```
p4 opened
//depot/dev/www/brochure.pdf - add (binary+l)
//depot/dev/www/diagram.pdf  - add (binary+l)
```

Before you submit files, you can change their type as often as you want with the reopen command. For example, to make the new PDF files always writable as well:

```
p4 reopen -t +w *.pdf
```

The one-size-fits-all reopen command can be used for files opened for editing as well.

Changing the type of existing files

When a file is submitted, Perforce records its type accordingly. That's the file type that stays with it from revision to revision, and it's the type inherited by files branched from it. You can use the filelog command to see a file's type history:

```
p4 filelog readme.txt
//depot/dev/www/readme.txt#2 - edit (text+kw)
//depot/dev/www/readme.txt#1 - add  (text)
```

Once a file exists in the depot, the only way to change its type is to open it for editing and submit it again. For example, to change the *readme.txt* file from text+kw to text+w:

```
p4 edit -t text+w readme.txt
p4 submit readme.txt
```

(Unfortunately there's no syntax to deduct a modifier from a base file type.)

This change now shows up in the file's history as well:

```
p4 filelog readme.txt
//depot/dev/www/readme.txt#3 - edit (text+w)
//depot/dev/www/readme.txt#2 - edit (text+kw)
//depot/dev/www/readme.txt#1 - add  (text)
```

 There are parameters you can set in your client spec that don't affect depot file types, but that do affect the way Perforce handles files in your workspace. Try:

```
p4 help client
```

for a summary of options that control:

- Whether workspace files are made writable as they are synchronized
- Whether unopened but writable workspace files can be clobbered
- What timestamp is set on workspace files as they are synchronized
- Whether line endings in text files follow local convention

Opening files after the fact

Although opening files before you change them is the polite thing to do, you don't have to work that way. You are free to change your local file permissions and make changes as you see fit. You do have to open files at some point—otherwise you won't be able to submit them to the depot—but you can always open them after the fact.

Opening files after the fact reconciles Perforce's record of what's open in your workspace with what's actually changed. You simply open the files you've created, modified, or removed by running add, edit, or delete, respectively. In "Adding an entire directory tree of files," earlier in the chapter, you saw how to open new files for adding by piping a list of files to the add command. Opening modified and deleted files after the fact works the same way:

Opening modified files after the fact
To open files that have been modified locally since you synchronized them, run:

```
p4 diff -se | p4 -x- edit
```

(The diff -se command lists unopened files that don't match their depot counterparts. You've seen the -x- flag before—it makes edit operate on the list of files in the standard input stream instead of a command argument.) Opening files for editing after the fact doesn't change the content of your workspace files. However, it will make files writable if they aren't already.

Opening deleted files after the fact
Earlier in this chapter you saw how to list missing files so that they could be resynchronized. But if files are missing because you removed them as part of an

intentional change, you have to open them for deleting before you can submit that change to the depot. To open missing files for deleting, use:

```
p4 diff -sd | p4 -x- delete
```

Normally the delete command removes files from the workspace, but in this case it will have no effect on the workspace at all.

Reverting files

Reverting files is how you discard changes you've made to local files, rather than submitting them. For example, to revert the index.html file in the current directory:

```
p4 revert index.html
```

(The revert command doesn't have a default argument—it won't revert all the files in your workspace, for example, unless you give it an argument whose view is that large.) Reverting takes files off your pending changelist and replaces workspace files with copies from the depot. Files you have opened for editing are restored to their original, read-only versions.

 The revert command doesn't save backup copies of your changed workspace files. It simply overwrites them with fresh copies from the depot. In other words, *you will lose your local changes* when you revert files.

When you revert files opened for deleting, the depot copies are restored to your workspace. Reverting files opened for adding has no effect on files at all, other than to take them off your pending changelist.

Working with Pending Changelists and Submitting Files

As you open files, they are associated with a *pending changelist*. Your local changes don't affect the depot until you submit your files. What you submit to the depot is not individual files, really, but the entire pending changelist.

Submitting a pending changelist

Use the submit command to submit a changelist:

```
p4 submit
```

By default, submit operates on the default pending changelist. (You can have more than one changelist, as you'll see in a moment.) Like the client command, submit launches an editor so that you can fill out a form. The form comes prefilled with the list of files in the changelist. All you really have to fill out for submit is the Description field. For example:

```
p4 submit
```

Description	Added feature and price list pages for the new web site.
Files	//depot/dev/www/index.html#1 - add
	//depot/dev/www/price.html#1 - add

Once you save and exit the editor, Perforce begins sending your new and changed files to the depot. Submitting files goes very quickly—about as quickly as the files can be transferred over the network to the server. When all content has reached the server, and assuming you ran into no problems with permissions or triggers, new file revisions are created in the depot and your changelist description is recorded permanently.

Preventing unchanged files from being submitted

It often comes as a surprise to new users that *all* the files in their changelists are submitted, even the ones that haven't been changed. New revisions whose contents are the same as their unchanged predecessors are created in the depot. If this behavior strikes you as unacceptable, you can revert your unchanged files before submitting them with:

```
p4 revert -a
```

Note that even though a file's content is unchanged, revert -a won't revert a file if you've resolved it or done anything to change its type.

Creating additional changelists

Changelists are meant, among other things, to document files changed together as a single unit of work. However, it's easy to end up with unrelated files in your default pending changelist. If that happens, consider splitting your files into changelists that can be submitted separately.

You can create additional changelists with the change command. This command brings up a spec form, just like submit. The form will list all the files opened in your default changelist. Simply fill in a description and save the form to move files to the new changelist.

```
p4 change
```

Change	new
Description	Tighten up page layout
Files	//depot/dev/www/template.xml#4 - edit
	//depot/dev/www/globals.xml#7 - edit

Saving the form doesn't submit the files. Instead, it creates another pending changelist, this one identified with a number:

```
p4 change
Change 1453 created with 2 open file(s).
```

Do I have more than one pending changelist?

The `changes -s pending` command lists pending changelists. Normally it lists *all* the pending changelists in the system, which is rarely what you want to see. To list the pending changelists for your workspace, run `changes -s pending -c` with your workspace name. For example:

```
p4 changes -s pending -c Bill-WS
Change 1453 by bill@Bill-WS *pending* 'Tighten up page layout'
Change 1406 by bill@Bill-WS *pending* 'Test offsite links'
```

This shows us that there are two pending changelists in the Bill-WS workspace in addition to the default. (Every workspace has a default pending changelist.)

Moving files from one changelist to another

Once you have more than one pending changelist, you can use the `reopen` command to juggle open files between them. For example, to move all your opened XML files to the default changelist:

```
p4 reopen -c default //.../*.xml
//depot/dev/www/template.xml#4 - reopened; default change
//depot/dev/www/globals.xml#7 - reopened; default change
```

To move the current directory's *template.xml* file to pending changelist 1453:

```
p4 reopen -c 1453 template.xml
//depot/dev/www/template.xml#4 - reopened; change 1453
```

In P4V, moving files between changelists is simply a matter of dragging and dropping. Figure 2-3 shows pending changelists displayed by P4V.

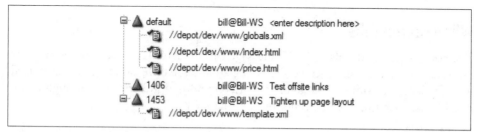

Figure 2-3. Pending changelists displayed by P4V

What's in this changelist?

Use opened -c to list the files in a cparticular changelist. For example:

```
p4 opened -c default
//depot/dev/www/globals.xml#7 - edit default change (text)
```

```
p4 opened -c 1406
File(s) not opened on this client.
```

Submitting a numbered pending changelist

You can submit a numbered pending changelist by giving a changelist number to the submit command:

```
p4 submit -c 1453
```

Getting rid of empty changelists

Empty pending changelists can be deleted with change -d. For example:

```
p4 change -d 1406
Change 1406 deleted.
```

Submitting a subset of opened files

You can also submit files separately by supplying a filespec to the submit command. For example, to submit all the files in the *www/img* path:

```
p4 submit www/img/...
```

This effectively splits your default changelist in two. The first new changelist, containing the files that match the filespec, is submitted. The rest of your opened files remain open, in what is now your new default changelist.

Note that you can do this only with the default pending changelist. Numbered pending changelists can be submitted only in their entirety.

When submit fails

The submit command fails with the message Out of date files must be resolved or reverted if it detects that files you're trying to submit have not been synchronized with the latest revisions. This failure is perfectly normal in Perforce, although it can be a bit disconcerting the first time you see it happen:

```
p4 submit
Change 6412 created with 2 open file(s).
Submitting change 6412.
//depot/dev/www/index.html - must resolve before submitting
//depot/dev/www/index.html - must resolve #3
Out of date files must be resolved or reverted.
Submit failed—fix problems above then use 'p4 submit -c 6412'.
```

What's happened here is that you synchronized and opened revision 2 of the *index. html* file. Before you could submit it, someone else submitted revision 3. Now you can't submit yours without *resolving* the file.

Because Perforce detected a problem with one of the files in your pending change-list, it didn't submit any of them. Instead, it assigned a number to your pending changelist. As the error message tells you, you'll have to resolve the out-of-date file and then submit the changelist with:

```
p4 submit -c 6412
```

If you lose track of the pending changelist's number, remember that you can list pending changelists with `changes -s pending -c`:

```
p4 changes -s pending -c Bill-WS
Change 6412 by bill@Bill-WS *pending* 'Fix typos'
```

The `opened` command shows pending changelist numbers as well:

```
p4 opened
//depot/dev/www/contact.html#9 - edit change 6412
//depot/dev/www/index.html#3 - edit change 6412
```

Resolving files

When someone else has submitted changes to the same files you're working on, you will have to resolve your open files. There's a lot more to be said about resolving files and it will be said in Chapter 3. For now, however, we'll just point out that you resolve files using the `resolve` command:

```
p4 resolve
```

The `resolve` command cycles through the files in your workspace that need resolving. It lets you choose what to do about each one's updated depot file. You can merge the depot file's changes into your file, copy the depot file to your file, or ignore the depot file.

Only when you've resolved all your unresolved files can you submit your changelist successfully.

 Rather than letting a `submit` command fail, consider synchronizing your workspace regularly before you submit. Synchronizing doesn't affect your opened files—it simply lets you know that they need to be resolved. But it also updates the unopened files in your workspace so that it's easier for you to verify that you've resolved your opened files correctly. (It's usually easier to test for correctness when you've got a synchronized set of files.)

Listing unresolved files

At any time, you can list the files that need resolving with:

```
p4 resolve -n
```

Removing and Restoring Files

Removing files can mean a number of things in Perforce. Let's look at removing files—and restoring them, when possible—in three different contexts: removing workspace files, deleting depot files, and obliterating files.

Removing workspace files

In the first context, you're removing Perforce-managed files from your workspace. In this case, you don't want to affect the depot files in any way—you simply want your workspace to be rid of them. You could remove them yourself, of course, since you have control over them. But it you did that, Perforce would be unaware that they're no longer there. Your have list would be out of kilter. You can prevent that by using Perforce commands to remove files from your workspace.

In a GUI like P4V, this is simply a matter of selecting files or folders and clicking File → Remove from Workspace. With P4, however, removing files from your workspace is a little less intuitive. You do it by synchronizing to the symbolic revision *#none*. For example:

```
p4 sync c:\ws\dev\www\...#none
```

This command removes files previously synchronized, but only if they are not open. The open files produce a warning—to remove them you must revert first, *then* synchronize to *#none*.

To restore previously removed files to your workspace, simply resynchronize:

```
p4 sync c:\ws\dev\www\...
```

Deleting depot files

The next meaning of removing files is to delete them from the depot while keeping a history of their prior revisions intact. This operation does affect depot files, of course, and because it's a depot change, it requires you to synchronize the files, open them to be deleted, then submit a changelist. For example:

```
p4 sync c:\ws\dev\wwww\...
p4 delete c:\ws\dev\www\...
p4 submit
...
Change 4933 submitted
```

Perforce creates new head revisions of deleted files when you submit them—*deleted* revisions. Deleted file revisions have special properties. When people synchronize deleted revisions, Perforce removes the files from their workspaces. Deleted revisions also behave differently in resolve and integration operations, as we'll see in subsequent chapters.

You can restore deleted files by synchronizing with nondeleted revisions and adding them again. For example, we just saw a set of files deleted in changelist 4933. To restore this set of files, use:

```
p4 sync c:\ws\dev\wwww\...@4932
p4 add c:\ws\dev\www\...
p4 submit
```

The deleted revisions remain in the depot, superceded by the newly added revisions. You'll see evidence of this in file histories:

```
p4 filelog c:\ws\dev\www\...
...
//depot/dev/www/catalog/item3004.html
... #4 add by corey 'Restore deleted files'
... #3 delete by bill 'Remove obsolete items'
... #2 edit by corey 'Complete descriptions'
... #1 add by corey 'New catalog items'
...
```

Obliterating files

The third meaning of removing files is to obliterate them *and their history* from Perforce's database. This is something you'd resort to only if files had been added or branched by mistake, for example. Although deleted files can be restored from prior revisions, obliterated files are gone forever and completely. All revisions are removed from the depot and all references to them in changelists, labels, workspaces, and so forth are removed from the database.

> There is no easy way to restore obliterated files.
>
> There is no guaranteed way to restore obliterated files. (If you find yourself in the unfortunate position of having to restore obliterated files, contact Perforce Software. Their technical support team may be able to help you restore obliterated files from your system backups.)

Only privileged Perforce users can obliterate files. For more information, see the online help for the obliterate command:

```
p4 help obliterate
```

Useful Recipes

There are a couple of Perforce command recipes you may find yourself using often. One is the recipe for reconciling your workspace after working offline. The other is the recipe for backing out changes.

Reconciling offline changes

Once you've synchronized your workspace, you can do your development work completely offline. You could, for example, synchronize a workspace on your laptop before leaving the office, then work offline while riding the train home.

But your offline changes can't be submitted unless the files they involve are opened in a pending changelist. Once your laptop is back online, you'll have to reconcile your offline changes—the state of your local files, in other words—with your pending changelist.[*]

Reconciling offline changes is simply a matter of opening files after the fact. The formula is:

1. Find the files that were changed and open them for editing:

   `p4 diff -se | p4 -x- edit`

2. Find the files that were removed and open them for deleting:

   `p4 diff -sd | p4 -x- delete`

3. Find the files that are new and open them for adding. Assuming that you're in the top-level directory of your workspace, the Windows command to find files and add them is:

   `dir /s/b/a-d | p4 -x- add -f`

   On Unix that's:

   `find . -type f | p4 -x- add -f`

   (These `dir` and `find` commands list *all* the files in your local workspace tree and pipe them to P4's `add` command. The files that are truly new are opened for adding; the rest generate warnings but are ignored by `add`.)

Having done this, you can either submit your pending changelist or continue working on your opened files.

---

[*] Another need for reconciling offline changes arises when you run programs that modify files unbeknownst to you. Some artist tools and authoring tools are prone to doing this by modifying several related files when you save a single file or project.

Backing out a recent change

A change that has been submitted to the depot can be backed out by submitting another change that reverses it. There's a simple recipe for backing out a change. Assuming that C is the change number, the recipe is:

1. Synchronize with the pre-@C files.
2. Open C's deleted files for adding.
3. Open C's edited or integrated files for editing.
4. Synchronize with the latest files.
5. Open C's added or branched files for deleting.
6. Resolve files.
7. Submit the changelist.

This sequence of steps assures that the new change restores added, deleted, and edited files to their pre-C content and type.

For example, say you want to back out change 1245. Let's take a look at the files involved:

```
p4 files @=1245
//depot/dev/www/contacts.html#2 - edit change 1245 (text)
//depot/dev/www/index.html#12 - edit change 1245 (text)
//depot/dev/www/projects.html#5 - delete change 1245 (text)
//depot/dev/www/depts/eng.html#1 - add change 1245 (text)
```

(The *@=1245* filespec identifies file revisions submitted in change 1245. It's an undocumented syntax—you can read about it in the output of help undoc.) As you can see, two files were edited, one was deleted, and one was added in this change. No files were branched or integrated. To back out change 1245, you'd run:

```
p4 sync @1244
p4 add //depot/dev/www/projects.html
p4 edit //depot/dev/www/contacts.html //depot/dev/www/index.html
p4 sync
p4 delete //depot/dev/www/depts/eng.html
p4 resolve -ay
p4 submit
```

(The resolve -ay command preserves the content of files—you'll see how and why it works in Chapter 3.)

When a change involves a lot of files, you can filter the output of the files command to produce lists of files to open. Unfortunately, files can't be piped directly to other P4 commands because its format isn't acceptible to them. For example, a line of files output that looks like this:

```
//depot/dev/www/index.html#12 - edit change 1245 (text)
```

has to look like this when piped to the `edit` command:

```
//depot/dev/www/index.html
```

This can be fixed easily in a filter, however. If you're on Unix, for example, you can use sed. Here's the recipe again, this time using sed filters instead of specific file names:

```
p4 sync @1244
p4 files @=1245 | sed -n -e "s/#.* - delete .*//p" | p4 -x- add
p4 files @=1245 | sed -n -e "s/#.* - edit .*//p" | p4 -x- edit
p4 sync
p4 files @=1245 | sed -n -e "s/#.* - add .*//p" | p4 -x- delete
p4 resolve -ay
p4 submit
```

On Windows, the `for` command can be used to filter file lists. Ruby or Perl scripts would do just as well, of course.

In any case, this basic recipe works when the change you're backing out is the most recent change to the files involved. In Chapter 3 we'll look at backing out non-recent changes—that is, changes that have to be unmerged. And in Chapter 11, we'll see an example of using the recipe to back out changes involving branching and integration as well.

Resolving and Merging Files

The previous chapter blithely mentions that you may have to resolve and merge files before submitting them. *Resolving* instructs Perforce to take care of files that have been changed in parallel; *merging* is one way to resolve files. Resolving files is usually easy, and the result is usually exactly what you want, whether you understand how it came about or not. However, there are times when you do need to know exactly how files are resolved and merged. That is what this chapter is about.

This chapter starts out with a review of the Perforce resolve operation: what it's for, when you do it, and what you do with it. It nails down the meanings of "yours" and "theirs," the often-puzzling names Perforce gives to files being resolved. Next, it describes how Perforce actually merges text files. It shows how a merged file is constructed, and explains where and why conflicts are detected. (Merge results that seemed random to you before you read this chapter will seem completely predictable to you once you have read it.) This chapter also explains how to reconcile files that can't be resolved because they've been added, deleted, renamed, or moved. It offers tips for developers to resolve, merge, and reconcile files. Finally, it closes with a bit of arcana, including information about configuring alternate merge tools.

Resolving: When, What, and How

You must resolve files when:

- You have files opened for editing, and you synchronize them with newer revisions.
- You have files opened for editing, and your attempt to submit them fails because you aren't synchronized with the head revisions.
- You are integrating changes between branched files.

The first two cases will be the focus of this chapter. However, most of what you will read here applies to the third case as well, so consider it prerequisite reading for the next chapter, Chapter 4.

The Ambiguities of SCM Terminology

Merge, *conflict*, *resolve*, and *integrate* are words that exacerbate the ambiguities of SCM terminology. Before we go any further, let's get clear about what these words mean—at least in the context of this chapter:

- By *merge*, we mean merging the contents of one file into another. Much of this chapter dwells on how Perforce merges files. Don't confuse this with the concept of merging changes from one branch into another. Perforce can do this kind of merging, too, only Perforce calls it *integrating*. We'll cover integration in Chapter 4.

- If you and I both change *index.html*, that's a *parallel change*. Some SCM systems use the word *conflict* when they mean parallel change. But in this chapter, *conflict* means a condition that can be detected when parallel changes are merged. For example, if you changed "<img src=logo.gif>" to "<img src=img/logo.gif>," and I changed it to "<img src=newlogo.gif>"—that's a *conflict*.

- You have to tell Perforce what to do with parallel changes. That's called *resolving* files, and you use Perforce's resolve command to do it. Merging is one of the options you have when you resolve files; resolve can merge files for you. And, after merging, you may have to *resolve conflicts*. But the resolve command doesn't resolve conflicts. It alerts you to the presence of conflicts and launches an editor so that *you* can resolve conflicts by editing the merged file.

Are you in sync?

To lay the groundwork for resolving and merging, let's take another look at what it means to be "in sync" with the depot. When you synchronize, Perforce fetches files from the depot. For example:

```
p4 sync
//depot/projectA/doc/detail.html#9
//depot/projectA/doc/index.html#16
//depot/projectA/doc/sched.html#5
//depot/projectA/img/diag01.gif#3
//depot/projectA/img/diag02.gif#2
```

(Note that this is the abridged output of sync. Here, as in most of the P4 examples in this book, we've massaged the output to fit the page and to make the point at hand.)

Unless you specify otherwise, Perforce copies the head—that is, the newest—revisions to your workspace. We see this in Figure 3-1. The three most recent changes to the files we're working with are @1000, @1005, and @1009. We're synchronized with the head revisions (the bold outlines).

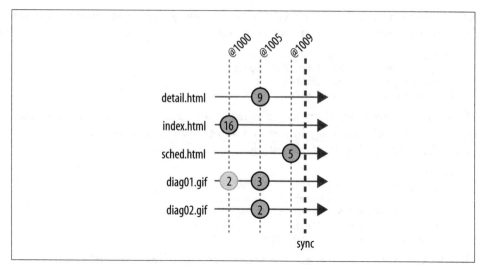

Figure 3-1. A workspace synchronized with head revisions

But the revisions you have in your workspace won't remain the head revisions forever. As soon as other people submit changes, your workspace gets out of sync.*
Figure 3-2 shows that since we last synchronized, more changes (@1014, @1015,
@1026, @1027, and @1032) have been submitted to the files we're working on.
We're no longer in sync with the head revisions of some of our files.

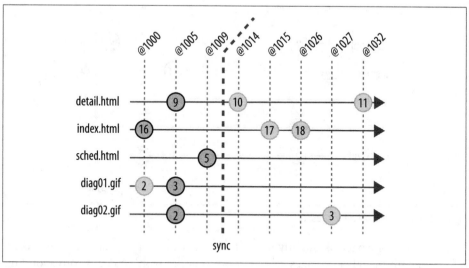

Figure 3-2. Files out of sync

---

* None of this applies to you if you are the only person using your Perforce system, of course. Nor is it relevant
if you are the only person working in a particular branch. However, if you're working in a branch, you'll
probably have to integrate your changes into another branch eventually, and that involves resolving and
merging files. So do read this chapter before going on to the next.

An out-of-sync workspace is no big deal—simply run sync again and your workspace files will be refreshed with newer depot versions:

```
p4 sync
//depot/projectA/doc/detail.html#11 - updated
//depot/projectA/doc/index.html#18 - updated
//depot/projectA/img/diag02.gif#3 - updated
```

Things are slightly more complicated when you've got opened files. In this case, resynchronizing refreshes only the files you don't have opened. For example, say you have *index.html* and *diag02.gif* opened when you resynchronize:

```
p4 sync
//depot/projectA/doc/detail.html#11 - updated
//depot/projectA/doc/index.html#18 - is opened
... must resolve #17,#18 before submitting
//depot/projectA/img/diag02.gif#3 - is opened
... must resolve #3 before submitting
```

The files you do have opened go into a state where they're considered synchronized but unresolved. (In the Perforce vernacular, they're scheduled for resolve.) In Figure 3-3 we see that we're now in sync with the head revisions again. However, the files we have opened for editing (shown in square outlines) need to be resolved.

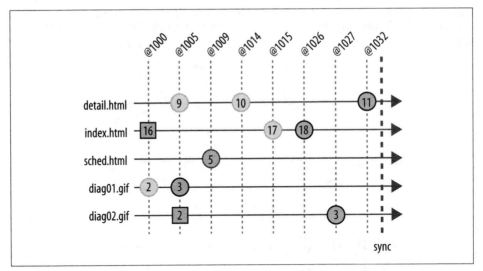

Figure 3-3. Files scheduled for resolve

Now, your workspace is slightly out of kilter. Your unopened files have been refreshed with the latest changes, but your opened files won't contain corresponding changes until you resolve them. So, until you resolve, you'll have problems compiling or using your files, because you don't really have all the changes you need.

Which files need resolving?

Note that you have to synchronize before you can resolve files. In the GUI programs it's easy to see which of your files are opened, which need synchronizing, and which need resolving, because they'll be marked with corresponding icons.

As you read in the previous chapter, you can use P4's sync -n command to see which of your files need synchronizing. After synchronizing, you can use resolve -n to see which files are as yet unresolved:

```
p4 resolve -n
c:\ws\doc\index.html -
   merging //depot/projectA/doc/index.html#17,#18
c:\ws\doc\img\diag02.gif -
   vs //depot/projectA/img/diag02.gif#3
```

Here we see that two workspace files are unresolved, *c:\ws\doc\index.html* and *c:\ws\doc\img\diag02.gif*. (You'll see what the rest of this output means shortly.)

Each time you resynchronize opened files, another resolve is scheduled. A file scheduled for more than one resolve is an indication that you've resynchronized more than once:

```
p4 resolve -n
c:\ws\doc\sitemap.html -
   merging //depot/projectA/doc/sitemap.html#9
c:\ws\doc\sitemap.html -
   merging //depot/projectA/doc/sitemap.html#10
c:\ws\doc\sitemap.html -
   merging //depot/projectA/doc/sitemap.html#11
```

Resynchronizing more than once is not a problem—the file can still be resolved. However, as we'll show in "Tips for Smoother Collaboration," later in this chapter, there are good reasons to resolve after each synchronization.

Resolving files automatically

After resynchronizing your workspace, you can resolve files interactively (that is, one by one) or automatically (all at once). Not all files can be resolved automatically, as you'll see. But nobody wants to spend all day resolving files interactively. So the practical thing to do is to first try to resolve as many files as you can automatically, then resolve the stragglers interactively.

The safest way to resolve files automatically (or to "auto-resolve" files, as we call it) is with resolve -as:

```
resolve -as
c:\ws\projectA\doc\ads.html
- merging //depot/projectA/doc/ads.html#3,#5
   Diff chunks: 0 yours + 1 theirs + 0 both + 0 conflicting
- copy from //depot/projectA/doc/ads.html
c:\ws\projectA\doc\index.html
```

```
- merging //depot/projectA/doc/index.html#17,#18
  Diff chunks: 2 yours + 4 theirs + 0 both + 0 conflicting
- resolve skipped
c:\ws\projectA\img\diag02.gif
- vs //depot/projectA/doc/img/diag02.gif#3
  Non-text diff: 0 yours + 0 theirs + 0 both + 1 conflicting
- resolve skipped
```

The -as flag directs resolve to handle only the files that can be resolved safely—that is, without compromising locally edited files. Files that would be compromised are skipped. The output shows which files were resolved and how. Before you attempt to interpret the output, let's look at what Perforce means by calling files "yours" and "theirs."

"Yours," "theirs," and "base"

Every unresolved file has three relevant variants. Perforce calls them "yours," "theirs," and "base":

Yours
> "Yours" is the file in your workspace. It is the file you will submit to the depot after you've finished whatever it is you're working on.

Theirs
> "Theirs" is the revision in the depot. It contains changes made in parallel with yours, and it's the one you would be synchronized with if the file weren't open in your workspace.

Base
> The "base" is the revision you were synchronized with when you opened the file. It's the one that was copied to your workspace, the starting point of the changes you've made locally.

Take the scenario shown in Figure 3-4, for example. *index.html#16* was synchronized in your workspace when you opened it for editing yesterday. In the meantime, other people have submitted changes to the depot and the newest revision is now *index.html#18*. Today you've resynchronized your workspace. If you were to resolve the file now, yours would be the file in your workspace, theirs would be *index.html#18*, and the base would be *index.html#16*.

And, in its own way, the resolve -n -o command shows us exactly which files these are:

```
p4 resolve -n -o index.html
c:\ws\doc\index.html
- merging //depot/projectA/doc/index.html#17,#18
  using base //depot/projectA/doc/index.html#16
```

(We use -o with resolve to make it display the base.) Here, yours is *c:\ws\doc\index.html* and theirs is *//depot/projectA/doc/index.html#18*. (The message shows the range of

---

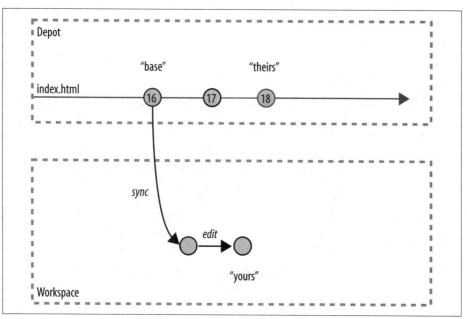

Figure 3-4. The three variants of an unresolved file

revisions, *#17* through *#18*, that resolve will take care of for you.) The base is */depot/projectA/doc/index.html#16*.

During integration, as you'll read in the next chapter, the revisions meant by yours, theirs, and base are subtly different from what we've just described here. However, whether your workspace file is opened for editing or integrating, the mechanics of the resolve operation are the same. For each yours-theirs-base triplet of files, one of three things happens during the resolve operation: theirs is copied into yours, theirs is ignored, or theirs is merged into yours.

Safe auto-resolving does only the first two of these things, copying theirs into yours or ignoring theirs. Files that can't be resolved this way are skipped. Let's first look at what resolving by copying or ignoring does, then at how to auto-resolve files by merging. Finally, we'll look at resolving files interactively.

Resolving files by copying theirs into yours

During auto-resolving, when Perforce encounters triplets where theirs has changed but yours has not, theirs is copied into yours. In other words, when there are files in your workspace that you've opened but have not gotten around to changing, auto-resolving them simply refreshes them with copies from the depot (see Figure 3-5). They're still open for editing, so you can make changes to them and eventually submit them.

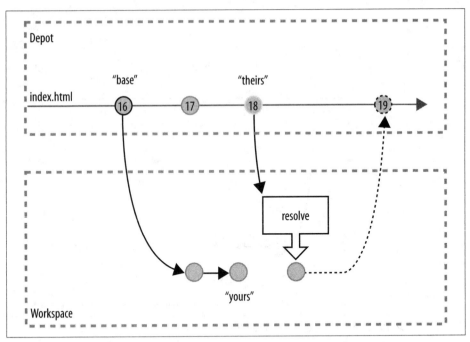

Figure 3-5. Copying theirs into yours

There are cases where you might want to replace your files with theirs even if yours *have* changed. For instance, you may have made local changes that you don't care about, or that are no longer relevant. You can use resolve -at for this. It auto-resolves files without looking, always copying theirs into yours:

```
resolve -at
c:\ws\doc\index.html
- vs //depot/projectA/doc/index.html#17,#18
- copy from //depot/projectA/doc/index.html
c:\ws\doc\img\diag02.gif
- vs //depot/projectA/doc/img/diag02.gif#3
- copy from //depot/projectA/doc/img/diag02.gif
```

(Think of -at for "always accept theirs" as a mnemonic.)

 As you can imagine, resolve -at is destructive—it overwrites your workspace files. Any local changes you've made will be lost.

Remember that you can use filespecs with the resolve command. You can use a command like this, for example, to replace all your opened, unresolved *.gif* files with theirs:

```
p4 resolve -at ...*.gif
c:\ws\doc\img\diag02.gif
- copy from //depot/projectA/doc/img/diag02.gif#3
```

Resolving files by ignoring theirs

The flip side of copying theirs into yours is to ignore theirs (see Figure 3-6). When you auto-resolve files, theirs is ignored in triplets where it is identical to the base. (In other words, there are no changes that need to be merged from theirs into yours.) Running resolve doesn't change your files, in these cases. It simply records the fact that they've been resolved. You can continue editing them, and submit them when you're ready.

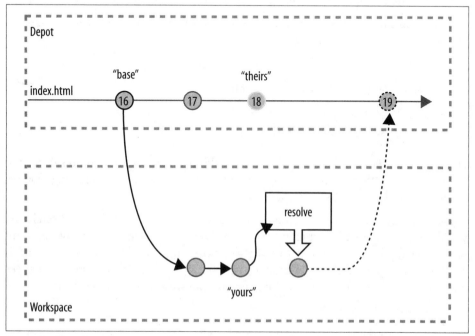

Figure 3-6. Resolving by ignoring theirs

It may seem odd that there can be newer versions of files in the depot that are exactly the same as previous versions. There are a number of reasons this could happen. One is that someone has submitted versions that back out previous changes. Another is that files' types have changed, but their content has not. Usually, resolving by ignoring theirs is the right thing to do; you can assume that the file you eventually check in will have the right characteristics. Read "Reconciling file type changes" later in this chapter to find out when you can't make this assumption and what to do about it.

There are also cases where you might want to resolve by ignoring theirs, even if theirs have changed and yours haven't. (In fact, you saw a use for this in Chapter 2.) To auto-resolve files by ignoring theirs, use resolve -ay:

```
resolve -ay
c:\ws\doc\index.html
```

```
- ignoring //depot/projectA/doc/index.html#18
c:\ws\doc\img\diag02.gif
- ignoring //depot/projectA/doc/img/diag02.gif#3
```

(For -ay, think of "always accept yours.")

Resolving files by merging theirs into yours

Finally, there is resolving files by merging theirs into yours. In this case, all three variants of the unresolved file are combined to produce a single result.

Note that during a safe auto-resolve, files are never merged. Instead, safe auto-resolving skips files that need merging:

```
p4 resolve -as
c:\ws\doc\index.html
- merging //depot/projectA/doc/index.html#17,#18
- resolve skipped
c:\ws\doc\img\diag02.gif
- vs //depot/projectA/doc/img/diag02.gif#3
- resolve skipped
```

Here, the *index.html* and *diag02.gif* files were skipped because there is no safe way to resolve them. In other words, resolving them requires merging, and merging requires updating your local files, so it's not considered safe.

Now, you *could* interactively resolve each file that can't be auto-resolved safely. As you'll see in a moment, interactive resolving gives you a chance to review the result of each merge before saving it to your workspace file. But interactive resolving is time-consuming. If you're comfortable with simply letting Perforce merge changes into your workspace files, you can save time by auto-resolving with merging:

```
p4 resolve -am
c:\ws\doc\index.html
- merging //depot/projectA/doc/index.html#17,#18
  Diff chunks: 1 yours + 2 theirs + 0 both + 0 conflicting
- merge from //depot/projectA/doc/index.html
```

(Think of -am as meaning "accept merged, when possible.") When you auto-resolve with merging, your workspace files are resolved only if they can be either resolved safely or merged without conflicts. In the latter case, Perforce reads files from your workspace and from the depot, merges them, and writes the merged result into your workspace files (see Figure 3-7). After files are merged, you can continue working on them.

When you auto-resolve files with merging, Perforce skips the files that have conflicting parallel changes. This behavior leaves them for you to resolve interactively.

Resolving files interactively

Files that need to be resolved on a case-by-case basis can be resolved interactively. From the command line, use resolve with no flags to get the interactive resolve

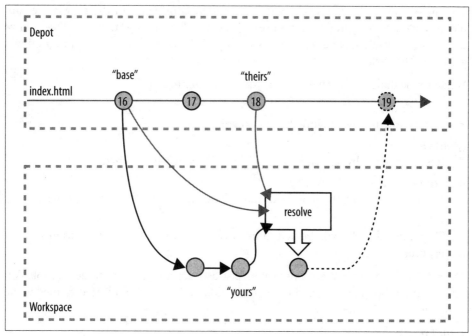

Figure 3-7. Resolving by merging

prompt. (The GUI programs have interactive resolve commands, too—look in the File menus for them.)

 In this chapter you'll see a few of the commands you can supply to the interactive resolve prompts. At any point, you can enter "?" to get the full menu of commands. You can also display the full menu of interactive resolve commands without actually entering the dialog itself, with this command:

> **p4 help resolve**

The interactive resolve prompt cycles through your unresolved files, showing information about the triplet of files involved with each one. Here, for example, the first unresolved file is *ads.html*:

```
p4 resolve
c:\ws\doc\ads.html
- merging //depot/projectA/doc/ads.html#3,#5
Diff chunks: 0 yours + 1 theirs + 0 both + 0 conflicting

Accept(a) Edit(e) Diff(d) Merge(m) Skip(s) Help(?) at:
```

You're now in resolve's interactive dialog. The dialog tells you which file it's on, and, if it's a text file, it summarizes the diffs it found when attempting to merge the file. (You'll find out what diff chunks are in the upcoming section "How Perforce Merges Text Files.")

The dialog always prompts you with a suggested command. In the previous example, it suggests you enter at, the terse abbreviation for "accept theirs." Once you've done that, your file will be replaced by a copy of theirs, and the resolve program will go on to the next unresolved file.

While in the dialog, you can enter the following commands:

at *(accept theirs)*
  Resolve the file by copying theirs into yours.

ay *(accept yours)*
  Resolve the file by ignoring theirs and leaving yours untouched.

am *(accept merged)*
  Resolve the file by merging. Your file will be replaced with the merged result.

s *(skip)*
  Skip this file. (It will be left unresolved for now. You'll have to resolve it eventually.)

The resolve dialog also offers a poor man's substitute for a graphical merge tool. You can use the following commands to show diffs and to view and modify files while resolving:

dt *(diff theirs)*
  In other words, diff their file with the base. This shows the changes *they* have made.

dy *(diff yours)*
  Diff yours with the base to show the changes *you* have made.

d *(diff)*
  Diff the merged file with your file. This command shows how your file will change if you resolve it by merging (that is, if you accept merged or accept edited).

e *(edit)*
  Edit the merged file. In other words, bring up the merged file in your text editor so you can edit the conflicts.

ae *(accept edited)*
  Resolve by replacing your file with the merged, edited result. (This is how you resolve a file after you've edited the conflicts.)

The Perforce GUI programs, P4V and P4Win, provide you with graphical tools to merge text files. As you would expect, it's far easier to merge files using a graphical tool than it is using a command-line tool. So, while we show many command-line resolve examples here, we expect that you'll be using P4V or P4Win to resolve files that need merging.

Perforce doesn't merge binary files

Files can be roughly classified into two types: text and binary. Text files contain bytes encoded in one of the many standardized character sets representing letters, numbers, and symbols. Perforce treats files as text if their filetype is text or unicode. (For more on this, see Chapter 1.) As far as Perforce is concerned, all other files are binary files. This is an important distinction that comes up when you resolve files, because Perforce merges only text files—it doesn't merge binary files. (Moreover, it merges text files only if all three files in the yours-theirs-base triplet have the same filetype, either text or unicode.)

 This is not to say that binary files can't be merged at all. They can, if you have a tool that resolve can use to merge them. See "Configuring an alternative merge tool" later in the chapter.

When resolving binary files, you must choose between copying and ignoring. Thus, resolve with binary files has its idiosyncrasies:

- A safe auto-resolve *will* work with binary files:

    p4 resolve -as

    With this command, binary files are treated the same as text files. In triplets where both yours and theirs have changed, the file is left unresolved.

- Auto-resolving by merging treats binary files exactly the same as does safe auto-resolving. Here, binary files are left unresolved in triplets where both yours and theirs have changed:

    p4 resolve -am

- Binary files that can't be auto-resolved by merging can be auto-resolved either by copying theirs into yours:

    p4 resolve -at

    or by ignoring theirs and leaving yours intact:

    p4 resolve -ay

- Resolving binary files interactively lets you choose how each file individually should be resolved. Even so, your choice is limited to copying or ignoring.

What's been resolved, and how?

The resolved command shows which of your opened files have already been resolved. It also shows how each file was resolved and which depot files were involved. For example:

```
p4 resolved -o
c:\ws\doc\ads.html
- copy from //depot/projectA/doc/ads.html#3,#5
```

```
   base //depot/projectA/doc/ads.html#2
c:\ws\doc\index.html
- merge from //depot/projectA/doc/index.html#17,#18
   base //depot/projectA/doc/index.html#16
c:\ws\doc\img\diag02.gif
- copy from //depot/projectA/doc/img/diag02.gif#3
```

(The -o flag makes the resolved command show which file was used as a base for each merge.)

How Perforce Merges Text Files

Any two files can be compared to reveal diffs. *Three* files are necessary to merge content: a starting version and two modified versions.

 Three-way file merging is an operation you'll find in many content-management tools. Perforce itself implements a three-way merge that operates on lines of text, not on characters, words, or other context-specific syntax. Some three-way merge tools *can* operate on characters, words, paragraphs, XML structures, HTML markup, programming language syntax, and so forth. If line-by-line merging isn't suitable for the kinds of files you're working with, you can configure Perforce to use another merge tool when resolving files. See "Configuring an alternative merge tool."

Chunks and conflicts

In Perforce's three-way merge, the "base" is the starting version and "yours" and "theirs" are the two modified versions of the file. Yours and theirs are each compared to the base so that lines in the three files can be grouped into "chunks." Each chunk in the base is determined to be changed or unchanged with respect to yours and theirs.* Chunks that are added or deleted are considered changed. Perforce constructs a merged file from the chunks using these rules:

- When a chunk is the same in all three files, it goes into the merged file.
- When a chunk has been changed in either yours or theirs, but not in both, the changed chunk goes into the merged file.
- When a chunk has been changed in both yours and theirs, and the change is identical, the changed chunk goes into the merged file.
- When a chunk is different in all three files, a conflict marker is placed at that location in the merged file. It will be up to you to decide what goes there.

---

* Prior to Release 2004.2, Perforce's merge algorithm treated contiguous lines with changes as single chunks. Consequently, parallel changes in lines adjacent to each other *always* produced a conflict. If you're seeing a lot of conflicts in your merged files, check to see whether you're using a pre-2004.2 version of Perforce. Upgrading to the latest release may make your merges easier.

A simple file merge

Figure 3-8 shows a simple file merge. When the base file is compared to yours and theirs, six chunks are detected. The merged file consists of:

- Chunks 1, 3, and 5 from the base. These are chunks of text neither you nor they changed.
- Chunk 2 from yours. (Or theirs—both of you made the identical change.)
- Chunk 4 from theirs. You made no change in that spot, but they did, so their chunk goes into the merged file.
- Chunk 6 can't be merged. Because they got rid of "aunts" and you changed "aunts" to "ants," the chunk is different in all three files. The spot where chunk 6 belongs is marked as a conflict in the merged file.

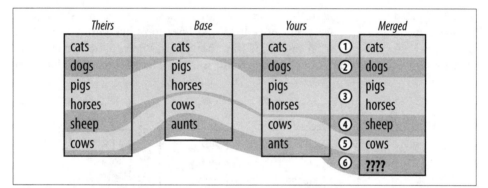

Figure 3-8. Chunks of a merged file

If you happened to be using the P4 resolve command, here's what you'd see when you edited the merged file:

```
cats
dogs
pigs
horses
sheep
cows
>>>> ORIGINAL
aunts
==== THEIRS
==== YOURS
ants
<<<<
```

It's up to you to remove the conflict markers and choose the text that should remain. As Figure 3-9 shows, P4V's merge tool presents the same merged file without visible conflict markers, but it's still up to you to choose the text that replaces the conflict.

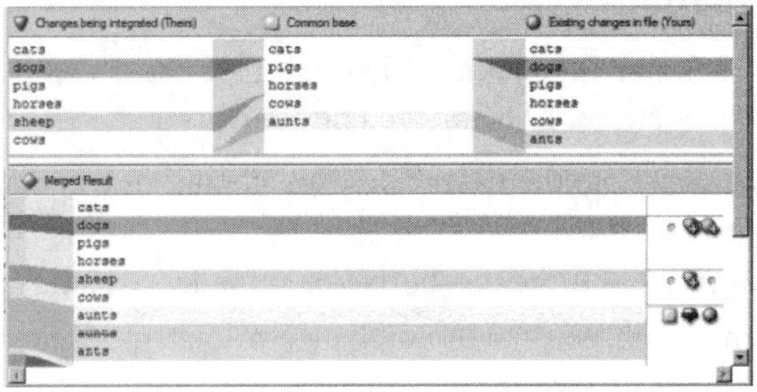

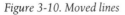

Figure 3-9. Merging in P4V

Merging moved lines

The Perforce file merge algorithm does not differentiate between lines that have changed and lines that have been moved. Moved lines look like chunks that have been removed in one location and added in another. In Figure 3-10, for example, they moved "cats" from the top of the file to the middle, whereas you moved it to the end.

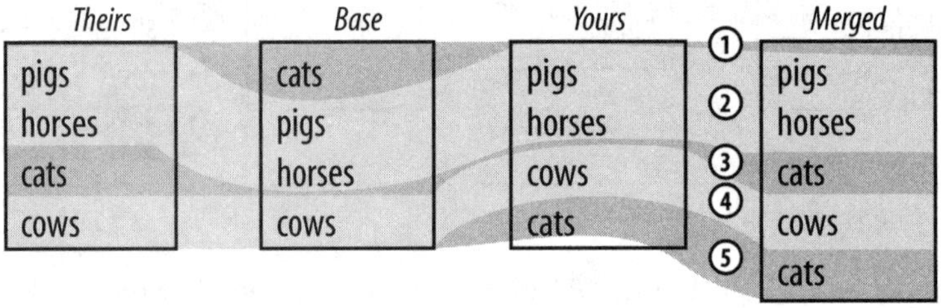

Figure 3-10. Moved lines

To Perforce, however, it looks like:

- In chunk 1, you and they both removed "cats," so "cats" is removed from the result.

- In chunk 3, they added "cats." You made no change to chunk 3, so their change goes into the result.

- Chunks 2 and 4 were changed by neither you nor them, and are therefore unchanged in the result.

- In chunk 5, you added "cats." They made no change to chunk 5, so your change goes into the result. Now there are two "cats."

As mentioned earlier, Perforce doesn't take syntax or context into account when merging files. And without more context, it's impossible to say whether this result is right or wrong. Suffice to say that parallel line-moves can have unexpected consequences. But the consequences can often be avoided altogether by resolving files via one changelist at a time, as you'll see later in the chapter.

A Notation for Discussing File Merging

Entirely independent of Perforce, there's a notation you can use to discuss the effects of files merges. Consider the example shown in Figure 3-8. In the figure we see it redrawn, this time using arbitrary letters of the alphabet to represent the chunks.

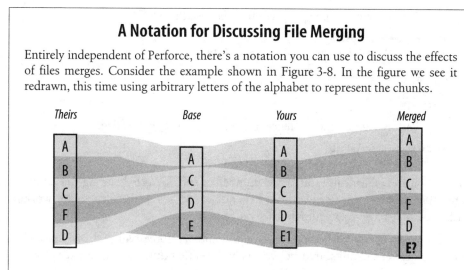

Each file can be represented by a bracketed set of chunks:

- The base is [A,C,D,E].
- Theirs is [A,B,C,F,D].
- Yours is [A,B,C,D,E1].
- The merged result is [A,B,C,F,D,E?].

This notation is easy to draw on a whiteboard and it's easy to use in writing.

Comparing whitespace

Whitespace characters—spaces and tabs, that is—are normally significant when Perforce diffs and merges files. You can control this, to some extent. Commands that compare files (diff, diff2, and resolve) have flags that change Perforce's diff algorithm.

For example, consider this diff case:

```
p4 diff myscript.rb
==== //depot/myscript.rb#1 - c:\ws\myscript.rb ====
3c3
< puts     a(b)
---
> puts a(b)
6c6
< c( d, e )
```

```
---
> c(d,e)
```

In the first pair of unequal lines, some whitespace was changed. In the second, some whitespace appears in only one of the two lines.

To make Perforce ignore *changes* in whitespace, use the -db flag:

```
p4 diff -db myscript.rb
==== //depot/myscript.rb#1 - c:\ws\myscript.rb ====
6c6
< c( d, e )
---
> c(d,e)
```

To make Perforce ignore the *existence* of whitespace, use the -dw flag:

```
p4 diff -dw myscript.rb
==== //depot/myscript.rb#1 - c:\ws\myscript.rb ====
```

The -db and -dw flags can reduce the number of diffs detected during file comparisons. *Which* of the two flags you use depends on what's in the files you're working with. You may have to experiment to get a good result.

If you use -db or -dw with the resolve command, Perforce will pick "yours" when choosing between chunks. In other words, in lines that differ by whitespace only, the merged result will match your workspace file.

Note that line-ends are always significant. You can't make Perforce ignore them for diffing and merging purposes.[*]

Reconciling Structural Changes

Parallel changes that affect depot structure can't be resolved in the same way as can parallel changes to file content alone. Among the changes that can't be resolved are changes where files have been added, deleted, renamed, moved, or combined. Perforce won't schedule files for resolving when:

- You have files opened for editing and you synchronize with newer depot revisions that are deleted. (In other words, someone else has deleted files you are working on.)

- You have files opened for deleting and you synchronize with newer, edited depot revisions. (In other words, someone else has edited the files you are about to delete.)

---

[*] Although you can't make Perforce ignore line-ends, you can use resolve -dl to make it ignore the difference between Unix-style CR line-ends and Windows-style CR/LF line-ends. This is not something you'd need to do unless your workspace is on a disk shared by both Unix and Windows machines or you're using local tools that write files with non-native line-end characters.

- You have files opened for adding or branching, and you synchronize with non-deleted depot revisions of files with the same names. (In other words, someone else has already added or branched files before you.)

Perforce does warn people who are opening files if other users have the same files opened. And people should heed these warnings, especially if they're opening files for refactoring or other structural changes. But sometimes they just don't realize that structural changes can't be resolved, and sometimes they have reasons to submit their changes anyway. All is not lost—there are ways to reconcile structural changes.

 The advice that follows works best if you make a habit of synchronizing, resolving, and reconciling changes incrementally, as described in "Tips for Smoother Collaboration" later in the chapter.

Someone adds the files you were going to add

Let's start with a simple case: you opened some files for adding, and in the meantime, someone else has added files with the same names to the depot. You have resynchronized, but that doesn't affect these files in your workspace. You still have them opened for adding, and you won't be able to submit them.

To detect files in this state, look for files that are both opened for adding and already in the depot:

```
p4 opened diag04.gif
//depot/dev/www/img/diag04.gif#1 - add default change
```

```
p4 files diag04.gif
//depot/dev/www/img/diag04.gif#1 - add change 4761
```

Here, for example, you were going to add *diag04.gif*, but someone has already added a file with the same name. Your next move depends on the nature of your work:

You can abandon your changes

You can simply abandon your plan to add the file, of course, by reverting it:

```
p4 revert diag04.gif
//depot/dev/www/img/diag04.gif#none - was add, abandoned
```

Note that reverting files you opened to add doesn't remove them from your workspace. Be sure to remove the file yourself to keep it from affecting your local tests.

You can use different names for your new files

To add your new file with a different name, rename your local file, open it to add it with its new name, and revert it with its old name. On Unix, for example:

```
mv diag04.gif diag05.gif
```

```
p4 add diag05.gif
//depot/dev/www/img/diag05.gif#1 - opened for add
```

p4 revert diag04.gif
```
//depot/dev/www/img/diag04.gif#none - was add, abandoned
```

You can submit new revisions of existing files

You may choose to submit the file you were going to add as a new revision of the file someone else added. To do that, first revert the file you planned to add. (Remember, reverting files opened for adding leaves them intact in your workspace.) Then use the `sync -k` command to make Perforce think you've already synchronized with the depot revision, and open the file to edit it. For example:

p4 revert diag04.gif
```
//depot/dev/www/img/diag04.gif#none - was add, abandoned
```

p4 sync -k diag04.gif
```
//depot/dev/www/img/diag04.gif#1 - added as c:\ws\www\img\diag04.gif
```

p4 edit diag04.gif
```
//depot/dev/www/img/diag04.gif - opened for edit
```

Now you'll be able to submit your file as a revision of the file already added.

Someone deletes the files you were going to delete

In this situation, you opened files for deleting and Perforce removed them from your workspace. While you had them open, someone else deleted them in the depot. Resynchronizing these files has no effect on your workspace. The files are still on your changelist, however, and you won't be able to submit them.

To detect files in this state, use revert -n and look for files that would be "cleared":

p4 revert -n //...
```
//depot/dev/www/blank.html#none - was delete, cleared
```

 Be sure to use the -n flag with the revert command. Otherwise it *will* revert your files—including the files you've edited—and your local changes will be lost.

It's trivial to reconcile files that are opened for deleting in your workspace with files that were deleted in the depot—all you have to do is revert them:

p4 revert //depot/dev/www/blank.html
```
//depot/dev/www/blank.html#none - was delete, cleared
```

Someone renames the files you were editing

In this situation, you opened files to edit them, and in the meantime, someone has renamed them. Resynchronizing, in this case, adds the newly named files to your workspace, but doesn't do anything with the files you were editing. To reconcile these files, you'll have to do two things. First, you'll have to merge your local changes into the newly named files. Second, you'll have to revert the original files.

To detect files that were renamed while you were editing them, look for files that would be deleted if you were to revert them:

```
p4 revert -n ...
//depot/dev/www/ads.html#none - was edit, deleted
```

Then check the recent history of any such files:

```
p4 filelog -m2 ads.html
//depot/dev/www/ads.html
... #6 change 6341 delete by bill "Clean up promo"
... #5 change 6340 edit by jim "Correct links"
... ... branch into //depot/dev/www/promo.html#1
```

(The -m2 flag limits filelog output to the two most recent revisions of each file.)

In the history of *ads.html*, we see that its highest revision is a delete, and that its last-known content was branched into *promo.html*. In other words, *ads.html* was renamed *promo.html*. And because you have resynchronized, you now have both *ads. html* and *promo.html* in your workspace. This is convenient, because the first step in reconciling this change is to open the newly named file for editing:

```
p4 edit promo.html
//depot/dev/www/promo.html#1 - opened for edit
```

Now, you could simply copy the original file into the new file, then revert the original file. But this doesn't account for the fact that the new file may have been modified as it was renamed. If you're working with text files, a better way to reconcile old with new is to *merge* your changes into the new file. Start by making a local copy of the original file as it was in the depot before it was deleted:

```
p4 print -q ads.html#5 > orig
```

Use this file as the base for a three-way merge with your edited file and the renamed file. Move the merged result into the newly named file and discard the copy of the original. On Windows, for example:

```
p4 merge3 -r orig ads.html promo.html > merged
move merged promo.html
del orig
```

(Here we use merge3—another undocumented P4 command—but you could just as well have used a graphical tool like P4Merge or P4WinMerge for this. The -r flag was used to keep merge3 from annotating every chunk in the file—only the conflicting chunks will be annotated.)

The newly named file now contains the merged result. If you used merge3 to create it, you'll have to use a text editor to straighten out any conflicts. (Look for strings like "CONFLICT" in the file.) When you're satisfied with the result—and *only* when you're satisfied with the result—revert the original file:

```
p4 revert ads.html
//depot/dev/www/ads.html#none - was edit, deleted
```

Reverting the original file removes it from your workspace.

Someone moves the files you were editing

This situation is exactly like the one in which someone renames the files you were editing, and can be reconciled in exactly the same way. The only difference is that the files may have been moved to a depot location outside of your workspace's client view. If so, you will have to modify your view in order to reconcile the change. (You saw how to do this in Chapter 2.)

Someone combines the files you were editing with other files

In this situation, you had files opened to edit them. Meanwhile, someone has merged their content into other files and deleted them. Resynchronizing doesn't affect your workspace files, but because their depot counterparts were deleted, you won't be able to submit them. Moreover, you probably don't want to submit them. You want to edit and submit the files that now contain their content.

This situation is also just like the one where someone renames the files you were editing, and it can be reconciled in the same way. The only difference is that the files you merge your changes *into* may be considerably different from the ones you started out with. Merging your changes into them might be messy.

Someone deletes the files you were editing

In this situation, you had files opened for editing and someone else deleted them in the depot. After you resynchronize, your files are still opened for editing but you won't be able to submit them.

To detect files in this state, look for files that would be deleted from your workspace if you were to revert them:

```
p4 revert -n ...
//depot/dev/www/beta.html#none - was edit, deleted
```

Here we see that *beta.html* was deleted while you were editing it. Check its history to make sure it wasn't renamed:

```
p4 filelog -m2 beta.html
//depot/dev/www/beta.html
... #4 change 6341 delete by bill "Clean up promo"
... #3 change 6340 edit by jim "New beta look"
```

Because there is no evidence that it was branched or merged into another file, we can assume *beta.html* was just plain deleted. How you reconcile this change depends on the nature of this file and the work you're doing:

You can abandon your changes
    To choose to abandon your changes to the now-deleted file, just revert it:

```
p4 revert beta.html
//depot/dev/www/beta.html#none - was edit, deleted
```

(Don't do this unless you really mean to abandon your changes. Reverting this file removes it from your workspace!)

You can reinstate deleted files

If you choose to reinstate the deleted file, you'll have to reopen it for adding and submit your version of it. However, you can't reopen the file for adding until you've reverted it and resynchronized with the last nondeleted version. There's a trick to doing this without losing your local edits:

```
p4 revert -k beta.html
//depot/dev/www/beta.html#none - was edit, deleted
```

```
p4 sync -k beta.html#3
//depot/dev/www/beta.html#3 - updating c:\ws\www\beta.html
```

 Be sure to use revert -k and sync -k, as shown. If you don't, you'll lose your local changes! The -k keeps revert and sync from modifying your workspace copy of the file.

```
p4 add beta.html
//depot/dev/www/beta.html#3 - opened for add
```

Now, when you submit your changelist, your workspace version will be copied to the depot and the file reinstated.

Someone edits the files you were going to delete

This situation, where someone else submits new revisions of files you are about to delete, is very difficult to detect after resynchronizing. For one thing, when you resynchronize, Perforce doesn't schedule resolves for the files you opened to delete. Nor does it prevent you from submitting those files. For another, once you've resynchronized, there's no way to tell which revisions you originally opened. At this point, there are no commands you can run to tell you if you are about to delete files without taking someone's prior changes into account.

If you follow the upcoming guidelines set out in "Tips for Smoother Collaboration," however, you'll be able detect this situation *before* you resynchronize. Then, after you resynchronize, you can choose your course of action:

You can delete anyway

If you choose to delete the files anyway, you don't need to do anything special. Just submit your changelist and the files will be deleted.

You can revert

If you decide that, under the circumstances, you shouldn't be deleting these files, revert them before submitting your changelist.

Someone edits the files you planned to rename or move

In this situation, you opened files to branch and delete them in order to rename them. (As you read in Chapter 2, this is how you rename files.) Meanwhile, someone has edited the files you planned to rename—that is, the ones you opened for deleting.

This situation is the same as if someone had edited files you planned to delete, and it's just as difficult to detect. However, once you've detected it, you can reconcile it by merging their changes into the files you are branching.

For example, assume you planned to change a file's name from *misc.html* to *topics.html*. You have *misc.html* opened for deleting, and *topics.html* opened for branching:

```
p4 opened
//depot/dev/www/misc.html#2 - delete
//depot/dev/www/topics.html#1 - branch
```

By the way, you can use the resolved command to confirm that these files are related:

```
p4 resolved
c:\ws\www\topics.html - branch from //depot/dev/www/misc.html#1,#2
```

Meanwhile, Jim has submitted a new revision of *misc.html*:

```
p4 filelog -m1 misc.html
//depot/dev/www/misc.html
... #3 change 6320 edit by jim "Fix javascript popup"
```

To merge Jim's changes into your newly named file, you'll need a local copy of the original file (*misc.html#2*) and a local copy of the one Jim submitted (*misc.html#3*):

```
p4 print -q //depot/dev/www/misc.html#2 > orig
p4 print -q //depot/dev/www/misc.html#3 > jims
```

Now, merge Jim's file into the new file, using the original as the base:

```
p4 merge3 -r orig jims topics.html > merged
```

Next, you'll need to reopen the new file for adding. This step makes it writable in your workspace (and tells Perforce that the file you'll be submitting is not identical to the one from which it was branched):

```
p4 add topics.html
//depot/dev/www/topics.html#1 - reopened for add
```

Finally, move the *merged* file into the new file and remove the local copies. On Windows, for example:

```
move merged topics.html
del orig jims
```

Now you can test Jim's changes in place and submit the files when you're ready.

Reconciling file type changes

Every file revision has a type associated with it. As you learned in Chapter 1, changing a file's type is a matter of opening a file, assigning a new type to the opened file, and submitting it. You can see how a file's type has evolved by looking at its filelog output. Here we see a file whose context type has changed from text to text+k:

```
p4 filelog misc.html
//depot/projectA/www/doc/misc.html
... #4 change 1756 edit 2004/11/01 (text+k)
... #3 change 1613 edit 2004/10/19 (text)
... #2 change 1602 edit 2004/10/18 (text)
... #1 change 1183 edit 2004/10/11 (text)
```

Changes to file type can be a bit of a wrench in the works when it comes to collaborative development. Like structural changes, type changes can't be resolved. Here's how a file's type behaves in your workspace:

- When you open a file, your opened workspace file takes on the type of the depot file's *head revision* rather than that of the revision you synchronized.

- Neither synchronizing nor resolving a file after you've opened it changes its type in your workspace.

- When you submit a file, the new head revision of the depot file takes on the type your opened workspace file had.

What this means is that even if you're in the habit of regularly synchronizing and resolving your files, you can still inadvertently back out someone else's change to a file's type.

For example, consider the *misc.html* file in the preceding example. You opened the file when its head revision was *#2*. Your opened file's type is text. After other changes, the latest revision is *misc.html#4*. The depot file's type is now text+k. You resynchronize and resolve, and your opened file's type is still text. You submit the file. Whether you meant to or not, you've just changed it back to a text file.

Before you submit a file, you can detect a pending file type change by looking at the file's fstat details:

```
p4 fstat misc.html
... depotFile //depot/projectA/www/doc/misc.html#4
... headType text+k
... type text
```

If fstat shows that type and headType are different, you'll be changing the file's type when you submit it.

To correct the type of a file you have opened, use reopen:

```
p4 reopen -t text+k misc.html
```

If you didn't get a chance to correct the file's type before submitting it, you can submit another version. Use the edit command to open the file and correct its type, and submit the file again. For example:

```
p4 edit -t text+k misc.html
p4 submit misc.html
```

Tips for Smoother Collaboration

An SCM tool can do only so much to make collaborative development possible. The rest is up to developers. Here are some things developers can do to keep collaboration going smoothly.

Keep your workspace synchronized

When you're working on files in parallel with other developers, resynchronize your workspace regularly. The longer you put off resynchronizing, the harder it is to get caught up. And if you're not caught up, you can't submit files.

Also, instead of resynchronizing individual files, resynchronize all the files in the scope of your work. (The scope could be a directory, several directories, or even your entire workspace.) This keeps your files in sync with each other and assures that when you try to compile or test, you'll have a set of files known to work together.

When you're working in a heavily concurrent environment, it's easier to resolve or otherwise reconcile changes *before* you attempt to submit files than it is after a submit command fails. So, before you submit, check to make sure you're synchronized:

```
p4 sync -n
```

If you're not, synchronize and resolve one changelist at a time, as described in the next section, *then* submit your files.

If resynchronizing regularly is going to make it difficult for you to do your work, consider working in a private branch. See Chapter 10.

Synchronize and resolve one changelist at a time

We tend to speak of synchronizing as a way to get caught up with the current state of the depot. But in fast-moving, parallel development projects, many changes can occur in a short time. Simply synchronizing to the latest revisions puts you in a position of having to resolve many people's changes at once. This can be confusing, if not downright hellish.

If smooth collaboration is your goal, synchronize, resolve, and reconcile *one changelist at a time*. Here's a recipe for changelist-by-changelist synchronization. Run these commands from the root of the file tree that encompasses the scope of your work:

1. Determine the changelist you're currently synchronized with:

   ```
   p4 changes -m1 ...#have
   Change 9284 on 2004/03/01 by jim 'Swap project names'
   ```

2. Find out what's happened in the depot since you last synchronized:

   ```
   p4 changes "...@>9284"
   Change 9306 on 2004/03/05 by ann 'Fix menus on interactive'
   Change 9301 on 2004/03/05 by ron 'Update training schedule'
   Change 9299 on 2004/03/05 by ann 'New menu bar for interac'
   ```

   (The @>9284 syntax means changelist numbers greater than 9284. You can read about it in help undoc. It's in quotes to keep the command shell from treating it as file redirection syntax.)

   The lowest changelist on the list—9299 in this case—is the one you want to synchronize with next.

3. Get acquainted with the change you are about to synchronize. Read the changelist description, note the files that were updated, and look for parallel changes to files you're working on. (Pay particular attention to changes to files you plan to delete!) These commands are useful for this:

   ```
   p4 describe -s 9299
   p4 sync -n ...@9299
   ```

4. Synchronize with the change:

   ```
   p4 sync ...@9299
   ```

5. Were files added, deleted, or branched in this change? Are any of those the files you're working on? If so, refer to "Reconciling Structural Changes" earlier in this chapter, and reconcile those files now.

6. Auto-resolve the files that don't have conflicts, then resolve the rest of the files interactively:

   ```
   p4 resolve -am
   p4 resolve
   ```

   (Use resolve -as instead of resolve -am if you want to defer the merges to the interactive step.)

7. Test the state of your workspace. Were files merged correctly? Can you compile? If not, fix the problem before doing anything else.

Now, repeat the whole thing for the next changelist. Seems like a lot of work, but it's a lot easier than trying to merge everybody's changes at once.

Be on the lookout for changes that can't be resolved

There are two kinds of changes that Perforce doesn't handle by resolving: structural changes, and changes to a file's type. There's no reason these changes can't be done in parallel, but if done unawares, collaboration can become exasperating.

A little advanced planning could save hours or days of trying to reconcile work in progress later:

- If you're making a structural change—that is, you're making a change that involves renaming, moving, deleting, splitting, or combining files—get in touch with users who have the same files opened. Remember that you can see who has files opened with opened -a. For example:

  ```
  p4 opened -a *.html
  //depot/www/projectA/index.html#13 - also opened by bill
  //depot/www/projectA/misc.html#2 - also opened by ann
  ```

- Check the file type of your opened files before you submit them. Make sure you're not undoing someone else's file type change.

Submit logical changelists

Changelists let you organize your work into logical changes. Use them to help other developers reconcile their work in progress with your contributions. Here are some ways to be helpful:

- Don't combine several tasks into one changelist.
- Don't submit files one at a time if they depend on changes to other files.
- When you're renaming or moving files, in particular, be sure to submit the corresponding deleted and branched files in the same changelist.
- Use the changelist description to warn other developers of anything in your change that might be tricky to reconcile.
- If you're making structural changes, say so in the changelist description.
- Don't mix refactoring with functional changes. All the reasons that make this a good idea for development make it a good idea for SCM, too.
- Don't mix gratuitous whitespace changes with other changes. If you have a compulsion to line up all the margins in a source file, for example, don't do it as you are fixing a bug. Instead, submit the bug fix first, then submit your redecorating in a separate changelist.

Check your merged files

Merging is where many mistakes are introduced in collaborative projects. The mechanics of merging are not so difficult, but verifying that the result is correct can

Conflicts, Context, and Text

Merging can introduce errors whether conflicts are detected or not. Consider a file that contains these lines of text:

```
You must bring your
birth certificate
when you register.
```

Let's say you open the file for editing and add a few lines at the end:

```
You must bring your
birth certificate
when you register.
(You may bring a
photocopy instead
of the original.)
```

Meanwhile, someone else has submitted a new version of the file that looks like this:

```
You must bring your
parent or guardian
when you register.
```

As far as Perforce can tell, there is no conflict between your changes and theirs. When you resolve the file and merge in their changes, you'll end up with:

```
You must bring your
parent or guardian
when you register.
(You may bring a
photocopy instead
of the original.)
```

This looks like a perfectly formed English paragraph, but it makes no sense, of course. After merging files, and before submitting them, you should always verify that they were merged correctly by testing them in their intended contexts.

be. Here are a few things you can do to prevent bad merges from slipping through undetected:

- Don't assume that nonconflicting merges are correct merges. As you saw in "Merging moved lines," earlier in the chapter, the correctness of a merge is a matter of context.

- If you have a not-too-large number of files to merge, use P4V or P4Win to resolve your files interactively. The graphical merge tools in these GUIs show diffs in context, making mismerged results far easier to detect with the naked eye. (You can also configure the P4 interactive resolve command to use P4V's graphical merge tool, P4Merge. See "Configuring P4 to use P4Merge" later in the chapter for details.)

- Before merging, make local backup copies of your opened files. If subsequent testing shows a problem, backup copies give you the option of restoring your files to their premerged states and merging them again.

- Compare *your* diffs before and after resolving. (*Your* diffs being the diffs that show your local changes to files.) You can do this by capturing before and after diffs in temporary files and then comparing the files.

  For example, say you've just synchronized with changelist @2104. Previously, you were synchronized with @2103. Before you resolve, capture your diffs:

  ```
  p4 diff @2103 > before.diffs
  ```

  Resolve your files as you see fit. For example, you might choose to auto-resolve your files by merging, then resolve the stragglers interactively:

  ```
  p4 resolve -am
  p4 resolve
  ```

  Capture your diffs again:

  ```
  p4 diff > after.diffs
  ```

  Now compare these two files, *before.diffs* and *after.diffs*. Except for the line numbers, they should be identical, *except* where they reflect conflicts you had to edit. In other words, your diffs should be essentially the same before and after you've merged in someone else's change. If *after.diffs* contains something that's not in *before.diffs*, and you don't recognize that something as a change you made while editing conflicts, you may have inadvertently backed out someone else's change. And, if vice versa, you may have inadvertently backed out a local change of your own.

The Arcana of Merging

What you've read so far may be all you need to know about resolving and merging files for your day-to-day work. In this section we'll take a look at a few advanced and arcane topics that may prove useful in special situations.

Forced merging

Earlier you read that when you auto-resolve files with merging, Perforce skips files if it finds parallel changes that conflict. There is a way to force Perforce to auto-resolve all files with merging even when there are conflicts. Use:

```
p4 resolve -af
```

The -af flag makes resolve work the same way as -am, but instead of skipping files with conflicts, it goes ahead and merges changes, leaving conflict markers in the resulting files. Forcing a merge of the files in "A simple file merge" earlier in this chapter, for example, writes this result to your workspace file, as:

```
cats
dogs
pigs
horses
sheep
cows
>>>> ORIGINAL
aunts
==== THEIRS
==== YOURS
ants
<<<<
```

The advantage of forcing merges is that you can resolve everything at once and edit the conflicts later. But this small advantage may be outweighed by several disadvantages:

- Forced merging overwrites your workspace files with files that are never syntactically correct. Until you edit them, they won't compile or behave properly in any way.

- Once you've resolved a file by forcing a merge, the file is ready to submit, as far as Perforce is concerned. There's nothing in Perforce that warns you that you've left conflict markers in files you are submitting.

- If you forget to edit the conflict markers in a file before resynchronizing and merging newer changes to it, the conflict markers will themselves be treated as file content. And if these lines conflict with the newer changes, the result will be very, very confusing.

Can you undo or redo a resolve?

You can't undo a resolve. Once you've resolved a file, it's resolved:

```
p4 resolve -am index.html
c:\ws\doc\index.html
- merging //depot/projectA/doc/index.html#17,#18
merging from //depot/projectA/doc/index.html

p4 resolve -am index.html
No file(s) to resolve.
```

Even if you synchronize a resolved file to a newer revision, it stays resolved with respect to previously resolved revisions.

There is a resolve flag, -f, that purports to re-resolve resolved files. But remember, resolving modifies your workspace files. Once your workspace files are modified, there's no way for Perforce to recover their previous versions. So resolve -f doesn't actually redo the *first* resolve. Instead, it resolves files again, this time using your modified workspace files as input.

You may find resolve -f useful if you've resolved files by ignoring and now want to re-resolve them by some other method. You might also get some use out of it if you've previously resolved by any method and now want to re-resolve by copying.

Here, for example, *index.html* is first resolved by ignoring and then the same file is re-resolved by copying:

```
p4 resolve -ay index.html
c:\ws\doc\index.html
- vs //depot/projectA/doc/index.html#17,#18
ignoring //depot/projectA/doc/index.html
```

```
p4 resolve -f -at index.html
c:\ws\doc\index.html
- vs //depot/projectA/doc/index.html#17,#18
copying //depot/projectA/doc/index.html
```

The only reason this approach works, of course, is that resolving by copying doesn't need reference to pre-resolved versions of your workspace files.

Can you undo a merge?

A merge that happens during a resolve *can* be undone, but with difficulty. As long as you didn't have to edit conflicts when you resolved by merging, you should be able to undo the merge cleanly.

For example, say you've resolved *index.html* by merging. First, find out which revisions were involved in the merge:

```
p4 resolved -o index.html
c:\ws\doc\index.html
- merge from //depot/projectA/www/doc/index.html#17,#18
  base //depot/projectA/www/doc/index.html#16
```

This shows us that *index.html#18* was merged with your *index.html* file using *index. html#16* as the base. You can effectively undo this merge by merging your current *index.html* with *index.html#16* using *index.html#18* as the base. You'll need temporary copies of *index.html#18* and *index.html#16* for this:

```
p4 print -q //depot/projectA/www/doc/index.html#16 > old.base
p4 print -q //depot/projectA/www/doc/index.html#18 > old.theirs
```

Now, merge to undo the previous merge:

```
p4 merge3 -r old.theirs old.base index.html > new.merged
```

If all went well, the *new.merged* file will look like your workspace *index.html* did before you did the first merge. At this point, you can copy it into *index.html* and remove the temporary files.

If the resulting *new.merged* file doesn't look right, try the same merge with P4Merge. This method won't change the merge result, but the graphical display may help you see how it came about. It also makes it easier to edit the result in context. On Windows, you can launch P4Merge for this example with:

```
p4merge old.theirs old.base index.html new.merged
```

On Unix, that's:

```
p4v -merge old.theirs old.base index.html new.merged
```

What happens when you revert files?

When you revert workspace files, Perforce replaces them with *the revisions you last synchronized*, not the revisions you last resolved. This behavior can be a little confusing if you're not expecting it.

For example, let's say you opened *index.html#16* for editing, and *index.html#18* is now the head revision. Resynchronizing schedules your file for resolve, without changing its contents. Your local copy still looks like *index.html#16* (with any local changes you have made). But if you revert the file, it will be replaced with *index.html#18* instead of *index.html#16*, whether you resolved the file or not. Why? Because it was the revision you last synchronized.

Another way to schedule a resolve, however, is to attempt to submit unsynchronized files. The submit command will fail, and the files involved will be scheduled for resolve with their corresponding head revisions. You will be able to resolve just as if you'd synchronized. But in this case, since you've never actually resynchronized the files, reverting them at this point would restore them to their original revisions rather than to the revisions scheduled for resolve.

For example, assume you have *index.html#16* opened for editing. You attempt to submit it even though *index.html#18* is now the head revision. The submit command schedules it for resolve with *index.html#18*, without synchronizing it. Whether you resolve the file or not, reverting it now will replace it with *index.html#16*, not *index.html#18*. Why? Because *index.html#16* was the revision you last synchronized.

Backing out changes, revisited

In Chapter 2, you saw the recipe for backing out a change. That was the basic recipe; it works when the affected files have not been modified by changes subsequent to the one you're backing out.

Now that you are familiar with resolving and merging, you'll see that the basic recipe can be extended to work even when subsequent changes are involved. To back out change C, the recipe is:

1. Synchronize with the pre-@C files.

2. Open C's deleted files for adding.

3. Open C's edited or integrated files for editing.

4. Synchronize with @C.

5. Open C's added or branched files for deleting.

6. Resolve files by ignoring.

7. Synchronize with the latest files.

8. Resolve files by merging.

9. Submit changelist.

Let's revisit the example, backing out change 1245. And in this scenario, let's say the files edited in change 1245 were also edited in subsequent changes. Here's how the extended recipe is applied to this case:

```
p4 sync @1244
p4 files @=1245 | sed -n -e "s/#.* - delete .*//p" | p4 -x- add
p4 files @=1245 | sed -n -e "s/#.* - edit .*//p" | p4 -x- edit
p4 sync @1245
p4 files @=1245 | sed -n -e "s/#.* - add .*//p" | p4 -x- delete
p4 resolve -ay
p4 sync
p4 resolve
p4 submit
```

The first resolve uses the -ay option to ignore theirs—that is, to prevent the *@1245* versions of the files from being merged in. The second resolve is interactive, giving you a chance to make sure the changes that occured *after* change 1245 are merged in correctly.

(And yes, we're using the Unix sed command to filter the output of the P4 files command. Why a filter? See "Backing out a recent change" in Chapter 2. Why sed? Because it's compact. If you're on Windows, and you have no sed, you can use Ruby, Perl, Python, or the recondite for command.)

 Remember to use this recipe in a workspace that doesn't already have these files open. As you are backing out a changelist, be aware that if any of the changelist's edited files were later deleted, you'll have to adjust the recipe per the instructions in "Someone deletes the files you were editing," earlier in this chapter. And if any of the files' types were changed later, you'll have to adjust the recipe per the instructions in "Reconciling file type changes," earlier in this chapter.

Configuring P4 to use P4Merge

Perforce lets you configure an alternate merge tool to be used when resolving files interactively. If you're a P4 user, this is great—it means you don't have to look at inscrutable text diffs or edit files marked up with ugly, text-delineated conflicts. Instead, you can configure P4 to use P4Merge, the same graphical merge tool that P4V provides.

Unix users can set the P4MERGE environment variable to tell P4 to invoke `p4v -merge`. For example:

```
export P4MERGE='p4v -merge'
```

(The exact command you use depends on your shell, of course.)

If you're on Windows, use P4's set command to set P4MERGE in the Registry. The command to invoke is `p4merge`:

```
p4 set P4MERGE=p4merge
```

Now, when you run `resolve` interactively, use `m` to invoke P4Merge instead of using `e` to edit the merged file manually. For example:

```
p4 resolve
c:\ws\doc\misc.html
- merging //depot/projectA/doc/ads.html#3,#5
Diff chunks: 1 yours + 1 theirs + 0 both + 2 conflicting

Accept(a) Edit(e) Diff(d) Merge(m) Skip(s) Help(?) e:
  m
```

Issuing this command launches P4Merge, where you can point and click to view (and modify) the merged file. Once you save the merged file and close P4Merge, `resolve` will prompt you to accept the result:

```
Accept(a) Edit(e) Diff(d) Merge(m) Skip(s) Help(?) ae:
```

Choose the prompt's default (ae, in this example) to copy the file P4Merge saved for you into your workspace file.

P4 can also be configured to use P4Merge for the `diff` command. Just set the P4DIFF in the environment or registry the same way you did P4MERGE.

Perforce invokes alternative merge tools only during interactive resolving and diffing. Regardless of how you've configured your environment, Perforce will use its own merge tool, not yours, when you auto-resolve files.

In the "more than you needed to know" category, here's the reason: the auto-resolve merges are done by the Perforce Server. The `resolve -am` command sends your workspace files to the server program, the server does the merge and sends files back to the client program, and the client puts them in your workspace files. There's no way to configure the server to run a different merge program than its own.

Configuring an alternative merge tool

There are reasons beyond the pleasure of a graphical experience for which you might want to use an alternative merge tool. For example, if you're working with XML, you might want to use a tool that can recognize XML syntax and merge XML files intelligently. Likewise, if you're working with Java or C++ source, you might want to use a tool that can merge programming constructs defined in those languages. Whatever your reason, you can use Perforce client programs with the merge tool of your choice.

Many commercial merge tools provide a way to configure themselves for use with Perforce. Those that don't can be configured by you—all Perforce requires is that your merge tool can be launched from a command shell, and that when it exits, it has saved or output a merged file.

Perforce will invoke a merge tool with four positional arguments, each naming a file:

> *file1*: the base file
> *file2*: their file
> *file3*: your file
> *file4*: the merged file

(Other than your file, the files passed to the merge tool are temporary copies generated by Perforce for the current operation.) Your merge tool will need to be able to merge *file2* and *file3*, using *file1* as the base, and save the result in *file4*. You may have to wrap your merge program in a script that rearranges the order of the arguments Perforce passes to it or that provides additional command flags.

For example, let's look at what it takes to configure KDiff3[*] as your merge tool on Windows. The kdiff3 program expects to be invoked with these arguments:

```
kdiff3 file1 file2 file3 -o file4
```

To use KDiff3 as P4's merge tool, you'll need to create a wrapper script that invokes it correctly. On Windows, the wrapper script would look something like this:

```
set path=%path%;c:\program files\kdiff3
kdiff3.exe %1 %2 %3 -o %4
```

Call this script *kdiff3p4merge.bat* and put it in the *C:\Program Files\Perforce* directory. Now use P4's set command to set P4MERGE in the registry:

```
p4 set P4MERGE=kdiff3p4merge.bat
```

To configure P4V to use KDiff3 as its merge tool, fill in P4V's Tools → Preferences → Merge dialog, as shown in Figure 3-11.

If all goes well, you should now be able to launch KDiff3 when interactively resolving files with P4 or P4V.

---

[*] See *kdiff3.sourceforge.net*. KDiff3 doesn't have any syntax- or context-specific merging features. We're using it here simply because it's a readily available example of an alternative merge tool that works with Perforce.

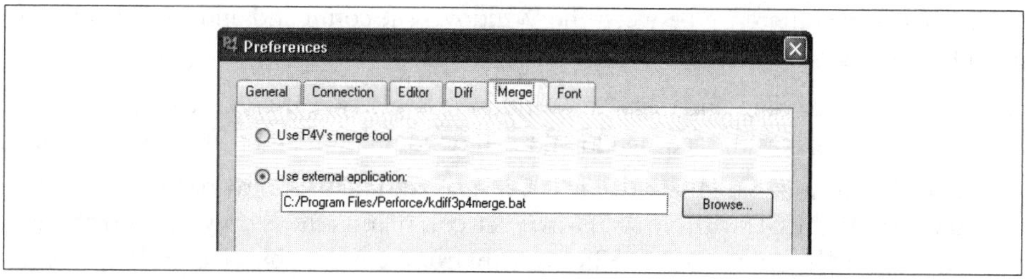

Figure 3-11. P4V's merge Preferences dialog

Merging nontext files

As you know, Perforce can't merge nontext files. But if *you* have a tool that can merge nontext files, you can coerce the `resolve` command into handling them as text and passing them to your merge tool.

For example, say the **.dat* files you work with contain binary data peculiar to the software you develop. You have a program called `datamrg` that can do three-way merging of files in this format, and you've configured Perforce to use this program as your alternative merge tool. While you were editing *spin.dat#3*, someone submitted a new revision. To resolve your file with the changes in *spin.dat#4*, you can use this command:

```
p4 resolve -t spin.dat
c:\ws\data\spin.dat
- binary merge //depot/projectA/data/spin.dat#4

Accept(a) Edit(e) Diff(d) Merge(m) Skip(s) Help(?) e:
  m
Accept(a) Edit(e) Diff(d) Merge(m) Skip(s) Help(?) ae:
```

Normally, Perforce doesn't offer to let you merge binary files. But in this case, because you used the -t flag, `resolve` is handling *spin.dat* as if it were text. When you answer m to its prompt, it invokes your `datamrg` program to do the merge. And after `datamrg` is done, `resolve` prompts you to save the file it produced (or, in `resolve`'s words, to "accept the edited file").

Setting P4MERGE

The `resolve` command, as you've seen, uses P4MERGE to determine which merge tool to run. If you're using a specialized merge tool, like the `datamrg` program in the preceding example, you might want to wrap the `resolve` command in a script that sets its own P4MERGE. A Windows script, for example, might look like this:

```
@setlocal
set P4MERGE=c:\special\datamrg
p4 resolve %1 %2 %3 %4 %5 %6 %7 %8 %9
@endlocal
```

And what is the difference between the Windows set command and the P4 set command? It is this:

- The P4 set command sets a Windows Registry variable. Using it to set P4MERGE makes the setting global to all of your command prompt windows.

- The Windows set command, on the other hand, sets an environment variable. Setting P4MERGE with the Windows set command affects only the current window or batch script. To P4, Windows environment variables trump Registry settings.

On Unix, there is no Registry and the P4 set command doesn't set anything. P4MERGE can be set in a Unix shell session or script just like any other environment variable.

CHAPTER 4

Branching and Integration

In the course of software development, we *branch* files to do concurrent, parallel work on them, and we *integrate* files to combine the results of such work. In this chapter, we'll look at how to do branching and integration with Perforce

This chapter won't dwell on reasons to branch, what to branch, or how to work with different kinds of branches. Not that those things aren't important—they are, and they'll be given due consideration in Part II. But for now, we'll limit our discussion to the mechanics of branching and integrating.

More Terminology

In this book, we use the term *branch* to mean a set of files that is a variant of another, each set evolving independently. (*Codeline* and *stream* are other words for this set.)

Don't confuse the term *branch* with the P4 branch command. The command creates Perforce database objects called "branches," but these objects are not branches at all. They're really *branch views*. We'll discuss branch views later in this chapter.

It's common to hear people in the software development world say they *merge* changes from one branch into another. In Perforce, we say we *integrate* changes from one branch into another. This is not a capricious choice of words. It's based on the notion that even when two branches are closely related, not all changes in one branch *can* be merged into the other. Even so, every change has to be accounted for when you're trying to figure out what needs merging. ("*Why was this change never merged? Is it not applicable? Or did someone simply forget to merge it?*")

The business of accounting for every change is what Perforce calls *integrating*. A change can be integrated from branch to branch by merging, when appropriate, or by simply deciding that it should be ignored. In either case, the change is considered *integrated* when you've decided what to do about it and Perforce has recorded your decision.

The Classic Case for a Branch

Of all the uses for branching, the one best understood is that of branching recently developed software for a product release. For example, assume that we are Ace Engineering and that we've been working on a software product called Ace. We're gearing up to make the first release of Ace available. Our plan is to release Ace Version 1.0 while simultaneously developing new features for a future release. For this, we're going to have to make a branch.

So far, there's one tree of files that constitutes the Ace product. It's in the //Ace/ MAIN directory path of our depot. Until now, we've all worked together on the files in the //Ace/MAIN tree, shown in Figure 4-1.

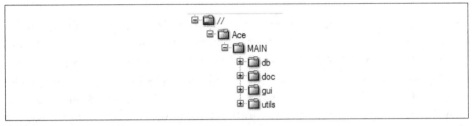

Figure 4-1. One tree of files

With Perforce, we can simply clone the //Ace/MAIN file tree into a new //Ace/V1 file tree. This allows us to continue working on new features in the //Ace/MAIN tree. Meanwhile, those of us testing and stabilizing the 1.0 release can work in the //Ace/ V1 tree. The two file trees are shown in Figure 4-2.

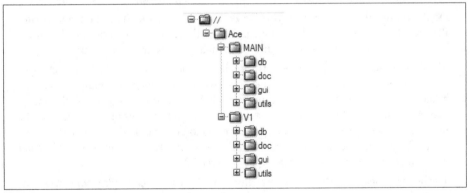

Figure 4-2. Cloning //Ace/V1 from //Ace/MAIN

At the outset, every file in the //Ace/MAIN tree has an identical counterpart in the //Ace/V1 tree. Over time, content diverges between the two trees as new development proceeds. The //Ace/V1 tree holds the stable, 1.0 version of the product, and the //Ace/MAIN tree holds the bleeding-edge, unreleased version.

This notion of cloning a tree of files from another is the essence of branching in Perforce. We clone a tree of files so that we can make changes to either tree—or branch—without affecting the other. The two file trees are peers in the depot hierarchy. Moreover, every file is a full-fledged file in its own right. Files in either branch can be edited, added, deleted, renamed, or moved. And changes made in one branch can be merged or otherwise integrated into the other.

Behind the scenes, Perforce keeps track of branching. Although every branched file is a file in its own right, its lineage is stored in the Perforce database. Perforce keeps track of a file's integration history as well. As we successively integrate changes between a pair of branches, Perforce uses file history to keep us from having to re-merge changes we've already merged.

Even more important is that Perforce can tell us the integration history of a branch. Given a pair of branches, Perforce can tell us which changes have already been integrated from one into the other, and which have yet to be integrated.

If all of this were as simple as it sounds, you wouldn't need this book. Many branch and integration operations in Perforce *are* quite simple, of course, but some of the simplest ones are a bit unintuitive and one or two of the essential ones just aren't that simple. The goal of this chapter is to front-load you with knowledge to keep you from making the common mistakes the first time out. And if it's too late for that, this chapter will at least help you understand your prior missteps.

We'll use the classic branch-for-release use case throughout this chapter to demonstrate Perforce commands and their consequences. However, the classic case is certainly not the only use to which Perforce branching can be applied. Later in this book, you'll see how Perforce branching can be used to configure products, distribute software, trace object origins, and shepherd web content, among other things.

Creating Branches

As with all operations that affect depot files, creating a branch is a two-step process in Perforce. First you use integrate to open files for branching, then you use submit to make them appear in the depot.*

Opening files for branching

So, back to our Ace example. We can think of the evolution of *//Ace/MAIN* as a single timeline, punctuated by submitted changelists (see Figure 4-3).

Now it's time to branch *//Ace/MAIN* into *//Ace/V1*. (We'll call these branches *MAIN* and *V1*, for short. See Figure 4-4.)

---

* "Open," as you recall, is Perforce's term describing files you plan to submit.

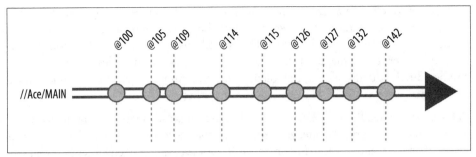

Figure 4-3. The evolution of //Ace/MAIN

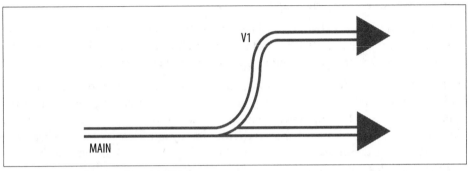

Figure 4-4. Branching V1 from MAIN

Making the branch is simply a matter of using integrate to clone one directory from another:

```
p4 integ //Ace/MAIN/... //Ace/V1/...
//Ace/V1/db/Jamfile#1 - branch/sync from //Ace/MAIN/db/Jamfile#1,#32
//Ace/V1/db/dbAcc.cpp#1 - branch/sync from //Ace/MAIN/db/dbAcc.cpp#1,#3
//Ace/V1/db/dbDefN.cpp#1 - branch/sync from //Ace/MAIN/db/dbDefN.cpp#1,#7
...
```

(What's integ? An alias of integrate.) The integrate command takes two filespecs as arguments.* The first identifies the donor files and the second identifies like-named target files—the files that will be created, in this case.

> Whether it's used to branch, rename, or integrate files, the higher calling of integrate is to propagate change. Change comes from "donor files" and flows to "target files." Thus the integrate command always involves a pair of filespecs, one being the donor and the other the target.

As you can see, every file in *MAIN* is branched into a corresponding file in *V1*. For example, donor file *//Ace/MAIN/db/Jamfile#32* is branched into target *//Ace/V1/db/Jamfile#1*. From integrate's output, we can infer that *#32* is the head revision of the

---

* To refresh your understanding of filespecs, see Chapter 1.

donor. The message `branch/sync ... Jamfile#1,#32` lets us know that revisions *#1* through *#32* of the donor are going on record as having been integrated into revision *#1* of the target.

Perforce bootstraps the new branch by copying donor files from the depot into target files in your workspace. (That's what the `branch/sync` messages in the output of integrate mean.)

 The target files, even though they don't exist yet in your workspace or in the depot, *must be mapped in your workspace client view*. The donor files need not be. This is commonly misunderstood.*

For example, to run

```
p4 integ //Ace/MAIN/... //Ace/V1/...
```

you must have a client view that encompasses the *//Ace/V1* files. But it doesn't matter whether your view encompasses the *//Ace/MAIN* files.

Chapter 2 showed how to configure client views. We'll see many more examples in this chapter and in the chapters that follow.

Branching from a point in time

The integrate command normally branches each donor file from its head revision. In other words, it branches from the current point in time (see Figure 4-5).

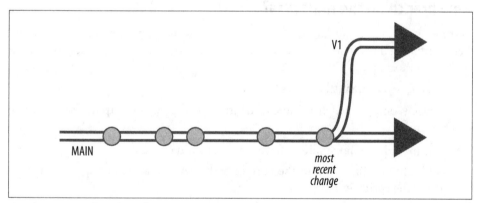

Figure 4-5. Branching from the current point in time

You can make integrate branch from a previous point in time by providing a revision in the donor filespec. For example, to branch *MAIN* from its 12 October 2004 state, you could use:

```
p4 integ //Ace/MAIN/...@2004/10/12 //Ace/V1/...
```

---

* The root of this misunderstanding may be that the integrate command always cites donor files rather than target files in error messages about views. For example, say you're integrating *a/foo.c* into *b/foo.c*. You'll get the message `a/foo.c - no target file(s) in both client and branch view` if the *b/...* path is not in your view.

As far as depot evolution is concerned, changelist numbers *are* points in time. So you could just as well use a changelist number as a branch point. For example:

```
p4 integ //Ace/MAIN/...@3109 //Ace/V1/...
```

Figure 4-6 illustrates the result in either case.

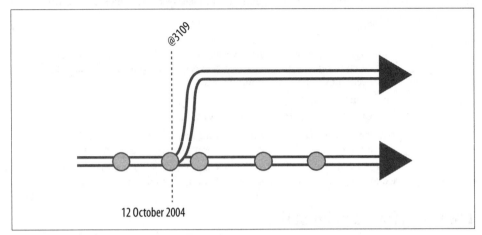

Figure 4-6. Branching from a previous point in time

Am I branching the right files?

Perforce is usually quite happy to let you run any integrate command you want. Before running an actual integrate, you can run it with -n to see a preview of what it will do. For example:

```
p4 integ -n //Ace/MAIN/... //Ace/V1/...
```

The preview output, which is almost identical to the actual output, will help you assure that:

- You aren't branching more or fewer files than you expected.
- You're branching files into the correct paths. (And that you've spelled the new pathname correctly!)
- All of the target files are in your client view.
- You have permission for the operation.

Oops, I branched the wrong files!

Even if you've already run the integrate command, you always have the option of reverting files instead of submitting them. For example:

```
p4 revert //Ace/V1/...
```

removes the newly branched //Ace/V1 files from your workspace and takes them off your pending changelist.

It's not a branch until the files are submitted

Like other Perforce commands that work on files, integrate doesn't actually affect the depot. Instead, it simply opens files to be branched. The new branch doesn't appear in the depot until you've submitted the files:

```
p4 submit //Ace/V1/...
...
Change 3372 submitted.
```

In the timeline of the new branch, the changelist you submitted is the first event, as shown in Figure 4-7.

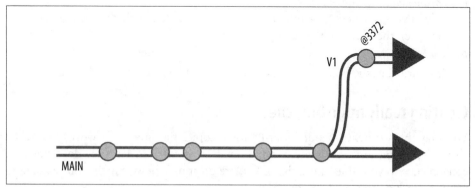

Figure 4-7. The first event in the timeline of a branch

> ## Lazy Copying
>
> Once you submit branched files, other users will be able to see them in the depot, browse them, synchronize with them, and so forth. But Perforce doesn't actually store new file content in its repository when you submit branched files. Instead, it uses internal logic to fetch their content from the storage of the files they were branched from. Only when someone *changes* the content of a branched file does new content get stored in the repository. (You will see this referred to as "lazy copying" in the Perforce product documentation.) Why do you care? Because it means you can branch very large file trees without worrying about consuming unnecessary repository space.

Can you undo and redo a branch?

Once you've submitted branched files, they're a permanent part of depot history. In other words, you can't undo a branch. However, you can effectively redo a branch, in a way that satisfies most of the reasons you'd want to:

Wrong files branched

For example, you branched files from *//Ace/MAIN/...* into *//Ace/V1-R1.0/...* when you meant to branch from *//Ace/V1/...*. To fix the problem, delete the branched files, then branch the correct files:

```
p4 delete //Ace/V1-R1.0/...
p4 submit
p4 integ -d //Ace/V1/... //Ace/V1-R1.0/...
p4 submit
```

(The -d option tells Perforce to go ahead and branch new files on top of deleted ones.)

Files branched to wrong place

If you've branched files into the wrong place, delete the branched files and rebranch the files into the right place.

Branch not needed

If it turns out the branch wasn't needed after all, delete the branched files.

Creating really huge branches

You may think it heavy-handed that Perforce copies files into your workspace when all you're trying to do is create a new branch in the depot. Perforce does this as a convenience to you. It assumes that if you are creating a new branch, you're going to want to work on the newly branched files.

However, if you're branching a really huge tree of files, a copy of the whole thing in your workspace may be the last thing you want. You can optionally skip the workspace copying. The -v flag on integ does that:

```
p4 integ -v //Ace/MAIN/... //Ace/V1/...
//Ace/V1/db/Jamfile#1 - branch from //Ace/MAIN/db/Jamfile#1,#32
//Ace/V1/db/dbAcc.cpp#1 - branch from //Ace/MAIN/db/dbAcc.cpp#1,#3
//Ace/V1/db/dbDefN.cpp#1 - branch from //Ace/MAIN/db/dbDefN.cpp#1,#7
...
```

(The -v is for virtual as opposed to real files in your workspace.) When you use integ -v, you'll still need the target path in your client view, you'll still have files open for branching, and you'll still have to submit a changelist. But the branched files themselves won't appear in your workspace. If you do want them in your workspace, you'll have to synchronize with them after submitting them.

Working in a new branch

People can begin working in a new branch as soon as you submit the branched files. Working in a new branch is the same as working with files in any depot path. All that's needed is a workspace with a client view that includes the new branch.

For example, if Bill wants to configure his Bill-V1 workspace for working in the new V1 branch, he can set up this client view:

```
p4 client Bill-V1
```

Client	Bill-V1
Root	c:\ws-v1
View	//Ace/V1/... //Bill-V1/...

The P4V screenshot in Figure 4-8 shows the scope of the Bill-V1 workspace.

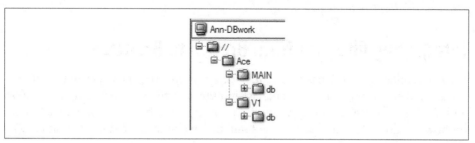

Figure 4-8. A view of the V1 branch

You don't have to have the whole branch in your client view, of course. In fact, you can even mix and match branch subdirectories in your workspace. Ann, for example, is doing some analysis that requires her to have the *db* subdirectories from both branches, *MAIN* and *V1*, in her workspace. She has her client view set up like this:

```
p4 client Ann-DBwork
```

Client	Ann-DBwork
Root	/usr/team/ann/dbtests
View	//Ace/MAIN/db/... //Ann-DBwork/MAIN/db/...
	//Ace/V1/db/... //Ann-DBwork/V1/db/...

The Ann-DBwork workspace's client view is shown in Figure 4-9.

Figure 4-9. A view of files in two branches

Browsing branch history

You can use the changes command to display the history of a branch. For example:

```
p4 changes //Ace/V1/...
Change 3459 on 2004/10/05 by pete 'Fix titles of...'
```

```
Change 3456 on 2004/10/04 by rob 'Delete junk files...'
Change 3372 on 2004/10/04 by bill 'Branch V1...'
```

P4V can show you the history of a branch with its Folder History command.

Comparing branches

You can use diff2 to compare branches. It lists and diffs the files that are no longer identical:

```
p4 diff2 -q //Ace/MAIN/... //Ace/V1/...
==== //Ace/MAIN/doc/Jamfile/#7 - //Ace/V1/doc/Jamfile#4 ==== (content)
==== //Ace/MAIN/doc/index.html#1 - <none> ====
==== //Ace/MAIN/utils/readme#8 - <none> ====
```

(The -q option suppresses the actual diffs.)

In P4V you can use Tools → Diff files to bring up an expanding, side-by-side comparison of the two branches. Figure 4-10 shows an example.

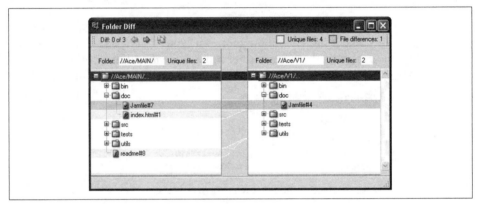

Figure 4-10. Using P4V to compare branches

Integrating Changes from Branch to Branch

So, Ace Engineering now has two branches, *V1* and *MAIN*. New development continues in *MAIN* as bugs are fixed and last-minute changes are submitted in *V1*. *When* and *why* to integrate are topics we'll discuss later in the book. For now, we'll focus on how it's done. In this case, let's assume that we're interested in integrating *V1*'s changes into *MAIN*.

Which changes need integrating?

The changes command tells us how the *V1* branch has evolved:

```
p4 changes //Ace/V1/...
Change 3470 on 2004/10/05 by rob 'New threshold for...'
Change 3459 on 2004/10/05 by pete 'Fix titles of...'
Change 3456 on 2004/10/04 by rob 'Delete junk files...'
Change 3372 on 2004/10/04 by bill 'Branch V1...'
```

Not all of these changes need integrating into *MAIN*. Changelist 3372, as you recall, was the change that *created* the branch. To find out which changes do need integrating, we can use `interchanges`:[*]

```
p4 interchanges //Ace/V1/... //Ace/MAIN/...
Change 3456 on 2004/10/04 by rob 'Delete junk files...'
Change 3459 on 2004/10/05 by pete 'Fix titles of...'
Change 3470 on 2004/10/05 by rob 'New threshold for...'
```

Whereas `changes` shows all changes to a branch, `interchanges` shows only the changes that are not accounted for in a target branch. (See "What interchanges really tells us" later in the chapter.) In this example we see that of the three changes made to *V1* since it was created, none have been integrated into *MAIN*. Figure 4-11 shows these changes.

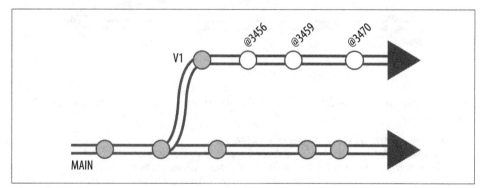

Figure 4-11. V1 changes not yet accounted for in MAIN

Integrating changes incrementally

A very practical way to integrate changes between branches is incrementally—changelist by changelist, in order. This method preserves logical changes as they're propagated from branch to branch. It also keeps the problems of reconciling, resolving, and merging files to a minimum. It's a good technique to start off with, if you're not sure how to go about integating changes between branches.

Incremental integration is similar to branching from a point in time, using a changelist number instead of a date. Each time we integrate, we use `interchanges` to find out which changelist number to use.

---

[*] interchanges is a new Perforce command; it's still nominally undocumented. (It's actually documented in p4 help undoc, but it's not guaranteed to behave the same way, or even be available, in future releases.)

Returning to the scenario in the previous example, here are the *V1* changes as yet unaccounted for in *MAIN*:

```
p4 interchanges //Ace/V1/... //Ace/MAIN/...
Change 3456 on 2004/10/04 by rob 'Delete junk files...'
Change 3459 on 2004/10/05 by pete 'Fix titles of...'
Change 3470 on 2004/10/05 by rob 'New threshold for...'
```

From this we see that changelist 3456 marks the next increment to integrate, as shown in Figure 4-12.

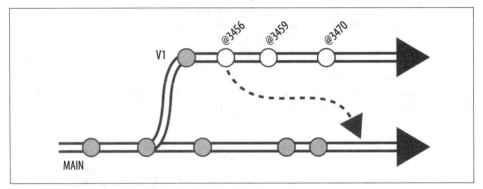

Figure 4-12. Integrating one changelist at a time

Before doing the actual integration, let's run `integ -n` to get a preview of what's involved:

```
p4 integ -n //Ace/V1/...@3456 //Ace/MAIN/...
//Ace/MAIN/doc/issues#7 - delete from //Ace/V1/doc/issues#2
//Ace/MAIN/doc/readme#10 - integrate from //Ace/V1/doc/readme#2
//Ace/MAIN/doc/setup.gif#1 - branch/sync from //Ace/V1/doc/setup.gif#1
//Ace/MAIN/qa/t102.pl#4 - integrate from //Ace/V1/qa/t102.pl#2
//Ace/MAIN/src/Jamfile#32 - integrate from //Ace/V1/src/Jamfile#2
```

Here we see that integrating change 3456 from *V1* to *MAIN* will involve merging three files, branching one, and deleting another. (Remember that `integrate`'s *target* files must be in your client view. In other words, you'll need *//Ace/MAIN/...* in your view for this `integ` command to work.)

Note that Perforce isn't actually operating on a changelist. It's operating on file revisions. However, when you put a changelist number on the donor filespec, Perforce considers only the file revisions that existed as of the changelist's point in time. What we're really doing here is asking Perforce to treat the donor branch as if it had not yet evolved past the point in time represented by *@3456*.

Perforce assumes that if you added files in the donor branch, you'll want to add them in the target branch when you integrate. Trying to be helpful, it branches new target files from new donors. Ditto for deleted files—if you deleted files in the donor, Perforce assumes you'll want to delete them in the target as well. If Perforce has assumed correctly, you're all set. But if you *don't* want these changes propagated to the target branch, you'll have a bit of reconciling to do before you submit your changelist. See "Reconciling Structural Changes," later in this chapter.

Once you've familiarized yourself with what `integrate`'s going to do, run it for real (that is, without -n):

```
p4 integ //Ace/V1/...@3456 //Ace/MAIN/...
```

We're not listing `integrate`'s output here because it's nearly identical to that of the preview we just saw. It shows us that Perforce has:

- Found files in *V1* that have been modified since they were branched, and opened corresponding *MAIN* files for integrating.

- Found files that are new in *V1* and branched them into corresponding *MAIN* files. (Strictly speaking, it opened new *MAIN* files for branching.)

- Found files in *V1* that have been deleted and opened corresponding *MAIN* files for deleting.

To complete the integration, you'll now have to resolve the files that are open for integrating and submit your pending changelist:

```
p4 resolve
p4 submit
```

(In upcoming sections we'll take a look at the finer points of resolving files opened for integrating.)

Integrations won't be repeated

So now you've integrated change *@3456* from *V1* into *MAIN*. Look what happens when you try to integrate the same change again:

```
p4 integ //Ace/V1/...@3456 //Ace/MAIN/...
... - all revision(s) already integrated.
```

You'll get this message from the `integrate` command when Perforce detects that relevant revisions in the donor branch have already been accounted for in the target branch. This behavior is dictated by integration history. (See "The mechanics of integration" later in the chapter for the gory details.)

And notice that `interchanges` no longer reports that change 3456 needs integrating:

```
p4 interchanges //Ace/V1/... //Ace/MAIN/...
Change 3459 on 2004/10/05 by pete 'Fix titles of...'
Change 3470 on 2004/10/05 by rob 'New threshold for...'
```

If you proceed to integrate each of the remaining *V1* changelists into *MAIN*, you'll eventually reach a point where all *V1* changes are accounted for, as shown in Figure 4-13.

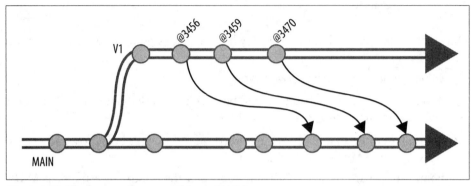

Figure 4-13. V1 changes all accounted for in MAIN

Now here's something even more interesting. What if we now try integrating in the other direction? Which changelists does Perforce think need integrating? *Not* the ones created by integrating *V1* into *MAIN*, it turns out. When we flip the *V1* and *MAIN* arguments, `interchanges` omits the integration changes. It lists only the *MAIN* changes that *didn't* come from *V1*:

```
p4 interchanges //Ace/MAIN/... //Ace/V1/...
Change 3381 on 2004/11/05 by sue 'New attributes...'
Change 3461 on 2004/11/05 by jan 'Optional flag for...'
Change 3465 on 2004/11/05 by jan 'Fix precedence...'
```

The output of `interchanges` is illuminated in Figure 4-14.

When Perforce detects that a change was integrated *from* a target, it keeps you from integrating it back *into* the target. Again, for the gory details, see "The mechanics of integration."

Which files need resolving? (And why?)

The `integrate` command can open target files for branching, deleting, or integrating.[*] Files opened for integrating have to be resolved before you can submit them. Why?

---

[*] In fact, `integrate` can even open files for importing from another Perforce domain, if the donor path is in a remote depot. See Chapter 6.

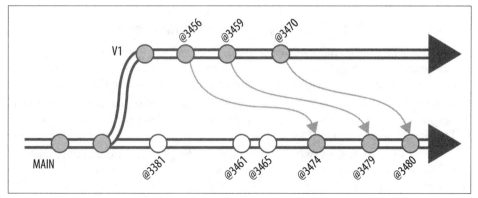

Figure 4-14. Changes in MAIN that didn't come from V1

Because, for each target file opened for integrating, Perforce needs to know whether you want to:

- Merge the donor file into the target file
- Copy the donor file to the target file
- Ignore changes that were made in the donor file

You can use resolve to see which files need resolving. For example:

```
p4 resolve -n -o
C:\ws\MAIN\readme - merging //Ace/V1/doc/readme#2
    using base //Ace/V1/doc/readme#1
C:\ws\MAIN\qa\t102.pl - merging //Ace/V1/qa/t102.pl#2
    using base //Ace/V1/qa/t102.pl#1
C:\ws\MAIN\src\Jamfile - merging //Ace/V1/src/Jamfile#2
    using base //Ace/V1/src/Jamfile#1
```

(The -n flag makes resolve give you a preview. -o makes it display the base files.)

"Yours," "theirs," and "base," revisited

Resolving, as you know, is how you tell Perforce what you want done with parallel changes to files. In Chapter 3, you read about how the files you have opened for editing can be resolved with newer revisions submitted by other people.

Resolving files during integration is almost exactly the same, only in this case files in a target branch are resolved with newer revisions in a donor branch. And, as with files you're editing, Perforce uses the same "yours," "theirs," and "base" terminology to identify three variants of each file. This terminology can be a little confusing when you're integrating, however:

- "Yours" is the target file, the file being integrated *into*. This is the file integrate opens in your workspace, and it is the file you will submit.

Auto-Resolve or Resolve Interactively?

Files opened for integrating can be resolved automatically or interactively, just as can files opened for editing. If you're unclear on the difference between automatic resolving ("auto-resolving") and interactive resolving, take another look at Chapter 3.

As with files opened for editing, your best bet is to auto-resolve first, then resolve the stragglers interactively. (The stragglers are the files that Perforce can't resolve for you.) There are two ways to auto-resolve first:

- If you're comfortable with letting Perforce merge files automatically, auto-resolve by merging first, then resolve interactively:

  ```
  p4 resolve -am
  p4 resolve
  ```

- If you'd prefer to merge files individually—which lets you inspect each merged result before accepting it—do a "safe" auto-resolve first, then resolve interactively:

  ```
  p4 resolve -as
  p4 resolve
  ```

Note that merging is inherently less risky when you're integrating than it is when you've resynchronized files you're editing. That's because files you're integrating aren't already opened and modified by you. Everything in the target files can be restored from depot copies if you notice a bad merged result after resolving.

- "Theirs" is the donor file, the file you are integrating *from*. (Even when the donor file contains changes *you've* made, Perforce still calls it theirs!)
- The "base" is a file that will be used to compute the merged result, if you choose to merge the donor into the target.

Although the integrate command allows you to operate on entire branches, Perforce is actually processing files individually. Each file opened for integration has its own yours-theirs-base triplet of files to resolve.

For example, *readme* is a file open for integration from *V1* into *MAIN*. *V1*'s *readme#1* was originally branched from *MAIN*. Its revision as of changelist 3456 is #2. In *MAIN*, *readme#10* is the head revision. Resolving will involve a triplet of files—*MAIN*'s #10 as yours, *V1*'s #2 as theirs, and *V1*'s #1 as the base (see Figure 4-15).

When you resolve *readme*, you'll choose whether you want to ignore theirs, copy theirs into yours, or merge theirs into yours. All this happens in your workspace, of course. Once your workspace file is resolved, you can submit it. That creates *readme#11* in the *MAIN* branch.

Perforce normally selects the head revision of the target file as "yours" so that you'll be merging changes into the most up-to-date file. If your workspace copy is not

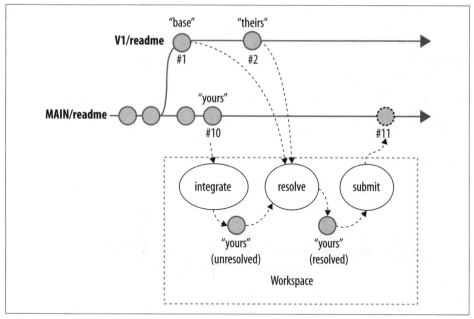

Figure 4-15. Yours, theirs, and base when integrating

already synchronized with the head revision, the integrate command resynchronizes for you. The revisions Perforce selects as theirs and the base depend on revisions you supply to the integrate command and on recorded integration history, as you'll see in "The mechanics of integration," later in this chapter.

Merging the donor file into the target

Text files can be resolved by merging. In fact, resolve's default behavior is to merge text files when necessary. For example, let's say the *readme* file has been edited in both branches since it was branched from *MAIN* into *V1*, as illustrated in Figure 4-15. Integrating from *V1* into *MAIN* opens the *MAIN/readme* file:

```
p4 integ -o //Ace/V1/...@3456 //Ace/MAIN/...
...
//Ace/MAIN/readme#10 - integrate from //Ace/V1/readme#2
    using base //Ace/V1/readme#1
...
```

(The -o flag on integrate causes the base revision to be listed.) As in the previous example, *MAIN/readme#10* is yours, *V1/readme#2* is theirs, and *V1/readme#1* is the base. Let's assume auto-resolving merges the file without conflict:

```
p4 resolve -am
...
C:\ws\MAIN\readme - merging //Ace/V1/readme#2
Diff chunks: 2 yours + 3 theirs + 0 both + 0 conflicting
```

```
- merge from //Ace/V1/readme
...
```

(Recall that the -am flag tells resolve to accept merges.) Your workspace file now contains the merged result. When you submit your changelist, the file is sent to the depot and *MAIN/readme#11* is created:

p4 submit
```
...
//Ace/MAIN/readme#11 - integrate
...
```

P4V's Revision Graph illustrates this, as Figure 4-16 shows.

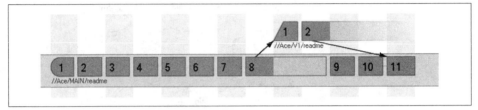

Figure 4-16. Merging the donor file into the target

The filelog command shows the integration history:

p4 filelog -m1 //Ace/MAIN/readme
```
//Ace/MAIN/readme
... #11 change 5420 integrate 2004/10/15 rob 'Pull in V1...'
... ... merge from //Ace/V1/readme#2
...
```

Had there been conflicts, you would have had to resolve the file interactively and edit it. And, because you'd edited it, the submitted file would have had a slightly different integration history:

p4 filelog -m1 //Ace/MAIN/readme
```
//Ace/MAIN/readme
... #11 change 5420 integrate 2004/10/15 rob 'Pull in V1...'
... ... edit from //Ace/V1/readme#2
...
```

Copying the donor file into the target

You can resolve files by copying donors to targets. Auto-resolving will do this for you, in cases where the donor file has changed and the target file has not. When Perforce encounters these conditions during interactive resolving, you'll be prompted you to resolve by copying.

For example, assume *MAIN/readme#8* was branched into *V1/readme#1*. Since then, someone has submitted *V1/readme#2*. *MAIN/readme* hasn't changed.

Browsing a File's Integration History

As you submit files, Perforce records a history of file revisions that were integrated and how they were resolved. You'll see integration history as you examine file history. For example, the *//Ace/MAIN/readme* file was branched into *//Ace/DEV/readme*. Here's its history:

```
p4 filelog //Ace/MAIN/readme
//Ace/MAIN/readme
... #8 change 3712 integrate ...
... ... copy from //Ace/DEV/readme#3'
... #7 change 3710 edit ...
... #6 change 3709 integrate ...
... ... ignored //Ace/DEV/readme#2
... #5 change 3708 edit ...
... #4 change 3707 edit ...
... #3 change 3703 edit ...
... ... branch into //Ace/DEV/readme#1
... #2 change 3702 edit ...
... #1 change 3701 add ...
```

The reciprocal details show up in the history of *//Ace/DEV/readme*:

```
p4 filelog //Ace/DEV/readme
//Ace/DEV/readme
... #3 change 3711 edit ...
... ... copy into //Ace/MAIN/readme#8
... #2 change 3705 edit ...
... ... ignored by //Ace/MAIN/readme#6
... #1 change 3704 branch ...
... ... branch from //Ace/MAIN/readme#1,#3
```

Another way to dig up integration history is with the integrated command. For example:

```
p4 integrated //Ace/DEV/readme
//Ace/DEV/readme#1 - branch from //Ace/MAIN/readme#1,#3
//Ace/DEV/readme#2 - ignored by //Ace/MAIN/readme#6
//Ace/DEV/readme#3 - copy into //Ace/MAIN/readme#8
```

P4V's Revision Graph produces a great bird's-eye view of a file's integration history, with succinct symbols that show how file revisions were created and integrated. The figure shows the legend of Revision Graph symbols.

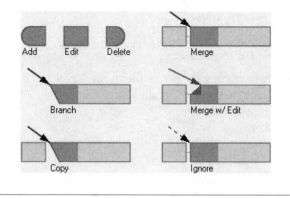

Here are the commands that integrate from *V1* into *MAIN*:

```
p4 integ //Ace/MAIN/...@3456 //Ace/V1/...
...
//Ace/MAIN/readme#8 - integrate from //Ace/V1/readme#2
...

p4 resolve -am
...
C:\ws\MAIN\readme - merging //Ace/V1/readme#2
Diff chunks: 0 yours + 1 theirs + 0 both + 0 conflicting
- copy from //Ace/V1/readme
...
p4 submit
...
integrate //Ace/MAIN/readme#9
...
```

Integrating from *V1* into *MAIN* opens *MAIN/readme#8* in your workspace, resolving copies *V1/readme#2* to the *MAIN/readme* file in your workspace, and submitting creates a *MAIN/readme#9* in the depot whose content is the same as *V1/readme#2*.*

The Revision Graph for the preceding example is shown in Figure 4-17. Compare this figure with Figure 4-17 to see the subtle difference in the symbol for *MAIN/readme#11*.

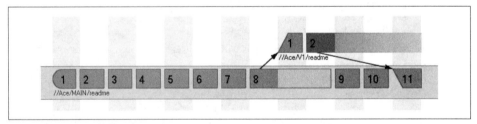

Figure 4-17. Copying the donor file into the target

The history of *MAIN/readme* shows how *V1/readme* was integrated:

```
p4 filelog -m1 //Ace/MAIN/readme
//Ace/MAIN/readme
... #9 change 5420 integrate 2004/11/17 rob 'Pulling in V1... '
... ... copy from //Ace/V1/readme#2
```

You can also make resolve copy the donor file to the target regardless of whether the target file has been changed. (This is called copy-integrating.) Use the -at flag for this. For example:

```
p4 resolve -at
...
```

---

* When you submit files that have been resolved by copying, Perforce doesn't actually send your workspace files to the depot. It simply makes lazy copies, as described in Chapter 4.

```
C:\ws\MAIN\readme - vs //Ace/V1/readme#2
Diff chunks: 1 yours + 1 theirs + 0 both + 0 conflicting
- copy from //Ace/V1/readme
...
```

Ignoring the donor file's changes

Perforce normally resolves by ignoring when it detects that nothing has changed in the donor file—that is, when the base and theirs have the same content.

 If the donor still has the same content that it had when it was branched, isn't the donor accounted for in the target? Not necessarily. For example, the donor file may have been edited simply to change its file type. Or it may have been changed twice—the second time to back out the first change.

You have the option of resolving by ignoring even when the donor file has changed. You'd do this when integrating a change that, for one reason or another, isn't applicable to the target branch.

For example, assume *V1*'s change 3456 is not accounted for in *MAIN*:

```
p4 interchanges //Ace/V1/... //Ace/MAIN/...
...
Change 3456 on 2004/10/05 by pete 'Promo for release...'
...
```

And let's say you plan to ignore change 3456 because it's not applicable to the *MAIN* branch. Still, you integrate it, so that you have a record of the fact that it's not applicable. One of the files opened for integrating is *readme*:

```
p4 integ //Ace/V1/...@3456 //Ace/MAIN/...
...
//Ace/MAIN/readme#10 - integrate from //Ace/V1/readme#2
...
```

Now you auto-resolve, using the "accept yours" option:

```
p4 resolve -ay
c:\ws\MAIN\readme - vs //Ace/V1/readme#2
- ignored //Ace/V1/readme
```

("Accept yours" is the same as "ignore theirs.") When you resolve this way, your workspace file is left unchanged. Even so, you must submit it in order to record the integration:

```
p4 submit
...
integrate //Ace/MAIN/readme#11
...
```

The Revision Graph is shown in Figure 4-18.

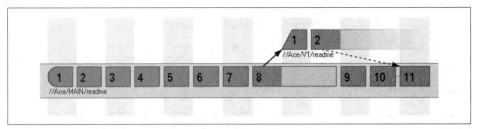

Figure 4-18. Integrating and ignoring the donor file's changes

History now shows that *V1/readme#2*'s change has been ignored, yet accounted for, in *MAIN/readme*:

```
p4 filelog //Ace/MAIN/readme
... #11 change 5420 integrate 2004/11/17 rob 'Ignoring promo...'
... ... ignored //Ace/V1/readme#2
```

As you would expect, there's no content difference between *MAIN*'s *readme#10* and *readme#11*:

```
p4 diff2 //Ace/MAIN/readme#10 //Ace/MAIN/readme#11
==== //Ace/MAIN/readme#10 - //Ace/MAIN/readme#11 ==== identical
```

Editing files as you're integrating them

As you know, you can edit files in the course of resolving them. But what if you need to edit files *after* you resolve them? You can do this; you simply need to reopen the files for editing first, to make them writable.

For example, *src/Jamfile* is one of the files in changelist 3456. Integrating changelist 3456 will open *MAIN*'s *src/Jamfile*. There's nothing to keep you from reopening it for editing before you submit it:

```
p4 integ //Ace/V1/...@3456 //Ace/MAIN/...
p4 resolve
p4 edit //Ace/MAIN/src/Jamfile
```

In fact, you can run edit and integrate in any order. A file that is already opened for editing can be opened for integrating, and a file that is already opened for integrating can be opened for editing.

Integrating by subdirectory

When feasible, you can limit the scope of the integrate command to a particular subdirectory. For example, let's say we're interested in integrating changes to the *db* subdirectory. To find out which *db* changes in *V1* need to be integrated into *MAIN*, we use:

```
p4 interchanges //Ace/V1/db/... //Ace/MAIN/db/...
Change 3470 on 2004/10/05 by rob 'New threshold for...'
```

This lists all the changes in *V1* that involved as-yet unintegrated file revisions in the *db* subdirectory. It shows us that the next change to integrate is 3470. Now we double-check to make sure change 3470 affects no files *outside* of the *db* subdirectory:

```
p4 describe -s 3470
Change 3470 by rob on 2004/10/05
    New threshold for db page allocation ...

...
... //Ace/V1/db/dbLng.cpp#2 edit
... //Ace/V1/db/Jamfile#2 edit
```

This is good; we see that changelist 3470 references *db* files only. (To find out why this is so important, see the upcoming section "Don't break up changelists.") To integrate the change, we use:

```
p4 integ //Ace/V1/db/...@3470 //Ace/MAIN/db/...
p4 resolve
p4 submit
```

Cherry-picking changes to integrate

"Cherry-picking" integration is where you integrate a single change, or sequence of changes, out of order, from one branch into another. For example, assume these are the changes that currently need integration from *V1* into *MAIN*:

```
p4 interchanges //Ace/V1/... //Ace/MAIN/...
Change 3456 on 2004/10/04 by rob 'Delete junk files...'
Change 3459 on 2004/10/05 by pete 'Fix titles of...'
Change 3470 on 2004/10/05 by rob 'New threshold for...'
```

Let's say you want to integrate Pete's change before integrating the other two changes (see Figure 4-19).

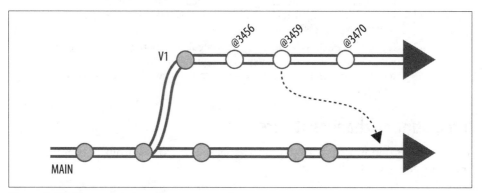

Figure 4-19. Cherry-picking a change to integrate

You can cherry-pick a change to integrate by using its changelist number in a *revision range*, like this:

```
p4 integ //Ace/V1/...@3459,@3459 //Ace/MAIN/...
//Ace/MAIN/gui/opRList.cpp#12 - integrate from //Ace/V1/gui/opRList.cpp#3,#3
//Ace/MAIN/gui/opRList.h#9 - integrate from //Ace/V1/gui/opRList.h#3,#3
```

The *@n,@n* revision syntax[*] restricts the operation to the files that were involved in changelist 3459. Two files were involved; their *MAIN* counterparts are now open for integrating. All you have to do now is resolve the files, submit them, and voilà, change 3459 is integrated into *MAIN*.

That's the good news. The bad news is that interchanges is not always able to detect cherry-picked changes. Thus, even after you've submitted integrated change 3459 from *V1* to *MAIN*, the change may *still* show up as unintegrated because it's nested between two changes that really do need integrating:

```
p4 interchanges //Ace/V1/... //Ace/MAIN/...
Change 3456 on 2004/10/04 by rob 'Delete junk files...'
Change 3459 on 2004/10/05 by pete 'Fix titles of...'
Change 3470 on 2004/10/05 by rob 'New threshold for...'
```

This is an idiosyncracy of the interchanges command, not of integration history. (See "What interchanges really tells us.") If you were to try to cherry-pick the same change again, you would see that it is already accounted for:

```
p4 integ //Ace/V1/...@3459,@3459 //Ace/MAIN/...
... - all revision(s) already integrated.
```

 There are often good reasons to integrate a single change out of sequence. But unless the change is small and self-contained, cherry-picking may create more problems than it solves. What if the change builds on a previous change? If you're not careful, you could end up integrating half of the previous change along with all of the current one. What if the change involves a renamed file? If you've skipped past the change in which the rename occured, should you propagate the new name or not?

It's hard enough to keep collaboration going smoothly when changes are integrated in order. Integrating changes out of order adds complexity. Complexity, in turn, makes it more likely that something will go wrong.

Integrating all changes at once

You have the option of integrating all changes, all at once, from one branch into another (see Figure 4-20).

---

[*] @3459, @3459 is syntactically equivalent to @=3459. However, because the former syntax can be used to select a sequence of revisions, it's often more useful than the latter for cherry-picking.

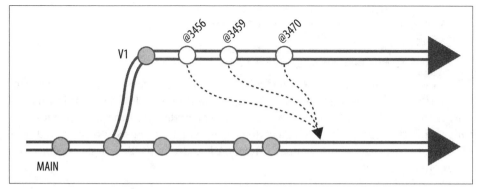

Figure 4-20. Integrating changes all at once

Be aware, though, that integrating everything at once can be a challenge. For one thing, it puts you in a position of having to merge several changes at the same time. The more you're merging at once, the bigger your diffs, and the bigger your diffs, the more likely it is that merge errors will slip in unnoticed. For another, structural changes that are easy to reconcile piecemeal can be impossible to reconcile when combined with other changes. You'll understand why after reading "Reconciling Structural Changes" later in this chapter.

For all-at-once integration, you don't need to specify a donor revision. To integrate all of *V1*'s changes into *MAIN*, for example, you'd use:

```
p4 integ //Ace/V1/... //Ace/MAIN/...
p4 resolve
p4 submit
```

Because you didn't give a revision on the integ command's donor argument, Perforce assumes you want changes up to and including the most recent *V1* change to be considered for integration. (Of course, as it considers changes, Perforce opens only the files that *need* integrating. So if you run this sequence of commands frequently, it's pretty much the same as integrating incrementally.) The single change submitted to the target will effectively account for all the corresponding changes in the donor.

Which changes were integrated?

If you have comm and sort programs available[*] you can use them with changes to show changes that have been integrated into a branch. For example, to list the V1 changes that have been integrated into *MAIN*:

---

[*] comm is a program that compares lists. It comes with Unix; several Windows toolkits offer it as well. The comm command requires alphabetically sorted input; hence the need for sort. Both Windows and Unix have sort commands that can be used to filter the output of P4 commands.

```
p4 changes //Ace/V1/... | sort > tempfile1
p4 changes -i //Ace/MAIN/... | sort > tempfile2
comm -1 -2  tempfile1 tempfile2
Change 3456 on 2004/10/04 by rob 'Delete junk files...'
Change 3459 on 2004/10/05 by pete 'Fix titles of...'
```

(The changes command reports changelists that refer to files in a given filespec. *tempfile1*, therefore, is a list of every change submitted to *V1*. The -i option makes changes include the changelists that have been integrated into the files in question. *tempfile2* is therefore a list of changes that were either submitted or integrated into *MAIN*. The comm command compares *tempfile1* and *tempfile2* and shows only the lines common to both.)

Don't break up changelists

You may recognize that if all of the files in changelist 3471 are within the *src* subdirectory, these two commands are the same:

```
p4 integ //Ace/V1/...@3471 //Ace/MAIN/...
p4 integ //Ace/V1/src/...@3471 //Ace/MAIN/src/...
```

But if changelist 3471 involves files outside of *src*, the commands are *not* the same. The first of the two integrates the entire change; the second breaks up the changelist.

There's nothing to stop you from breaking up a changelist—you can resolve and submit the *src* files whether or not other files were involved in changelist 3471. But you will have integrated only part of the change, not the entire change. The same thing can happen if you're using a workspace with a client view limited to the *src* subdirectory. The scope of your integrate commands is limited accordingly and you won't be able to integrate the entire change.

The unintegrated part of a change can always be integrated later, of course. But there are two problems with partially integrated changes. The first is the obvious one: you're breaking up a logical change. Whatever it may be, the reason files were changed together in the *V1* branch argues for integrating the entire change to the *MAIN* branch.

The second problem is that partially integrated changes can lead to false positives from some Perforce commands. If a change is only partially integrated, changes -i will report that it's been integrated, for example. Likewise, interchanges reports partially integrated changes as unintegrated. The jobs and fixes commands, which you'll read about in later chapters, can also yield false positives on partially integrated changes.

Reconciling Structural Changes

Earlier we said that files can evolve independently in their own branches. This is completely true. Files can be added, deleted, moved, renamed, split, or combined in one branch without affecting any other branch. However, structural changes like

---

these can't be resolved during integration. In fact, when you use the integrate command, Perforce simply matches donor and target files by name. The state of each donor file, whatever it is, is imposed upon the like-named target file. If the donor file was deleted, integrate deletes the target file. If the target file doesn't exist, it branches the donor file into it.

Matching donor and target files by name is normally quite effective for propagating structural changes. For example, say *MAIN/readme#8* was branched into *V1/readme#1* when you created the *V1* branch. Since then, the *V1/readme* file has been renamed to *V1/readme.txt* and edited a couple of times.

Now, as you integrate from *V1* into *MAIN*, here's what happens:

```
p4 integ //Ace/V1/... //Ace/MAIN/...
//Ace/MAIN/readme.txt#1 - branch/sync from //Ace/V1/readme.txt#3
//Ace/MAIN/readme#11 - delete from //Ace/V1/readme#3
```

So far, so good. Although Perforce gave you no choice in the matter, and nothing is left for you to resolve, the outcome is exactly what you wanted. When you submit your changelist, Perforce will delete *MAIN/readme* and branch *V1/readme.txt* into *MAIN*, effectively propagating both the content change and the structural change from *V1* to *MAIN*.

But what if you wanted to merge the content change and ignore the structural change? What if the structural change had occured in *MAIN* instead of *V1*? Neither integrate nor resolve offers a way for you to handle these cases. However, as with files you're editing, there are several ways to reconcile structural changes. One way is to provide Perforce with some guidance as to how branches correspond structurally. This is where *branch views* come in.

Using branch views

To save you from having to jot down your frequently used donor and target filespecs on a cocktail napkin, Perforce lets you save them in named, reusable *branch views*. Branch views are similar to client views in that they map one set of files to another. In branch views, depot files are mapped to other depot files instead of to workspace files. A branch view named V1toMAIN, that stores a mapping between *V1* and *MAIN*, for example, looks like this:

```
Branch      V1toMAIN
View        //Ace/V1/... //Ace/MAIN/...
```

To create or change a branch view, use the branch command. This is the command that created the branch view called V1toMAIN:

```
p4 branch V1toMAIN
```

Note that the branch command doesn't branch files—in fact, it has no effect at all on files.

A branch view is a spec, like client specs. When you run the `branch` command, you're given a form to fill out. Once you save the form, you can use your new branch view with the `integrate` command. Given the branch view definition shown earlier, these two commands will now do exactly the same thing:

```
p4 integ -b V1toMAIN
p4 integ //Ace/V1/... //Ace/MAIN/...
```

Branch views change the way you use revisions with `integrate`. For example, these commands are equivalent:

```
p4 integ -b V1toMAIN @3456
p4 integ //Ace/V1/...@3456 //Ace/MAIN/...
```

as are these commands:

```
p4 integ -b V1toMAIN @3459,3459
p4 integ //Ace/V1/...@3459,3459 //Ace/MAIN/...
```

What's happening here is that when you're using a branch view, the `integrate` command already knows which donor and target path to use. The revision you supply is applied to the donor path. (You can't put revisions in the branch view specs themselves, by the way.)

You can also use branch views with `interchanges` and `diff2`. The following commands are equivalent, for example:

```
p4 interchanges -b V1toMAIN
p4 interchanges //Ace/V1/... //Ace/MAIN/...
```

as are these:

```
p4 diff2 -q -b V1toMAIN
p4 diff2 -q //Ace/V1/... //Ace/MAIN/...
```

In a moment we'll show how to augment branch views to reconcile structural differences between branches.

Looking for a branch view

To list the branch views that have already been defined, use:

```
p4 branches
Branch V1toMAIN 2004/10/15 'Created by laura'
```

You can inspect a branch view's definition with `branch -o`. For example:

```
p4 branch -o V1toMAIN
Branch: V1toMAIN
View:
    //Ace/V1/... //Ace/MAIN/...
```

Branch views are reversible

You can use the same branch view to integrate changes in either direction. To apply a branch view in reverse, use `integrate -r`. For example, when the V1toMAIN branch view is defined as previously, these commands are equivalent:

```
p4 integ -r -b V1toMAIN
p4 integ //Ace/MAIN/... //Ace/V1/...
```

Mapping one directory structure to another

So, why all the fuss about branch views? They give us a way to coerce `integrate` into mapping the old directory structure in one branch to the new directory structure in another. For example, say that in changelist 3461, *V1*'s *readme* was renamed to *readme.txt*. As you just saw, simply integrating from *V1* into *MAIN* will replicate the structural change:

```
p4 integ -n //Ace/V1/...@3461 //Ace/MAIN/...
...
//Ace/MAIN/readme.txt#1 - branch/sync from //Ace/V1/readme.txt#1
//Ace/MAIN/readme#11 - delete from //Ace/V1/readme#4
...
```

But what if you *don't* want to replicate the structural change? What if, from here on, changes to *V1*'s *readme.txt* are to be integrated into *MAIN*'s *readme*? You can effect this behavior through a branch view. We'll use the V1toMAIN branch view in this example. We update the view to map *V1*'s new structure to *MAIN*'s old structure:

```
p4 branch V1toMAIN
```

```
Branch      V1toMAIN
View        //Ace/V1/...          //Ace/MAIN/...
            //Ace/V1/readme.txt   //Ace/MAIN/readme
```

Now, when we use the V1toMAIN branch view with `integrate`, look what happens:

```
p4 integ -b V1toMAIN @3461
... - all revision(s) already integrated
```

Perforce makes no attempt to integrate *V1*'s *readme* change into *MAIN*. Why not? Because it's now matching *V1*'s *readme.txt* to *MAIN*'s *readme*. *V1*'s *readme. txt@3461* has integration history that shows that it has not been edited since it was branched from its ancestor, *readme#10* in *MAIN*. Therefore, there is nothing to integrate.

Once *V1*'s *readme.txt* is edited, however, Perforce *will* find reason to open *MAIN*'s *readme* for integration. For example, say *V1*'s *readme.txt* was edited in change 3466.

Now, let's integrate *V1* into *MAIN*, again using the branch view:

```
p4 integ -o -b V1toMAIN @3466
...
//Ace/V1/readme#10 - integrate from //Ace/V1/readme.txt#2
```

```
- using base //Ace/V1/readme#3
...
```

As you can see, Perforce is matching *V1/readme.txt* to *MAIN/readme*. And, having found a revision of the former that is not accounted for in the latter, it opens the latter for integrating. You can resolve and submit the opened file as you would any other file opened for integrating.

Keeping added files from being propagated

You can also use branch views to prevent replication of added files. Normally, when integrate finds a new file in the donor branch, it branches it into the target branch. But you may have a situation where a file added in one branch is not appropriate for another.

For example, say the *v1promo.html* file that was added in *V1* is not appropriate for *MAIN*. Unless you do something about it, *v1promo.html* is going to be branched when you integrate from *V1* into *MAIN*. You can prevent this from happening by adding a line to the V1toMAIN branch view that excludes *v1promo.html*. For example:

p4 branch V1toMAIN

```
Branch      V1toMAIN
View            //Ace/V1/...              //Ace/MAIN/...
                //Ace/V1/readme.txt       //Ace/MAIN/readme
            -//Ace/V1/v1promo.html    //Ace/MAIN/v1promo.html
```

(A line that begins with "-" excludes files from the view.) Now the V1toMAIN branch view will effectively hide *v1promo.html* from commands that use it. That is, commands like interchanges and integrate will pay no attention to the file when you use them with the V1toMAIN branch view. If you're working in V1, of course, you'll still be able to see and work on *v1promo.html*.

Keeping target files from being deleted

Normally, when integrate sees that files in the donor branch were deleted, it assumes you want the corresponding targeted files deleted as well. You can use branch views to keep integrate from deleting target files.

You can do the same thing for files that have been deleted. Normally, when integrate sees that files in the donor branch were deleted, it assumes that you want the corresponding targeted files deleted as well.

For example, say *V1*'s *doc/issues* file has been deleted. When you integrate from *V1* to *MAIN*, Perforce either tells you that *MAIN*'s *doc/issues* will be deleted:

p4 integ -b V1toMAIN @3456

```
...
//Ace/MAIN/doc/issues#7 - delete from //Ace/V1/doc/issues#2
...
```

or it tells you that it wants to delete it:

```
p4 integ -b V1toMAIN @3456
...
//Ace/MAIN/doc/issues#8 - can't delete from
    //Ace/V1/doc/issues#2 without -d or -Dt flag
...
```

(The second behavior is what you'd see if *MAIN*'s *doc/issues* file had been changed recently.) In any case, let's assume that you *don't* want the *MAIN* file deleted. To keep Perforce from attempting to delete it, you can exclude it from the branch view:

```
p4 branch V1toMAIN
```

Branch	V1toMAIN	
View	//Ace/V1/...	//Ace/MAIN/...
	//Ace/V1/readme.txt	//Ace/MAIN/readme
	-//Ace/V1/v1promo.html	//Ace/MAIN/v1promo.html
	-//Ace/V1/doc/issues	//Ace/MAIN/doc/issues

Now when you run integrate using the branch view, Perforce will skip over the *doc/issues* file.

Preventing warnings about deleted target files

Deleted target files are usually of no concern to Perforce when you run integrate. Perforce cares only about propagating change from donor to target; the change that deleted the files is already accounted for in the target. But if the corresponding donor files have as-yet-unintegrated changes, Perforce warns you that something is amiss.

For example, say new development in *MAIN* has involved deleting the entire *db* directory. (Granted, this is an extreme example.) And say a recent bug fix in *V1* involved a change to files in *db*. Now, every time you integrate from *V1* to *MAIN*, Perforce will give you warnings about the deleted target files:

```
p4 integ -b V1toMAIN @3467
...
//Ace/MAIN/db/dbPgLoad.cpp—can't branch from
    //Ace/V1/db/dbPgLoad.cpp#2 without -d or -Dt flag
...
```

What Perforce is telling you is that it found a change to *V1*'s *db* files that isn't accounted for in *MAIN*. But when it looked for *db* files in *MAIN*, all it found was deleted files. It tells you that if you *really* want to propagate the change, it can oblige you by branching *V1*'s *db* files into *MAIN*. But you'll have to run integrate using the -d flag to get it to do that.

Chances are good, however, that new development in *MAIN* has made changes to *V1*'s *db* files irrelevant. Perforce emits warnings because it has no way of knowing that this is the case. If the warnings annoy you, you can exclude the *db* files from the branch view:

```
p4 branch V1toMAIN
```

Branch   V1toMAIN
View   //Ace/V1/...   //Ace/MAIN/...
                //Ace/V1/readme.txt   //Ace/MAIN/readme
                -//Ace/V1/v1promo.html //Ace/MAIN/v1promo.html
                -//Ace/V1/doc/issues   //Ace/MAIN/doc/issues
                -//Ace/V1/db/...   //Ace/MAIN/db/...

Henceforth your integrate commands will ignore the *db* files, as long as you use them with the V1toMAIN branch view.

The Arcana of Integration

(Heavens, it's all rather arcane, isn't it?)

Reconciling split and combined files

It's worth noting that there are ways to reconcile branches so that changes can be integrated between them even when files have been split or combined in one of them. Reconciling split and combined files is a bit of a parlor trick, but that it can be done at all is a distinguishing feature of Perforce.

Consider this case: after *V1* was branched from *MAIN*, *MAIN*'s *parse.cpp* was split into two files, *parse.cpp* and *eval.cpp*. Meanwhile, change 3472 has been submitted in *V1*, which affects *parse.cpp*.

As is your custom, you integrate change 3472 from *V1* into *MAIN* thus:

```
p4 integ -b V1toMAIN @3472
...
//Ace/MAIN/parse.cpp#5 - integrate from //Ace/V1/parse.cpp#2
...
```

MAIN's *parse.cpp* is opened for integrating, which is good. Maybe the change in *V1*'s *parse.cpp* should be merged into it. But what if the change should be merged into *MAIN*'s *eval.cpp*? What if part of the *V1* change should be merged into *MAIN*'s *parse.cpp* and part of it should be merged into *eval.cpp*?

Unfortunately, because nothing maps *V1*'s *parse.cpp* to *MAIN*'s *eval.cpp*, integrate has no way of knowing it should open the latter. Even if there were such a mapping in the V1toMAIN branch view, it would eclipse the mapping between the two *parse. cpp* files, because there can be only one mapping per file in a branch view. (When there is more than one, the last takes precedence.)

However, there's nothing to keep you from running more than one integrate command. If you know that part of *MAIN*'s *parse.cpp* has been spun off into *eval.cpp*, you can integrate change 3472 using a pair of integrate commands:

```
p4 integ -o -b V1toMAIN @3472
...
//Ace/MAIN/parse.cpp#6 - integrate from //Ace/V1/parse.cpp#2
  using base //Ace/V1/parse.cpp#1
...

p4 integ -o //Ace/V1/parse.cpp@3472 //Ace/MAIN/eval.cpp
//Ace/MAIN/eval.cpp#1 - integrate from //Ace/V1/parse.cpp#2
  using base //Ace/MAIN/parse.cpp#5
```

This sequence of commands opens two target files for integrating from the same donor file. When you resolve them—which you should do interactively—you'll have a chance to pick the correct merged result for each. Whether it's easy or hard to pick a merged result, and whether conflicts are involved, depends on how the *MAIN* file was split and how the *V1* file was changed.

Integration involving split and combined files is definitely in the category of things not to make a habit of. Nevertheless, software development being what it is, refactoring happens, and branches diverge. In Chapter 7 we'll look at ways to organize and use branches so that most change flows between fairly similar branches and changes that increase divergence don't have to traverse too many branches.

Integration history can't be undone

Integration history is permanent. Once integrated, changes won't come up for integration again. So what can you do if you've botched an integration?

For example, say you've been incrementally integrating changes from *V1* into *MAIN*. You've just integrated 3461 from *V1* into *MAIN*, creating change 3484 in *MAIN*. Now you find out that change 3461 wasn't applicable to *MAIN*.

You always have the option of undoing an integration by backing out the change. (You read about how to do this in Chapter 2.) For example, you can back out change 3484. This will restore the *MAIN* branch to what it was before you submitted the bad integration.

Backing out a change doesn't change integration history. When you next look for changes to integrate, 3461 won't show up. As far as Perforce knows, *V1*'s 3461 is accounted for in *MAIN*. Hopefully this is what you wanted, because there's nothing you can do to change it.

Forcing Perforce to redo an integration

But what if you *do* want to redo an integration? For example, let's say change 3461 *was* meant for *MAIN*. One file, *db/Jamfile*, was merged during the integration. Now you discover that in editing conflicts in the merged result, you managed to delete entire chunks of the file. And, in your haste, you submitted your integration before realizing what you'd done.

There are two ways to fix this. One way, of course, is to open *MAIN/Jamfile* for editing and put the missing chunks back in by cutting and pasting.

The other way to fix a bad merge is to coerce Perforce into redoing the integration. This gives you another chance at merging the orginal files.

Here's what you'll need to do:

1. Synchronize with the last good revision of the target file:

   ```
   p4 sync //Ace/MAIN/db/Jamfile@3483
   ```

2. Use this form of `integrate` to open the file for integrating:

   ```
   p4 integ -h -f //Ace/MAIN/db/Jamfile@3484,3484
   ```

   (-h makes Perforce use the revision you have as the target. -f forces Perforce to ignore previous integration history. The revision range, *@3484,3484*, makes Perforce use *@3483* as the merge base.)

3. Take another crack at resolving the file:

   ```
   p4 resolve
   ```

4. Resynchronize the file and resolve it by ignoring the depot version:

   ```
   p4 sync //Ace/MAIN/db/Jamfile
   p4 resolve -ay
   ```

   (The depot version, as you recall, is currently the mangled one.)

5. If you're happy with the result, submit the file:

   ```
   p4 submit
   ```

Note that you can redo only the parts of an integration that involve resolving files. With the procedure shown here, for example, you can redo a merge. But for integrations that involve branching or deleting files, you'll have to resort to backing out changes.

The mechanics of integration

Thanks to filespecs and changelist numbers, you can use `integrate` to operate on entire branches, complete changes, points in time, and various combinations thereof. But underneath it all, Perforce operates on individual file revisions. In this section we take a look at what happens to the files involved in integration operations.

When you run `integrate`, you provide filespecs that describe sets of donor and target files. You provide them as command arguments, in a branch view, or through a combination of both. Once `integrate` has analyzed donor and target files, it opens a subset of the target files. In other words, `integrate` operates on target files, not donor files.

Your workspace's client view limits the scope of the `integrate` command. No matter how you invoke it, `integrate` won't operate on files that aren't in your client view.

The target files don't necessarily have to be synchronized in your workspace, but they do have to be in your client view. The donor files, although they will be analyzed, will not be opened by integrate. So it doesn't matter whether the donor files are in your client view.

You can always use integrate -n to find out exactly which target files will be opened. For example:

```
p4 integ -n //Ace/MAIN/...@3456 //Ace/V1/...
```

The Perforce Server does quite a bit of analysis to figure out which files to open. It begins the analysis by:

- Making a list of the donor files that currently exist. (Note that a file exists even if its current revision is marked deleted.)
- Computing a target filename for each donor filename. This is done strictly by pattern-matching, using filespecs you provide in a branch view or as command arguments. File history has no bearing on matching target filenames to donor filenames.

Now Perforce has a list of donor-target file pairs to analyze. From here on, it analyzes each donor-target pair individually. So when we say *donor* and *target* in the explanation that follows, we mean the individual files, not the entire sets.

Perforce's next step is to assess the history of the donor—at least, as much of its history as is relevant to the current integrate command. The relevant history is tempered by:

- Whether the donor was ever deleted and re-added. For integration, Perforce usually treats the donor as if it had begun life when it was most recently re-added. (Rebranched revisions have the same effect as re-added revisions.)
- Whether you supplied a revision on the integrate command. When you integrate one changelist at a time, or cherry-pick changes to integrate, you're narrowing the relevant history of the donor.

In the context of its relevant history, the donor file is either a deleted file or not. Perforce can tell whether it needs to do anything, in some cases, without any further analysis:

- If the donor is deleted and the target does not exist, nothing happens. There is nothing to integrate.
- If the donor and target file are both deleted, nothing happens. There is nothing to integrate.
- If the donor is *not* deleted, and the target does not exist, the donor needs to be branched to the target. (This is the familiar "cloning" case.) The target file will be opened for branching.

These are the simple cases; even more analysis is needed for the rest. Perforce now takes stock of all the revisions in the donor's relevant history and inspects them to see which are already accounted for in the target.

A donor revision is accounted for if it was branched or integrated *into* the target, or if it was branched or integrated *from* the target without editing. (See "Why does editing matter?" a bit later in the chapter.) A donor revision may also be considered accounted for if it's related to the target indirectly by a trail of integration history. If all revisions of the donor have been accounted for in the target, nothing happens to the target—there is nothing to integrate.

If there are donor revisions not yet accounted for in the target, Perforce tests a number of factors to decide what to do with the target:

- If the donor is deleted and the target is not, Perforce assumes that you want to delete the target. But before doing anything, it asks itself, "Is the target evolving, too?" If the answer is yes, it warns you that if you really want it to delete a file that's been modified, you'll have to run integrate -d. If the answer is no, it opens the target for deleting.

- If the target is deleted but the donor is not, Perforce gives you a warning. It tells you that it can rebranch the donor file on top of the target, but you'll have to run integrate -d to force it to do so.

- And, finally, in the case where both donor and target exist, and neither is deleted, Perforce synchronizes the target in the workspace, opens it for integrating, and leaves it for you to resolve.

As you know, resolving a file involves three files, "yours," "theirs," and the "base." The donor's highest, unaccounted-for revision will be used as "theirs." The target file in your workspace will be used as "yours."

Perforce picks the base using a formula that takes into account previous integration history.[*] As you can imagine, it's a complicated formula; explaining it doesn't make anything clearer. Let's just say that:

- Usually the base is the revision of the donor you last integrated. This is excellent for three-way merging, because it keeps changes you've already merged from showing up as diffs.

- When you cherry-pick, the base is the donor revision that precedes the lowest revision in the range you specified. For three-way merging, this has the effect of making changes within a revision range look like "their" diffs.

---

[*] There is a big difference between Release 2004.2 and previous releases of Perforce when it comes to picking the revision to use as the base for merging. As of Release 2004.2, the Perforce Server uses the common ancestor as the merge base. In previous releases, it used either the closest revision of the donor that had already been integrated or—if nothing had ever been integrated from it—the first revision of the donor.

- Sometimes the base is a revision of the donor that is lower than the revision you last integrated. This happens when you're integrating changes that were skipped by previous cherry-picking.

- Sometimes the base is a revision of the file the donor was branched from. This makes it possible to merge changes to and from renamed files.

- Sometimes the base is a file only indirectly related to both donor and target. Perforce picks a base like this when the donor has never been integrated into the target. This makes it possible to merge changes that have occurred since a distant branch point.

- When Perforce can't find anything better, it uses the donor's revision *#1* as the base.

Finally, new integration history is recorded when you submit the target file. The lowest and highest of the donor revisions as yet unaccounted for are associated with the new revision of the target. The next time you integrate between donor and target, these revisions will be taken into account.

What interchanges really tells us

As you read in "Cherry-picking changes to integrate," earlier in this chapter, interchanges can imply that a change needs integrating when in fact the change has already been cherry-picked. Once you've fathomed the mechanics of integration, you'll see why the interchanges command behaves this way.

Perforce isn't keeping track of changelists as they are integrated from donor to target files. Instead, it's keeping track of individual file revisions. When you run the integ command, it operates on the individual revisions that haven't been integrated. (As you've seen in this chapter, you can run integ -n to get a list of these revisions.)

The problem with integ -n is that it yields too much information. When you're trying to figure out what to integrate next, an itemized list of file revisions isn't that helpful. What *is* helpful is a list of changelists—logical units of work submitted by developers—that need integrating.

The interchanges command meets this need by analyzing the donor-target integration history that would be recorded if its operands were used by integ. As you just read in "The mechanics of integration," each donor file has a lowest and highest revision that will be associated by integration with the new revision of its target. Each low-to-high range involves one or more file revisions, and each file revision has one changelist associated with it. The interchanges command aggregates all of the revisions in all of the low-to-high ranges and reports the sorted list of unique changelists associated with them. If a low-to-high range includes revisions previously integrated by cherry-picking, previously integrated changelists can show up in the output of interchanges.

However, as long as you're careful about integrating changelists in order and in their entirety, interchanges will give you useful output. And as it turns out, there are other good reasons to integrate changelists in order and in their entirety. We'll get to that in Chapter 8.

Decoding integration history

In the output of various Perforce commands, you may have noticed integration history described in terms like "add from" and "edit into." This looks like English, but what it really is is a very terse vocabulary of integration events. The actual output depends on the commands emitting them, but once you recognize the keywords, it's easy to interpret. Table 4-1 explains the keywords.

Table 4-1. Integration history keywords and their meanings

Keywords	Explanation
branch	You branched a file. Content-wise, the file is identical to its donor.
branch+add	You branched a file and modified it before submitting it. The branched file may or may not be identical to its donor.
integrate+merge	You integrated a file and resolved it by merging. You submitted the file Perforce constructed; you didn't edit the merged result.
integrate+edit	You integrated a file and modified it before submitting it. You may have edited it to resolve merge conflicts, or you may have reopened it for editing before or after resolving it.
integrate+copy	You integrated a file and resolved it by copying the donor to it. The file is identical to its donor.
integrate+ignore	You integrated a file and resolved it by ignoring the donor.
delete from/into	You integrated a deleted file. (That is, you used `integrate` to delete a file.)
branch+import	You branched a file from a remote depot. The file is identical to its donor.

Why does editing matter?

During integration, content can be merged into a file with or without your intervention. Likewise, content can be copied to a file during branching with or without your intervention. In either case, you have the option of editing the file before submitting it. (And you may not have a choice, as when editing a file to resolve merge conflicts.)

When you edit a file—that is, if you change any of its actual content—you're doing something to it that can't be derived by copying or merging another file.[*] So, as Perforce records integration history, it notes whether you've edited files. It uses this distinction later, to determine which donor revisions can be considered accounted for in targets.

For example, look at this integration history:

---

[*] Editing a file simply to remove conflict markers is not considered a change to the content of a merged file.

```
p4 integrated apples
...
apples#9 - merge from fruit#4
...
apples#1 - branch from fruit#1,#3
```

Here, *apples#1* was branched from *fruit#3*. Nothing in its content was introduced by the user. And *apples#9* was created by integrating from *fruit* into *apples* and resolving by merging. Because no editing was involved in creating either *apples#1* or *apples#9*, both revisions of *apples* are considered accounted for in the history of *fruit*.

Now look at this history:

```
p4 integrated oranges
...
oranges#9 - edit from fruit#4
...
oranges#1 - add from fruit#1,#3
```

Here, *oranges#1* was branched from *fruit#3*. Add from tells us it was edited before it was submitted. And, although *oranges#9* was created by integrating from *fruit*, edit from tells us it was edited before it was submitted. In any case, neither *oranges#1* nor *oranges#9* is considered accounted for in the history of *fruit*, because both contain content edited by a user.

The curious syntax of the integrate command

Finally, the last bit of arcana is for command-line users. It's about using branch views, filespecs, and revisions together on the integrate command.

When you use a branch view with integrate, the branch view dictates the donor files. You can pass filespecs as command arguments, and when you do, the filespecs are assumed to be target files.

For example, let's say that you want to integrate the *src* directory's changes from *V1* into *MAIN*. You can use the V1toMAIN branch view and supply *MAIN*'s *src* directory as a command argument:

```
p4 integ -b V1toMAIN //Ace/MAIN/src/...
```

The donor files, in this case, are the files in *//Ace/V1/src*, as dictated by the V1toMAIN branch view.

Now, what if you wanted to cherry-pick and integrate *V1*'s change 3488 while limiting the scope to the *src* directory? Surprisingly, the syntax is:

```
p4 integ -b V1toMAIN //Ace/MAIN/src/...@3488,3488
```

This is a surprise, because the filespec *//Ace/MAIN/src/...@3488,3488* is an empty set. The revision range *@3488,3488* refers to files in *V1*, not *MAIN*. No files in *MAIN* were involved in changelist 3488.

The `integrate` command is special in that when you use a branch view, target filespecs, and donor revisions together, you must combine each donor revision with its target filespec. This quirky syntax overloading applies *only* when you use a branch view. Without a branch view, you must supply both a donor and a target filespec; the donor revision is attached to the donor filespec, as you would expect:

```
p4 integ //Ace/V1/src/...@3488,3488 //Ace/MAIN/src/...
```

CHAPTER 5

Labels and Jobs

Software configuration management is not complete without a way to save snapshots of file configurations so we can restore them later. Nor is it complete without a way to link external issues like bug reports, change requests, and to-do lists to the work we do on files. In this chapter, we'll look at how to do these things in Perforce, including using *labels* and *jobs*.

Saving Important Configurations

There are a number of ways to mark and restore file configurations in Perforce:

- You can use changelist numbers. Every changelist number *is* a snapshot of the depot.

- You can use dates and timestamps. Perforce knows the state of the depot at any point in time.

- You can use labels. Labels can be applied to depot snapshots and to workspace-synchronized revisions as well as to arbitrary collections of files at mix-and-match revisions. And because labels can have descriptive names, they are easier to recognize than changelist numbers.

- You can use jobs. Jobs can be linked to changelist numbers, giving you a way to mark the depot snapshots that are important to you. Like labels, jobs can have descriptive names.

Each of these methods has its pros and cons, as you'll learn from reading this chapter.

Changelists and dates: the automatic snapshots

Every time a user submits files to Perforce, a snapshot of the depot is created automatically. The changelist number created at submit time is effectively a global revision number. It can be used to reference any file or set of files in the depot snapshot.

For instance, Ann submits a changelist:

```
p4 submit
Locking 2 files ...
edit //depot/www/index.html#9
add //depot/www/products.html#2
Change 5624 submitted.
```

As you can see, Ann's changelist contained only two files. However, by submitting it, she has created the revision identifier @5624.

This identifier can be used with *any* filespec to refer to the depot snapshot created when Ann submitted her files. Weeks later, for example, Roy might want to use it to synchronize his workspace with a snapshot of *//depot/appserver* as of that moment:

```
p4 sync //depot/appserver/...@5624
```

Dates or dates with a timestamp can also be used as snapshot revisions. Perforce supports two date formats:

- YYYY/MM/DD
- YYYY/MM/DD:HH:MM:SS

For example, to synchronize your workspace with a snapshot of the *//depot/ourproject* files as of October 12, 2004, you'd use:

```
p4 sync //depot/ourproject/...@2004/10/12
```

 If you don't specify a time, Perforce assumes you mean the *beginning* of the 24-hour day. If what you really want is a snapshot that includes work done by the *end* of the day, use the next day's date. Also, the Perforce Server assumes you're referring to *its* time zone, not yours. (The P4 info command can tell you what time zone your Perforce Server is in.)

The depot does not change continuously over time. Rather, it changes in discrete events, with each event marked by a changelist number. When you use a date to refer to a snapshot of the depot, what you get is a version of the depot marked by the last-submitted changelist as of that date. For example, if changelist 1200 was submitted on February 13, 2004, and changelist 1201 wasn't submitted until February 16, these three snapshots would be identical:

```
//depot/ourproject/...@1200
//depot/ourproject/...@2004/02/14
//depot/ourproject/...@2004/02/15
```

Comparing snapshots

There are several ways to compare snapshots. One is to use diff2 to list the files that have changed. For example, here we list the files that changed in the *//depot/www* path between 6:00 a.m. on March 15, 2004 and 6:00 p.m. of the same day:

```
p4 diff2 -q //depot/www/...@2004/03/15:06:00:00 //depot/www/...@2004/03/15:18:00:00
==== //depot/www/cgi-bin/login.rb#4  - //depot/www/cgi-bin/login.rb#5 ====
==== //depot/www/doc/index.html#8 - //depot/www/doc/index.html#9 ====
==== <none> - //depot/www/doc/contest/index.html#1 ====
```

Or, you can use the changes command to list the changes that were made to a file collection in the interval between two snapshots. For example:

```
p4 changes //depot/www/...@2004/03/15:06:00:00,@2004/03/15:18:00:00
Change 3407 on 2004/03/15 by roy 'Fix the login script...'
Change 3398 on 2004/03/15 by roy 'Publish web contest...'
```

You can also use P4V's Folder Diff tool to compare snapshots. Right-click on a folder and select Folder History, and you'll see the changes that were made to the folder. Drag any folder revision to another and you'll get the Folder Diff view (see Figure 5-1), where you can expand highlighted subfolders and drill down to individual file diffs.

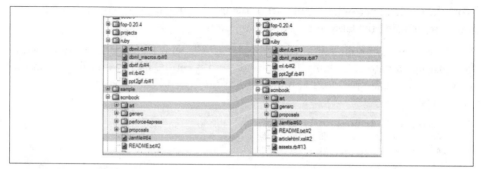

Figure 5-1. P4V's Folder Diff view

Using Labels

In Perforce, as in many SCM systems, you can tag files with a label. A label lets you use memorable names like "REL2.0.1" or "Best_JPEGs_for_t-shirts" to refer to specific configurations of file revisions.

Applying a label to files

Use tag to apply a label to files. For example, to tag all the files in the *//Ace/Products/R2.0/* path with the label Rel2.0.1_Beta1, you would use:

```
p4 tag -l Rel2.0.1_Beta1 //Ace/Products/R2.0/...
```

In P4V this is simply a matter of selecting a folder or a file, then picking the Label command from its context menu.

Normally, tag applies a label to the head revisions—that is, the newest revisions—of files. You can tag older revisions by supplying a revision to the file argument. For example, this command tags the revisions that were newest as of 6:00 a.m. on February 1, 2004:

```
p4 tag -l Rel2.0.1_Beta1 //Ace/Products/R2.0/...@2004/02/01:06:00:00
```

A label can't have an all-numeric name, and it can't be the same as an existing workspace name. To list the labels already in existence, use:

```
p4 labels
```

Referring to labels

Once a label has been applied, it can be used as shorthand to refer to an entire collection of files. For example, to synchronize a workspace with the files labeled Rel2.0.1_Beta1, you would use:

```
p4 sync @Rel2.0.1_Beta1
```

Note the @ character—that's not part of the label name; it's the syntax that tells Perforce you're using the label as a symbolic revision.

You read about symbolic revisons in Chapter 1. A label is a symbolic revision identifier, just like a date or a changelist number, and it can be used with filespecs in the same way. For example, let's assume the Rel2.0.1_Beta1 label has been applied to these files:

```
//Ace/Products/R2.0/app/db/fileA.cpp#3
//Ace/Products/R2.0/app/db/fileB.cpp#4
//Ace/Products/R2.0/app/ui/fileC.cpp#2
```

Any of these files can now be referred to with the symbolic revision @Rel2.0.1_Beta1. For example:

```
//Ace/Products/R2.0/app/db/fileA.cpp@Rel2.0.1_Beta1
```

refers to:

```
//Ace/Products/R2.0/app/db/fileA.cpp#3
```

Wildcards can be combined with labels. For example:

```
//Ace/Products/R2.0/app/db/*@Rel2.0.1_Beta1
```

refers to:

```
//Ace/Products/R2.0/app/db/fileA.cpp#3
//Ace/Products/R2.0/app/db/fileB.cpp#4
```

Which files did I label?

You can use files to see a list of labeled files. For example, to see which files are labeled Rel2.0.1_Beta1, use:

```
p4 files @Rel2.0.1_Beta1
//Ace/Products/R2.0/app/db/fileA.cpp#3 - edit change 1931 (text)
//Ace/Products/R2.0/app/db/fileB.cpp#4 - edit change 1904 (text)
//Ace/Products/R2.0/app/ui/fileC.cpp#2 - delete change 1980 (text)
```

Locking a label

When you tag files with a label, you're creating a label spec. (A spec, as you recall, describes an object in the Perforce database.) Normally the spec simply exists behind the scenes and you can pay no attention to it. A situation where the spec is important, however, is when you want to lock a label. You can do this only by updating the label spec and changing its unlocked option to locked. For example:

p4 label Rel2.0.1_Beta1

Label	Rel2.0.1_Beta1
Owner	dave
Options	locked

Any user can apply or remove an unlocked label. Once a label is locked, it can't be applied or removed by anyone, including its owner! (That's meant to keep us from inadvertently reapplying a label.) As the owner of a label, you can unlock the label by editing its spec and changing locked to unlocked.

Do you really need a label?

Labels aren't always the most efficient way to save file configurations. Say you label a depot snapshot thus:

p4 tag -l Rev2.3.1-Beta-Mar06 //depot/project/...@1245

This snapshot can now be referenced with either of these filespecs:

```
//depot/project/...@1245
@Rev2.3.1-Beta-Mar06
```

The labeled reference is obviously more meaningful (to the people involved with the project, at least). However, Perforce has to store the association between the label and the file revisions it tags. Labeling files consumes database space, and making new labels frequently to tag a huge collection of files can consume noticeable database space.

To keep track of huge configurations, consider using changelist snapshots instead of labels. Changelist numbers aren't as descriptive as label names, of course, so you lose that convenience when you rely on them. (However, jobs can help you keep track of the changelist numbers that are important to you; see "Jobs as Changelist Markers," later in this chapter.)

The case where changelist snapshots won't work, however, is when you need to record a configuration of files at revisions that are not contemporaneous. For example, say you are trying to compile a program from the files in *//depot/project*. You've synchronized a build workspace with the latest revisions, but a recent change to one of the files has made it impossible to compile the program. You've found that you can compile only if you synchronize the errant file with an earlier revision.

Once you do that, however, the files in the workspace aren't uniformly synchronized with the head revisions—one file matches a previous revision. Thus you'll not be able to use a changelist number or a date as a snapshot to restore this build configuration. You'll have to label the current workspace configuration to be able to refer back to the mix-and-match collection of revisions in it.

Labeling the current workspace configuration

Labeling the current workspace configuration is easy, although it takes two steps:

1. Use the label command to create a label spec:

   p4 label BobsWorkspaceMar06

   (Just save the label spec as is—there's no need to modify it.)

2. Use the labelsync command to apply the label to files:

   p4 labelsync -l BobsWorkspaceMar06

The preceding labelsync command labels all the files in the workspace, at the revisions synchronized in the workspace. If you ever need to restore this particular configuration to a workspace in the future, all you have to do is run this command:

p4 sync @BobsWorkspaceMar06

What's the difference between tag and labelsync?

Now that you've seen both tag and labelsync, you may be wondering what the difference is.

The tag command is meant to be used to apply a label to a set of files:

- You must give tag a filespec to tell it which files to label.
- If the filespec doesn't have a revision, tag applies the label to the head revisions.
- Using tag to apply a label to a set of files doesn't remove the label from files outside of the set.
- It doesn't matter whether a spec for the label exists yet; tag creates the label spec on the fly if needed.

The labelsync command, by contrast, is meant to make one labeled configuration match another. When you use it you'll find that:

- If you don't give labelsync a filespec, it applies the label to the files synchronized in the current workspace.
- Unless you specify a revision, labelsync applies the label to the currently synchronized revisions, not to the depot's head revisions.
- labelsync is an exclusive operation. As it applies a label to a set of files, it removes the label from files outside of the set.
- You can't use labelsync with a label that doesn't have a spec yet.

There are subtle differences in the implicit arguments and the default behaviors of these two commands. If you need to know more, see the online help:

```
p4 help tag
p4 help labelsync
```

Finding and comparing labels

Use labels to see which labels have been applied to a particular set of files. For example, the following command lists labels that have tagged files in *//depot/main/ project*:

```
p4 labels //depot/main/project/...
Label GoodBuild...
Label Branched-to-Dev-Titan...
Label Branched-to-Rel2.0...
Label Branched-to-Rel1.0...
```

Labeled configurations can be compared. The diff2 command lists the file revisions that differ between two configurations:

```
p4 diff2 -q //...@Branched-to-Rel2.0 //...@Branched-to-Dev-Titan
==== //depot/main/project/src/db.c#13 - //depot/main/project/src/db.c#14 ====
==== //depot/main/project/src/ws.c#9  - //depot/main/project/src/ws.c#8 ====
```

Earlier, you saw how to list changes that took place between two snapshots. You can't do that with labels, because labeled configurations are not guaranteed to be contemporaneous. In other words, you'd be looking for the changes that took place between two points in time, but labels are not points in time. (Perforce does allow you to use labels as end-points in a revision range, but the results you get when you do that are rarely what you were looking for.)

Reusable labels (rolling labels)

Labels can be reused. For example, the GoodBuild label can be reapplied every time a new build is successful:

```
p4 tag -l GoodBuild //depot/project/...
```

Rolling labels like this give developers a convenient, consistent revision identifier to use in the course of their work. For example, to keep their workspaces synchronized with the latest known good build, they'd simply get in the habit of using:

```
p4 sync @GoodBuild
```

Note that Perforce doesn't keep a history of previously labeled configurations. When you reapply a label to a file revision, the label is removed from any other revision of the file it may have previously tagged. (Only one revision of a file can be tagged with a given label.) What this means is that a rolling label can represent only one configuration at a time. There's no way to restore any of the configurations it previously tagged—unless you've archived them somehow.

Archiving rolling labels with unique labels

One way to archive rolling label configurations is to tag each one with a unique label. For example, you can make a GoodBuild2004/02/01 label that tags the configuration represented by today's GoodBuild label:

```
p4 tag -l GoodBuild2004/02/01 @GoodBuild
```

You can tag the GoodBuild configuration every week to archive it. To restore the current GoodBuild label to one of its archived configurations, you'd use:

```
p4 labelsync -l GoodBuild @GoodBuild2004/02/01
```

This effectively reapplies the GoodBuild label to the same files it labeled back on February 1, 2004. The labelsync command is used here in place of the tag command in order to make sure the label is applied exclusively.

Archiving rolling labels in files

If your labeled configurations are large—hundreds of thousands of files, say—you may not want to bloat the Perforce database with unique labels that replicate your rolling label's configurations. As an alternative, you can use a file to archive the configurations. In other words, you can save a list of tagged files in a file itself and submit it every time you reapply the label.

For example, to tag files with the GoodBuild label and check in the list of files you've just tagged, use a sequence of commands like this:

```
p4 tag -l GoodBuild //depot/project/...
p4 edit GoodBuild.save
p4 files @GoodBuild > GoodBuild.save
p4 submit GoodBuild.save
```

By checking in the *GoodBuild.save* file every time you roll the GoodBuild label, you have a concise history of your labeled configurations at hand. To compare any two archived configurations, simply diff two versions of the file:

```
p4 diff2 GoodBuild.save@2004/01/01 GoodBuild.save@2004/02/01
```

On the rare occasion that you need to restore a rolling label from a configuration saved in a file, you can do so by piping the file to labelsync. You'll have to use a filter, however, because the files output saved in the file isn't acceptable to the labelsync command. Whereas files outputs lines like:

```
//depot/project/src/main.cpp#12 - edit change 3432 (text)
```

the labelsync and tag commands expect lines like:

```
//depot/project/src/main.cpp#12
```

If you're on Unix, for example, you can use sed as a filter. To restore the GoodBuild label from a configuration saved in a file:

```
p4 print -q GoodBuild.save@2004/02/01 | \
    sed -e "s/ - .*//" | p4 -x- labelsync -l GoodBuild
```

The print command outputs the contents of the February 1, 2004 version of the *GoodBuild.save* file. This output—itself a list of file revisions—is filtered and piped to the labelsync command to reapply the GoodBuild label. This effectively restores the label; if you use @*GoodBuild* as a revision identifier now, it will behave as it did on February 1, 2004.

Labels have views, too

Like client specs and branch view specs, label specs have View fields. A label's view restricts the scope of the label—that is, it limits the files that may be tagged with the label.

When the tag command creates a label spec behind the scenes, it assigns a default view of the entire repository:

```
Label       Rel2.0.1_Beta1
View        //Ace/...
```

(In this example, the entire repository is a single depot named "Ace.")

There are times where it's useful to create a label view first, *then* tag files. (In fact, you'll see examples of this in Part II.) You can use the label command to create a new label spec and enter one or more filespecs in the View field. For example:

p4 label Rel3.0.1

```
Label       Rel3.0.1
View        //Ace/Products/R3.0/...
```

With a view like this, the only files that can be tagged with the Rel3.0.1 label are those in the *//Ace/Products/R3.0* path.

Note that changing a label's view doesn't change the files already tagged. Nor does it prevent already-tagged files from being referenced using the label as a revision. All it does is restrict the scope of the label's future tag and labelsync commands.

Removing a label

You can remove an unlocked label from files with tag -d. For example:

p4 tag -d -l GoodBuild //depot/project/...

removes the GoodBuild label from the files in the *//depot/project* path.

Note that a label can exist as a spec even if it tags no files. After untagging files, you can leave the label spec intact, for reuse, or you can delete the label spec:

p4 label -d GoodBuild

This command removes the GoodBuild label from *all* the files it tagged *and* removes the label spec named GoodBuild.

Labels, snapshots, and workspaces

As with label names—and changelist numbers, and dates—workspace names can be used as symbolic revisions. When used as a revision, a workspace name refers to the revisions currently synchronized in the workspace. For example, if Roy-Mac-Dev is the name of a workspace, *//depot/www/index.html@Roy-Mac-Dev* refers to the revision of *//depot/www/index.html* with which the Roy-Mac-Dev workspace is synchronized. (Now you see why Perforce doesn't allow workspaces and labels to have the same names.)

Because workspace names can be used as symbolic revisions, it's very easy to compare workspaces to labels or snapshots. For example, to find out how different the *//depot/project* files in the Roy-Mac-Dev workspace are from the ones labeled Good-Build, we could use:

```
p4 diff2 //depot/project/...@Roy-Mac-Dev //depot/project/...@GoodBuild
```

Anyone, using Roy's workspace or not, can do comparisons like this. However, when a workspace name is used as a revision for comparison purposes, Perforce is not actually getting content from files in a workspace. It's getting content from depot files, referring to the revisions synchronized in the workspace. Thus a comparison like the example one here doesn't show us what Roy has changed in his workspace. It merely shows how the revisions that his workspace is synchronized with are different from the revisions tagged by the label.

You can use the diff command to compare your actual workspace files to labels and snapshots, as long as you are running commands *from your own workspace*. For example, to compare the *//depot/project* files in your workspace to the files labeled GoodBuild, you could use:

```
p4 diff -f //depot/project/...@GoodBuild
```

Or, to compare your files to a date snapshot:

```
p4 diff -f //depot/project/...@2004/03/15
```

In this kind of comparison, you *will* see how your local workspace files compare to depot file revisions as of the snapshot or label. Perforce is able to do this for you, because as long as you are running commands from your workspace, it has access to your workspace files.

 If you're using Perforce from the command line, you should be aware that there are two diff commands, diff and diff2. The diff command compares actual workspace files to files in the depot, while diff2 compares two versions of depot files. If you're using a Perforce GUI, you may be blissfully ignorant of this distinction, thanks to the menus and dialogs that guide you to the comparison you seek.

Using Jobs

A *job* is an object in the Perforce database that can be used to tie development activity to external information. Jobs can be used for anything—requirements, project plans, to-do lists, milestones—but their most common use is for defect tracking.

As you read this section, you might begin to wonder whether the commands that operate on jobs are too cumbersome and inconvenient for developers to use. The real power of jobs comes not from their convenience to users, but from their ability to provide a smart, persistent, Perforce-side data store for external defect-tracking systems. A number of open source and commercially available defect-tracking software systems work with Perforce jobs. (For more on this, go to the Perforce web site and navigate from Product Info to Defect Tracking.)

In this section we'll take a look at the underlying Perforce commands that support external defect-tracking systems. Why? For one thing, you can use these commands to automate your SCM procedures. For another, they're the key to being able to detect bug fixes as they migrate from codeline to codeline, as you'll find out in Chapter 8.

What is a job?

A job is an instance of a data structure that consists of name-value pairs. Job data is stored in the Perforce database. Jobs may mirror external data, but no external database is actually required to support Perforce's job storage.

Here is an example of a job:

```
Job          job000321
Type         bug
Status       open
User         miriam
Date         2005/02/10
Description  Login dialog is wrong size.
Product      AcePack 3.0.1
Category     GUI
```

The fields in a job are determined by a site-wide template. A Perforce superuser can use the jobspec command to customize the template:

p4 jobspec

jobspec opens a specification form in which you can define fields and default values. We won't go into the details of customizing the job template, but here are the salient points:

- Various data types (selection lists, multiple lines, and so forth) can be configured in the template, as can field names, default values, allowable values, and required fields.
- There is *one* job template in the Perforce database. This means that all jobs in your system will conform to the same structure of fields, data types, defaults, and allowable values.
- Perforce assigns new job names according to its own convention (e.g., "job000021"). But you don't have to go with Perforce's convention. You can use a different naming convention, or use the naming convention of an external defect-tracking system to name jobs.
- Use of jobs can be controlled by triggers. As superuser, you can set up trigger scripts to fire when jobs are created, updated, or deleted. (See Chapter 6.)

Customizing the job template is not difficult. To find out how to do it, see the *Perforce Administrator's Guide*.

You can create and use jobs whether or not the job template has been customized. Uncustomized, a job contains only a handful of fields:

Job
> The unique job ID.

Status
> Either open or closed.

User
> The Perforce user who created the job.

Date
> The date the job was created.

Description
> An arbitrary chunk of text. You'll see the first 30-odd characters of the Description field, along with the job ID, in the output of many P4 commands that list jobs.

Creating jobs

To create a new job use the job command. This gives you a job spec form to edit:

```
p4 job

Job           new
Status        open
User          carl
Description    <enter description here>
```

Unless you provide a job ID, Perforce assigns one for you. If you want to create a job with a specific ID, *BUG100.10* for example, you'd use:

```
p4 job BUG100.10
```

(It's unusual for Perforce users to have to create or update jobs using the Perforce-provided job spec forms. What's more typical is that users enter bug reports into an external defect-tracking system; the defect-tracking system passes data to Perforce via the job command.)

Searching for jobs

As jobs are stored in the Perforce database, their field values are indexed for fast searching and reporting. Simple search expressions can be used to find jobs by field values. You can enter expressions in the job search dialog of a GUI or in the p4 jobs command:

```
p4 jobs -e "status=open user=carl"
```

Job search expressions can contain keywords, logical operators, and wildcards:

```
p4 jobs -e "status=open user=carl|usr=ann login window|dialog siz*"
```

The jobs command by itself will list all the jobs in the system. This command's output could be large; you can limit the number that will be listed with the -m flag:

```
p4 jobs -m30
```

The search expression you supply to the jobs command is known as a *jobview* in Perforce. To find out more about job search expressions, consult the online help:

```
p4 help jobview
```

Linking jobs to changelists

As you submit changelists to check in the files you've changed, you have an opportunity to link jobs to them. There's a Jobs field in the changelist form into which you can enter a job name. (You can enter several, actually.) If you're using a GUI, you can point and click to select job names from the results of a search dialog. In a text editor, you have to type job names in manually.

```
p4 submit

Changelist    new
User          pete
Description   Bigger login dialog.
Jobs          job000021
```

Linking a job to a changelist does two things. First, it records the fact that a particular set of file changes fixes a bug. (It creates a *fix* record in the Perforce database to store the link between the changelist and the job.)

Second, linking a job to a changelist causes the Perforce submit command to automatically update a job's Status field. When a job is created, its status is set to "open," by default. When your changelist is submitted, its status will be changed to "closed."

Preselecting your own jobs

Of course, having to type job names into your submit forms is not very practical. You may prefer to have the jobs that appear in your submit forms preselected so that all you have to do is pick the ones that apply before saving the form.

You can do that through your user spec. (Users are objects in the Perforce database, just as clients, labels, and jobs are.) Use the P4 user command to update your user spec and enter a job search expression in the Jobview field. If you're Pete, for example, you could set your Jobview thus:

```
p4 user
```

```
User        pete
Jobview     status=open user=pete
```

Now, when you submit files, the Jobs field in your submit form will be prefilled with the jobs that match the search expression "user=pete status=open," along with a short description of each one.

```
p4 submit
```

```
Change       new
Description   <enter description here>
Jobs         job00021 # Fix size of login dialog.
             job00028 # Remove 'Are you sure?' popup.
```

Before saving the submit form, you'll have to trim the jobs you didn't fix from the Jobs field. But at least you've been spared the legwork of looking for your work-in-progress jobs.

Linking jobs to changelists after the fact

Jobs can also be linked to changelists after changelists are submitted, using the p4 fix command. For example, to record the fact that changelist 324 fixed job000021, use:

```
p4 fix -c 324 job000021
```

The fix command also updates a job's status—to "closed," by default, if the changelist has already been submitted. You can use the -s option to make fix change a job's status to another value, if you wish:

```
p4 fix -c 324 -s suspended job000021
```

If a submitted changelist is only a partial fix for the bug described by the job, or if it turns out not to be a fix at all, you can sever the association between the changelist and the job by using fix -d:

```
p4 fix -d -c 324 job000021
```

Searching for job fixes

The p4 fixes command lists job-changelist associations. For example, to list the jobs that are linked to changelist 3501, use:

```
p4 fixes -c 3501
```

Conversely, to list the changelists that are linked to job000021, use:

```
p4 fixes -j job000021
```

The jobs command can be used to list jobs associated with changelists submitted to a depot path. If you use jobs to report bugs, and if you link jobs with changelists that fix bugs, you can use a job search to list bugs fixed in a release branch. For example, to list the jobs linked to changelists that involve files in the *//depot/REL3.0/* path:

```
p4 jobs //depot/REL3.0/...
job000219 on 2005/04/13 by bill *closed* 'RTool missing from ...'
```

Better yet, you can use jobs -i to to list bug fixes that have been *integrated* into a release. For example, the following command lists all bug fixes in the *//depot/REL3.0* path, including the ones that were integrated into it from other paths:

```
p4 jobs -i //depot/REL3.0/...
...
job000177 on 2005/01/17 by tony *closed* 'Scroll bar not working...'
job000206 on 2005/03/08 by ann  *closed* 'Need thumbnail view...'
job000219 on 2005/04/13 by bill *closed* 'RTool missing from ...'
...
```

Strictly speaking, this output lists jobs linked with changelists that affect file revisions, that either are in the *//depot/REL3.0* path or have integration history that connects them to files in the *//depot/REL3.0* path. As you can imagine, this listing is *very* useful for finding out which bugs are fixed in which releases. For more on this, see Chapter 8.

Deleting and restoring jobs

You can delete a job with job -d. For example:

```
p4 job -d job000123
```

Deleting a job removes all data related to it, including fixes. (Fixes are the database records that associate jobs with changelists. The changelists themselves aren't affected when you delete a job.)

If you have the spec depot set up, you can restore deleted jobs from versioned specs, as described in Chapter 6. Note that restoring a job doesn't restore its fixes.

Jobs can't be locked

Unlike labels, jobs can't be locked. Normally, any user can change or delete them. With triggers, however, you can have complete control over who gets to change or delete jobs. You'll read more about triggers in Chapter 6.

Jobs as Changelist Markers

You read earlier in the chapter that changelist numbers are more efficient than labels for accumulating large configurations. But changelist numbers have a drawback—there's nothing in their identifiers that makes them easy to recognize. When a thousand new changelists have accrued over the past week, how can you tell which ones are the nightly build snapshots? You could record important changelist numbers on a cocktail napkin, but you don't have to. You can mark them with jobs.

Marking changelist numbers

To use a job to mark changelist numbers, first create the job. You can give a job any name, as long as it's unique (and as long as it doesn't contain spaces or the character #, %, *, or @). If you don't supply a job name, Perforce will come up with one for you. For example, to create a job called NightlyBuilds, use:

```
p4 job NightlyBuilds

Job            NightlyBuilds
Description    Nightly builds of //depot/project/...
```

Once you've created the job, you can use the `fix` command to mark a changelist with it. Here we use the NightlyBuilds job to mark changelist 1245:

```
p4 fix -c 1245 NightlyBuilds
```

Looking up changelist numbers by job

You can't use a job name to refer directly to files, because unlike labels, jobs can't be used as revision identifiers. However, you can query a job to find a changelist number, then use the changelist number to refer to file revisions:

```
p4 fixes -j NightlyBuilds
job NightlyBuilds fixed by change 1245 on 2004/02/18
```

This tells us that if we want to restore the nightly build configuration as of February 18, 2004, we should use *@1245* as the revision identifier. For example:

```
p4 sync //depot/project/...@1245
```

Note that jobs can be associated with more than one changelist number. This means that you can use the same job to mark snapshots of recurring configurations. For example, the NightlyBuilds job can be fixed with a new changelist every night. At the end of the week, you'd have a list of snapshot revisions you can use to refer to the nightly build configurations:

```
p4 fixes -j NightlyBuilds
job NightlyBuilds fixed by change 1245 on 2004/02/18
job NightlyBuilds fixed by change 1301 on 2004/02/19
job NightlyBuilds fixed by change 1384 on 2004/02/20
job NightlyBuilds fixed by change 1420 on 2004/02/21
job NightlyBuilds fixed by change 1532 on 2004/02/22
```

Of course, after a few weeks this list would get large. Luckily the fixes command lets you use a date range to limit its output. For example, if you had a need to find a changelist number to refer to the nightly build of work done by February 20, you would use:

```
p4 fixes -j NightlyBuilds @2004/02/19,@2004/02/20
job NightlyBuilds fixed by change 1384 on 2004/02/20
```

The dates you provide to the fixes command are shorthand for time 00:00:00 on those dates. In other words, using @2004/02/20 as an ending range limits output to changelists submitted before 2004/02/20:00:00:00. The dates *output* by the fixes command, on the other hand, are rounded up. A changelist submitted at 2004/02/19:14:20:00, for example, will be output with a date of 2004/02/20. Thus the previous example finds the changelist number that refers to the work done *before* February 20, not the work done by the *end* of February 20.

CHAPTER 6

Controlling and Automating Activity

Now that you've seen the nuts and bolts of how Perforce works, it's time to look at ways to control and automate what it does. This chapter focuses on aspects of control and automation, starting with a look at controlling depot and file access, including access to files in other Perforce domains. It describes using the depot to store specs as versioned files and restoring specs from saved versions. It describes setting up automatic change notification, and demonstrates how users can monitor depot activity. It offers tips on using Perforce in scripts, explains how scripts can mine for data efficiently, and touches on using triggers to invoke scripts. Lastly, it surveys the behind-the-scenes Perforce client programs with an eye to bringing even the most reluctant developers into the SCM fold.

Depot and File Access

We don't intend for this book to cover Perforce system administration, but there is one place where system administration overlaps with what this book is about, and that is where it concerns access to depots and depot files. Only Perforce superusers can create depots and control file access. We'll assume that you're a superuser.

 In a brand-new Perforce installation, every user is a superuser until one of them runs protect. The first user to run protect becomes the one and only superuser, and only he or she can change other users' access to files. This is not as limiting as it sounds; the first superuser can also make other users superusers. For the complete details of how this works, see the "Protections" chapter in the *Perforce System Administrator's Guide*.

Creating a new depot

As you read earlier, the root of a file tree in the Perforce repository is a depot. (And yes, the entire repository is often called "the depot.") Perforce comes with one depot by default; its name is "depot" and its path is *//depot/*....

There can be more than one depot—that is, more than one file tree root—in a repository. As a Perforce superuser, you can create new depots with the depot command. For example, to create a depot called "Ace":

```
p4 depot Ace

Depot       Ace
Type        local
Address     local
Map         Ace/...
```

Just save the form as is to create a normal depot. Now users will be able to add files in the //Ace/... depot path.

To list your depots:

```
p4 depots
Depot Ace  2004/08/01 local Ace/...   'Created by super'
Depot depot 2004/04/11 local depot/...  'Default depot'
```

To delete an empty depot:

```
p4 depot -d depot
```

(Perforce won't let you delete a depot if files have already been submitted to it. To get rid of it, you'll have to obliterate its files first. Alternatively, you could simply use depot protections to hide it from view.)

Depot protections

In Perforce, access to depot files is controlled by the protect command. Running the protect command opens up a form that keeps track of users, the files they can access, and the types of commands they can run. Here's an example:

```
p4 protect

Protections     super user  super   *   //...
                read  group ace     *   //Ace/...
                write group ace     *   //Ace/MAIN/...
                write group ace     *   //Ace/REL1/...
```

There's only one field in the protection spec, called Protections. Lines in the Protections field contain these tokens:

```
[level] [type] [name] [address] [path]
```

Each token has its own purpose:

level

A keyword that sets a level of file access. The read level allows users to run commands that read files. The write level allows them to run commands that change files. There are more access levels that can be set; these are just the most common.

type
> A keyword that is either user or group.

name
> The name of a Perforce user or group. If this is "*", the access level applies to any user or group.

address
> An IP address. If this is "*", the access level applies to users connecting from any network location.

path
> A filespec that defines a depot path. The access level applies to this path.

Thus, each line in the protection spec equates a depot path with a user (or a group) and a level of access. (Optionally, it can limit the scope to the user's IP address as well.) You'll see examples of this later in the book.

Unlike many things in Perforce that look tricky but aren't, protections look simple, but in fact they're a bit tricky. If you're planning on being a Perforce superuser, take the time to read about protections in the *Perforce System Administrator's Guide*.

Groups

So, what are these *group* things? Groups are groups of users. If you're a superuser, you can define a group with the group command. This too gives you a spec form to edit, allowing you to add or remove users in the group. For example, to define a group called "dev":

```
p4 group dev

Group       dev
Users       ann
            bill
            ron
            bob
```

You can use protect to assign file access levels to the dev group. The file access levels of the dev group will be available to users ann, bill, ron, and bob as well.

Accessing Files in Other Domains

As you know, a Perforce Server manages a repository and a database. These three things together—the server, its repository, and its database—can be thought of in the abstract as a *domain*. When you run a P4 command or launch a Perforce GUI program, you are entering a Perforce domain. Your username is checked against the list of users authorized for the domain. If you create a client workspace, its name— which must be unique in the domain—is added to the domain. Likewise, if you create files, their names—which must be unique within the domain—are added to the domain. Labels, jobs, branch views, and depots are also objects that can be defined within the domain. Descriptions of all the objects in the scope of a domain are stored in the domain's database, and versions of all the files in a domain are archived in the domain's depots.

In large companies, independent business units are likely to install and host their own Perforce domains. A Perforce feature called *remote depots* can be used to make one domain's versioned files visible in another.

Switching domains

Note that you don't need the remote depot feature to switch between Perforce domains. Perforce users can enter any Perforce domain, as long they have authorization and network access to it, by changing their P4PORT settings. (See Appendix A for an example of how P4PORT is used.)

But habitual switching between Perforce domains can be awkward. For example, say Bob normally works in the pilot:1666 domain—that is, his P4PORT is set to pilot:1666 (see Figure 6-1). Every now and then he sets P4PORT to scout:1666 to get access to files in the scout:1666 domain. The user bob and its client workspace BobWS are instantiated as objects in the database of each domain.

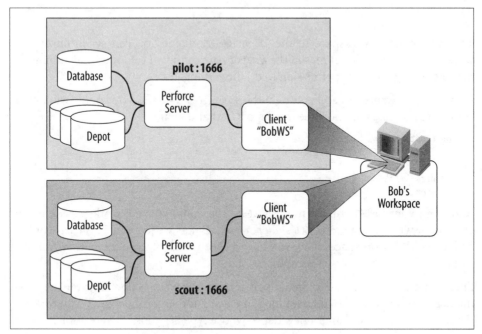

Figure 6-1. Working in two Perforce domains

Unfortunately, the Perforce Servers at `pilot:1666` and `scout:1666` know nothing about the users and workspaces in one another's domain. Each Perforce Server guides Bob's activities as if the other domain didn't exist. If Bob synchronizes his workspace while connected to `scout:1666`, he could inadvertently overwrite files that came from `pilot:1666`. Because he's switching domains, it's up to him to remember which files in his workspace came from `pilot:1666` and which came from `scout:1666`.

It would be easier for Bob if Perforce could keep track of which workspace files are from `pilot:1666` and which are from `scout:1666`. That is, in effect, what remote depots enable the Perforce Server to do.

How remote depots work

Let's assume, for example, that your current domain is controlled by the Perforce Server listening at `pilot:1666`. The `depots` command lists depots in the domain you are connected to:

```
p4 depots
Depot depot 2004/04/11 local depot/... 'Default depot'
```

The preceding output shows one depot, named "depot," in the current domain. If it contains files—and if you have permission to access them—this depot also shows up as a top-level directory in the domain's repository:

```
p4 dirs '//*'
//depot
```

You can create a workspace in the `pilot:1666` domain. You can synchronize your workspace to get copies of files in the *//depot* path, and you can open and submit the files (assuming you have permission to do these things).

Now, say you wanted to access files in the `scout:1666` domain. You could switch your `P4PORT` to `scout:1666`, and now see the depots in that domain:

```
p4 depots
Depot depot 2003/09/21 local depot/... 'Default depot'

p4 dirs '//*'
//depot
```

And, with your `P4PORT` still set to `scout:1666`, you could create a workspace and synchronize it with files in `scout:1666`'s *//depot* path. But as we just saw in the case of Bob and his BobWS workspaces, now you have to keep track of the domain that you're in and make sure your workspaces don't overlap.

Enter remote depots. As a Perforce superuser in the `pilot:1666` domain, you can make the depot in the `scout:1666` domain look like just another local depot. To do this, use the `depot` command to define a new depot whose type is remote. For example:

```
p4 depot scout

Depot        scout
Type         remote
Address      scout:1666
Map          //depot/...
```

(Note the Address field in the preceding spec form—it points to the remote server, a server outside of the current domain.) Once you have defined the remote depot, users in the `pilot:1666` domain will see both depots:

```
p4 depots
Depot depot  local  depot/...    'Default depot'
Depot scout  remote //depot/...  'Created by super'

p4 dirs '//*'
//depot
//scout
```

The *//scout* path is now an alias for the *//depot* path in the `scout:1666` domain. To refer to files in the `scout:1666` depot, users will have to use *//scout* as the path root.* Aside from that, however, any combination of wildcards and revisions—as long as it's a valid filespec—will work with files in the *//scout* path. For example:

```
p4 files //scout/dist/...
//scout/dist/toolkit/README#4
//scout/dist/toolkit/kit2-1.tar#1
```

You can't submit changes to files in a remote depot path. However, you can copy or branch files from the remote depot into the local depot. For example:

```
p4 integ //scout/dist/toolkit/... //depot/import/toolkit/...
p4 submit
```

The nice thing about this is that each domain's Perforce Server keeps track of where its files came from:

```
p4 filelog //depot/import/toolkit/kit2-1.tar
//depot/import/toolkit/kit2-1.tar
... #1 change 2533 add on 2004/04/18 by bob 'Get toolkit...'
... ... branch from //scout/dist/toolkit/kit2-1.tar#1
```

Distributed software...

Before getting carried away with remote depots, you should know that in addition to being read-only, remote depots are inherently inefficient. Your local Perforce Server doesn't cache remote depot files or metadata. Consequently, commands involving remote depot files can be satisfied only by transferring data—usually a large amount

---

* See Chapter 8 for a suggestion about naming depots that are intended to be accessed remotely.

of data. While this may be acceptable for special cases, it's certainly not something you want happening for run-of-the-mill user activity.

The real value of remote depots lies in being able to periodically integrate software from another domain and keep track of what you've integrated. In other words, remote depots are a great way to import distributed software.

...versus distributed software development

Perforce's remote depot feature gives you access to files in other domains' depots but it doesn't let you update them. Nor does it give you any information about who is working on the files, who changed them, or why. In other words, with remote depots, you get the files but not the metadata.

But it's the metadata—who's working on what, which files are opened, which files are locked, and so forth—that makes development collaboration possible. So, while remote depots are a good solution for software distribution, they're not a solution for distributed software development.

For distributed development, you want all your developers in the same domain. They don't have to be in the same geographic location, of course. Developers and their workspaces can be anywhere as long as they have network access to the machine on which the Perforce Server is running.

Saving and Restoring Specs

Specs, the Perforce database structures that represent workspaces and other nonfile objects, aren't normally versioned. However, they can be, if you set up a *spec depot*. A spec depot is managed entirely by the Perforce Server; it's used solely to store specs.

Setting up a spec depot

To set up a spec depot, use the depot command to create it. This gives you a form to edit; enter "spec" in the Type field of the form. For example, to set up a spec depot named "specs":

```
p4 depot specs

Depot      specs
Type       spec
```

Once you've saved this form, your spec depot will be created. (Note that you have to be a Perforce superuser to create depots.)

From now on, every time a spec for a label, client, user, or any other object is saved, a copy of its spec form will be saved to a file in the spec depot.

The Perforce Proxy

You can use the Perforce Proxy to extend a single Perforce domain to the far reaches of your network. The proxy—which behaves just like a Perforce Server, as far as client programs can tell—builds up its own cache of depot files. It gives its nearby developers much faster access to files than they'd have if they connected directly to the Perforce Server.

At each geographic location, a Perforce Proxy runs on a machine easily accessible to developers there. Developers near the domain's hub connect their client programs directly to the Perforce Server, while developers at distant locations connect to a Perforce Proxy. The figure shows an example.

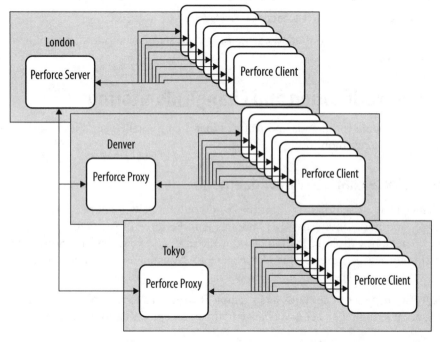

For more information about the Perforce Proxy, see the *Perforce Administrator's Guide*.

Neither the Perforce Server's remote depot feature nor the Perforce Proxy costs extra, by the way. Your company pays for the same number of Perforce users regardless of how your depots, domains, and proxies are configured.

Restoring a spec

You can restore a deleted or badly edited spec from the last good revision of the corresponding file in the spec depot.

For example, we'll restore a job named job000123. First we look for the spec's file in our specs depot:

```
p4 files //specs/...job000123...
//specs/job/job000123.p4s#4 ...
```

Next we check the recent history of the file:

```
p4 filelog //specs/job/job000123.p4s
//specs/job/job000123.p4s
... #4 default change delete on 2004/04/28
... #3 default change edit on 2004/03/04
... #2 default change edit on 2004/02/05
... #1 default change add on 2004/02/05
```

Finally, we recreate the job from the last good revision of the spec file:

```
p4 print -q //specs/job/job000123.p4s#3 | p4 job -i
```

(The -i flag on the job command causes p4 to read standard input instead of launching an editor.)

Change Notification and Change Monitoring

Perforce has some commands and features that are especially useful for change notification and change monitoring.

The Perforce change review daemon

A change review daemon is a script that runs continuously to check for recent depot changes and notify interested users about them. Perforce provides a sample change review daemon, written in Python. To download it, go to the Perforce Software web site (*http://www.perforce.com*) and navigate to Downloads → Related Software → Review Daemons. The script is *p4review.py*.

The *p4review.py* script contains a few simple instructions for installing and starting it up. Once it's running, it sends a change notification email that looks like:

From	sue@ace.com
To	don@ace.com
Subject	PERFORCE change 1254 for review
Message	Change 1254 by sue@sue-ws 2005/01/28 13:30:20

```
                    Fix highlighting on active items so that
                    even when all are lit you can see where the
                    borders are.

          Affected files ...

          ... //Ace/DEV/gui/active/mlpen.cpp#9 edit
          ... //Ace/DEV/gui/active/fmgr.cpp#3 edit
```

Note that the mail appears to come from the person who made the change. If Don replies to this message, for example, his reply will go to Sue.

Subscribing as a depot path reviewer

To receive email from *p4review.py*, you can use the user command to subscribe to the depot paths you're interested in reviewing (in other words, the depot paths you want to hear about when changed). The user command gives you a spec form to fill out. In its Email field you can give an address to which notifications should be sent, and in the Reviews field you can list depot paths you're interested in. Here, for example, is how Don's user spec is set up:

```
p4 user

User        don
Fullname    Don Quixote
Email       don@ace.com
Reviews     //Ace/DEV/gui/...
            //Ace/MAIN/gui/...
```

Don will receive a *p4review.py*-generated email message for each change that affects files in the *//Ace/DEV/gui* and *//Ace/MAIN/gui* paths. Also, *p4review.py* will use the Fullname and Email values in Don's user spec to generate email notifications of the changes Don submits.

Review daemon commands

If the Perforce-provided review daemon doesn't suit the needs of your site, you can write one yourself. A few simple Perforce commands support change review daemons:

counter

> The counter command stores a number as a named value. Your script can use this to store the last changelist number it has already processed. For instance, to store the number 1250 in a counter named "mydaemon":
>
> ```
> p4 counter mydaemon 1250
> ```

review

> The review -t command lists submitted changelists higher than a given counter, along with the username, email address, and full name of the users who submitted them. For example, to list changelists higher than the one stored in the mydaemon counter:
>
> ```
> p4 review -t mydaemon
> 1254 sue <sue@ace.com> (Sue Z. Queue)
> 1255 sue <sue@ace.com> (Sue Z. Queue)
> 1258 don <don@ace.com> (Don Quixote)
> ```

(Note that email addresses and full names are valid only if users have entered this information correctly in their user specs.)

reviews

The reviews command lists users who have subscribed to any of the depot paths affected by a submitted changelist. For example, to list the users who subscribed to paths affected by changelist 1254:

```
p4 reviews -c 1254
don <don@ace.com> (Don Quixote)
penny <penny@ace.com> (Penny Wise)
sue <sue@ace.com> (Sue Z. Queue)
```

(As you saw earlier, users can subscribe to depot paths with the user command.)

describe

The describe command shows information about a changelist. Use it with the -s flag to prevent it from including file diffs in its output:

```
p4 describe -s 1254
Change 1254 by sue@sue-ws 2005/01/28 13:30:20

        Fix highlighting on active items so that
        even when all are lit you can see where the
        borders are.

Affected files ...

... //Ace/DEV/gui/active/mlpen.cpp#9 edit
... //Ace/DEV/gui/active/fmgr.cpp#3 edit
```

The typical review daemon wakes up every 5 or 10 minutes. It gets a list of unreviewed changelists and, for each changelist, gets a list of users to notify, gets the changelist description, and emails the changelist description to each user. When it's done it saves the last changelist it processed in a counter and goes back to sleep.

Note that the counter, review, and reviews commands can't be run by ordinary users; review permission is required to run them. In other words, a review daemon script must be set up to run as a user with review permission. (See "Depot protections," earlier in this chapter.)

Using P4Web and browser bookmarks to monitor changes

To those of us who already get enough email, the prospect of receiving an email message every time a change is submitted is not a pretty one. We have many ways to monitor changes, however. We can simply run the changes command, of course. For example:

```
p4 changes -m10 //Ace/MAIN/gui/...
Change 1254 on 2005/01/28 by sue 'Fix highlighting on active...'
Change 1253 on 2005/01/27 by mo  'Add samples to installer...'
...
```

A more convenient way of keeping abreast of changes to certain areas of the depot is with P4Web bookmarks. You can point your browser to P4Web, navigate to a particular depot path, and select Submitted to get a page showing the latest changes submitted to the path. An example is shown in Figure 6-2. This page can be bookmarked; every time you return to it you'll get an updated report.

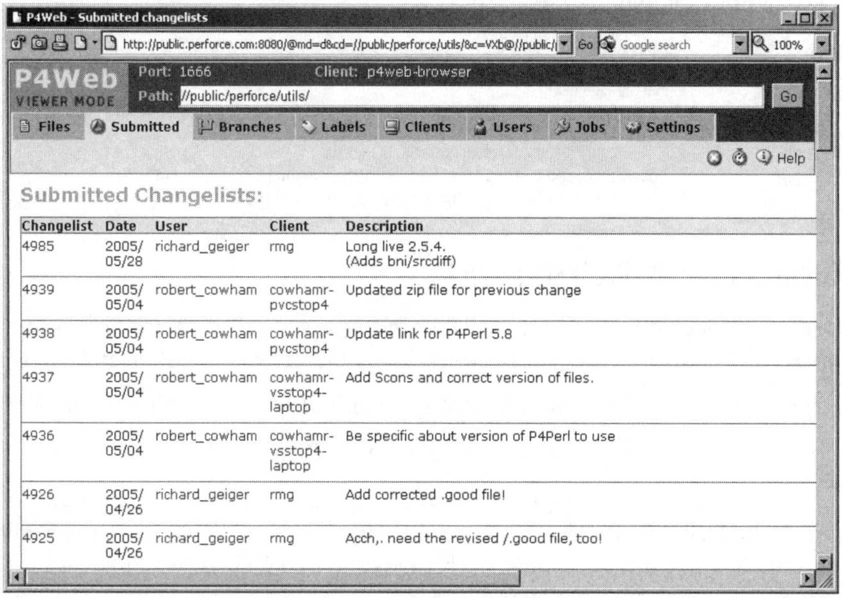

Figure 6-2. P4Web's Submitted Changelists page

You can have as many P4Web page bookmarks as you want to monitor activity in the depot paths that are important to you.

Hyperlinks to Perforce files and objects

P4Web is a standalone Perforce client program. It has two basic modes of operation. In "standard mode" it functions as a user-driven workspace manager with a web browser interface. A standard-mode P4Web serves a single user; it typically runs on the user's machine.

P4Web's other mode of operation is called "viewer mode." The P4Web viewer is, in fact, a little web server. It can serve multiple users; users point their web browsers to it just as they would to any other web server. Unlike any other web server, however, P4Web can serve up information about what's going on in the Perforce system.

For example, if P4Web is set up to run as a viewer on port 80 of a machine named *intranet.ace.com*, documents and email can use URLs that begin with *http://intranet.ace.com* to hyperlink to Perforce files and objects.

P4Web URLs for files and directories are very simple. For example, the URL that links to the *//Ace/DEV/gui/active/mlpen.cpp* file is:

> *http://intranet.ace.com//Ace/DEV/gui/active/mlpen.cpp*

There are also P4Web URLs you can use to display directory structure, change history, file diffs, and so forth, making it possible to link to them in email and other documents. For example:

From	don@ace.com
To	tim@ace.com
Subject	Have you seen these changes?
Message	Tim -- check out these changes: http://intranet.ace.com/Ace/DEV/gui/mapwin/...?ac=43 Is the test driver going to be able to handle these?

Undocumented P4Web URL tricks

Although not documented, P4Web URL syntax is easy to infer from the links within the pages P4Web displays in your browser. The general form of a P4Web URL is:

> *http://ourhost:8080/@parameters@//depot/path/file@rev?ac=n&arg=val*

You can break down the general form to compose a P4Web URL of your own:

- The root of the URL, `http://ourhost:8080/`, indicates the host and port address at which the P4Web viewer is available. In this case, the P4Web viewer is available on port 8080 of a host named ourhost. (When P4Web is listening on port 80, you don't need to supply a port number.)

- The string that appears between `/@` and `@/` is not needed. You'll see it in P4Web-generated URLs, but it doesn't have to be present in a P4Web URL that you compose.

- The portion of the URL that looks like *//depot/path/file* is a Perforce filespec. It can be a file (as it is in this case), or a path alone (that is, with no file). The P4Web URL syntax for a path is *//depot/path/* but in most cases the familiar *//depot/path/*... will work just as well.

- `@rev` is a symbolic revision identifier. As it turns out, almost any Perforce filespec will work—wildcards and all—as long as you use a symbolic revision rather than an absolute file revision. (You can't use absolute file revisions because the # delimiter has special meaning to browsers.)

- You can specify a P4Web action code with the syntax `?ac=n`. There's an action code for each type of page P4Web produces. For example, `?ac=43` specifies the Submitted Changelists page. If you don't provide an action code, P4Web displays either an actual file (if you gave a filename) or a depot tree page (if you did not).

- You can pass arguments for the specified action with the `&arg=val` syntax, as you'll see in the following examples. You can also use this form to pass absolute file revisions.

As you poke around with P4Web, you'll find other useful URLs. Here are some examples you can try for yourself with the P4Web viewer at the Perforce Public Depot:

http://public.perforce.com:8080//public/jam/
  Shows what's in the *//public/jam* path

http://public.perforce.com:8080/public/jam/?ac=43
  Shows the change history of the *//public/jam* path

http://public.perforce.com:8080//2564?ac=10
  Shows the details of changelist 2564

http://public.perforce.com:8080//public/jam/src/RELNOTES?ac=19&rev1=50&rev2=51
  Shows the diffs between revisions #50 and #51 of *//public/jam/RELNOTES*

http://public.perforce.com:8080//public/…/index.html
  Lists the *index.html* files in the *//public* path

When documents link to each other with relative URLs, P4Web can show entire sites as they appeared at previous points in time ("sites" being collections of files stored in the Perforce depot, of course). This is a P4Web feature called Back-in-Time Browsing.™

Try Back-in-Time Browsing in the Perforce Public Depot. The following URLs, for example, point to the 2002 and 2004 versions, respectively, of the RevML project site in the Public Depot:

  http://public.perforce.com:8080//public/revml/index.html@2002/01/01
  http://public.perforce.com:8080//public/revml/index.html@2004/01/01

Scripting Tips

As you may have gleaned from what you've read so far, and as you'll certainly see in the chapters that follow, there are some very useful things you can do with hard-to-type P4 commands and P4Web URLs. Scripts, of course, can hide complicated syntax and command sequences. Scripts have an even more important role, however, and that is in customizing and automating your SCM procedures. In the subsections that follow are a few tips to get you started using P4 commands in scripts.

The fstat command

Many Perforce commands—files and opened, for example—give you abridged information about files. The fstat command gives you everything, and its output format is easier for scripts to parse. For example:

```
p4 fstat //public/revml/vcp.pl
... depotFile //public/revml/dist/vcp.pl
```

```
... headAction add
... headType xtext
... headTime 1079646286
... headRev 4
... headChange 4235
```

fstat has a cornucopia of flags that control the scope and detail of its output. See the *Perforce Command Reference* for details, or run this command:

```
p4 help fstat
```

for more information.

Tagged output

Almost any Perforce command can produce output as verbose as fstat's if you use the -ztag flag on p4. For example:

```
p4 -ztag describe 4417
... change 4417
... user barrie_slaymaker
... client VCP_barries_winXPpro_dev
... time 1092971510
... desc - Adapt to "estimated values" messages
      - Adapt to more accurate test suite
... status submitted
... depotFile0 //public/revml/bin/gentrevml
... action0 edit
... type0 xtext
... rev0 56
... depotFile1 //public/revml/lib/VCP/TestUtils.pm
... action1 edit
... type1 text
... rev1 65
```

(Compare this to the readable but difficult-to-parse output shown in the depot browsing examples in Chapter 1.)

For more information on tagged output, run:

```
p4 help usage
p4 help undoc
```

Marshalled output

You can make p4 marshal its tagged output for Ruby or Python.[*] For example, p4 -R produces marshalled Ruby output:

```
ruby -e "p Marshal.load( `p4 -R describe 4417` )"
{"action3"=>"edit", "status"=>"submitted",
```

---

[*] Many scripting languages have formats for exchanging data structures between scripts; formatting data for script-to-script exchange is called "marshalling."

```
"user"=>"barrie_slaymaker", "action4"=>"edit",
"time"=>"1092971510", "code"=>"stat", "type0"=>"xtext",
"depotFile0"=>"//public/revml/bin/gentrevml",
"client"=>"VCP_barries_winXPpro_dev", "type1"=>"text",
"depotFile1"=>"//public/revml/lib/VCP/TestUtils.pm",
"change"=>"4417", "type2"=>"text",
"depotFile2"=>"//public/revml/t/91cvs2revml.t",
"rev0"=>"56", "desc"=>"- Adapt to \"estimated values\" messages\n
- Adapt to more accurate test suite\n",
"type3"=>"text", "depotFile3"=>"//public/revml/t/91vss2revml.t",
"rev1"=>"65", "type4"=>"text",
"depotFile4"=>"//public/revml/t/95cvs2p4.t", "rev2"=>"16",
"action0"=>"edit", "rev3"=>"7", "action1"=>"edit",
"rev4"=>"30", "action2"=>"edit"}
```

P4's help usage and help undoc commands will tell you what marshalled output is available.

Dates and times

Perforce stores dates and times as epoch values—that is, as the number of seconds since 00:00:00 GMT January 1, 1970. The p4 program normally converts epoch values to a human-readable form. But for output that is meant for scripts, dates and times are converted to epoch-value strings. (You can see examples of this in the previous examples.) This leaves it up to your scripts to convert them to appropriate formats when displaying them.

In Ruby, for example, epoch strings can be handled like this:

```
str = Marshal.load( `p4 -R describe 4417` )[ "time" ]
puts Time.at( str.to_i ).to_s
```

to produce output like this:

```
Thu Aug 19 20:11:50 Pacific Standard Time 2004
```

Specs and spec forms

To keep commands like p4 change and p4 submit from launching an editor, use them with -i and -o. For example, in a command shell you'd run this single command to create a pending changelist:

p4 change

This command launches an editor that contains the changelist's spec form. To keep from launching an editor, a script would have to run these commands:

p4 change -o
p4 change -i

(The -o flag makes change write the unedited changelist description to stdout. The -i flag makes change read a changelist description—one that is presumed to be edited already—from stdin.)

How a script runs these commands depends on the scripting language and what the script is doing. For example, here's a Ruby script that creates a pending changelist; the pending changelist's description is taken from the script's command line:

```
specform = `p4 change -o`
specform.gsub!( /<enter description here>/, ARGV.join(" ") )
IO.popen( 'p4 change -i', "w" ){ |f| f.puts( specform ) }
```

Scripting language extensions

The Perforce C++ API has been embedded in a number of scripting languages. With P4API extensions, scripts can access Perforce without having to pass p4 commands to the system. This Ruby script, for example:

```
require 'p4'
p4 = P4.new
p4.tagged
p4.connect
p p4.run_describe( 4417 )
p4.disconnect
```

produces this output:

```
[{"status"=>"submitted", "user"=>"barrie_slaymaker",
"time"=>"1092971510", "rev"=>["56", "65", "16", "7", "30"],
"type"=>["xtext", "text", "text", "text", "text"],
"action"=>["edit", "edit", "edit", "edit", "edit"],
"client"=>"VCP_barries_winXPpro_dev", "change"=>"4417",
"desc"=>"- Adapt to \"estimated values\" messages\n
- Adapt to more accurate test suite\n",
"depotFile"=>["//public/revml/bin/gentrevml",
"//public/revml/lib/VCP/TestUtils.pm",
"//public/revml/t/91cvs2revml.t",
"//public/revml/t/91vss2revml.t",
"//public/revml/t/95cvs2p4.t"]}]
```

The advantages of using a P4API extension are that error handling is easier, command results are packaged into very nice structures, and you can create persistent connections to the Perforce Server. The disadvantages are that you may have to build extension modules yourself, and your scripts aren't as portable once they rely on them.

Various P4API extensions are available from various sources. Go to *http://www. perforce.com*, and navigate to **Downloads** → Related Software → API Tools to find links to them.

Don't swamp your server

You can do a lot with Perforce in scripts. In fact, you can do too much. A common mistake is to stick Perforce commands in tight loops. For example, your script might run p4 users and then iterate through the results running p4 user -o on each file. If you have 500 users, that's 500 p4 user -o commands.

When your script fires off commands far faster than users can run commands from client programs, the Perforce Server enthusiastically tries to accommodate you. The effect of this is that users have to wait for your scripts to finish before their commands get any response.

In most cases, however, you don't need to run more Perforce commands as you iterate through results. The tagged output of Perforce commands contains more data than you think. (Don't base your assumptions on what you've seen plain p4 commands produce. They display only a fraction of the relevant data.) For example, instead of running p4 users and then p4 user -o on each result, just run p4 -ztag users once. It will give you all the data you need.

The same goes for files. If you want detailed information about files, there's usually a command you can run on an entire set of files that will give you what you need. For example, to get the integration history of a set of files, try running p4 -ztag integrated or p4 -ztag filelog on the entire set instead of running each command on every file in the set.

For more on this topic, see "Preventing Server Swamp" in the *Perforce Administrator's Guide*.

Triggers

Triggers are custom programs that run when users invoke certain commands. As a Perforce superuser, you can set up triggers to control and automate the things that your developers do with Perforce.

In Perforce, triggers are run by the Perforce Server; they don't interact directly with the user. They're typically written in scripting languages, but any executable program can be a trigger as long as it can run on the server's machine. Because they reside on the machine the Perforce Server is running on, they must be installed by someone with access to that machine.

Perforce triggers fall into two categories—spec triggers and file triggers:

Spec triggers
> Fire when users run commands that produce or update specs (commands like client and job, for example). They can intercept spec forms on their way from the server to the user and on their way from the user back to the server. Thus you can use spec triggers both to prefill spec fields and to validate or post-process what the user entered in them. You can also use spec triggers to prevent objects like jobs, labels, and branch views from being created, modified, or deleted.

File triggers

Fire when users run `submit`. They can be used to examine the content of files, to enforce changelist and job dependencies, and to launch server-side programs that run after changes are committed to the database. File triggers can also be used to prevent files from being created, modified, or deleted. However, they can't prevent users from accessing or opening files—for that, you have to use depot protections.

The `triggers` command allows you to define when and how the Perforce Server runs triggers. (You must be a Perforce superuser to run `triggers`.) This book won't go into detail about all the ways you can define triggers, but here's a taste of what it looks like:

p4 triggers

```
Triggers        WorkspaceCheck in client "clientcheck.rb %user% %client% %formfile%"
                WebReview submit //depot/www/...  "reviewpages.rb %changelist%"
```

In this example, two triggers are defined, named WorkspaceCheck and WebReview:

- WorkspaceCheck is a spec trigger that runs after a `client` command completes (that is, when a user saves a workspace client spec). It runs *clientcheck.rb*, passing to it the name of the user, the name of the client spec, and the name of a temporary file containing the spec form saved by the user.

- WebReview is a file trigger that runs as a user submits files in the *//depot/www* path. It runs the *reviewpages.rb* script, passing to it a number that can be used to access the user's changelist.

If one of these triggers were to fail, the user would see an error message prefixed by the trigger name. The error message itself is generated by the script. For example:

```
WebReview:
There is no opened job associated with the changelist you are submitting.
Did you forget to open a job? Or to link an opened job to your changelist?
Please fix the problem and submit your changelist again.
```

The only way a trigger can prevent users from doing what they shouldn't do is by failing. (That is, by exiting with a nonzero return code.) A client spec trigger must fail, for example, to prevent a user from changing a workspace view. A file trigger must fail in order to keep the user from submitting files.

A trigger that fails intentionally is fine; it is preventing users from doing what they shouldn't do. But a trigger that fails because the script isn't working is dangerous—it will prevent users from doing the things they *should* do. Before you install them in a production environment, be sure to exercise triggers thoroughly in a test environment.

See the "Triggers and Daemons" chapter in the *Perforce System Administrator's Guide* for detailed information about configuring triggers to fire at certain points, passing data to triggers, and consequences of trigger failure.

Behind-the-Scenes Version Control

"Don't bore me with 'client' and 'sync'—just give me the blinkin' file!"

—Anonymous

While we may agree among ourselves that it's all software and we're all software developers, not everyone we work with does. We're all software developers until it's time to learn how to use version control, at which point some of us suddenly become artists, lawyers, or chief executives with no head at all for technical details.

For these busy Luddites, behind-the-scenes version control can gently encourage SCM participation. It lets them access and update Perforce files using applications familiar to them—like Microsoft Word—with commands they understand—like "Save." In this section we'll take a look at the Perforce components that can be set up to work behind the scenes.

WebKeeper, a Perforce module for Apache

WebKeeper is a Perforce module that can be compiled and linked into the Apache HTTP Server. With WebKeeper in place, a file in the depot called *//Ace/WEB/index.html* can be accessed from a web browser with a URL like:

http://intranet.ace.com/Ace/WEB/index.html

(This example assumes that Apache is configured at port 80 of a machine called *intranet.ace.com*, of course.)

When a web browser sends Apache a URL, Apache checks its configuration parameters to see whether the URL refers to Perforce content. If it does, it lets its WebKeeper module convert the URL to a depot filename and fetch file content from the Perforce depot. Apache then sends the file content back to the user's browser. The depot files served up by WebKeeper are entirely under the control of Apache—to Apache, the depot looks like a file system. You can use the same redirects, path aliases, and authentication for depot files as you would for any other files managed by the Apache server.

P4Web, Perforce's own web server

Like WebKeeper, the P4Web viewer lets you access a file in the depot called *//Ace/WEB/index.html* with a URL like:

http://intranet.ace.com/Ace/WEB/index.html

And, as you read previously, there are P4Web URL tricks you can use to link to all kinds of Perforce information. None of these tricks will be of much use to naïve or reluctant Perforce users, of course. However, they can be of great use to Perforce-savvy project leads and configuration managers—P4Web URLs inserted into web pages and email can give naïve users a portal to information they would otherwise be oblivious to.

How are WebKeeper and P4Web different?

WebKeeper and the P4Web viewer are alike in that both allow users to get to Perforce through a web browser. And neither WebKeeper nor the P4Web viewer allows users to update depot files. Each simply shunts file content from the Perforce depot to users' web browsers.

WebKeeper and the P4Web viewer are not the same, however, when it comes to:

Metadata
> The P4Web viewer lets you browse changelists, jobs, and other Perforce metadata. WebKeeper does not.

Older revisions
> WebKeeper always gives you the most recent document revisions. P4Web can serve up older revisions.

Access control
> If you're using WebKeeper, Apache controls access to depot files. With a P4Web viewer, Perforce controls access to depot files. (You just read a bit about this at the beginning of the chapter in "Depot and File Access.")

Installation and administration
> WebKeeper is distributed as C++ source and must be compiled and linked into an Apache module. However, once that's done, the Apache server does double duty as a Perforce document server. A P4Web viewer, on the other hand, is available as a prebuilt binary program for a large number of operating systems. It needs no compiling or linking, but it does need to be started up and managed as a separate server.

Perforce via FTP

Thanks to FTP, users of word processing and multimedia authoring applications need not know about Perforce even if they do need write access to files in the depot. P4FTP, the Perforce FTP plug-in, can be installed by a system administrator in place of an FTP server.

To FTP clients, P4FTP looks like a normal FTP server. To a Perforce Server, P4FTP looks like a garden-variety Perforce client. P4FTP intercepts requests from FTP clients and converts them to Perforce requests. For example, when a Windows

Explorer user expands an FTP site folder, P4FTP requests a directory list from the Perforce Server. When a user saves a file to an FTP site folder, P4FTP submits the file to the Perforce depot.

P4FTP does quite a bit of Perforce work behind the scenes to support naive users. It creates workspaces, synchronizes, opens, submits, and reverts files, and generates canned change descriptions. Users have practically no control over any of the Perforce operations performed by P4FTP on their behalf.

Nevertheless, P4FTP's transparent access to Perforce makes it easy to draw reluctant contributors into the fold. It requires no Perforce software installed on user machines, it works with user applications on any operating system, and, best of all, users don't have to know anything about Perforce to get their changes into the depot.

Note that P4FTP gives users no way to resolve concurrent changes. Like other FTP servers, P4FTP simply accepts files sent to it by users and archives files as it receives them. Each version of a file replaces the previous version. P4FTP, however, archives files by submitting them to Perforce; if one user inadvertently overwrites another's changes, the original files can always be recovered.

Windows applications and Perforce plug-ins

Windows users who want more control over their files can meet Perforce halfway. Perforce plug-ins that integrate with a number of Windows applications can be installed on users' machines to offer Perforce commands in the context of those applications. The P4OFC plug-in, for example, adds Perforce menus to Microsoft Word, Excel, and PowerPoint. For visual artists and game developers, the P4GT plug-in integrates Perforce with popular graphical tools like Adobe Photoshop. With Perforce plug-ins installed, users can use comfortable commands like "Check Out" and "Check In" to make applications synchronize workspaces, open files for editing, and submit changelists behind the scenes.

The plug-ins expect users to know how to set up their workspaces. Truly naïve or timid users may need help getting over this hump, but will be able to comfortably navigate on their own henceforth.

Perforce as ODBC data source

Finally, for a different breed of non-Perforce user, there's P4Report, the Perforce Reporting System. P4Report can be installed on a user's Windows machine to make a Perforce Server look like an ODBC data source. With P4Report installed, reporting and data visualization tools like Crystal Reports and Microsoft Access can draw on metadata from the Perforce database. This is a boon to managers and administrators who want to keep an eye on Perforce activity but who are not Perforce users themselves.

P4Report is distinct from the other behind-the-scenes solutions mentioned in this section in that it provides no access to files. It's meant to provide access to metadata only. And although it takes no Perforce command expertise to work with P4Report, it does take some understanding of what's stored in changelists, jobs, and fixes.

CHAPTER 7

How Software Evolves

Just as there's more to driving than knowing how to operate a car, there's more to SCM than knowing how to use an SCM tool. Mastering SCM starts with understanding how software evolves and recognizing how team collaboration, defect management, parallel releases, and distributed development affect the software life cycle. For just as road maps and rules of the road are the bigger part of driving, the software life cycle is the bigger part of SCM.

In this chapter we take a step back from Perforce to look at the roadmap of the software life cycle: the mainline model. We'll identify the codelines that form the mainline model and describe the rules of the road for change flowing between them. This chapter sets the stage for the chapters that follow, each of which demonstrates using Perforce to manage codelines of a particular type.

The Story of Ace Engineering

Consider the story of Ace Engineering, a fictitious software company. After a year of intensive startup development, the company introduced a new product, AcePack 1.0. Sales were successful; the customer base grew. Alas, so did the bug report database. Within six months Ace had produced a point release—essentially the same product but with many bug fixes and small enhancements—as AcePack 1.1. For a while, the company supported customers on either version, but at the end of the second year it announced that AcePack 1.0 was being discontinued.

During this time Ace developers had started working on two new features, code-named Saturn and Pluto. The plan had been to include both features in the AcePack 2.0 release. Midway through the third year Pluto was done, but Saturn turned out to be much more work than anticipated. (In fact, the company ended up doubling the size of the Saturn development team, with half the team working on an unforseen adjunct now code-named Saturn Plus.) AcePack 2.0 was ultimately released without the Saturn feature.

The 2.0 release did well, although it too had its share of problems. It was hard to get customers to upgrade, and Ace ended up having to fix showstopping bugs in both available releases, 1.1 and 2.0. However, it was able to produce a very stable release, AcePack 2.1, about six months later. Shortly after that, support for AcePack 1.1 was discontinued.

Finally the Saturn and Saturn Plus development projects were completed. The Saturn feature will be in AcePack 3.0. Meanwhile, customers have upgraded to AcePack 2.1, AcePack 2.0 has been retired, and Ace developers have started working on yet another new feature, codenamed Rocket. Figure 7-1 shows the development history of Ace's product.

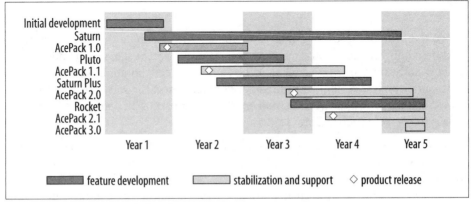

Figure 7-1. Ace Engineering's first five years

The Ace Engineering story illustrates typical problems of the software life cycle:

- At any point in time there is likely to be more than one supported product version available to customers. Ace must be prepared to field customer calls, diagnose problems, and fix critical bugs in all of its currently supported versions.

- Not all development tasks have the same urgency. Some are expected to yield results immediately while others are targeted for distant future releases.

- Software development is not entirely predictable; some projects go according to plan, others get mired in unforeseen difficulties.

What Ace Engineering makes is "shrinkwrapped"* software. Other kinds of software—web-hosted, embedded, open source—evolve differently and have life cycle problems of their own. What all of them have in common is that their software life cycle problems can be solved by parallel development. Ace, for example, solved its

---

* Shrinkwrapped software is software that is distributed in periodic releases. The provider decides when to make new releases available; users decide when to upgrade. As a consequence, there can be several releases in use at the same time and the provider may have to support many or all of them concurrently.

---

problem of having to support customers on two releases by putting some developers to work on the old release while others developers worked in parallel on the new relese.

Software development is complicated enough; *parallel* software development can be even more complicated. But it doesn't have to be. In the next section, we'll look at how the mainline model can be used to keep the complexities of parallel development in check.

The Mainline Model

A *codeline* is, for the most part, the same as a branch. But though the term *branch* can mean any set of files created by branching, *codeline* is imbued with slightly more significance. Codelines have a purpose, a strategic role in the development of software. Together, codelines form a model of software evolution.

In the Perforce view of software configuration management, one model—the *mainline model*—is most effective. This chapter discusses codelines and software evolution in the context of the mainline model. It's not a Perforce-specific discussion, by the way—the mainline model is a general concept, not a Perforce feature. But it is the concept on which much of the design of Perforce is based.

From ideal world to real world

In the ideal world, there are no bugs, no schedule crunches, no personnel changes, no market shifts, and no technology revolutions. Software in the ideal world is simply developed and released—that is, new features are developed, and when they're ready, a new version of the software is released (see Figure 7-2). Each release contains features that work perfectly.

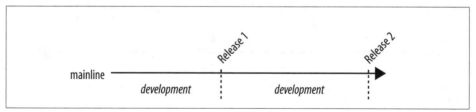

Figure 7-2. The mainline in the ideal world

If there were such an ideal world, we probably wouldn't need an SCM system. Even so, we'd have a collection of files evolving together in a codeline. This codeline embodies the evolution of our software; it is our *mainline*. In the ideal world it would be the only codeline we'd ever need.

A sad fact of the real world is that the software we develop isn't perfect. Because of that, we subject software to a testing phase before release, during which bugs are invariably found. We could do all this in the mainline if development could halt for the testing phase, and if all bugs could be found and fixed during testing. But all bugs are *not* found during testing; many are found after software is released. And we can't hold off on new development during the testing phase, because we face deadlines and market pressures to face. So we branch completed software from the main codeline into a release codeline.

Branching release codelines allows us to do two different kinds of software development at once. One kind is bug fixing—euphemistically known as *stabilization*—and the other is new feature development. In the release codeline, we stabilize a version of our software—both before and after release—while in the mainline we get on with developing new features. As we stabilize the release version, we can make point releases—that is, we can rerelease the software—without the risk of releasing untested new development.

Another problem with the real world is that our customers expect us to fix bugs in old versions of our software even as we are developing and stabilizing new versions. To deal with this, we branch a new codeline for each release, leaving our old release codelines intact for more bug-fixing. Now the typical shrinkwrapped software evolution model begins to take shape. A mainline charts the course of the overall development, while release codelines sprout as new versions are ready (see Figure 7-3). When releases are no longer supported, the codelines designated for them cease to evolve, but the mainline persists.

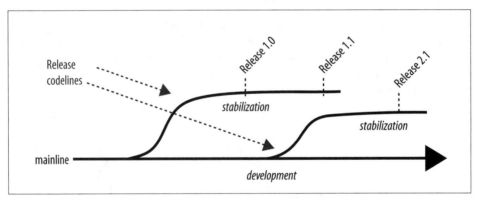

Figure 7-3. Release codelines

In the ideal world, all development projects are completed on schedule. No matter how many new features are slated for the next release, developers in the ideal world get them all done on time. In the real world, a single incomplete project can hold up an entire release if it's in the same codeline as completed projects. To decouple development projects from one another in the real world, we can branch the mainline into one or more development codelines. Development projects are delivered to the mainline as they're completed, and when enough development is completed to warrant it, a new version is branched for release stabilization (see Figure 7-4).

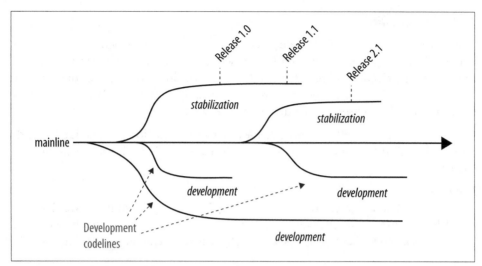

Figure 7-4. *Development codelines*

Thus our mainline evolves as new development is completed, although development does not necessarily take place in the mainline.

And there you have it. The mainline model is a necessary deviation from the ideal world. It seeks to preserve the intent of the ideal world while accommodating the constraints of the real world.

Why We Don't Drive Through Hedges

Why not just branch a development codeline into a release codeline? Or merge a bug fix straight from a release codeline into a development codeline? Well, just as there is no law of physics that keeps you from driving through hedges to get on and off the freeway, there's nothing in Perforce that keeps you from integrating changes any which way you please.

One has only to look at traffic on a freeway to see why entrances and exits are controlled. Clearly, driving would be inefficient and unpredictable if they weren't. Because we can't see the flow of change, it's not so easy for us to understand that we must control change for the same reason: parallel development would be inefficient and unpredictable if we didn't.

Think of the mainline model as the freeway system of parallel development. It's a fast and reliable way to get somewhere, but only if we resist the temptation to drive through the hedges.

The flow of change

The closer we are to the ideal world, the simpler our SCM is. When our ideal-world intent to work together is thwarted by real-world constraints, we branch one codeline into another and make our changes there. But we don't lose sight of the fact that our changes in the second codeline are really meant for the first. We pull changes from the second codeline into the first as soon as we can.

It is this flow of change between codelines that brings us closer to the ideal world. Each codeline type—mainline, release, and development—has a role in the flow of change:

Mainline

The mainline is the clearing-house for all changes to the software we develop. Whether we submit changes directly to the mainline or integrate changes to it from other codelines, all change eventually reaches the mainline (see Figure 7-5).

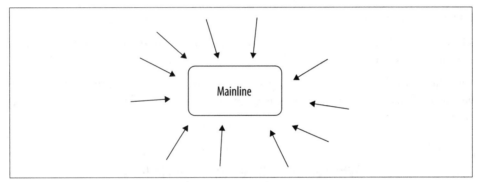

Figure 7-5. All change flows to the mainline

However, the mainline isn't a free-for-all. It holds the software that's complete enough to enter the release stabilization cycle. So the flow of change to the mainline is tempered by the state of the codelines from which change flows.

Release codelines

Change flows continually from release codelines to the mainline. Every time a bug is fixed in a release codeline, the change that fixed it is integrated into the mainline, as Figure 7-6 shows. This doesn't compromise the mainline, because every change coming from a release codeline has already been reviewed and tested. Moreover, release codeline changes are changes that fix broken things. Thus, merging release codeline changes to the mainline is bound to have a stabilizing effect. It brings the mainline closer to perfection, as is our ideal-world intent. This flow of change continues until the mainline has evolved so much that the bug fixes in a release branch are no longer relevant to it. (In Chapter 9 we'll take a closer look at this.)

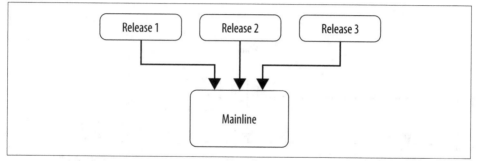

Figure 7-6. Bug fixes flowing to the mainline

Release codelines are not normally open to changes from the mainline. For one thing, every change to a release codeline should be a change that stabilizes and finalizes the release. For another, the mainline is changing constantly—it will never be perfect. We don't want the increasing perfection of a release codeline to be sullied by the inherent imperfection of the mainline.

(Although release codelines are not normally open to mainline changes, the unexpected can happen. If we're in the unfortunate position of having to support several releases concurrently, a bug fix in one release may have to be applied to another. That is, we'll have to cherry-pick a change from either a release codeline or the mainline and integrate it into another release codeline. In Chapter 9 we'll cover this in more detail.)

Development codelines

There's also a constant flow of change from the mainline to the development codelines branched from it, as shown in Figure 7-7. In other words, a development codeline is continually updated with changes from its parent codeline. Thus even development codelines benefit from release stabilization. As we fix a bug in a release, we merge the bug fix into the mainline. As the mainline changes, we merge its changes into development codelines.[*]

In some cases, bugs can be fixed right in the mainline. Because the mainline is guaranteed to be stable, development codelines can be continually updated with these bug fixes. This featuregives project teams the benefit of working with the latest, improved code. It also forces them to integrate sooner, rather than later, with development happening outside of their control.

What about the flow of change from development codelines to the mainline? A development codeline can be a hotbed of untested new development. There may be periods of time when a development codeline doesn't build, or when it builds nothing but a basket case. The valve is closed on the flow of change from the development codeline to the mainline during these periods.

---

[*] Who is this "we," you ask? See Chapters 8 and 9.

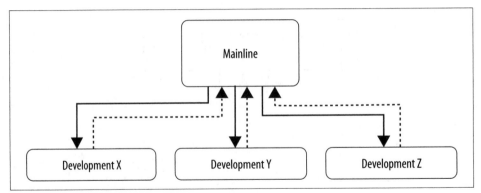

Figure 7-7. Flow of change between the mainline and development codelines

But when the development codeline is stable—when new development is complete or at a deliverable state—the valve opens. At these points the development codeline software is delivered to the mainline. Thus change flows from development codelines to the mainline at points of completion. And, because development codelines are always open to mainline changes, other development codelines will receive the completed new development as well.

Development and release codelines can themselves be branched. Quite often they're branched into short-lived, task-specific sub-branches to accommodate unplanned changes. A release codeline can be branched to make a patched version of a released product, for example, and a development codeline can be branched to isolate work on a specific problem or behavior.

Branching from release codelines

In the ideal world, our customers upgrade to our latest release without complaint. In the real world, customers have reasons they can't do that, and we have reasons to keep our customers happy. Reality occasionally puts us in the position of having to patch a previously released version. We do this by branching a release codeline into a patch branch.

The flow of change between a patch branch and its release codeline parent is exactly the same as the flow of change between a release codeline and its mainline parent. In other words, the release codeline is continually updated with changes from the patch branch. (Not that there's likely to be much change in the patch branch.) This gives the release codeline the benefit of the patch branch's bug fix. No change flows from the release codeline to the patch branch because the whole point of making the branch was to reproduce and patch an earlier version.

For example, one extremely important customer, still using Release 1.0, finds a critical bug and demands a patch that doesn't require an upgrade to our latest point release, 1.1. To accommodate this customer, we take the 1.0 version of the Release 1 codeline and branch it into a patch branch. We fix the fussy customer's bug in the patch branch and build a new version from a snapshot of the branch. This is the version we give to the customer. (Figure 7-8 shows the patch branch.)

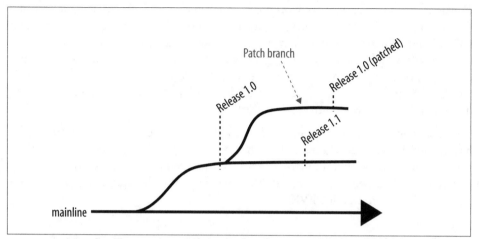

Figure 7-8. A patch branch

The changes we made in the patch branch are merged into the Release 1 codeline. This gives the Release 1 codeline the benefit of the patch. Release 1 changes flow into the mainline, of course, bringing the patch with them (see Figure 7-9).

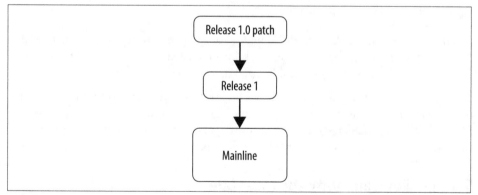

Figure 7-9. Patch branches and the flow of change

Branching from development codelines

Development codelines branched into sub-branches also inherit the flow-of-change roles of their parents; change flows continually from development codelines to their sub-branches so that work in a sub-branch is always up to date with the parent codeline. Change flows in the other direction only at points of completion. When work in a sub-branch is completed, it's delivered to the development codeline. Thus, each development codeline acts as a mainline for its sub-branches, and each sub-branch behaves like a development codeline.

Consider a team of developers working on an application. They're using a codeline they've named DEVX to develop a major new feature. Two developers plan to help out by overhauling a part of the new feature known as the the Z-widget. It's going to be a ground-up rewrite; the Z-widget won't be working right again for weeks. But a broken Z-widget will make it impossible for other developers to work in the DEVX codeline. (They could simply relax and play ping-pong for two weeks, but that doesn't go over very well in the real world.)

To satisfy constraints of the real world, the DEVX codeline is branched into a codeline named DEVZ (see Figure 7-10). The two Z-widget developers complete their overhaul in the DEVZ sub-branch. The rest of the developers continue their work in its parent, DEVX, with an old but stable Z-widget. (And they promise not to touch any of the Z-widget files in DEVX.)

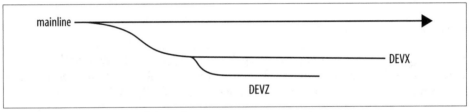

Figure 7-10. A development sub-branch

As changes are made in DEVX, the Z-widget developers pull them immediately into DEVZ. They don't put their changes back into DEVX, however, until their overhaul is done and the new Z-widget is stable (see Figure 7-11).

To the Z-widget developers, this satisfies the ideal-world intent to build upon other developers' changes, as if they were working right in DEVX. To the developers working in DEVX, this satisfies the ideal-world expectation that they won't lose project time waiting for broken components to work again.

Soft, medium, and firm: the tofu scale

Every codeline has a characteristic ranking on the "tofu scale." And what is this tofu scale? It's an informal assessment of stability and quality that takes into account:

- How close software is to being released
- How rigorously changes must be reviewed and tested

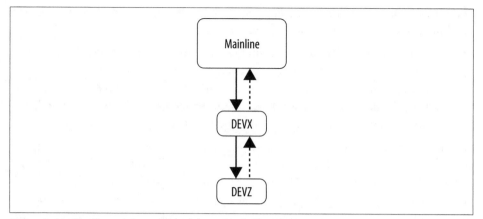

Figure 7-11. The flow of change to and from development codelines

- How much impact a change has on schedules
- How much a codeline is changing

As shown in Figure 7-12, release codelines are highest on the tofu scale; they are "firm." They don't change much, and even the slightest changes to them can impact release schedules because of their rigorous review and testing requirements. The mainline is "medium"—changes do require testing, but release is further out and schedules are more accommodating of them. Development codelines are "soft"—they're changing rapidly, the software in them is farthest from release, and there may not even be tests yet for their newest development.

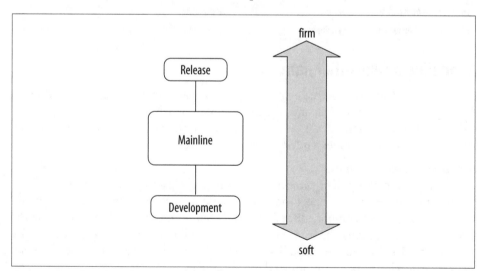

Figure 7-12. The tofu scale

The flow-of-change rules tell us *when* file content should be propagated from one codeline to another. The tofu scale tells us *how*:

- In the firm-to-soft direction, file content can be merged. The target, being softer, is more able than the donor to absorb the risk and effort of merging.

- In the soft-to-firm direction, file content should be copied. The target is more at risk than the donor in this case. Files should be merged from the firmer codeline to the softer one first, then copied from the softer codeline to the firmer one.

The unwritten contract of collaborative development says that we don't impose unstable changes and we always accept stable changes. The tofu scale gives us a way to tell unstable from stable changes before we impose or accept them.

There's a uniformity to the mainline model that can be described in terms of flow of change and the tofu scale. Aside from the mainline, which is in a category of its own, there are essentially only two codeline types: release codelines and development codelines. No matter how many codelines you have, if you know each codeline's type, you know exactly how and when file content should be propagated between those codelines. This is summarized in Table 7-1; you'll see how this plays out in the chapters that follow.

Table 7-1. How change is propagated

	Release codeline	Development codeline
Tofu rank	Firmer than parent	Softer than parent
Change flows *to* parent	Continually	At points of completion
Change flows *from* parent	Never	Continually
File content is propagated	By merging	By copying

A codeline by any other name…

…is still a codeline. If you're saying to yourself that a mainline and a handful of development and release codelines are not going to satisfy your SCM needs, you're right. In fast-paced, large-scale development environments, the fundamental codeline types are adapted and extended to a variety of uses:

Active development streams
> Sometimes development projects aren't all that clear-cut. One use of development codelines is to support long-lived, ongoing development work on components. This gives component developers a common, persistent codeline to work in without requiring them to create a new codeline for each task or feature. In Chapter 10, for example, you'll see how a development codeline is used as an active development stream for a GUI component.

Task branches
> Task branches are very short-lived codelines branched from either development codelines or release codelines. They can be used to protect release codelines

from untested interim changes, or to protect development codelines from desta-bilizing re-engineering. (The DEVX development codeline described earlier in this chapter in "Branching from development codelines" is a task branch.) In Chapter 9 you'll see how a task branch is used to permit a bug fix to be reviewed and tested before it's introduced into a release codeline.

Staging streams
Staging streams allow you to make extremely frequent releases without having to branch a new codeline for each release. (They're commonly used to support web development. You'll see an example of this in Chapter 11.) A staging stream is essentially a reusable release codeline. Each staging stream is used for a particu-lar stage of release stabilization. Once the stage is completed for a particular release, the codeline is immediately redeployed for the next release.

Private branches, ad hoc branches, and sparse branches
Private branches make it possible for each developer's changes to be reviewed before they are submitted to shared codelines. Private branches can also be used to isolate experimental or proof-of-concept work. Ad hoc branches are created on the fly to give users a place to check in changes they thought they were going to be able to check in elsewhere but found out they couldn't. Sparse branches can be used in any of the aforementioned cases to piggy-back a few changed files onto a full codeline. Examples of all of these will come up in later chapters.

One-way codelines

We also recognize another fundamental codeline type: the "one-way" codeline. One-way codelines house software, but not software development. The following are examples of one-way codelines:

Third-party codelines
Third-party codelines provide a place to store vendor drops—software and source code obtained from external suppliers. Code is typically copied or merged from third-party codelines into development codelines.

Remote depot codelines
In Chapter 6 you read about how you can access depots in other Perforce domains as *remote depots*. Codelines in remote depots are always one-way code-lines—files can be branched, copied, or merged from them, but not into them.

Packaging and distribution streams
Packaging streams can be used to assemble customer-specific configurations of software from released components. Distribution streams can be used to offer released products to customers. (They're the vendor's side of the vendor drop.) Software is delivered from release codelines to packaging and distribution streams; nothing is ever copied or merged in the opposite direction.

We'll revisit one-way codelines in Chapters 9 and 10.

Codelines that aren't codelines

Finally, while we're cataloging codeline species, it's worth recognizing that some codelines aren't really codelines at all:

Porting branches
Porting branches contain architecture-specific variants of source code and built objects.

Custom-code branches
Custom-code branches contain source and built objects configured for hardware, customers, locales, and other deployment targets.

Branches like these aren't codelines in their own right. Although it's often difficult to recognize the fact, they're really modules that belong in development codelines, release codelines, and the mainline.[*]

Musings on codeline diagrams

Codeline and flow diagrams help us visualize software evolution. We have all, at one time or another, sat in a room with our colleagues and drawn or pondered diagrams on a whiteboard. Here are some things to keep in mind when you find yourself doing the diagramming:

- When you're drawing a timeline, put release codelines above their parents and development codelines below them. This orders codelines on the tofu scale, with the firmest on the top and the softest on the bottom. (See Figure 7-13.)

  The tofu scale shows the impact of a change at a glance. A change made to a codeline at the top of the diagram, for example, will reach customers soonest, at the greatest risk to quality and scheduling. A change made to a codeline at the bottom of the diagram, on the other hand, doesn't pose a great risk, but it will be a while before it is available to customers.

- Remember the time axis when you're drawing timelines. Plot codeline beginnings and endings in time order. That way, any vertical line you draw will tell you how many active codelines you'll have at that point in time. (See Figure 7-14.)

- If the timelines in a diagram are getting congested, try using slightly parabolic lines instead of horizontal ones (see Figure 7-15). Parabolic lines also imply divergence—the greater the vertical distance to the mainline, the more the codeline is likely to have diverged from the mainline.

---

[*] For a real-world example of how custom-code branches can become errant codelines, see *Changing How You Change* (*http://www.ravenbrook.com/doc/2003/03/06/changing-how-you-change/*), a white paper presented by Peter Jackson and Richard Brooksby at the 2003 Perforce User Conference.

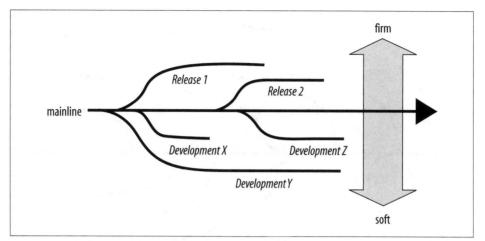

Figure 7-13. Ordering codelines on the tofu scale

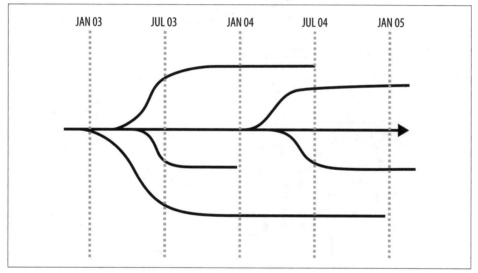

Figure 7-14. Ordering codeline beginnings and endings on the time axis

- Remember that *historical* flow of change isn't the same as *intended* flow of change. Use flow diagrams in addition to timelines to help people understand how change is intended to flow between codelines. Show the tofu scale in flow diagrams as well, as shown in the example in Figure 7-16.

- Finally, recognize that if your codeline diagram is complicated, your SCM process is going to be complicated. Simplifying the diagram may be a good first step in reducing the complexity of your SCM plan.

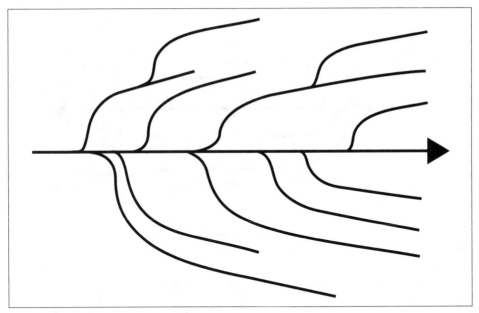

Figure 7-15. Using parabolic lines to reduce congestion in a diagram

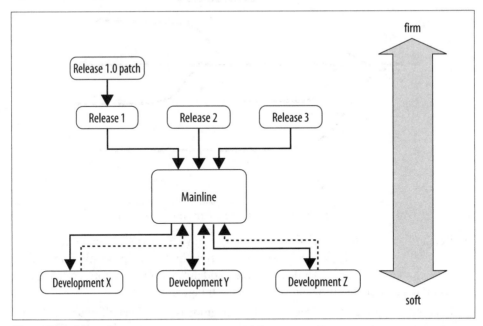

Figure 7-16. A flow diagram

Ace Engineering Revisited

Let's look at the mainline model as employed by Ace Engineering. Once an initial body of development was begun, it formed the MAIN codeline. As you read, the first AcePack versions released were 1.0 and 1.1. However, Ace engineers did not plan their schedule around two first-generation (1.X) releases. In fact, they didn't know how many 1.X releases they would make. Their strategy was simply to make periodic point releases to fix bugs and tidy loose ends until the next major release was ready. To support the as-yet-undetermined number of 1.X releases, MAIN was branched into REL1 (see Figure 7-17).

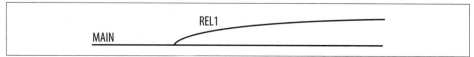

Figure 7-17. REL1 branched from MAIN

AcePack 1.0 and AcePack 1.1 were released from the REL1 codeline. REL1 was used for ongoing fixing before and after the releases were made. When AcePack 1.0 customers required patches, the AcePack 1.0 version of the REL1 codeline was branched into R1.0 (see Figure 7-18). The only changes allowed in R1.0 were fixes for critical, showstopping bugs; these were immediately merged into REL1. Thus, when Ace-Pack 1.1 was released, all the R1.0 fixes were already in it. The same strategy was used to patch AcePack 1.1—the REL1 codeline was branched into R1.1. No changes except for critical fixes were allowed in R1.1, and all R1.1 changes were merged immediately into REL1. Meanwhile, changes in REL1 were regularly merged to MAIN; thus the mainline always reflected the sum of improvements made in the 1.X releases.

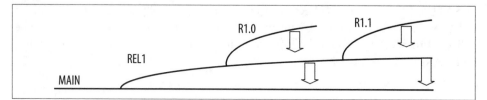

Figure 7-18. The 1.X release branches

R1.0 and R1.1 were fairly inactive codelines. Their entire purpose was to provide a place to fix showstopper bugs in released versions. As a result, neither R1.0 nor R1.1 deviated very much from their parent, REL1, and merging changes from them into REL1 was extremely easy.

You may be wondering why Ace used separate R1.0 and R1.1 codelines to patch released products instead of simply building patched releases from REL1. The reason is that while the releases were concurrently supported, developers had to be able to deliver critical bug fixes to both releases without requiring customers on either release to upgrade. (Ace Engineering is a very accommodating company.) And if you're wondering what REL1 was used for after R1.1 was released, recall that Ace engineers were not sure how many 1.X releases they would make. If all went well, the new features for the next major release would be ready soon and the REL1 codeline could be abandoned. But on the chance that the new-feature schedule would slip, developers continued fixing bugs in REL1 and merging their fixes into MAIN. That way they would have yet another 1.X point release ready to go if no 2.0 release were forthcoming.

To develop the new features slated for the 2.X release, the SATURN and PLUTO codelines were branched from MAIN, as shown in Figure 7-19. Giving each feature development project its own codeline ensured that the two could remain independent. Changes in MAIN were routinely merged into both SATURN and PLUTO, keeping the development codelines up to date with the latest bug fixes from the release codelines.

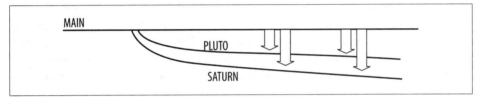

Figure 7-19. Branching for two development projects

As you recall, the Saturn feature turned out to be bigger project than anticipated. The SATURN development codeline was eventually branched into SATURNPLUS to keep the two Saturn development teams out of one another's hair. Feature development continued in SATURN while some much-needed infrastructure work was done in SATURNPLUS. The SATURN changes were continually merged to SATURN-PLUS, as shown in Figure 7-20. This made it very easy for SATURNPLUS work to be delivered to SATURN when the infrastructure work was completed. At that point, SATURNPLUS was retired.

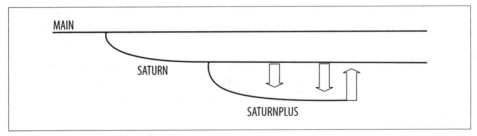

Figure 7-20. Isolating SATURNPLUS development

The Pluto team was the first to complete a new feature for the next major release. The PLUTO codeline's work was delivered to MAIN and PLUTO was retired (see Figure 7-21). At that point, the decision was made to defer the Saturn feature to a future release, and MAIN was branched to REL2 for the second major AcePack release. At about this time, development on another new feature was begun in a codeline called ROCKET that was branched from MAIN. All the while development continued in SATURN; MAIN changes were continually merged into SATURN to keep the latter from diverging.

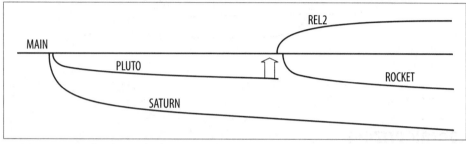

Figure 7-21. Branching REL2 and ROCKET from MAIN

Meanwhile, Ace produced two releases, AcePack 2.0 and AcePack 2.1, out of the REL2 codeline. In order that each release could be patched independently, REL2 was branched into R2.0 and R2.1, respectively, as shown in Figure 7-22. Critical, show-stopping bugs were fixed in the R2.0 and R2.1 patch branches, while REL2 formed a trunk for ongoing bug fixing and stabilization. Bug fixes in the patch branches were merged back into REL2, and REL2 changes were merged into MAIN (see Figure 7-22).

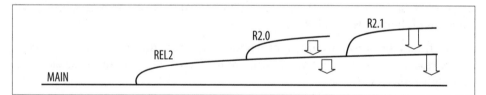

Figure 7-22. Branches for 2.X point releases

Once the Saturn development project was completed, work in the SATURN code-line was delivered to the mainline, and the mainline was in turn branched into REL3 in order to stabilize and build what will be AcePack 3.0 (see Figure 7-23).

Thus, Ace Engineering has produced and supported five releases using a total of 12 codelines. That seems rather a lot of codelines until you consider that only a handful were ever active at the same point in time. Moreover, because the mainline embod-ies all completed work so far, it serves as the single point of reference for future development. SCM is really no more complicated at Ace Engineering now than it was when the first release was made.

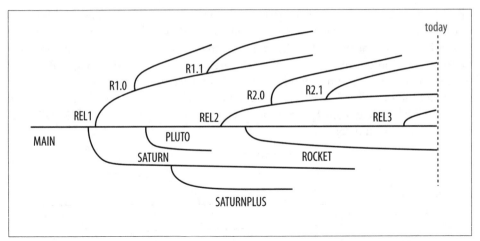

Figure 7-23. Ace's codelines today

Containerizing

In commerce, manufacturers control complexity by "containerizing." A truck driver doesn't know he's delivering 19 sofas, 400 chairs, and 80 tables to outfit a hotel in New York. All he knows is that he's delivering one shipping container from the factory to the shipyard. And when he arrives at the shipyard, he doesn't throw open the back of the truck and start counting out sofas. He merely confirms that the container is intact.

It's the same with branching and merging. The software we're working on involves far too many files for us to have to branch and merge them individually. We need to containerize so we can branch and merge mere handfuls of containers instead of hundreds of thousands of files.

Although they seem to have different names everywhere they're used, the file containers essential to software development are *modules*, *codelines*, and—for lack of a better term—*bodies of code*.

Modules

The files we work on are grouped into *modules*. At face value, a module is simply a set of files organized in a directory tree. (Other systems, and other writings on the topic, use terms like *source directory*, *component*, and *subsystem* for what we're calling a *module*.) What makes modules important is that they correspond to the file hierarchies needed on disk in order to work on specific parts of the software being developed.

In the development of the AcePack software, for example, the GUI module corresponds to the directory tree of C++ source files and Jamfiles* needed to build AcePack's GUI components. In order to work on the GUIs, a developer needs this directory tree on disk. Other modules support other areas of development. The database module, for example, contains the scripts and stored procedures needed on disk to work on AcePack's database component. The documentation module contains Frame files and generated HTML files for the AcePack manuals. The utilities module contains AcePack-specific scripts and configuration files common to all development tasks. (See Figure 7-24.)

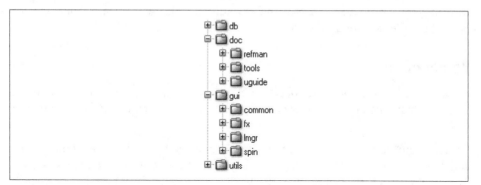

Figure 7-24. Top-level modules

Modules can contain other modules as well. For example, the AcePack GUI module is subdivided into a module of common code and a module for each of the AcePack GUI tools. The documentation module is subdivided into modules for each AcePack manual plus a module containing the tools used to build them. (Figure 7-25.)

Figure 7-25. Submodules

Modules are the raw materials of workspaces and builds. When a developer sets up a workspace, she sets it up in order to work with certain modules. When a build engineer builds software, his build tools process files in some modules and create files in others.

And although her workspace may be populated with many top-level modules, the changes a developer makes typically affect only one module at a time. A GUI

---

* Jamfiles are used by Jam, an open source build tool. Although Jam is available from Perforce Software, it is completely separate from Perforce.

programmer makes changes in the GUI module without affecting the database module or the utilites module, for example. Thus any change submitted by a developer is likely to affect no more than one module.

Codelines

A codeline contains modules evolving together in the same phase of development. (Another good word for codeline is *stream*; it emphasizes the point that not only is a codeline a container, it is a vessel that channels its contents toward completion.) Modules evolve together in a codeline because they contribute jointly to a specific version of an end product or suite of products. The 2.1 version of AcePack, for example, is made up of the 2.1 version of the GUI tools, the 2.1 version of the database, and the 2.1 version of the documentation.

Branching a codeline is really a matter of branching the modules contained by the codeline. Not all modules need to be branched, as you'll see in upcoming chapters. Depending on how closely software components are coupled, release codelines and development codelines may contain only the bare minumum of modules needed to support the work at hand.

Codelines also define the scope of build and test tools. A build script, for example, will be able to "see" only the files in a single codeline. Thus, even if a module won't be changed in the course of a codeline's evolution, its presence in a codeline may be needed in order for build tools to work.

Bodies of code

A *body of code* is the complete collection of codelines related to one another. In other words, a mainline and all the codelines related to it by branching form a body of code.

At Ace Engineering, for example, there is only one body of code. It encompasses the codelines that support development and release of the AcePack product suite. An Ace developer, whether working in the MAIN codeline, in the R1.0 release codeline, or in the SATURN development codeline, is always working with the AcePack body of code.

At large companies, it's likely that several bodies of code will coexist. Each body of code has its own mainline, its own development goals, its own release schedule, and its own collection of codelines. Products and packages built from one body of code can be imported into another, but each body of code is essentially independent.

CHAPTER 8

Basic Codeline Management

This chapter introduces conventions, policies, and techniques for managing code-lines in a Perforce system. It also exposes common pitfalls and missteps of codeline management that can easily be avoided.

Organizing Your Depot

You know by now that the Perforce depot is a hierarchical structure of directories and files, and that you are at liberty to organize it as you please. The question is: what is the *best* way to organize it? There is no one right answer, of course, but some factors and recommendations should be taken into consideration as you decide what goes where.

Filespecs as containers

Interestingly, Perforce doesn't know about containers like bodies of code, codelines, and modules. However, in Perforce we *can* containerize, and we do, with filespecs.*
Any set of files that can be described with a single filespec can be treated as a container with a life and a history of its own. Filespec-defined containers can be used in activities like navigating a depot tree, setting up a workspace, making a branch, and configuring a release. This, in turn, lets us treat these containers as true SCM objects—that is, as objects that can be versioned, compared, branched, merged, labeled, and restored.

For example, *//Ace/REL1/...* is the filespec that refers to Ace's Release 1 codeline. You can use this filespec to do things like display its recent history:

```
p4 changes -m3 //Ace/REL1/...
Change 9634 ... bob 'Fix installer ...'
Change 9632 ... bob 'Rebuild zip file...'
Change 9629 ... doug 'New screenshots...'
```

---

* Take a look back at Chapter 1 if you're not sure what a filespec is.

You can also refer to the REL1 codeline by revision. For example, to compare two of its revisions, use:

```
p4 diff2 -q //Ace/REL1/...@9634 //Ace/REL1/...@9629
```

This is all fairly easy, and in the next chapter you'll see quite a few more examples. (Our examples are admittedly simple—it's easy to remember //*Ace/REL1*. In real life, the filespec you'll need to use is likely to be a little less self-evident.)

Module filespecs work the same way. For example, *doc* is a top-level module in the REL1 codeline. It can be referenced with the //*Ace/REL1/doc/*... filespec. To see its recent history, for example, use:

```
p4 changes -m3 //Ace/REL1/doc/...
```

You can also refer to the *doc* module irrespective of the codeline, as long as it has a fixed location relative to the root of the codeline. For example, you overheard Doug saying he just checked in some great new diagrams. You don't know which codeline he checked them into, but you know they'll be in the *doc* module, so you run:

```
p4 changes -u doug -m3 //Ace/*/doc/...
Change 9607 ... by doug 'New screenshots...'
Change 9599 ... by doug 'Dynamite diagrams...'
Change 9592 ... by doug 'Fix callouts...'
```

(The -u option limits the output of changes to the changes made by a particular user.)

Tidy Views

For filespecs to work as containers, you have to have a pretty well-organized depot. One thing that helps is if every codeline and every module can be described by a "tidy view." A tidy view is *exhaustive*, *exclusive*, and *succinct*: exhaustive in that the view applies to all of the files that belong in the container, exclusive in that it applies *only* to the files that belong in the container, and succinct in that it can be expressed on a single line.

For example, this tidy view defines Ace's REL1 codeline:

```
//Ace/REL1/...
```

A tidy view makes a container easy to work with. Ace's REL1 codeline, for example, is easy to manipulate with tools like P4V and P4Win because it's all in one folder and everything in the folder is in the codeline. It's also easy to map this codeline to a workspace, to branch or label it, to peruse its history, and to compare it with other codelines whose views are this tidy.

The depot hierarchy

In Chapter 7 you read that files make up modules, modules make up codelines, and codelines make up bodies of code. Not surprisingly, the most useful way to organize your depot is roughly along these lines. The recommended depot layout, in a nutshell, is a hierarchy of:

- Depots
- Codeline groupings
- Codelines
- Modules

The scope of a depot

As you read in an earlier chapter, a depot is a named area of the Perforce repository hierarchy. Perforce comes with one depot already configured; its name is "depot." You can use the default depot as is, or you can create one or more depots with names of your own choosing.

 Once you've submitted files to a depot, that depot is here to stay. You can branch its files into a depot of another name, but you can't rename it,* nor can you move its history of changes to another depot.

The depot name is often used to identify an organization. For example, Ace Engineering, a small software company, uses "Ace" to name its one and only depot:

```
p4 depots
Depot Ace ... //Ace/... 'Ace Engineering, Inc.'
```

(As you can see, the depots command lists depots.)

Large companies can designate a depot to each of their business units. At Massively Large Media Corporation,† for example, you'll find these depots:

```
p4 depots
Depot Acme      //Acme/...    'Acme System Design'
Depot RedRiver  //RedRiver/... 'Red River Graphics'
Depot Tango     //Tango/...    'Tango Desktop Tools'
```

The rationale behind designating depots to independent organizations is two-fold. First, it provides areas in which organizations can create or branch codelines without

---

* Actually, a depot *can* be renamed, but not with Perforce. It's possible to rename a depot using checkpoint surgery—that is, by dumping a Perforce database to a checkpoint, editing the checkpoint yourself, and reloading the database. Checkpoint surgery is a do-it-at-your-own-risk remedy that is beyond the scope of this book to explain.

† Massively Large Media Corporation and Ace Engineering are fictional names made up for examples in this book. If there are real companies with these names, it is purely coincidence.

affecting one another. Second, it makes it possible to mirror depots, thanks to the inherent transparency of remote depots.

Depot Mirroring

It is not uncommon for a large company to host more than one Perforce domain. (A *domain*, in this context, is a Perforce Server, its repository, and its database.) For example, each of Massively Large Media Corporation's depots is hosted by a Perforce Server in a separate domain. However, that doesn't keep MLMC engineers from accessing files in one another's depots.

Every product released by MLMC is identified with a filespec. One of the Tango releases, for example, is identified thus:

```
//Tango/Dist/Rel05.1/...@2005/07/19:13:20:00
```

Perforce users in any MLMC division can use this filespec to download the release from their own Perforce Server. The same filespec works across divisions, because the Tango Desktop Tools division's *//Tango/Dist* depot path is configured as a remote depot named *//Tango/Dist* in the other Perforce domains within MLMC. This kind of mirroring is a snap when depot names are unique throughout the network of Perforce domains.

You can find out more about remote depots in Chapter 6.

Note that the Perforce spec forms for workspaces, labels, and branch views seed View fields with a line for each depot. If you have only one depot named Ace, for example, you'll get something like this when you configure a new workspace:

```
p4 client my-new-ws

Client       my-new-ws
View         //Ace/...      //my_ws/...
```

Whereas at MLMC, where there are three depots, you'd get something like this:

```
p4 client my-new-ws

Client       my-new-ws
View         //Acme/...       //my_ws/Acme/...
             //RedRiver/...   //my_ws/RedRiver/...
             //Tango/...      //my_ws/Tango/...
```

Codeline grouping

As it turns out, an entire body of code is rarely the target of a single operation. Codelines grouped by functional type, however, are often such targets. (For example, distribution codelines may be mirrored as a single remote depot.) If you have—or expect to have—a large number of codelines, consider using the top level of a depot

---

to group them. The Tango depot at MLMC, for example, has the following paths in its top level:

//Tango/Prod

> Contains the shared codelines that support Tango's desktop product suite. The suite's mainline, its release codelines, and its shared development codelines are all contained within this depot path. Each codeline has a subdirectory of its own:
>
> ```
> //Tango/Prod/MAIN/...
> //Tango/Prod/REL4.0/...
> //Tango/Prod/REL4.0P1/...
> //Tango/Prod/REL4.1/...
>     ...
> ```

//Tango/Web

> Contains the codelines that support the Tango division's web site development.

//Tango/Task

> Contains task branches (the sparse, short-lived branches used to isolate specific tasks). They are grouped here to reduce the clutter in the product and web paths.

//Tango/Priv

> Contains the private branches used by developers for informal and shelved work.

//Tango/Dist/

> Stores the files Tango makes available through its online product distribution system. When internal customers download Tango's products, they're getting files from this path. When external customers get Tango's products, the web distributions that they download come from this path.

//Tango/Import

> Stores downloads of third-party software used in Tango's products. When Tango engineers need third-party software, they look in this path first to see which versions have already been downloaded. When they download new software from external suppliers, they put it in this path.

//Tango/Int

> Stores internal tools, internal documents, and intranet content at the Tango division.

Lineage versus location

Note that codelines relate to one another in two ways. One way is by their lineage. For example, say MAIN is branched into REL1. Later, MAIN is branched into REL2. Now there are three related codelines: MAIN is the parent codeline, and REL1 and REL2 are sibling codelines (see Figure 8-1).

The second way in which codelines relate to each other is by their location in the depot hierarchy. For example, the MAIN codeline is in the *//Tango/Prod/MAIN* path,

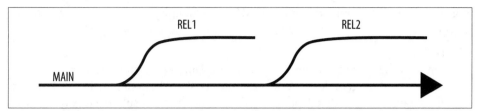

Figure 8-1. Branching lineage relationship

REL1 is in   *//Tango/Prod/REL1*, and REL2 is in *//Tango/Prod/REL2*. In the depot hierarchy, all three codelines are siblings, located in the *//Tango/Prod* path, as shown in Figure 8-2.

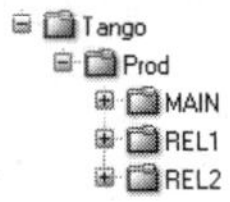

```
⊟ 🗁 Tango
   ⊟ 🗁 Prod
      ⊞ 🗁 MAIN
      ⊞ 🗁 REL1
      ⊞ 🗁 REL2
```

Figure 8-2. Depot location relationship

There's no reason that a codeline's location in the depot hierarchy *should* match its branching lineage. Nevertheless, the fact that it doesn't can be a source of confusion to new Perforce users.

Depot path naming conventions

You may wish to establish a naming convention to differentiate depot path levels. The following naming convention is applicable to most development environments. It is by no means required, but depending on the nature of your development environment, it might be helpful:

Depot name
> The depot name needs no special distinction, because it's obvious—it's the root of the path. However, you may wish to adopt a naming convention for depots for aesthetic reasons. Our examples use capitalized names. For example:
>
> ```
> //Tango/...
> ```

Codeline grouping
> Also, capitalize the names of the depot paths used to group your codelines. For example:
>
> ```
> //Tango/Prod/...
> //Tango/Web/...
> ```

Codelines
> Use all-uppercase letters for the names of depot paths that are codeline root directories. For example:

```
//Tango/Prod/MAIN/...
//Tango/Prod/TITAN/...
//Tango/Prod/GAIA/...
//Tango/Prod/R01.1/...
//Tango/Prod/R02.0/...
//Tango/Prod/R02.OP1/...
```

With this convention, the codeline name stands out.

Top-level modules

Use all lowercase for the names of top-level modules (the modules that are not included by any other modules). For example:

```
//Tango/Prod/TITAN/app/...
//Tango/Prod/TITAN/website/...
//Tango/Prod/TITAN/book/...
```

Other modules

Beneath the top-level modules, the pathnames will depend on the tools you use for development. Java, for example, requires that paths used for package parts be all lowercase. Many C++ development environments use capitalized and mixed-case names for subdirectories.

This is only one of many possible naming conventions you could adopt. The point is that naming conventions can be used to make the filespecs that define modules and codelines more predictable. This, in turn, makes it easier to treat modules and codelines as self-contained objects.

Storing generated files

Although you won't check in all the files generated in the course of building your software, you'll check in some of them. In particular, you'll want to check in:

Software for distribution

If you're releasing software for internal or external distribution, you can use the depot both to store a reference copy of the release and to distribute the software. (This will be explored further in Chapter 9.)

Files generated by nightly builds

One of the reasons we do nightly builds is so that developers can have up-to-date versions of shared libraries and other generated files without having to build everything themselves. See "Nightly Builds" later in this chapter.

Generated files and source files should be segregated. In other words, you should put generated files in modules of their own instead of in modules that already contain source files. (This is, admittedly, a tall order for some build tools.) Knowing that a module contains either generated files or source files—but not both—makes the business of branching and merging *so* much easier.

At Ace Engineering, for example, each codeline contains a top-level module called *built*. The *built* module contains nothing but generated files, organized by target platform. There's a *built* module in the MAIN codeline, for example, that is a peer of the other modules in the codeline:

```
p4 dirs "//Ace/MAIN/*"
//Ace/MAIN/built/...
//Ace/MAIN/db/...
//Ace/MAIN/gui/...
...
```

Codeline proliferation

As software evolves, codelines tend to proliferate. A large, active company can accumulate dozens of codelines in a year and hundreds over the life of the software it develops. These codelines don't consume significant space in the Perforce repository[*] but they do add to the number of subdirectories in the depot hierarchy. Navigating a mature depot can be cumbersome simply because of the huge number of codelines. This is not a problem that can be solved by depot organization, because by

---

[*] Most of the files in branched codelines are merely *lazy copies*. See Chapter 4 for more about that topic.

the time the problem comes up, the depot structure is established and can only be changed by *reorganization*.

It's easier to reduce codeline clutter with *protections*. (You read about protections in Chapter 6.) With protections, you can hide old, inactive codelines from normal viewing. You can also restrict codelines so that they're visible only to certain developers or groups. In the Tango depot, for example, protections hide the web-related codelines from all users but those in the WebDev group:

p4 protect

```
Protections    ...
               list    user    *        *  -//Tango/Web/...
               write   group   WebDev   *  //Tango/Web/...
               ...
```

Users can be added to or removed from groups with the group command:

p4 group WebDev

```
Group    WebDev
Users    dan
         mia
         anja
         kim
         ...
```

How not to organize your depot

Much of the foregoing advice is meant to head off common mistakes of depot organization. Here are some things to look out for specifically:

Don't organize by ownership

You may be tempted to create codeline or module hierarchies that match the hierarchy of your development organization. With the exception of allocating depots to business units, organizing by ownership is a bad idea, for several reasons.

First, it's more work. If you require that your depot structure reflect your company structure, you'll have to reorganize your depot every time your company reorganizes. Although a company reorganization can make the company more efficient, reorganizing a depot is not likely to have much effect on the efficiency of either the company or the depot. For all that effort, there's very little payoff.

Second, ownership changes obscure functional changes. The history of a module or a codeline in your depot can be a useful roadmap if you're trying to figure out where a bug was introduced and where and when it was fixed. For example, if a module has been unchanged for two years, you know not to look there for a bug that was introduced in the last month. You don't have that advantage when modules have been reorganized because of ownership changes. Not only do ownership changes obscure functional changes, but they can themselves introduce risk. Every change to a stable set of files reduces its stability somewhat.

Finally, you can discern useful information about trends in your software development process from depot history. For example, you may notice that files in a particular module have a high rate of change just after every release, perhaps indicating a problem in your release methodology. That's something you wouldn't easily notice if, due to ownership changes, those files appeared in different modules at every release.

Reorganizing a Depot

Reorganizing a depot is a bit like renaming a street. Changing street signs is easy, but it invalidates street maps and other references to the street. People with old street maps will be confused and annoyed when they end up lost. It's the same with depot reorganization. Moving codelines and modules around is fairly easy with the integrate command. But it can invalidate workspace views and branch views, among other things. One consequence is that users can be left with opened files that they can't submit because their workspace views refer to files that no longer exist. There are remedies (see "Someone moves the files you were editing" in Chapter 3) but they won't make you popular with your users.

That's not to say that a depot can't be reorganized. But if you do plan to reorganize a depot, let everyone know what you're doing, and give them a chance to check in files and adjust views.

Don't require modules to be reshaped with workspace views.

Perforce's workspace views allow you to reshape the way modules appear in your workspace. (The "shape" of a module is determined by the relative locations of its subdirectories and files.) For example, consider this workspace view:

```
Client      BobWS
Root        c:\ws
View        //Ace/REL1/app/src/...      //BobWS/app/src/...
            //Ace/REL1/app/helpfiles/... //BobWS/app/lib/helpfiles/...
```

Notice how this view mapping changes the relationship of subdirectories to each other. You may be tempted to use client view mappings like this when your development tools expect files to appear in a directory structure that's different than the depot's.

The problem with using view mapping to reshape modules is that it buries an important intellectual asset—the information about the shape the modules must take in order to be used. What would happen if a new version of a development tool required a different directory structure? You could certainly tell everyone to remap their workspace views, but that leaves no record of what was changed, by whom, and when. (That's no way to guarantee reproducible builds!)

Modules that need to be in a particular shape in workspaces should be stored that way in the depot, so that their relative location is part of their recorded history. Modules that need reshaping for specific uses—for example, to create a release—should be reshaped by running a script. The script itself should be stored in the depot.

Furthermore, just because it's easy to use workspace views to reshape modules doesn't mean it won't get complicated. Your development environment is probably complicated as is. Resist the temptation to add another layer of complexity. Instead, keep views simple, and store modules in the depot exactly as they should appear in workspaces.

Don't use depots to allocate disk space

Precocious Perforce superusers often discover that they can define depots in a way that distributes their Perforce repository across multiple filesystems or disk volumes. In the long run, using named depots to balance disk space is not a good idea. It hard-codes your current hardware resource allocation scheme into the depot pathnames that will be used to name your versioned files, codelines, releases, and so forth. As you know, hardware resources are likely to change. You wouldn't want hardware changes to invalidate or be constrained by the path names used by your build tools, your workspace and branch views, your depot protections, and the entire recorded history of your software's evolution.

There are ways to allocate disk space transparently—on Unix, for example, you can do it with symlinks. So instead of using named depots, consider using transparent, OS-provided disk allocation to distribute your Perforce repository.

General Care and Feeding of Codelines

In the chapters that follow, you'll see how to create and manage specific types of codelines. But first, let's begin with some general information about managing codelines with Perforce.

The codeline curator

Every codeline needs a curator. We say "curator" instead of "owner" because often codelines are owned collectively. But even a collectively owned codeline should have a single point-person to keep an eye on housekeeping tasks. This person may delegate tasks to others, but making sure the tasks get done is his or her responsibility.

Some of the codeline curator's tasks require special privileges. In particular, the tasks involving protections and triggers require superuser access, although these aren't tasks that are done often. As you plan codeline management, be prepared either to grant superuser access to codeline curators or to have someone with superuser access on hand who can run commands on behalf of codeline curators.

Naming a codeline

As far as Perforce is concerned, you're at liberty to use any name you want for a codeline. Bear in mind that:

- You'll use the codeline's name for its depot path and various other Perforce objects. The name should conform to your depot path naming rules.
- You can't easily change a depot pathname once you've created it.
- It's nice when a codeline's name can be used in conversation. So instead of using an inscrutable, data-derived string as a codeline name, consider using a pronounceable, recognizable nickname.
- Codelines can be reused. If you're planning on reusing a codeline, give it a name that describes its general scope, or that's not tied to any particular use.

Which modules go in a codeline?

The mainline typically contains many more modules than you'll need to branch into a single development or release codeline. In the following chapters you'll read about how a codeline's purpose dictates (or suggests) the modules to branch into it. In the meantime, bear in mind that:

- Modules in a given codeline are either "active" or "static." The active modules are the ones developers are working on—they're evolving right there in the codeline. The static ones aren't evolving in the codeline at hand—they've been branched to support development. (Inactive modules may be evolving in other codelines, though; the codeline at hand may need to be updated with their latest versions.)
- One reason that static modules are branched into a codeline is that it's so convenient to have everything you need all in one codeline. All developers have to do is put the codeline in their workspace views, and—poof!—synchronizing gets them all the source code, build scripts, test drivers, and tests they need to do their work.
- Alternatively, you can leave the static modules unbranched and require workspace views to map them from the parent codeline. These "virtual" modules don't actually exist in the codeline path but—thanks to label and client views—they *appear* to be there.

The master workspace

Every codeline should have a master workspace. The codeline curator creates the master workspace and uses it for codeline housekeeping tasks. Developers use the master workspace as a template for creating their own workspace views.

For example, the mainline at Ace Engineering has a master workspace called MAIN-master:

```
Client      MAIN-master
View        //Ace/MAIN/built/...    //MAIN-master/built/...
            //Ace/MAIN/db/...       //MAIN-master/db/...
            //Ace/MAIN/doc/...      //MAIN-master/doc/...
            //Ace/MAIN/utils/...    //MAIN-master/utils/...
            //Ace/MAIN/tests/...    //MAIN-master/tests/...
            //Ace/MAIN/gui/...      //MAIN-master/gui/...
```

Each module in the codeline is mapped explicitly in the master workspace's view. This gives developers a way to select the modules they need when they create their own workspaces. You'll see an example of how this works in Chapter 9.

The codeline's branch view

Every branched codeline—that is, every codeline but the mainline—should have a branch view. A branch view makes the `integrate`, `interchanges`, and `diff2` commands easier to use. It can also be used to reconcile structural differences between the codeline and its parent. The codeline curator creates the branch view and uses it to branch the codeline and to integrate changes between the codeline and its parent.

The branch view can be created or modifed using the `branch` command. A useful convention to follow is to use the branch view's name and mapping to point to the parent. For example, the branch view that maps Ace's PLUTO codeline to its parent, MAIN, is called PLUTO-MAIN. And in the View field of the branch view spec, the codeline's paths appear on the left and its parent's paths appear on the right:

p4 branch PLUTO-MAIN

```
Branch        PLUTO-MAIN
Description   PLUTO project development
View          //Ace/PLUTO/db/...      //Ace/MAIN/db/...
              //Ace/PLUTO/doc/...     //Ace/MAIN/doc/...
              //Ace/PLUTO/utils/...   //Ace/MAIN/utils/...
              //Ace/PLUTO/tests/...   //Ace/MAIN/tests/...
              //Ace/PLUTO/gui/...     //Ace/MAIN/gui/...
```

As with the master workspace view, the codeline's branch view itemizes modules—in this case, the modules branched from the parent. As long as the branch view is used consistently in integration operations, it prevents irrelevant modules from being branched later. It also documents the modules that are involved in the flow of change between the codeline and its parent.

Branching a codeline

In Perforce, a codeline doesn't exist until you branch files into it. To branch files, as you know, you use `integrate`. For example, Tango's PLUTO codeline was branched from MAIN using:

```
p4 integ -r -b PLUTO-MAIN
p4 submit
```

(Actually, this is a gross oversimplification. There are a few things you can do as you're creating a codeline to make it easier to work with and to make subsequent merges easier. You'll find out about them in the chapters that follow.)

Working in a codeline

A codeline is just another path in the depot. Once a codeline is branched, you can work on the files in it and add new files to it. The codeline's path must be included in your workspace view in order for you to do this, of course.

As a rule, you should work in one codeline at a time. (We use codelines to create order out of chaos; working in more than one codeline at once pulls us back toward chaos. It's like driving in two lanes at once.) This applies to developers and curators both.

For each codeline in which you work, create a separate workspace. You can have more than one workspace per codeline you work in, but you shouldn't use a single workspace to do work in more than one codeline.

The `client` command lets you use an existing workspace as a template to create a new workspace. For example, Bob creates a workspace called MAIN-bob, using the MAIN-master workspace as a template:

```
p4 client -t MAIN-master MAIN-bob
```

The `client` command gives Bob a spec form to edit, with a View field prefilled to match the MAIN-master workspace's view. All he has to do is fill in the workspace root and save the spec form.

 Command-line users, remember that you will also have to set your P4CLIENT variable to switch between workspaces. For more information, see Chapter 2.

Alternatively, Bob can use P4V, as follows, to create his new MAIN-bob workspace using MAIN-master as a template:

1. He uses View → Workspaces to find and select the MAIN-master workspace.

2. He uses Edit → Create Workspace from and enters MAIN-bob as the new workspace name.

About This Codeline

Developers need to know which codelines are available, where they are, who can use them, who their curators are, and so forth. By putting this information in an HTML file at the root of each codeline, you can keep developers informed *and* keep track of your codelines.

For example, in the Tango depot there's a file called *Codeline.html* at the root of the mainline file hierarchy. As a codeline is branched from the mainline or any of its progeny, the *Codeline.html* file is branched with it. Codeline curators update the branched *Codeline.html* files with current and relevant information. As developers navigate the depot tree with P4V, they can click the *Codeline.html* files to launch them in their browsers.

The *Codeline.html* files do more than document codeline purpose and status. As the files command shows, they mark codeline locations in the depot:

```
p4 files //Tango/.../Codeline.html
//Tango/Prod/MAIN/Codeline.html#2
//Tango/Prod/REL4/Codeline.html#1
//Tango/Prod/REL4.0P1/Codeline.html#1
//Tango/Prod/REL4.1/Codeline.html#1
...
```

Because each *Codeline.html* file marks a codeline, the list of these files is itself a handy summary of the Tango codelines. Even handier, the inherited history of the *Codeline.html* files reveals the lineage of Tango's codelines. This filelog output, for example, shows that the REL1.0 codeline was branched from MAIN, and REL1.0.1 and REL1.2.1 were branched from REL1.0:

```
p4 filelog -i //Tango/Prod/REL1.0/Codeline.html
//Tango/Prod/REL1.0/Codeline.html
...
... #2  edit on 2004/03/13 by daria 'New codeline info'
... ... branch into //Tango/Prod/REL1.2.1/Codeline.html#1
... #1  branch on 2004/03/13 by daria 'Create REL1.0'
... ... branch into //Tango/Prod/REL1.0.1/Codeline.html#1
... ... branch from //Tango/Prod/MAIN/Codeline.html#3
...
```

—continued—

3. He enters a root directory in the workspace form and clicks Save.

4. He uses Connection → Choose Workspace to switch to the MAIN-bob workspace.

Codeline lineage is much easier to see in P4V's Revision Graph, as the figure shows.

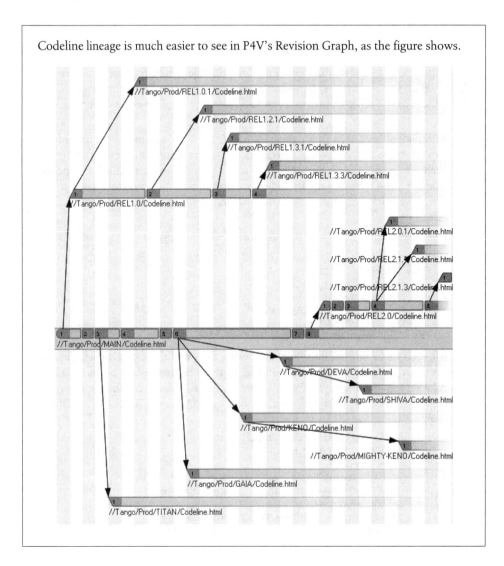

Controlling access to a codeline

If you're concerned about who can check files into a codeline, you can set up a permission group and use the group to define codeline access permissions. (See Chapter 6.)

For example, we can set up a group called REL1-dev to identify the developers working in Ace's REL1 codeline:

```
p4 group REL1-dev

Group        REL1-dev
Users        ann
             doug
             sue
```

This puts Ann, Doug, and Sue in the REL1 group. We use the protect command to configure depot protections so that the *//Ace/REL1* path is visible to all, but writable only to members of the REL1-dev group:

```
p4 protect

Protections   ...
              read    user    *               *    //Ace/REL1/...
              write   group   REL1-dev         *    //Ace/REL1/...
              ...
```

There are many ways you can set up groups and group hierarchies, of course. This is but a simple example.

Retiring a codeline

You don't really have to do anything to retire a codeline. It will always be part of your depot history, and that is a good thing. There are a couple of things you can do to keep developers from stumbling onto it and using it, however, aside from simply declaring that it has been retired. One is to set depot protections to prevent check-ins to it. The other is to use protections to block it from view entirely. You'll see examples of this in Chapter 9.

Nightly Builds

The firmer a codeline is, the more likely it is that you'll be setting up a nighty build of the software in it. (Although we call it a "nightly" build, we mean any recurring, automated process that resynchronizes and rebuilds.) In this section we'll look at how a nightly build script can use Perforce to synchronize a workspace with a codeline, open and submit generated files, and label the codeline.

The nightly build workspace

Nightly build workspaces are used by build engineers and their build scripts. As a rule of thumb:

- Each combination of codeline and target platform should have its own nightly build workspace.
- Each nightly build workspace should have a view of one and only one codeline.

At Ace, for example, a workspace called REL1-bld-linux is dedicated to the nightly builds of the REL1 codeline on Linux:

```
p4 client REL1-bld-linux
```

Client	REL1-bld-linux
Root	/usr/builds/REL1
View	//Ace/REL1/... //REL1-bld-linux/...

Synchronizing the nightly build

The first thing the nightly build script should do before synchronizing is to revert files that may been have left opened by a previous, failed build:

```
p4 revert //...
```

(The only files likely to be opened are generated files that will be submitted by the script. However, opened files can't be resynchronized, and unsynchronized files can't be submitted, so they should be reverted first.)

Next, your build script should identify the snapshot of the depot revision it is building. This is the build ID; it's the highest changelist number in the depot at the start of the build cycle. Your build script can get this number from the output of changes -m1:

```
p4 changes -m1
Change 7089 on 2005/01/21 by mei 'Fix size of pop-up for...'
```

If you trust your build tools to do incremental builds correctly, synchronizing the nightly build is easy. All the script has to do is synchronize with the build ID:

```
p4 sync @7089
```

Each time the workspace is synchronized this way, the only files that are updated are those that have changed since the last build; populating a nightly build area is very efficient if only a few files have changed and little needs rebuilding.

If, on the other hand, your build tools can't be trusted to rebuild things 100 percent correctly when files are updated, your nightly builds will have to be done from scratch. And for scratch builds, the build script will have to ensure that the workspace is pristine at the start. The simplest way to ensure this is to remove workspace files by brute force, then force Perforce to resynchronize the entire workspace. For example, in a Unix workspace whose root is */usr/builds/REL1*, the script would run:

```
rm -rf /usr/builds/REL1/*
p4 sync -f @7089
```

(The -f option forces sync to recopy files to the workspace regardless of the Perforce Server's record of what's already there.)

Opening generated files

Nightly build scripts typically submit generated files. Before a nightly build script can submit the files it has generated, it will have to open them.

Files not yet in the depot will have to be opened for adding. For example:

```
p4 add acepack.so
```

As the build script adds files to the depot, it can designate the +w filetype so that generated files will be writable in workspaces. This will simplify the script's work, because it won't have to open the files for editing first in subsequent builds. (It will also make it easier for developers to work with generated files; they won't have to do anything special to rebuild them incrementally.) To designate *acepack.so* workspace-writable as it is opened for adding, for example, the script uses:

```
p4 add -t +w acepack.so
```

Files being updated will have to be opened for editing, then submitted. Workspace-writable files can be regenerated first, then opened for editing. Read-only files will have to be opened before the build script regenerates them. In either case, the familiar edit is used to open files. For example:

```
p4 edit acepack.so
```

Submitting generated files

By the end of the build procedure, a number of generated files will be opened in the workspace's default changelist, ready to be submitted. As you saw in Chapter 6, the trick to submitting a changelist is to get the text of the changelist form from change -o, filter it to insert a changelist description, and pipe the result to submit -i.

It's a good idea to record the build ID in the changelist description. A build script written in Ruby, with the build ID revision stored in a variable called build_ID, for example, can insert the description into the changelist form thus:

```
spec = `p4 change -o`
spec.gsub!(
    /<enter description here>/,
    "Nightly build as of #{build_ID}"
    )
IO.popen( 'p4 submit -i', 'w' ){ |f| f.puts spec }
```

Your script can insert a more detailed description, of course. As long as the build ID is mentioned in the description's lead-in, nightly builds show up nicely in a codeline's history:

```
p4 changes -m10 //Ace/REL1/...
Change 7093 on 2005/01/12 ... 'Nightly build as of @7089'
Change 7089 on 2005/01/12 ... 'Fix typo in installer dialog'
Change 7086 on 2005/01/12 ... 'Add verbose tool-tips in the'
Change 7085 on 2005/01/11 ... 'More efficient find-file alg'
```

```
Change 7077 on 2005/01/11 ... 'Nightly build as of @7068'
Change 7068 on 2005/01/11 ... 'Hidden files now included in'
...
```

Labeling nightly builds

Among its final tasks, the nightly build script typically tags its workspace configuration with a rolling label. For example:

```
p4 labelsync -l REL1-nightly
```

(The `labelsync` command is preferred over `tag` for this use, because it also removes the rolling label from files not in the current workspace configuration.)

Note that `labelsync` works only with pre-existing, unlocked label specs. To ensure these conditions, the script can reinitialize the label spec beforehand using `label -i`. In a Ruby script, for example:

```
IO.popen( 'p4 label -i', 'w' ){ |f| f.puts <<EOF }
Label: REL1-nightly\n\n
Description: REL1 nightly build\n\n
Options: unlocked\n\n
View: //Ace/REL1/...\n\n
EOF
```

Using the nightly build label

The nightly build label can be used to compare the nightly build configuration with other configurations. For example, Bill, a developer, finds that he can't complete a build in his Bill-WS workspace. He compares the the latest nightly build to his workspace configuration:

```
p4 diff2 -q //...@REL1-nightly //...@Bill-WS
...
==== //Ace/REL1/db/minst/Jamfile#1 - <none> ====
==== //Ace/REL1/db/minst/st.cfg#1 - <none> ====
...
```

The preceding output shows Bill that his workspace isn't completely in sync with the nightly build—two files are missing. To synchronize his workspace with the nightly build configuration, he can use:

```
p4 sync @REL1-nightly
```

Is Bug X Fixed in Codeline Y?

When a codeline is branched, a new variant of the software it contains is born. As work proceeds, changes are submitted independently to each codeline and, depending on how and when changes are merged between them, the variants diverge. Eventually, each variant becomes distinct in its quality and functionality. Sooner or later the question is bound to come up, "Is bug X fixed in codeline Y?"

In simple cases, branching diagrams can reveal the answer. It's easy to see that if a bug is fixed in one codeline at some point in time, the same bug will be fixed in any codeline subsequently branched from that codeline, as illustrated in Figure 8-3. But what about the case where a bug fix is *merged* from one codeline to another? What if several bug fixes are merged together? What if the fix was backported to a distantly related codeline? In a production development environment, where there are many codelines and many merges, branching diagrams would show so many relationships that the end result would be impossible to interpret.

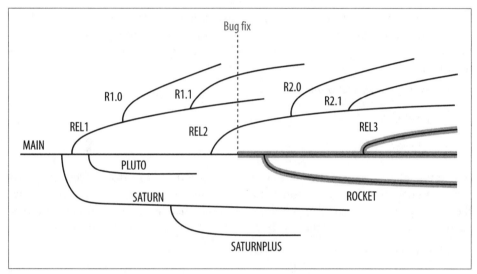

Figure 8-3. The ramifications of a bug fix

Perforce, it turns out, is innately capable of answering the question, "Is bug X fixed in codeline Y?" Under the right conditions, a merged bug fix can be detected regardless of the codeline it originated in, how many intermediate codelines it passed through, when it was merged to each codeline, and the sequence in which it was merged before reaching the codeline in question. Using integration records stored in its database, the Perforce Server can detect trails of merges emanating from file revisions associated with changelists. A bug fixed in one codeline and merged into a second, third, and fourth codeline, for example, leaves just such a trail of merges.

In this section we'll look at how Perforce detects merged bug fixes, and the factors that make detection more accurate.

Inside the Perforce database

Before looking at the logic behind Perforce's bug fix tracking ability, let's take a look at some of the objects modeled in the Perforce database. We'll start with the changelist. Submitted changelists* are recorded in the Perforce database when users submit files. The submitted changelist object associates file revisions with a changelist. For example:

```
p4 describe 6340
Change 6340 ... on 2004/08/19 21:06:09
Affected files ...
... //Ace/REL1/utils/regen.rb#1      add
... //Ace/REL1/utils/docfind.rb#6    edit
... //Ace/REL1/utils/orphaned.rb#19 integrate
```

A file revision is an object in the Perforce database uniquely identified by the file's name and a revision number. File revision records hold, among other things, an updating action (add, edit, integrate, etc.), a changelist number, and file type information:

```
p4 fstat //Ace/REL1/utils/orphaned.rb#19
... depotFile //Ace/REL1/utils/orphaned.rb
... headAction integrate
... headType text
... headRev 19
... headChange 6340
```

Integration records associate a starting and ending revision of a donor file with a revision of a target file. They also store a changelist number and information about how the target file was created or resolved. For example, here is an integration record that shows that revision 19 of *orphaned.rb* was copied from revision 21 of *listall.rb*:

```
p4 integrated //Ace/REL1/utils/orphaned.rb
//Ace/REL1/utils/orphaned.rb#19
- copy from //Ace/REL1/utils/listall.rb#1,#21
```

Every integration into a file creates two integration records in the database. One records the actual integration, as shown previously. The other is a pseudorecord that ensures that the integration will be accounted for in the opposite direction as well:

```
p4 integrated //Ace/REL1/utils/listall.rb
//Ace/REL1/utils/listall.rb#1,#21
- copy into //Ace/REL1/utils/orphaned.rb#19
```

The symmetry of integration records is easier to see in the tagged output of the integrated command:

```
p4 -ztag integrated //Ace/REL1/utils/orphaned.rb
... toFile //Ace/REL1/utils/orphaned.rb
```

---

* The database also records pending changelists, which are subtly different from submitted changelists in ways that aren't relevant here.

```
...  fromFile //Ace/REL1/utils/listall.rb
...  startToRev #18
...  endToRev #19
...  startFromRev #none
...  endFromRev #21
...  how copy from
...  change 6340

p4 -ztag integrated //Ace/REL1/utils/listall.rb
...  toFile //Ace/REL1/utils/listall.rb
...  fromFile //Ace/REL1/utils/orphaned.rb
...  startToRev #none
...  endToRev #21
...  startFromRev #18
...  endFromRev #19
...  how copy into
...  change 6340
```

Commands that detect merged bug fixes

There are three Perforce commands that are capable of reporting whether a particular bug fix is in a particular codeline: changes, jobs, and fixes. All three commands have an optional flag, -i, that causes them to report the presence of merged bug fixes.

For example, say we know that changelist 1200 fixed a bug. To find out whether that bug fix was merged into the PLUTO codeline—that is, to the files in the *//Ace/PLUTO* path—we run:

```
p4 changes -i //Ace/PLUTO/...
Change 1234 on 2003/03/20 by bruce
Change 1220 on 2003/03/18 by ann
Change 1200 on 2003/03/14 by henry
Change 1106 on 2003/02/23 by tracy
Change 1095 on 2003/02/12 by kip
...
```

Changelist 1200 appears in the output. But when we examine changelist 1200 we see that it refers only to files in the *//Ace/REL1* path. In other words, this bug was first fixed in the REL1 codeline:

```
p4 describe -s 1200
Change 1200 on 2003/03/14 by henry
Affected files:
...  //Ace/REL1/conf/db.cfg#4
...  //Ace/REL1/db/foo.c#3
...  //Ace/REL1/db/bar.c#9
```

Perforce traced the integration records emanating from files in the *//Ace/PLUTO* path and found a trail to the file revisions created in changelist 1200. Thus it reports that changelist 1200 has been merged into *//Ace/PLUTO*. From this we can infer that the bug is indeed fixed in the PLUTO codeline.

Two Perforce database objects, jobs and fixes, make merged bug fixes a little easier for us humans to find. (You may remember reading about jobs and fixes in Chapter 5.) For example, here's a job used to describe a bug report:

```
p4 job -o Bug90
Job:         Bug90
Status:      closed
User:        ron
Date:        2003/01/15
Description: Icons very jaggy.
```

With jobs and changelists linked by fixes, you can do better than the changes -i command. You can use fixes -i and jobs -i to narrow the search for bug fixes. Whereas changes -i outputs *all* the changelist numbers it finds, fixes -i can limit its output to changelists linked to a specific job:

```
p4 fixes -i -j Bug90 //Ace/PLUTO/...
Bug90 fixed by change 1200 on 2003/01/14
```

Likewise, jobs -i can limit its output to changelists that fix jobs matching a search expression you supply:

```
p4 jobs -i -e "icon*" //Ace/PLUTO/...
Bug90 ... *closed* "Icons very jaggy."
```

The jobs -i and fixes -i commands use the same logic as changes -i to report results. Starting with files in a codeline path, they follow trails of integration records looking for references to revisions submitted in changelists associated with jobs. In Figure 8-4, for example, REL1's changelist 1200 holds file revisions that have integration records leading to MAIN's changelist 1231. Changelist 1231 holds file revisions that have integration records leading to file revisions in PLUTO's changelist 1288.

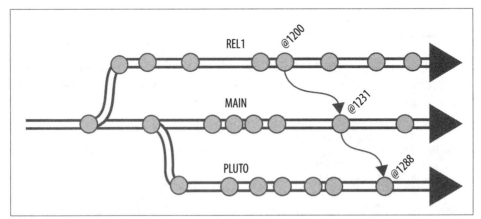

Figure 8-4. A trail of integration records

False positives

But what is Perforce actually telling you? Remember that codelines represent collections of files, each file having its own revision and integration history. If *any* of the revisions in the codeline you're inspecting is related by integration to the bug fix you're looking for, Perforce will report a positive result. What Perforce is reporting with fixes -i, jobs -i, and changes -i is the optimistic answer.

For example, looking at Figure 8-5, say a bug was fixed by change 1200 in the REL1 codeline. Changelist 1200 holds three file revisions; all three were integrated to MAIN in change 1231. For one reason or another, only one of the three file revisions in changelist 1231 was integrated from MAIN to PLUTO.

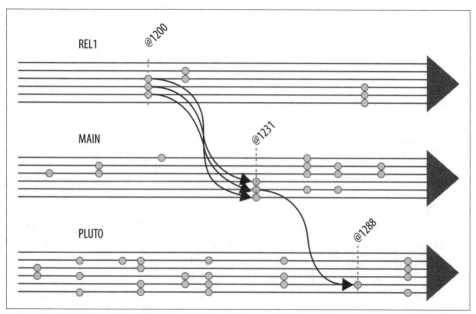

Figure 8-5. False positive due to partially integrated changelist

It would be nice to be able to assume that if Perforce reports that changelist 1200 was integrated into PLUTO, the *complete* changelist was integrated. But in fact, Perforce reports that changelist 1200 was integrated, even though only one of its three files has a trail of integration history leading all the way to the PLUTO codeline.

Perforce's optimistic reporting is based on the premise that content diverges between codelines. Because of that, not all revisions involved in a changelist are necessarily relevant when a bug fix is being merged into other codelines. Perforce assumes that if *some* of the revisions in a changelist have been merged, the unmerged revisions were left behind because they don't apply, not because they were forgotten.

Making merge detection more accurate

There are a number of ways you and your developers can decrease the likelihood of false positives from the `jobs -i` and `fixes -i` commands:

- Codeline scope should be succinct enough to be identified with a one-line Perforce filespec. In the same vein, codeline scope should be unambiguous. (See "Filespecs as containers," earlier in the chapter, for examples.)

- Developers should submit well-organized changelists.

  The following output shows, for example, that Ann and Henry have been careful to organize the files they submit into changelists that reflect points of integrity in their work. Each changelist they submit introduces a known condition into the repository: first some refactoring is completed, next a crash is fixed, next some icons are improved, and finally some copyright dates are updated.

  ```
  p4 changes -l
  Change 1234 on 2003/01/15 by ann
      Fix outdated copyright templates
      ...
  Change 1231 on 2003/01/14 by henry
      Fixed the jaggies on the file icons
      ...
  Change 1229 on 2003/01/12 by ann
      Fix crash on the file-not-found case
      ...
  Change 1227 on 2003/01/11 by ann
      Refactoring for found/not-found logic
      ...
  ```

The following is an example of poorly organized changelists, taken from a parallel universe. In this universe, Ann is bad; she has not been careful about organizing her changelists. To use any of her changelists to refer to a point of integrity would not be particularly useful, as none of her changelists refer to a point at which anything she worked on is complete. Even using Henry's changelist number to identify a point of integrity is impossible because his changelist was submitted between two of Ann's half-baked submissions.

```
p4 changes -l
Change 1234 on 2003/01/15 by ann
    Oops, some more .h files to fix crash
    ...
Change 1233 on 2003/01/14 by ann
    One more copyright template
    ...
Change 1231 on 2003/01/13 by henry
    Fixed the jaggies on the file icons
    ...
Change 1229 on 2003/01/12 by ann
    Work on crash and fix some copyright templates
    ...
```

(This is not to say you can't submit incomplete work. You can, in your private branch. See Chapter 10.)

- Entire changelists should be integrated when merging bug fixes. (See Chapter 4 for more on this.)

- By the same token, it's important to integrate changelists in order. (See Chapter 4.)

- Finally, when associating a job with a changelist, make sure it's the changelist that *really* fixes the bug. Say you fix Bug90 with changelist 1100. Then, you realize you missed something, so you submit changelist 1170, also to fix Bug90. Later, someone else finds a flaw in your work, so you fix it again with changelist 1200. That finally fixes it for good. As Figure 8-6 illustrates, Perforce is perfectly happy to create three fix records for you.

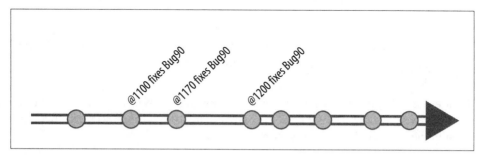

Figure 8-6. Too many fixes

Each fix record associates the job named Bug90 with a different changelist. But at what point in the life of the REL1 codeline is Bug90 really fixed? As of changelist 1200, of course. For the purpose of tracking bug fixes, the fix records that associated Bug90 with changelists 1100 and 1170 are red herrings. If the revisions in either of these changelists are integrated from REL1 into another codeline, Perforce will report Bug90 fixed in that codeline as well—another false positive. To prevent that from happening, you can use fix -d to remove fixes that aren't fixes. For example:

```
p4 fix -d -c 1100 Bug90
p4 fix -d -c 1170 Bug90
```

As the only change linked to Bug90, change 1200 now marks the point at which the bug is truly fixed, as Figure 8-7 shows.

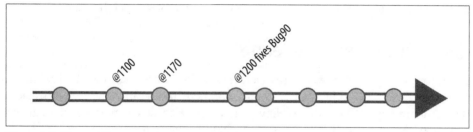

Figure 8-7. The real fix

CHAPTER 9

Release Codelines

It's June, the mainline abounds with completed development, and it's time to branch a new release. In this chapter we take a look at the care and feeding of release codelines.

We'll use Ace Engineering's repository for our examples. In fact, we'll put ourselves in the role of Ace Engineering's release manager for the example scenario that runs through the chapter. The filespecs of interest to us are:

//Ace/MAIN/...
> The mainline

//Ace/REL1/...
> The codeline that supports our 1.X releases

//Ace/REL2/...
> The codeline we're going to create and use for our second major release

The top-level modules that make up our release codelines are:

```
db/...
built/...
doc/...
gui/...
tests/...
utils/...
```

(Remember, these names, paths, and filespecs are shorter than you're likely to need in the real world. We keep them short here so the examples fit on the page.)

Creating a Release Codeline

In preparing to branch the new release codeline, we'll create a branch view and a label view, label the modules we're going to branch, and set up a master workspace. Before doing any of these things, however, we have to decide when to branch the codeline, what to call it, who owns it, and what belongs in it.

When should we branch?

As you read in Chapter 7, the mainline leaps (or creeps) forward with changes delivered from development codelines. When our development goals have been reached, we make a release.

Of course, software must be stabilized before it is released. (That is, it has to be tested, its showstopper bugs have to be fixed, and its loose ends have to be tied up.) We can't stabilize a release in the mainline, because the mainline must remain open for new development. The point at which new development conflicts with release stabilization work, therefore, is the point at which we branch a release codeline.

Who owns the release codeline?

The curator of the release codeline is typically the release manager, the person in charge of getting the release out the door. Every change to the release codeline is going to affect the release manager's schedule; it makes sense that the release manager controls the codeline.

Naming a release codeline

Every company has its own system for naming releases. Perforce doesn't impose any kind of release naming. In fact, visible release numbering systems have very little bearing on how software is managed in Perforce. We can pick any name we want for a release codeline without constraining externally chosen release identifiers.

At Ace Engineering, we take the following into account:

- We may not know the exact ID of the release we're working on. Even if we do, the final release number may change in the course of stabilization. (For example, we may be planning to release AcePack 2.0.0, but by the time we get there, it could be AcePack 2.0.3. Or UltraPack 2.0.3, for that matter.) This is a good reason not to use the actual, intended release ID as a codeline name.

- A single codeline can be used for a series of incremental releases. (For example, we'll be releasing AcePack 2.0-Beta and AcePack 2.1 from our new codeline. And we may produce point releases—AcePack 2.1 and so forth—from the same codeline.) This is another reason a specific release ID isn't suitable for a codeline name.

- If any of our source files use keyword expansion, the name of the release codeline may be visible to users.[*] In other words, if the AcePack software emits version strings generated from the expanding keyword Id, customers will see the full name of the depot path from whence the source files came. This is a good reason not to use anything tasteless or offensive for a codeline name.

---

[*] Run `p4 help filetypes`, or see "Perforce File Type" in *The Perforce Users Guide*, for more information about RCS-style keyword expansion.

Ideally, a release codeline's name identifies a set of potential releases, not any single release. At Ace Engineering, for example, we'll name our release codeline REL2 because it will be used to stabilize the "2.X" family of releases. The filespec for the REL2 codeline is:

```
//Ace/REL2/...
```

(As you can see, Ace Engineering has a very flat depot hierarchy.)

Which modules should we branch?

A release codeline, with its extremely high quality and stability requirements, should include all the modules that are needed to produce the release—that is, everything developers need to work on, build, and test their bug fixes. (If developers have to fix bugs in a workspace composed of modules mixed and matched from various codelines, the release codeline will never be stable.) This means that even inactive modules should be branched into a release codeline. If a module is needed to build or test the release, we'll branch it into the release codeline.

On the other hand, we don't have to branch modules that are *created* in the course of a build. For example, each of Ace's codelines contain a *built* module that stores the files created by nightly builds. There's no point in branching the *built* module from MAIN to REL2; the first nightly build in REL2 will create it.

We branch modules from MAIN, and only from MAIN. In other words, we won't be branching modules from development codelines or other release codelines directly into REL2. (This process normalizes the flow of change. It also makes it more likely that dependency problems will be caught *before* releases are branched.) These are the MAIN modules we'll branch into REL2:

//Ace/MAIN/db/…
   Source files for the database component of the product

//Ace/MAIN/gui/…
   Source files for the GUI component of the product

//Ace/MAIN/doc/…
   Files that contribute to the product's user documentation

//Ace/MAIN/tests/…
   Tests used to validate built components

//Ace/MAIN/utils/…
   Scripts and configuration files used for nightly builds and tests

A branch view for the release codeline

Now that we know which MAIN modules to branch into the REL2 codeline, let's create a branch view to keep track of them. In this case, we'll create a branch view named REL2-MAIN. The `branch` command creates a branch view:

```
p4 branch REL2-MAIN

Branch        REL2-MAIN
Description   Rel 2.X stabilization.
View          //Ace/REL2/db/...      //Ace/MAIN/db/...
              //Ace/REL2/doc/...     //Ace/MAIN/doc/...
              //Ace/REL2/gui/...     //Ace/MAIN/gui/...
              //Ace/REL2/tests/...   //Ace/MAIN/tests/...
              //Ace/REL2/utils/...   //Ace/MAIN/utils/...
```

Our REL2-MAIN branch view follows these conventions:

- The name of the branch view is of the form *childname-parentname*.
- A terse description shows the codeline's purpose. (It's terse so that the whole thing is visible in the output of the `branches` command.)
- The view is mapped "toward the mainline." (That is, the mainline's modules are listed on the righthand side of the mapping.)
- Each top-level module in the release codeline is represented by a line in the branch view.

Notice that thanks to our convention for naming and describing branch views, the `branches` command can tell us at a glance what we need to know about the REL2-MAIN branch view:

```
p4 branches
...
Branch REL2-MAIN 2004/11/10 'Rel 2.X stabilization.'
...
```

The master workspace

The master workspace serves both as a place for the curator to do maintenance tasks and as a template for creating developer workspaces. We use the `client` command to set up a master workspace called REL2-master:

```
p4 client REL2-master

Client    REL2-master
Root      /usr/relmgr/REL2
Options   locked
View      //Ace/REL2/db/...      //REL2-master/db/...
          //Ace/REL2/built/...   //REL2-master/built/...
          //Ace/REL2/doc/...     //REL2-master/doc/...
          //Ace/REL2/gui/...     //REL2-master/gui/...
          //Ace/REL2/tests/...   //REL2-master/tests/...
          //Ace/REL2/utils/...   //REL2-master/utils/...
```

This view puts the REL2 files in the */usr/relmgr/REL2* directory. The locked option ensures that only the workspace's owner can use it and change its parameters. (The owner of a workspace is the person who creates the client spec.) By explicitly mapping each of the codeline's modules in the view, we make it easier for developers to select the modules they'll need in their workspaces.

Are we branching the right files?

With a branch view created, and with REL2-master as our current workspace, we now check to make sure we'll be branching the right files. We use the integrate command to preview the branching operation:

```
p4 integ -n -r -b REL2-MAIN 1> tempfile1 2> tempfile2
```

(-n is the preview-only option, and -r reverses the branch view mapping.) *tempfile1* contains the list of files that will be branched. *tempfile2* contains error messages. We capture the output of this preview in temporary files, because it can be huge.

We check the preview output to make sure of the following:

- Target files are in view. We can confirm this by making sure there are no view errors captured in *tempfile2*. (See "Diagnosing View Errors," later in this chapter, if there are.)

- Target files are in the right depot location. (For this example, the target files are the files we're creating in the REL2 codeline.) A glance at *tempfile1* should confirm this—all the files listed in it should appear under the *//Ace/REL2* path.

- We're branching the modules we need. One way to check this is to do a quick count of the files in each of the modules we're interested in. On Unix, for example, we can do that with grep and wc:

```
grep //Ace/REL2/db/ tempfile1 | wc -l
      1483
grep //Ace/REL2/doc/ tempfile1 | wc -l
      5743
[... And so forth.]
```

A label view for the branch point

Next we create a REL2 label spec that identifies the MAIN modules that will be branched:

```
p4 label REL2
```

Label	REL2
Description	Branch from MAIN
View	//Ace/MAIN/db/...
	//Ace/MAIN/doc/...
	//Ace/MAIN/gui/...
	//Ace/MAIN/tests/...
	//Ace/MAIN/utils/...

By convention, the label name is the same as the codeline name. This label will be used to tag the branch point in MAIN, as you'll see in a moment. It also serves to document the scope of the REL2 codeline.

Diagnosing View Errors

`integrate`'s `no target files in both client and branch view` message can be caused by a number of problems:

- Once possibility is that *//Ace/REL2/*... is not within the client view of our current workspace. (Is the current workspace set to REL2-master? Could there be a typo in the REL2-master client view?)
- Perhaps `integrate`'s target is something other than *//Ace/REL2/*.... (A typo in the REL2-MAIN branch view, perhaps? Did we forget the `-r` on the `integrate` command?)
- Maybe depot protections hide *//Ace/MAIN/*... or *//Ace/REL2/*... from our view. (See Chapter 6.)

Remember that `integrate` always cites the *donor* filespec in view errors, even when it's the *target* filespec that's the problem.

Labeling the branch point

In the ideal world, all the modules we need would be ready for us to branch as is. In a more realistic scenario, we'd probably find ourselves branching some modules from specific points in the mainline's evolution. This is where the branch point label comes in handy. We check with each of the developers involved, and as we find out what versions of their modules to branch, we tag them with the REL2 label:

- MAIN's *doc* and *utils* modules are good to go as of right now. We tag their head revisions with the REL2 label:

  ```
  p4 tag -l REL2 //Ace/MAIN/doc/... //Ace/MAIN/utils/...
  ```

- We are informed that the *db* module should be branched at changelist 6590. We tag MAIN's *db* module accordingly:

  ```
  p4 tag -l REL2 //Ace/MAIN/db/...@6590
  ```

- The *gui* module should be branched as of @6595:

  ```
  p4 tag -l REL2 //Ace/MAIN/gui/...@6595
  ```

- The *tests* module is, in fact, not *quite* ready to branch yet. So we don't tag it now. (We've contrived this situation to demonstrate that everything doesn't have to be tagged and branched at once. We'll come back to *tests* later.)

Creating the release codeline — really!

We've set up a branch view, a master workspace, and a branch point label. Finally, we are ready to actually branch MAIN's files and submit them into our new release codeline. It's quite simple now:

```
p4 integ -r -b REL2-MAIN @REL2
p4 submit
```

(The -b flag tells integ to use the branch view to determine donor and target paths. The -r flag tells it to use the branch view's mappings in reverse. @REL2 is the label that tells integ what revision of the donor files to branch.)

Once we've done this, the new REL2 codeline is ready to use. Developers can synchronize their workspaces with it and stabilization of the release can commence.

Branching more files later

Wait—remember the *tests* module that wasn't ready to branch? A few days later we hear from the developer that as of changelist 6608, *tests* is finally ready to go. It's easy to branch this straggler into the new codeline now. First we tag the module in MAIN:

```
p4 tag -l REL2 //Ace/MAIN/tests/...@6608
```

Then we branch the module. We can use exactly the same integrate command as before. Since the @REL2 versions of the other modules are already branched, this operates only on the as-yet unbranched tests module:

```
p4 integ -r -b REL2-MAIN @REL2
p4 submit
```

Working in a Release Codeline

The release codeline exists in order to perfect already-developed software. It is typically used to test thoroughly, fix bugs, finalize installers and documentation, and generally tie up loose ends. Although these things may involve changes to program source files, these are small changes—no refactoring, and no changes to intended functionality. What all this adds up to is that development in the release codeline is a matter of close collaboration between coders, tech writers, testers, the build czar, and the release manager.

Now, if you'll take off your codeline curator hat and put on your software developer hat, we'll talk about points pertinent to working in a release codeline.

The developer's workspace

The people working on releases are on very tight schedules, and release codelines are held to high levels of quality. In the grand scheme of things, release codelines are at the top of the tofu scale. You, as a developer, don't want to be the one to throw a wrench in the works by checking in mismatched files or untested changes. You can reduce the chance of that happening by dedicating a workspace to release stabilization work.

To work on stabilizing REL2, for example, set up a workspace dedicated to working in REL2. You can use the REL2-master workspace as a template, as we'll see in a moment. This gives your workspace a view that encompasses all the REL2 modules you'll need on disk in order to build and test your changes.

For example, Sue is going to create a workspace called REL2-sue for her REL2 bug fixes. Sue is working on Unix; the workspace will be rooted in her */usr/team/sue/ REL2* directory. Of the modules in the REL2 codeline, Sue needs only the *doc* and *utils* modules on disk for her work.

Sue creates a client spec using the REL2-master workspace as a template. The `client` command gives her a spec form to edit. The form comes prefilled with a list of REL2 modules in its View field. She edits the form, entering her workspace root and removing the view lines for the modules she doesn't need:

```
p4 client -t REL2-master REL2-sue

Client        REL2-sue
Root          /usr/team/sue/REL2
View          //Ace/REL2/doc/...      //REL2-sue/doc/...
              //Ace/REL2/utils/...    //REL2-sue/utils/...
```

After saving the spec form and setting REL2-sue as her current workspace, Sue synchronizes the workspace:

```
p4 sync
```

Sue's */usr/team/sue/REL2* directory now contains the files she needs to work on the REL2 codeline.

As a developer, it's important to keep your workspace up to date when working in a release codeline. For one thing, there can be dependencies between your changes and the changes recently submitted by other developers. You'll want to find out what they are before you submit your changes, not after.

Another reason is that any tests you run are really valid only in a completely up-to-date workspace. You can certainly remain synchronized with an earlier point in time while you're still debugging, but once you've found the bug, resynchronize so you're not testing with stale code.

You may recall reading in Chapter 3 that it's a good idea to synchronize your workspace with new changes incrementally. If you resynchronize frequently, you are in effect synchronizing incrementally.

What to document in the change descriptions

When you're checking in a change to a release branch, you should write a change description that helps everyone working on the release understand the impact of your change. For example:

- Did you make a user-visible change? People working on user documentation and release notes will need to know this.

- Did you change any program interfaces? Other programmers will need to know.

- Did you add a test for your change? How do you know your change is working as expected? Testers will need this information to confirm that your change is in the build.

- Did you rename, move, or delete any files? (Hopefully not—this is a release branch, not a development branch!) The REL2 curator will need to know about this in order to update the REL2-MAIN branch view. (See "Keeping the branch view up to date," later in this chapter.)

Fixing a bug? Fix a job!

In Chapter 5 you read about using *jobs* for bug tracking. Most work done in a release codeline is to fix bugs. If you're using jobs to track bugs, make sure you link jobs to your release codeline changes.

For example, Sue's working on the bug described by job016551:

```
Job            job016551
Description    Diagram 8.1 in DBA Guide has unreadable text.
```

She's made a local change to fix the bug. Now she submits her change, and as she fills out the changelist form she enters *job016551* in the Jobs field:*

```
p4 submit

Change         new
User           sue
Description    Clearer flow diagram for the database re-org section.
...
Jobs           job016551

Change 8847 submitted.
```

---

* The job may already be listed in the changelist form. See Chapter 5.

Now her change is associated with the job. Perforce automatically changes the job's status to closed when the changelist is submitted.

It's no big deal to forget to enter a job in a changelist form. Jobs can be linked to changelists after the fact. For example, to link job016551 to changelist 8847:

```
p4 fix -c 8847 job016551
```

What if I can't check in a change?

You can find yourself in a Catch-22 situation working in a release codeline: you know that you can check in changes only if they're tested and proven correct. But what if testing a change fully means you have to test it on other machines? You can't get your change onto other machines unless you've checked it in, and you can't check it in because you haven't tested it.

Do not despair—you can check your change into an ad hoc task branch first. Then, once you've validated your change, you can pull it into the release branch. You'll see how to do this later in the chapter in "Task Branches and Patch Branches."

Keeping the branch view up to date

While developers are working in the release codeline, the codeline curator makes sure the branch view stays up to date. Let's step back into our codeline curator role and see what this entails.

The REL2-MAIN branch view, as you recall, is used to map release codeline files to corresponding mainline files. Over time, the structure of the mainline may change. We'll have to update the branch view from time to time to reconcile the old file structure in the release codeline with the new file structure in the mainline. In other words, when files in MAIN are renamed, moved, added, or deleted, we'll have to update the REL2-MAIN branch view. This will make it fairly painless for developers working in REL2 to integrate their changes into MAIN.

To update the branch view:

1. We look for any changes that have occured in MAIN since the branch point. The easiest way to do this is to list descriptions of the MAIN changes that aren't accounted for in REL2:

   ```
   p4 interchanges -l -r -b REL2-MAIN > tempfile
   ```

   (The -l option causes changelist full descriptions to be output. The -r and -b flags behave the same for interchanges as they do for integrate.)

   The output is piped to a temporary file because it could be large.

2. We skim through the temporary file looking for evidence of renamed, moved, or deleted files. If developers have been good about documenting them, the structural changes we need to know about will be evident. For example:

```
Change 8845 on 2004/10/11 by bill
    New test driver for DB procedures.
    Slight reorg of test directories so that...
    ...
    MOVED: db/proc/td/... => tests/db/proc/td/...
    ...
Change 8849 on 2004/10/19 by bob
    Fixed icon name conflict.
    RENAMED: gui/img/spin.png => gui/img/sp.png
    ...
Change 8850 on 2004/10/19 by sue
    Got rid of old setupApp, now that the installer is
    working.
    ...
    DELETED: db/setup/...
    ...
Change 8859 on 2004/10/20 by tim
    Consolidate color preferences.
    ...
    Nothing renamed, moved, or deleted. Relax.
```

3. We add lines to the REL2-MAIN branch view to reconcile these structural changes. (For more details on how and why to do this, see Chapter 4.)

   For example:

   p4 branch REL2-MAIN

   ```
   View     //Ace/REL2/db/...           //Ace/MAIN/db/...
            //Ace/REL2/doc/...          //Ace/MAIN/doc/...
            //Ace/REL2/gui/...          //Ace/MAIN/gui/...
            //Ace/REL2/tests/...        //Ace/MAIN/tests/...
            //Ace/REL2/utils/...        //Ace/MAIN/utils/...
            //Ace/REL2/db/proc/td/...   //Ace/MAIN/tests/db/proc/td/...
            //Ace/REL2/gui/img/spin.png //Ace/MAIN/gui/img/sp.png
           -//Ace/REL2/db/setup/...     //Ace/MAIN/db/setup/...
   ```

   The last three lines map the old structure in the REL2 codeline with the new structure in MAIN.

4. Finally, we add a comment to the branch view description to record the version of MAIN for which we've adjusted the mapping:

   p4 branch REL2-MAIN

   ```
   Description  Rel 2.X stabilization.
                Adjusted for MAIN/...@8859.
   ```

We may have to repeat this sequence of steps from time to time as the mainline evolves. By entering a changelist number in the description, we're leaving ourselves a breadcrumb for the next time we update the branch view. We can use the last-recorded changelist number to make the interchanges command skip past the changes we've already seen. The next time we repeat this procedure, for example, we'll start with:

```
p4 interchanges -l -r -b REL2-MAIN "@>8859" > tempfile
```

(The revision @>8859 means the next revision after @8859.* It's in quotes so that the command shell doesn't trip on the > symbol.)

Integrating Changes into the Mainline

Developers, you're not off the hook once you've submitted bug fixes to the release codeline. Your changes need to be integrated from the release codeline into its parent. In this section we take a look at what you need to know and do to integrate your changes.

Which changes should be integrated?

All changes in the release codeline should be integrated into the mainline. This step is almost always safe, because release codelines are inherently more stable than their parents. When it's not safe is when the mainline has evolved so much since the release was made that massive architectural differences make it difficult or impossible to merge files. In "How much has the mainline changed?" a bit later in the chapter we'll look at how to gauge the feasibility of an impending integration.

Even when a release codeline change has no relevance to the mainline—it updates release-specific configuration files, for example—it should be integrated into the mainline. It can be resolved by ignoring the change. As you read in Chapter 4, this creates integration history that shows that the change has been at least accounted for, if not actually merged, in the mainline.

When should changes be integrated?

Ideally, changes should be integrated into the mainline as they occur. In practice, there's always an interval of uncertainty between the time a change is submitted to a release codeline and the point at which it's proved valid. The reality is that each change should be integrated as soon as it's validated.

Who does the integration?

The best person to integrate a change into the mainline is the person who made the change in the release. Why? Because the person who made the change understands the content of the files involved. If there are any conflicts to resolve, he or she will know how to resolve them. If there are problems with compiling or testing, he or she will know how to fix them.

---

* The > syntax is undocumented; see p4 help undoc for information about it.

A workspace for integrating into MAIN

To integrate your changes to the parent codeline, you'll need a workspace with a view of the parent codeline. The procedure shown in "The developer's workspace," earlier in this chapter, works to set up a workspace for the parent codeline as well. Sue, for example, sets up her MAIN-sue workspace as follows:

```
p4 client -t MAIN-master MAIN-sue
```

Client	MAIN-sue
Root	/usr/team/sue/MAIN
View	//Ace/MAIN/doc/... //MAIN-sue/doc/...
	//Ace/MAIN/utils/... //MAIN-sue/utils/...

With this view, the *//Ace/MAIN* files will go in Sue's */usr/team/sue/MAIN* directory. (And if you compare the MAIN-sue view to the MAIN-master view shown in Chapter 8, you'll see that Sue has again removed mappings for the modules not needed in her workspace.)

Finding unintegrated changes

As a developer, you'll be pulling your own changes into the parent codeline, by changelist number. If you're not sure which changes you submitted, you can check the history of the release codeline. For example, Sue checks REL2's history with:

```
p4 changes -u sue //Ace/REL2/...
Change 8847 by sue  "Clearer flow diagram for..."
```

(The -u sue flag makes changes list only Sue's changes.) Sue recognizes 8847 as the change she needs to integrate into MAIN.

It's also important to know how many changes are queued for integration and where your change fits in. The interchanges command can show queued changes; use it with the release codeline's branch view. For example, to see the changes in REL2 that are queued for integration into MAIN:

```
p4 interchanges -b REL2-MAIN
Change 8843 by jim  "Fix installer permission..."
Change 8847 by sue  "Clearer flow diagram for..."
Change 8862 by ann  "Fixed password errors in..."
```

Ideally, changes should be integrated incrementally, in order. The preceding example shows that the next REL2 change in line for integration into MAIN is change 8843, and Jim's the one who should do the integration. After that, Sue should integrate 8847, then Ann should integrate 8862.

You can also look for unintegrated changes in individual modules. For example, to find unintegrated *doc* changes:

```
p4 interchanges -b REL2-MAIN //Ace/MAIN/doc/...
Change 8847 by sue  "Clearer flow diagram for..."
```

When it's okay to integrate changes out of order

One reason that changes should be integrated in order is so that no integration brings along with it any part of a previous change that has not yet been integrated. As long as changes are integrated in order, this won't happen.

However, it doesn't hurt to integrate a change out of order if it has no dependencies on any previous changes. As it happens, Sue's change 8847 corrects some documentation. Sue knows that the documentation module is completely independent of the other modules. She can go ahead and integrate her change, even though Jim has not yet integrated his.

Hidden Dependencies Between Changes

Sometimes change dependencies are obvious: if change 100 affects file A and change 101 affects file A, change 101 is clearly dependent on change 100. Unless you integrate change 100 first, you'll probably break something having to do with file A.

But change dependencies can also be caused by file dependencies. Say change 100 affects file A and change 101 affects file B: if file B depends on file A, change 101 depends on change 100. Unless you integrate change 100 first, you'll probably break something having to do with files A *and* B.

Your best bet is to integrate changes in order unless you're absolutely sure they have no hidden dependencies.

Integrating a change

Sue's going to go ahead and integrate change 8847 from REL2 into MAIN. She's using the MAIN-sue workspace for this. Here's what she does:

1. She makes sure she currently has no files opened in her workspace:

   ```
   p4 opened
   File(s) not opened on this client.
   ```

2. She synchronizes her workspace with the current MAIN codeline:

   ```
   p4 sync
   ```

   This fills her workspace with the latest *doc* and *utils* files from MAIN. (The modules *doc* and *utils* are the only modules mapped in her workspace view.)

3. She checks to make sure all the *doc* changes *prior* to 8847 are already integrated from REL2 into MAIN:

   ```
   p4 integ -n -b REL2-MAIN "//Ace/MAIN/doc/...@<8847"
   //Ace/MAIN/doc/...@<8847 - all revisions already integrated.
   ```

(The -n is integ's preview only flag. The -b flag selects the REL2-MAIN branch view to use for this command. The @<8847 syntax means all changes up to but not including 8847.)

4. She integrates her change:

```
p4 integ -b REL2-MAIN //Ace/MAIN/doc/...@8847
```

This integ command opens *//Ace/MAIN/doc* files in her workspace.

5. She resolves the opened files:

```
p4 resolve
```

This command either copies or merges REL2 files into her workspace, depending on how she answered the resolve prompts.

6. Finally, she submits her change:

```
p4 submit
```

Her REL2 change is now in the MAIN codeline.

How much has the mainline changed?

While the release is being stabilized, the mainline continues to evolve. Sue's change was easy to integrate because MAIN had not evolved much since REL2 was branched from it.

If the mainline has evolved in leaps and bounds—or if it's been a long time since the release was branched—you may want to find out how much the mainline has changed. This can give you some insight into how hard it's going to be to integrate a change into it from the release codeline. (It can also tell you whether your release change is even relevant in the evolved mainline.)

There are several things you can do to gauge how much the mainline has changed. One is to simply see how many changes have been submitted to the mainline since it was branched into REL2. The interchanges command can tell you this:

```
p4 interchanges -r -b REL2-MAIN
```

Because interchanges uses the branch view, it's reporting only the changes that are relevant to the modules in the release. (Note the use of -r—that's the flag that tells interchanges to apply the branch view in reverse.)

Another is to preview the integrate command for the change you're going to integrate. For example, if you're integrating change 8843 from REL2 to MAIN, you can get a preview with:

```
p4 integ -n -b REL2-MAIN @8843
...
//Ace/MAIN/db/dbPg.cpp - branch/sync from
    //Ace/REL2/db/dbPg.cpp#4,#5
//Ace/MAIN/db/dbPgLoad.cpp - can't branch from
    //Ace/REL2/db/dbPgLoad.cpp#2 without -d or -Dt flag
...
```

Warnings like these—branch/sync from and can't branch from—tell you that files in MAIN have been renamed, moved, or deleted since REL2 was branched. These structural changes should have been reconciled in the REL2-MAIN branch view, but it's possible that the branch view is not being kept up to date. (Put on your codeline curator hat again and see "Keeping the branch view up to date," earlier in this chapter.)

You can also gauge divergence between codelines with the diff2 command. For example:

```
p4 diff2 -b REL2-MAIN > tempfile
```

It's a good idea to pipe diff2's output to a temporary file—the further MAIN has diverged from REL2, the larger its output will be.

Making a Release

Once a release codeline is stabilized—or stable enough, at any rate—we can make the release. ("We," in this context, refers to the release manager and release codeline curator.)

Building the release

The release should be built from a contemporaneous snapshot of the release codeline. In other words, the files that contribute to the release should be the head revisions as of a known point in time. Moreover, they should all come from the release codeline. (Mixing and matching codelines to build a release just invites confusion.)

A known point in time in Perforce equates to a changelist number, of course. The changelist number that identifies the snapshot of our first release out the REL2 codeline is 8901, as shown in Figure 9-1.

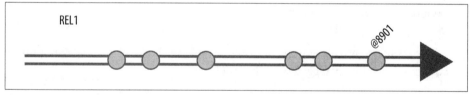

Figure 9-1. The release snapshot

The filespec *//Ace/REL2/…@8901* is the comprehensive, permanent, and unambiguous reference to the files that went into the release.

Labeling the release

It's not entirely necessary to label a release, but labels do have their advantages. For one thing, they have recognizable names, whereas changelist numbers don't. A label can be used to associate an external release identifier with a filespec.

The release we're making happens to be known to the rest of Ace Engineering as AcePack_2.0-Beta. To label our new release, we run:

```
p4 tag -l AcePack_2.0-Beta //Ace/REL2/...@8901
```

The revision @*AcePack_2.0-Beta* can now be used in place of a changelist number to identify files in the release (see Figure 9-2).

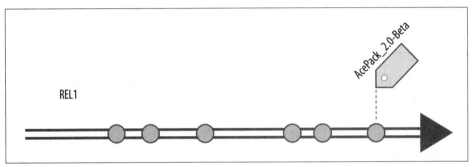

Figure 9-2. The release label

For our own reference, we can note the release point in the label description. We use the `label` command to bring up the label spec form, note the release snapshot changelist number in the Description field, and enter the release codeline's filespec in the View field:

```
p4 label AcePack_2.0-Beta
```

Label	AcePack_2.0-Beta
Description	Built from @8901
View	//Ace/REL2/...

This step is for documentary purposes only; changing the label spec does not affect the configuration already tagged with the label.

Making point releases

Having made a release is no guarantee that our bug fixing and release stabilization work is done. Au contraire—we're likely to get more bug reports than ever now. The release codeline will continue to be the venue for fixing bugs in the release. Eventually, we'll have a point release ready to produce from the same codeline.

For example, after producing the beta release from REL2, bugs have been fixed and minor improvements have been made. We're now ready to make the first production release from the REL2 codeline. AcePack 2.1, as it will be called, will essentially be a point release.

A Point Release by Any Other Name...

The term *point release* originates from a style of release numbering that is composed of a major version, a feature release, and a point release. For instance, V4.1.3 indicates a fourth major version, the first feature set based on it, and the third time the 4.1 release has been rebuilt after bug fixes.

With Perforce, you don't really have to number your point releases. You can simply use codeline names and changelist numbers instead. For example, REL2.8901 identifies the release built out of the *@8901* version of the REL2 codeline.

Making a point release is not really any different than making the initial release. We'll need to build from a new snapshot, identify the snapshot filespec, and label the snapshot.

In this case, say the new snapshot is *//Ace/REL2/...@9615* and that it's labeled AcePack_2.1. Now we have two release points in the REL2 codeline, as shown in Figure 9-3.

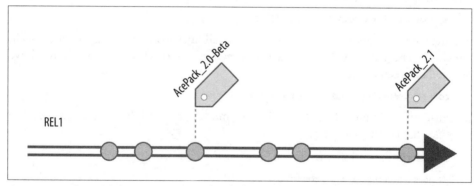

Figure 9-3. Release labels in REL2

The `labels` command, by the way, gives us a nice resume of our release codeline's accomplishments:

```
p4 labels //Ace/REL2/...
Label REL2              2004/11/10 Branch from MAIN
Label AcePack_2.0-Beta  2004/12/10 Built from @8901
Label AcePack_2.1       2005/01/09 Built from @9615
```

Generating release note information

In order to write release notes, we'll need to know which changes have gone into a release. If we're using jobs to track bugs and enhancement requests, we'll need to know what jobs were fixed in a release. These things are easy to determine with Perforce and filtering scripts.

As you know, changes can list changes in the history of a particular set of files. The exhaustive list of changes that have gone into the *//Ace/REL2* files, for example, can be generated with:

```
p4 changes -i //Ace/REL2/...
```

(The -i option causes changes to include changes inherited by branching and integration.) This list of changes will be huge, of course—too huge to be of much use for release notes, because it includes every change made since development began on the product. What we really need to know is what has changed in the interval between two releases.

For example, let's say that the last release notes we wrote were for the AcePack 1.3 release. That release was built out of the REL1 codeline and labeled AcePack_1.3. Now we are working on release notes for the upcoming 2.1 release, built out of REL2 and labeled AcePack_2.1.

First, we list the previous release's changes in *tempfile1*:

```
p4 changes -i @AcePack_1.3 > tempfile1
```

Next, we list the current release's changes in *tempfile2*:

```
p4 changes -i @AcePack_2.1 > tempfile2
```

Finally, with the handy comm* filter, we remove all lines from *tempfile2* that are also in *tempfile1*. The result, which we save in *tempfile3*, is the list of changes that have occured between the two releases:

```
comm -3 tempfile1 tempfile2 > tempfile3
```

(Because we've adhered to the mainline model, we can be confident that the *tempfile1* list is a subset of *tempfile2*.)

We can do the same thing with jobs:

```
p4 jobs -i @AcePack_1.3 > tempfile4
p4 jobs -i @AcePack_2.1 > tempfile5
comm -3 tempfile4 tempfile5 > tempfile6
```

tempfile6 contains the list of job fixes that occured between the two releases. (Be sure to read Chapter 8 for more on labeling releases.)

---

* comm is a program that compares lists. It comes with Unix; several Windows toolkits offer it as well.

Distributing Releases

At Ace Engineering, software is distributed to customers via FTP—the software is put on an external FTP site; customers use FTP to download it. The FTP site is simply a Perforce workspace kept constantly synchronized with the DIST codeline in the Ace's depot.

The DIST codeline is Ace's distribution stream. Its sole purpose is to control the software currently available to customers. Distributing a release at Ace Engineering, therefore, is a matter of copying built components from release codelines to the distribution stream. In the depot, Ace's distribution stream is in the *//Ace/DIST* path.

From release codeline to distribution stream

At this point, software in our REL2 codeline has been stabilized, finalized, built, and tagged with the AcePack_2.1 label. (By "built" we mean that all of the built components have been checked in to the release codeline itself.) At Ace, built files and installable objects are contained in the *built* module of each codeline. Of these, the files we'll be delivering to the distribution stream are:

```
//Ace/REL2/built/bin/win32/ap.zip
//Ace/REL2/built/bin/linux/ap.tar
```

These files will be copied from *//Ace/REL2/built* to *//Ace/DIST/AcePack* into files whose names identify the release. This is normally done by a script controlled by the release engineer, but for illustration, we'll do it manually.

Since we're going to be submitting files into the DIST codeline, we'll have to use a client workspace whose view includes the *//Ace/DIST* path. We've got that set up here, using a workspace called DIST-update:

```
Client        DIST-update
View          //Ace/DIST/...   //DIST-update/...
```

Now, using the DIST-update workspace, we copy the necessary files, using the AcePack_2.1 label to make sure we get the right ones:

```
p4 integ -d \
   //Ace/REL2/built/bin/win32/ap.zip@AcePack_2.1 \
   //Ace/DIST/AcePack/bin/win32/ap2.1.zip
p4 integ -d \
   //Ace/REL2/built/bin/linux/ap.tar@AcePack_2.1 \
   //Ace/DIST/AcePack/bin/linux/ap2.1.tar
p4 resolve -at
p4 submit
```

(We use -d with integrate in case we're replacing files previously deleted from the distribution stream. The -at flag on resolve is what makes this a copy, not a merge.) This is a lot of typing, of course, which is why the release manager uses a script to do it.

And that's that—our release is now in the distribution stream.

From distribution stream to FTP site

Ace Engineering's external FTP site resides on a Unix machine named zippy, in the */etc/ftp* directory. An FTP server running on zippy fields user requests for the files in the */etc/ftp* path.

However, the */etc/ftp* directory is not only the FTP site; it's the root of a Perforce client workspace called DIST-zippy:

Client	DIST-zippy
Host	zippy
Root	/etc/ftp
View	//Ace/DIST/... //DIST-zippy/...

As you can see, the DIST-zippy workspace has a view of the DIST codeline. A "sync daemon" program running on zippy synchronizes the workspace every five minutes using this familiar command:

p4 sync

This effectively fills the FTP site with the latest released software. As new releases appear in the DIST codeline, there's at most a five-minute delay before customers can download them.

Oops, we released the wrong build!

At Ace, releasing the wrong build is never an irreparable problem. If the wrong files are integrated to the distribution stream, there are a number of ways to recover:

- If there's a newer, more correct file in the release codeline, it can be copy-integrated into the distribution stream, replacing the version that was there. (To "copy-integrate" is to integrate, then resolve files by copying. See Chapter 4.) This causes the sync daemon to refresh the FTP site with the newer version.

- If a previous version in the distribution stream was correct but the current one isn't, the current one can be backed out. (See Chapter 2.) This causes the sync daemon to refresh the FTP site with the correct version.

- If it turns out there is no version ready to release, the errant files in the distribution stream can be deleted. This causes the sync daemon to remove them from the FTP site.

Using P4FTP as a sync daemon

By coincidence, the program that Ace uses as a sync daemon is P4FTP, the Perforce FTP Plug-in. (It's a coincidence in that P4FTP is not used for FTP in this case. P4FTP allows only Perforce users to connect, and Ace's external customers are not Perforce users—not in Ace's Perforce domain, at any rate.)

P4FTP can be configured to keep a specified workspace synchronized at specified intervals. At Ace, P4FTP was configured as zippy's sync daemon by starting it up thus:

```
p4ftpd -O autosync -c DIST-zippy -p ace:1666 -u auto-user
```

(DIST-zippy is the name of the workspace to synchronize, ace:1666 is Ace's Perforce Server address, and auto-user is the Perforce username designated for background processes.[*])

Breaking the Rules

Despite the most meticulous planning, we occasionally have no choice but to defy the rules of the codeline road. In this section we'll look at two ways to break the rule that says change does not flow to a release codeline from its parent.

Backporting a bug fix

When you're supporting several releases at once, you may find yourself in a situation where a bug fix made in one release has to be backported to another. For example, Jody, of Ace Engineering's QA team, has detected a subtle but severe data-corrupting bug during stabilization of the REL2 codeline. Ann, a developer responsible for the module in which the bug was found, fixed the bug in REL2 with changelist 8896. She then merged her fix to MAIN, using the procedure previously described in "Integrating Changes into the Mainline," earlier in this chapter. Change 8904 is the point at which REL2's change 8896 was incrementally integrated into MAIN. (The fact that the change was integrated incrementally is what's going to make this bug fix easy to backport.)

Jody now tests the currently available release, AcePack 1.3. She finds that it too is affected by the bug, although the problem had not been detected before. The bug is serious enough to merit a 1.3.1 point release. For this, the bug fix is going to have to be backported into the REL1 codeline. This action requires cherry-picking a change, either 8896 from REL2 or 8904 from MAIN, and integrating it into REL1, as shown in Figure 9-4.

Backporting either change will do the job, but integrating from MAIN to REL1 will be easier than integrating from REL2 to REL1. Why? Because at Ace, every release codeline has a branch view that reconciles its structure with its evolving parent codeline. (All the branch views follow the conventions described earlier in the chapter in "A branch view for the release codeline" and "Keeping the branch view up to date.") Because REL1 was branched from MAIN, there's a REL1-MAIN branch view. But there is no branch view that reconciles REL1's old structure with REL2's newer structure.

---

[*] By the way, you can get your Perforce license extended to cover a background user for free. Contact Perforce Software for more information.

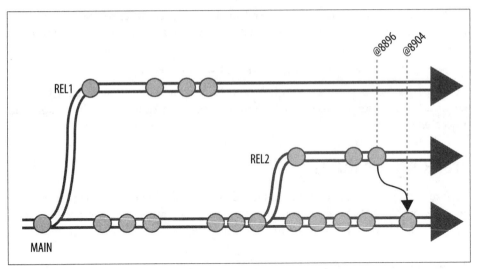

Figure 9-4. Choosing the change to backport

So, Ann chooses to integrate the bug fix from MAIN to REL1. In a workspace with a view of the REL1 codeline, she uses these commands:

```
p4 integ -b REL1-MAIN -r @8904,@8904
p4 resolve
p4 submit
```

(The -b flag causes integrate to refer to the REL1-MAIN branch view for the donor and target paths. By convention, REL1-MAIN maps toward the mainline, so the -r flag is used to reverse it. The revision range @8904,@8904 cherry-picks the bug fix change for integration.)

Note that it was Ann, not Jody, who backported the change. The comands are simple, but the resolve step may have required merging files. Ann, having made the original change, was best prepared to do the merging. Between the resolve step and the submit step, Ann took the opportunity to compile and test the result of the change in her workspace.

The effect of backporting change 8904 to REL1 is illustrated in Figure 9-5.

Pulling late-breaking development into a release

Missed deadlines can also put us in a position of having to bend the rules of the codeline road. Say, for example, that when the REL2 codeline was branched from the mainline, a certain feature wasn't ready. Its developers missed the deadline and the feature was deferred to a later release. Sometime later, the feature is finally finished and the decision is made to include it in the next REL2 release after all.

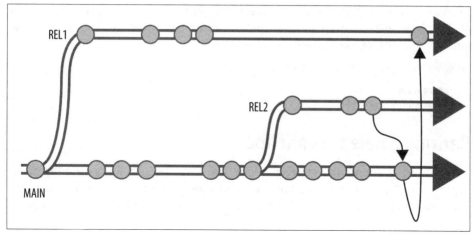

Figure 9-5. Backporting a change

Pulling late-breaking features into a release codeline isn't hard. In fact, it's often quite easy. The hard part is accepting the risk that it involves and understanding that it invalidates any testing done so far in the release codeline. In other words, pulling new development into a release resets the clock on the release stabilization schedule.

At any rate, we've reluctantly agreed to pull the late-breaking feature into the REL2 codeline. The feature, which involves the *gui* module, has just been integrated into MAIN from a development codeline. Revision *@6701* of MAIN's *gui* module contains the new feature. Now we are being entreated to pull this module into REL2 so that it can be part of the upcoming release.

If developers have been good about merging their REL2 bug fixes into MAIN, it should be trivial to pull MAIN's *gui* module into REL2. That is, there should be no merging involved, because every change in REL2 is already accounted for in MAIN. (Whether MAIN's *gui* is compatible with REL2's other modules is a different question entirely. We'll assume it is.)

At any rate, we can pull in the new feature by integrating revision *@6701* of MAIN's *gui* module into REL2. We do this using the REL2-master workspace. Before integrating, we make sure the workspace has no opened files and that it is synchronized with the latest REL2 files:

```
p4 opened
File(s) not opened on this client.
```

```
p4 sync //Ace/REL2/...
//Ace/REL2/... - file(s) up-to-date.
```

To integrate the *gui* module from MAIN into REL2 we run:

```
p4 integ -r -b REL2-MAIN //Ace/REL2/gui/...@6701
```

(Note the overloaded syntax. Although it looks like we're refering to revision @6701 of REL2's *gui* here, @6701 actually applies to the *gui* in MAIN. See "The curious syntax of the integrate command" in Chapter 4.)

Now we resolve and submit the opened files:

```
p4 resolve
p4 submit
```

Retiring a Release Codeline

As you read in Chapter 8, you can retire a codeline by setting protections on its depot path. Before doing that, however, you should make sure that no one's currently working in the codeline, and that all of its changes have been merged into its parent.

Who's still working in a release codeline?

Before retiring a release codeline, make sure that none of its files are checked out. For example, to see if any of REL1's files are still checked out:

```
p4 opened -a //Ace/REL1/...
```

(The -a flag extends opened's scope to files outside the current workspace.) You should contact these developers and let them know you're retiring the codeline. Once you set protections on REL1, they won't be able to check in their changes.

Are all changes integrated?

If you plan to use protections to hide a release codeline from view, you'll first have to make sure that all changes are integrated from it into its parent. Once you hide it from view, you won't be able to integrate changes from it. To see which of REL1's changes still need integrating into MAIN, use:

```
p4 interchanges -r -b REL1-MAIN
```

Any changes listed should be integrated before you set protections that hide REL1 from view. See "Integrating Changes into the Mainline," earlier in this chapter.

Setting protections to prevent changes

To prevent developers from submitting changes to a release codeline, restrict permission to read on the codeline's depot path. (Recall that you use the protect command to do this. See Chapter 6.) For example, to set read permission on REL1:

```
p4 protect

Protections       ...
                  read  user  *   *   //Ace/REL1/...
                  ...
```

This step prevents people from opening files in the *//Ace/REL1* path. It doesn't prevent them from seeing the files, synchronizing with them, or branching from them, however.

Setting protections to hide a retired codeline

There are a couple of reasons you might want to hide retired codelines altogether. One is that they'll show up in GUI file trees—the more retired codelines there are, the clumsier it becomes to navigate a file tree. The other reason is that the Perforce Server does less work if retired codelines are hidden from commands that scan the database.

You can hide a codeline from view by revoking list permission on it. Better yet, instead of revoking it, restrict the permission to a group no one is in. That way, anyone who does have a sudden need to see the codeline can be simply added to the group.

For example, to make the REL1 codeline visible to only the people in the archeology group, define access to it with this single line:

```
p4 protect

Protections    ...
               read   group   archeology   *   //Ace/REL1/...
               ...
```

Later, if Doug, say, has a burning need to poke around in the REL1 codeline, just create or modify the archeology group and make sure Doug's username is in the list:

```
p4 group archeology

Group    archeology
Users    ...
         doug
         ...
```

Annotating a release codeline's branch and label views

Finally, you can note a release codeline's retirement in the Description field of its branch and label views. (This is just for documentation—it has no effect on Perforce behavior.) For example:

```
p4 branch REL1-MAIN

Branch         REL1-MAIN
Description    **Retired**
               Rel 1.X stabilization.
```

```
p4 label REL1

Label          REL1
Description    **Retired**
               Branch from MAIN
```

Putting the word *retired* in the beginning of the descriptions ensures that it will appear in the terse output of the labels and branches commands:

```
p4 branches
...
Branch REL1-MAIN ... ** Retired ** Rel 1.X ...
Branch REL2-MAIN ... Rel 2.X stabilization ...
...
```

Task Branches and Patch Branches

As you read in Chapter 7, release codelines can themselves be branched. For example, a release codeline can be branched into a task branch to isolate a risky bug fix. Or, to patch an already-released version, a release branch can be branched into a patch branch. Task branches and patch branches have the following in common:

- Only a few files are actually changed.
- No structural changes are involved.

It often makes sense to implement task branches and patch branches as *sparse branches*. A sparse branch contains only a handful of files rather than a full complement of modules. To work in a sparse branch, you use a workspace client view to *overlay* the branch onto its parent codeline. You branch files as needed, instead of all at once at the outset. We'll look at how to do this in the subsections that follow.

Creating a task branch

A task branch is simply a short-lived, single-user codeline dedicated to a specific development task. Task branches are often used for fixing bugs in codelines too firm to allow developers to check in changes directly. As a developer, you create a task branch by branching the parent codeline; you make your changes in the task branch. This gives you a place to check in changes without affecting the parent directly, while giving reviewers a way to see what you have done. After your changes are approved, you can integrate them into the parent codeline.

For example, say Rob is fixing an AcePack bug known as BUG0422. The bug affects AcePack's database component. The fix will eventually go in the REL2 codeline, but Rob's going to submit it to a task branch first. Dee maintains the AcePack database code in released products. She will review Rob's fix, and if it passes muster, she'll integrate it into REL2.

At Ace Engineering, task branches are named after bugs. Rob's task branch will be called BUG0422; it will be located in *//Ace/BUG0422*. Figure 9-6 shows the timeline of the BUG0422 branch. It's very short.

Figure 9-7 shows the intended flow of change between the task branch and its parent, the release codeline.

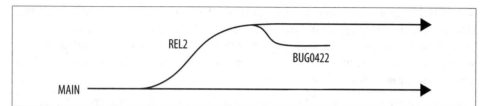

Figure 9-6. Timeline of a task branch

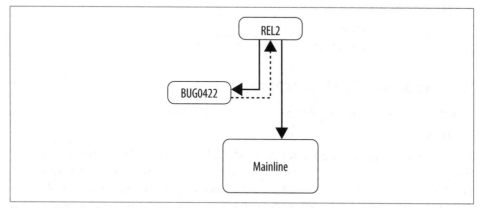

Figure 9-7. Flow of change between a task branch and its parent

In both Figure 9-6 and Figure 9-7, you'll notice, the task branch appears *below* the release codeline. That's because it's the softer of the two codelines.

The first thing Rob does is create a workspace for his bug fix. He's going to name the workspace BUG0422-rob; it will be rooted in the *c:\bugfix* directory on his local machine. (Rob's working on a Windows machine.) He creates his workspace client spec using the REL2-master workspace (shown in "The master workspace," earlier in this chapter) as a template:

```
p4 client -t REL2-master BUG0422-rob
```

Client	BUG0422-rob	
Root	c:\bugfix	
View	//Ace/REL2/db/...	//BUG0422-rob/db/...
	//Ace/REL2/built/...	//BUG0422-rob/built/...
	//Ace/REL2/tests/...	//BUG0422-rob/tests/...
	//Ace/REL2/utils/...	//BUG0422-rob/utils/...
	+//Ace/BUG0422/...	//BUG0422-rob/...

You'll notice that Rob has edited the view lines to select the REL2 modules he needs. He has also added one line to the template's View field. It's an *overlay mapping*—a mapping line that begins with a +. The result is that the REL2 files and the BUG0422 files are mapped into the same *c:\bugfix2* directory on Rob's local disk.

An overlay mapping has no effect on the workspace unless there are depot files that match the mapping. Right now there aren't any files in the BUG0422 task branch. When Rob synchronizes his workspace, it will be filled with files from REL2. In fact, as long as there are no files in BUG0422, Perforce will treat Rob's workspace as if the overlay mapping weren't there.

Rob also creates a simple branch view that maps his task branch to its parent codeline:

```
p4 branch BUG0422-REL2

Branch     BUG0422-REL2
View       //Ace/BUG0422/...  //Ace/REL2/...
```

Working on files in a task branch

To get started on his bug fix, Rob synchronizes his workspace:

```
p4 sync
```

This command fills the workspace with REL2 files. Now Rob can browse, debug, and build with these files. He doesn't use the edit comand to open files, however. Instead, he branches files in a way that puts them in the BUG0422 branch and leaves them open for editing in his workspace. For example, here's how he does this with the *db/lock.cpp* file:

```
p4 sync db/lock.cpp#none
p4 integ -r -b BUG0422-REL2 db/lock.cpp
p4 add db/lock.cpp
```

Here's what this sequence of commands does:

1. The sync command removes REL2's *db/lock.cpp* from Rob's workspace.

2. The integ command uses the BUG0422-REL2 branch view to open the file for branching into BUG0422. Thanks to the overlay mapping in Rob's workspace view, it also restores the file to the workspace.

3. The add command reopens the file for adding, making it writable in the workspace. (It also tells Perforce that the submitted file will not be the same as the one that was branched.)

Rob can continue opening files this way as he works on files. When his bug fix is complete, he submits his opened files:

```
p4 submit
```

If it turns out that Rob needs to change the same files again, he can simply use the edit command now. In other words, as long as a file has already been branched, Rob is free to edit it. He can use the have command to see whether unopened files have been branched:

```
p4 have db/...
...
```

```
//Ace/REL2/db/acc.cpp#2      - c:\bugfix\db\acc.cpp
//Ace/BUG0422/db/dset.cpp#2  - c:\bugfix\db\dset.cpp
//Ace/BUG0422/db/lock.cpp#2  - c:\bugfix\db\lock.cpp
//Ace/BUG0422/db/rset.cpp#2  - c:\bugfix\db\rset.cpp
//Ace/REL2/db/writ.cpp#2     - c:\bugfix\db\writ.cpp
...
```

Keeping a task branch and its workspace up to date

While he works, Rob remembers to keep his workspace synchronized. This ensures that he has the latest REL2 files to work with. However, synchronizing his workspace doesn't update the files in his task branch. For that, he'll have to integrate changes from REL2 into his task branch.

Unfortunately Rob can't simply integrate the entire REL2 codeline into his task branch—that would branch all of the REL2 files, and his branch would no longer be sparse. Instead, he must restrict the integration donors to the REL2 files that have counterparts in the task branch. A further complication is that Rob can't integrate to files unless they are *already* in his task branch. So if he has branched, unsubmitted files in his workspace, he'll have to submit them first.

It so happens that Rob has already submitted his workspace files. The `files` command can be used to list the files in his task branch:

```
p4 files //Ace/BUG0422/...
//Ace/BUG0422/db/dset.cpp#1 - add change 8997
//Ace/BUG0422/db/lock.cpp#1 - add change 8997
//Ace/BUG0422/db/rset.cpp#1 - add change 8999
```

This list of files can be piped to `interchanges` and `integrate`, but only after filtering. Here Rob uses the Windows `for` command[*] as a filter:

```
p4 files //Ace/BUG0422/... > tempfile1
for /f "delims=#" %i in (tempfile1) do @echo %i >> tempfile2
```

tempfile2 now contains:

```
//Ace/BUG0422/db/dset.cpp
//Ace/BUG0422/db/lock.cpp
//Ace/BUG0422/db/rset.cpp
```

To see if there are recent REL2 changes that need integrating to the task branch files, Rob uses:

```
p4 -x tempfile2 interchanges -r -b BUG0422-REL2
```

(This form of `interchanges` treats each file in the *tempfile2* list as a target per the reversed BUG0422-REL2 branch view mapping.) If the `interchanges` output shows

---

[*] You could write a more elegant filter in any scripting language, of course.

that there are changes to integrate, Rob pulls them into his task branch with the following commands:

```
p4 -x tempfile2 integ -r -b BUG0422-REL2
p4 resolve
p4 submit
```

(This integ command also treats the files in *tempfile2* as targets per the reversed branch view.)

Now, Rob's task branch is up to date with its parent codeline. Moreover, it's ready to be reviewed and, if acceptable, integrated into the parent codeline.

Reviewing and integrating task branch changes

Once Dee hears from Rob that his bug fix is ready, she reviews it. She peruses Rob's changelist descriptions with this command:

```
p4 changes -l //Ace/BUG0422/...
```

(The -l flag produces long changelist descriptions.)

Dee looks at the diffs between the task branch and its parent branch using:

```
p4 diff2 -b BUG0422-REL2
```

Finding Rob's bug fix acceptable, Dee proceeds to integrate it into the REL2 codeline. She uses a workspace she already has set up for working in the REL2 codeline; it currently has no opened files. She synchronizes her workspace and pulls changes from the BUG0422 branch into it:

```
p4 sync
p4 integ -b BUG0422-REL2
p4 resolve -as
p4 submit
```

The resolve -as command will fail if the files in Rob's task branch were not up to date with the REL2 codeline. If this happens, Dee reverts the opened files and has a word with Rob. Otherwise, if resolve -as suceeds, Dee exercises the same due diligence and caution as she would if she were submitting a bug fix directly into the REL2 codeline. In particular, she rebuilds and tests the built result thoroughly afer resolving and before submitting files.

Creating a patch branch

A patch branch can be created much the same way as a task branch. Files in a patch branch, however, are branched from a snapshot (that is, a label, a date, or a changelist number) instead of from the head revisions of the parent files.

For example, Dee is going to patch the AcePack 2.1 release. As you recall, this release was built out of the REL2 codeline and labeled @*AcePack_2.1*. The REL2 codeline has evolved, of course, since the release was made. However, a customer using the

AcePack 2.1 release has a critical need for the patch and can't upgrade to the current release.

Dee will branch the *@AcePack_2.1* version of REL2 into a patch branch called REL2.1. The patch branch will be located in the depot's *//Ace/REL2.1* path. It will be a sparse branch, containing only the files that need to be changed.

Dee sets up the patch branch using the following procedure:

1. She creates a workspace using the REL2-master workspace as a template. In the client spec form, she adds an overlay mapping for the *//Ace/REL2.1* path:

   ```
   p4 client -t REL2-master REL2.1-dee
   ```

Client	REL2.1-dee	
Root	/usr/team/dee/patch2.1	
View	//Ace/REL2/db/...	//REL2.1-dee/db/...
	//Ace/REL2/built/...	//REL2.1-dee/built/...
	//Ace/REL2/doc/...	//REL2.1-dee/doc/...
	//Ace/REL2/gui/...	//REL2.1-dee/gui/...
	//Ace/REL2/tests/...	//REL2.1-dee/tests/...
	//Ace/REL2/utils/...	//REL2.1-dee/utils/...
	+//Ace/REL2.1/...	//REL2.1-dee/...

2. She makes a branch view for the patch branch:

   ```
   p4 branch REL2.1-REL2
   ```

Branch	REL2.1-REL2	
View	//Ace/REL2.1/...	//Ace/REL2/...

3. After switching to her REL2.1-dee workspace, she synchronizes with the *@AcePack_2.1* version of the REL2 codeline:

   ```
   p4 sync @AcePack_2.1
   ```

Now Dee can proceed to work on files. As she finds files that need changing, she branches them from the REL2 codeline into the REL2.1 patch branch first. For example, here she branches *db/acc.cpp*:

```
p4 sync db/acc.cpp#none
p4 integ -r -b REL2.1-REL2 db/acc.cpp@AcePack_2.1
p4 add db/acc.cpp
```

Note that Dee branches the file at the *@AcePack_2.1* revision. Otherwise, the preceding commands are the same as the ones Rob used in "Working on files in a task branch," earlier in this chapter. When she has completed her changes, she submits her opened files:

```
p4 submit
```

Dee's workspace contains all the REL2 files except for the ones she's replaced with REL2.1 files. Thus, she can build and test a patch release right in her workspace. And the patch release—executable files, tar files, and so on—can be submitted to the REL2.1 branch as well.

After Dee has built, tested, and submitted a patch release, she labels her workspace configuration. As a formality, she creates a label spec first and uses the Description field to note the release being patched:

```
p4 label AcePack_2.1_01
```

Label   AcePack_2.1_01
Description   Patch for @AcePack_2.1

To apply the label to the files synchronized in her workspace, Dee runs:

```
p4 labelsync -l AcePack_2.1_01
```

The label can now be used to compare the patch release to the release it patches:

```
p4 diff2 -q //...@AcePack_2.1 //...@AcePack_2.1_01
```

Dee, mindful of the flow of change and the mainline model, remembers to pull the REL2.1 changes into its parent branch, REL2. She does this in her REL2 workspace:

```
p4 sync
p4 integ -b REL2.1-REL2
p4 resolve
p4 submit
```

Because the donor codeline, REL2.1, was carefully tested in the course of making the patch release, Dee is confident that the changes she is pulling in are stable enough for the target codeline, REL2. However, she may have to resolve changes in files that have evolved since that point. And because the REL2 codeline is a release codeline, she tests her opened and resolved files carefully before submitting them. In other words, she again exercises the same due diligence pulling her patch into the REL2 codeline as she would if she were making a bug fix directly in the REL2 codeline.

CHAPTER 10

Development Codelines

As you read in Chapter 7, development codelines provide a place to check in incremental work on projects without destabilizing the mainline. In this chapter, we look at creating development codelines, working in development codelines, keeping development codelines up to date, and delivering completed development work into parent codelines.

 With the exception of the mainline, every codeline has a *parent*; the parent is the codeline it was branched from.

Creating a Development Codeline

Creating a development codeline is a matter of creating a branch view and a master workspace, and using them as branching files. The curator of the development codeline does these things, after deciding what to name the codeline and which modules to branch. First we'll look at the factors and steps involved in creating a development codeline.

Why a development codeline?

The purpose of a development codeline is to isolate potentially disruptive coding and to decouple project schedules. Ideally, we wouldn't need development codelines—all development would take place in the mainline, and when it was done, we'd make a release. Realistically, we have to isolate projects from the mainline and decouple them from one another because:

- We don't really know how long it will take to completely code each new feature or behavior. By decoupling the work on them, we can release new software as soon as any of them is done instead of having to wait until they're all done.

- Interim changes made in the course of development can break software. By decoupling projects, we can limit the breakage so that it affects individuals or small coding teams instead of our entire development staff.

- Decoupling projects lets us test to see what we've broken without having to worry about whether the breakage is related to features and behaviors introduced by concurrent projects.

- We need the mainline to remain stable so that it can serve as a reference point of quality and compatibility for all new features and behaviors.

What goes on in a development codeline?

What goes on in a development codeline depends on the nature of the project. Unlike release codelines, development codelines can be veins of significant change. Component rearchitecture, code refactoring, file restructuring—all of these things are likely to happen in a development codeline.

Development codelines are continually updated from the mainline. The mainline, in turn, receives completed work from other development codelines, and that work may have been significant. Thus, change flowing *into* a development codeline can also bring with it rearchitecture, refactoring, and restructuring. Does this result in total chaos? No, not as long as:

- The software you're developing is partitioned intelligently enough that the scope of any given project is limited to a single component. Parallel development works best when a given component of the software is the subject of only one major project at a time. (A component is a part of the software that functions within the whole but that is developed and tested on its own.)

- Each development codeline is dedicated to work on one component or subcomponent. A development codeline can contain many components, but only one should be the subject of active development. The modules that make up this component are the active modules in the development codeline, as you'll see presently.

- Each development codeline respects the flow of change of the mainline model. In other words, a development codeline should always be open to changes from its parent, and it should not impose any changes on its parent that are not up to its parent's standards.

- Developers are good about documenting changes that can cause integration problems. One way they can do this is to use changelist descriptions to clearly announce when they've restructured or reformatted files, or refactored or rearchitected code. (You'll see examples in a moment.) Changelist descriptions are the turn signals of the codeline road—they let us know what is about to happen.

Who owns the development codeline?

A development codeline is usually under the control of the lead developer on the project. There's nothing to keep the lead developer from delegating codeline curator tasks to someone else, but it's the lead developer who makes the decisions. He or she decides things like the scope of the project, who can work in it, its quality requirements, and so forth.

For example, Ann is the lead programmer of a team of developers working on the GUI component of the AcePack product. She's going to be the curator of a development codeline dedicated to a GUI makeover scheduled for the next major release.

Naming the development codeline

When deciding on a name for a development codeline, first take into account the considerations described in Chapter 8, then consider these points:

- Upcoming product release IDs shouldn't be used to name development codelines. For example, don't use a name like Dev4.1 for a development codeline. If your project misses the deadline for its intended release, you and the rest of your team will be reminded of it every time the development codeline's name comes up.

- Project nicknames and codenames—names like PLUTO and SATURN, for example—can make good development codeline names. They're pronounceable, they aren't tied to release IDs, and and they're familiar to everyone involved with the projects they represent.

- You can keep codelines from proliferating by reusing development codelines. If this is what you plan to do, come up with a name for the codeline that reflects its general scope rather than the specific project at hand.

Ann's going to call her development codeline "AGUI." This name conforms to Ace's all-uppercase requirement for codeline names. Since it's not tied to a particular project name, it will be suitable for reuse for future AcePack GUI development projects. And it's a name that's easy to say (and short enough to be used in the examples that follow without running off the page).

Which modules should we branch?

Development codelines are typically branched from the mainline, and the mainline typically contains many modules. The modules in Ace Engineering's mainline, for example, are shown in Figure 10-1.

It's rarely the case that you want to branch the entire mainline into a development codeline. Instead you'll want to branch only the necessary modules. The rest can be

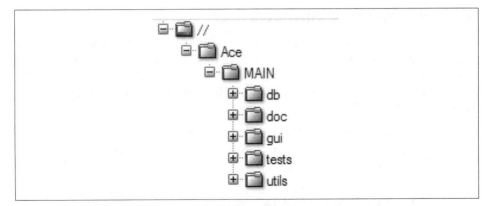

Figure 10-1. Modules in Ace Engineering's MAIN codeline

virtual, private, or omitted entirely. For the purposes of branching and working in a development codeline, modules can be categorized as follows:

Active modules

You'll branch some mainline modules to work on them. These will be the active modules in your development codeline. They're the ones developers will submit changes to in the course of your project.

Static modules

You'll branch some mainline modules simply in order to have stable versions of them. These will be the static modules in your development codeline. They won't be changed by developers working on the project, although they will appear in developer workspaces.

Virtual modules

Some modules you don't need to branch because the mainline versions will suffice. However, because they will be needed in developer workspaces, they'll be mapped to the parent codeline as virtual modules. Client views will make them appear to developers as if they were in the codeline. Developers won't be submitting changes to virtual modules.

Private modules

Some modules you won't branch because they'll be created anew in the development codelines. These are the private modules in your codeline. Developers may submit changes to these modules, but there is no flow of change between private modules and their counterparts in the mainline.

Unneeded modules

Some modules you won't need in your codeline at all. They're simply not relevant to your project.

For example, Ann has sorted through the modules in Ace Engineering's mainline and figured out which ones she needs to branch into the AGUI development codeline:

- *gui* and *tests* will be branched for active development. The bulk of AGUI work will take place in the *gui* module. Minor development may occur in the *tests* module. The changes to these modules will be delivered to the mainline when the makeover is complete.

- The *db* module will be branched, but it'll be static. In other words, it won't be affected by AGUI development. It is needed merely to provide a stable base for testing.

- The *utils* module will be a virtual module. It will appear in developers' workspaces as if it were in the AGUI codeline, but it will be synchronized with files that are actually in the mainline.

- The *built* module won't be branched. It *is* needed, but it will be recreated as a private module as soon as builds in the AGUI codeline are set up. Nothing in AGUI's *built* module will be integrated into the mainline.

- The *doc* module won't be in the codeline at all. It's not relevant to the AGUI makeover project.

 A module, as you know, is simply a directory path in a Perforce depot. And in Perforce, you don't create directories explicitly—they just appear when you add new files. So if you need a new module for developing a new feature, how do you create it before adding new files to it? You don't! The module doesn't exist until you add its files to the depot.

Why branch static modules?

Inactive modules, as you have read, are modules developers don't change but do use to build and test their work. Developers can use views to make these modules appear in their workspaces even though they were never branched from the parent codeline. Or you can branch these modules to create real, static copies of them in the development codeline. Why branch a module you're not going to change? Two reasons:

- A static module gives you an airlock between parent codeline changes and your project. For example, *db* is used only for regression testing in the AGUI codeline. In the mainline, however, the *db* module could change. If *db* changes in MAIN, Ann can choose when to pull the new version into AGUI. She may decide to wait a few days until her developers sort out regressions they've already caused. She doesn't have this kind of control when her developers are synchronizing with modules outside of her development codeline.

- The development codeline itself can serve to document the modules—specifically, their versions—that support the project environment. Branching and integration make a permanent record of what's needed to reproduce software in the development codeline at any point in time.

That being said, there are also good reasons to *not* branch static modules:

- Someone will have to update static modules by periodically integrating changes to them from the parent codeline. That someone is probably you, the codeline curator.
- If the static modules are extremely large, or if your depot holds an extremely large number of development codelines, repeated instances of static modules could bloat the Perforce database. The threshold at which this actually becomes noticeable is very high, but it's something to keep in mind.

The alternative to branching static modules is to use virtual modules—that is, modules mapped from the parent codeline into workspaces used for the development codeline. You'll see the difference between static and virtual modules in the examples that follow.

A branch view for the development codeline

A branch view is a handy tool for keeping track of the parent codeline modules that have counterparts in the development codeline. Here, for example, Ann creates a branch view called AGUI-MAIN. In it, she maps each active and static module in the AGUI codeline to its counterpart in MAIN. Following Ace's branch view convention, the mapping is toward the mainline—that is, MAIN appears on the righthand side of the view lines:

```
p4 branch AGUI-MAIN

Branch        AGUI-MAIN
Description   AGUI development
View          //Ace/AGUI/gui/...    //Ace/MAIN/gui/...
              //Ace/AGUI/tests/... //Ace/MAIN/tests/...
              //Ace/AGUI/db/...     //Ace/MAIN/db/...
```

Branch views don't alter files, of course. They are merely a convenience, like stored preferences. They're used for branching codelines, as we'll see in a moment, and for integrating and comparing codelines.

Creating a master workspace

As curator of a development codeline, you should set up a master client workspace for routine codeline maintenance tasks. You'll use it at the outset to branch the codeline, and from time to time to keep the codeline up to date with its parent. Developers will use it as a template for the workspaces they create.

For example, Ann creates a workspace called AGUI-master for this purpose:

```
p4 client AGUI-master

Client   AGUI-master
Root     c:\ws\agui
View     //Ace/AGUI/...         //AGUI-master/...
         //Ace/MAIN/utils/...   //AGUI-master/utils/...
```

With this view, AGUI modules will appear in the *c:\ws\agui* directory on Ann's machine. Notice the view mapping for the *utils* module—*utils* is a virtual module, inherited from the MAIN codeline. It will appear in the *utils* subdirectory of Ann's *c:\ws\agui* path, however, as a peer of the other modules in the AGUI codeline. And, since the AGUI-master workspace will be used as a template by developers working in the AGUI codeline, the same mapping will apply to the workspaces they create.

Aside from the virtual module, the AGUI-master workspace doesn't map modules explicitly. Instead, it maps the entire AGUI codeline to the workspace. There are two reasons for this. One is that Ann has already chosen the subset of the mainline's modules that will be branched to AGUI; developers will need all of them in their workspaces. The other is that it's conceivable that the AGUI project may give birth to another top-level module. (And in fact it will, as you'll see in a bit later in this chapter in "Working with Third-Party Software.") New top-level modules can be added only via a workspace that has an unrestricted view of the top of the codeline hierarchy.

Branching the development codeline

Once you have a branch view and a master workspace, you're ready to branch main-line modules into the development codeline.

Ann, for example, branches the AGUI modules thus:

```
p4 integ -v -r -b AGUI-MAIN
p4 submit
```

As you can see, she uses the AGUI-MAIN branch view with the `integ` command. Because the branch view maps modules *from* the development codeline *to* the main-line, she uses `integ`'s -r (reverse mapping) flag. Also, because she doesn't want to fill her workspace with copies of the newly branched files, she uses the -v (virtual) flag.

Thus the *//Ace/AGUI* directory is created in the depot and populated with files (see Figure 10-2). Each file in *//Ace/AGUI* is a clone of its *//Ace/MAIN* counterpart. Developers will now be able to browse the AGUI codeline, synchronize their workspaces with it, and submit changes to it.

Working in a Development Codeline

Once files have been branched into a development codeline, developers can begin to work in the codeline. Let's take a look at aspects of working in a development code-line that are of interest to developers.

The developer's workspace

Developers should set up separate workspaces for each development codeline in which they work. (If you're both curator and developer for the codeline, make sure

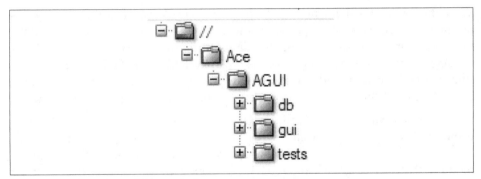

Figure 10-2. The AGUI codeline in the depot

you have a separate workspace for your own development work. It's easier to do routine codeline maintenance when you don't have to worry about interfering with your own development work in progress.)

Bob, for example, has a workspace set up for working in AGUI. It's called AGUI-bob and it's rooted in the */usr/team/bob/ws* directory on his workstation. He creates it using the AGUI-master workspace as a template:

```
p4 client -t AGUI-master AGUI-bob
```

Client	AGUI-bob	
Root	/usr/team/bob/ws	
View	//Ace/AGUI/...	//AGUI-bob/...
	//Ace/MAIN/utils/...	//AGUI-bob/utils/...

Once his workspace is configured, he can fill it with AGUI files by running:

```
p4 sync
```

Workspace file filters

Often there are depot files that you don't want copied to your workspace, or workspace files you don't want added to the depot. You can use your workspace view to filter these files out of the scope of Perforce commands.

If you're a Vim user, for example, your workspace may be littered with Vim backup and swap files; these files have names that end in ~ and *.swp*. You can hide them from Perforce with exclusion lines in your workspace view. Bob has done this by adding two exclusion lines to his AGUI-bob workspace view:

```
p4 client
```

Client	AGUI-bob	
View	//Ace/MAIN/...	//AGUI-bob/...
	-//Ace/...~	//AGUI-bob/...~
	-//Ace/....swp	//AGUI-bob/....swp

(The exclusion lines are the ones that begin with -.) With this exclusionary mapping in effect, Perforce client programs will ignore files whose names end with ~ and *.swp*. When Bob uses the add command, for example, Perforce won't open these files to be added to the depot.

The same trick can be used to prevent unwanted files from being copied to your workspace when you synchronize. If your workspace is on a FreeBSD machine, for example, you probably have no use for binaries built for other operating systems. Bob has inserted two more lines in his workspace view to filter out unneeded binaries:

```
p4 client

Client     AGUI-bob
View        //Ace/MAIN/...                     //AGUI-bob/...
           -//Ace/MAIN/built/bin/...           //AGUI-bob/built/bin/...
            //Ace/MAIN/built/bin/freebsd4/...  //AGUI-bob/built/bin/freebsd4/...
           -//Ace/...~                         //AGUI-bob/...~
           -//Ace/....swp                      //AGUI-bob/....swp
```

Here, an exclusionary mapping hides files in the *//Ace/MAIN/built/bin* path. It's followed by a mapping that reveals files in the *//Ace/MAIN/built/bin/freebsd* path. (In Perforce view maps, later lines always take precedence.)

The exact mapping to use depends on the organization and contents of your depot, of course.

Writing helpful changelist descriptions

As a developer working in a development codeline, keep in mind that your sweeping changes can cause integration problems in the future and in distantly related codelines. You can make such problems easier to deal with by using changelist descriptions to make very clear what you've done, *especially* when you've:

- Changed component interfaces or architecture.
- Moved, renamed, or deleted files.
- Prettied up files by changing things like indentation, line breaks, and bracketing.

During initial development, it's a great idea to go through the files you've added and pretty them up with consistent bracketing, uniform indentation, and other formatting changes. New development is the right time to get source files into conformance with a coding style used by your team.

But *don't* pretty up mature source files! The source files that have been around for a while have counterparts in other codelines, including release codelines. Unless you are absolutely certain that your changes won't conflict with parallel changes to the same file in other codelines, don't make gratuitous formatting changes. It's just not worth the complicated merging it causes.

When other developers are integrating changes, they'll be skimming changelist descriptions looking for advanced warning of these things. A helpful changelist description, for example, might look like this:

```
Change 9345 on 2005/03/02 by bill
    New test driver for GUI applications.
    ...
    MOVED: gui/spin/test/... => tests/gui/...
    ...
```

This description will jump out at people as they're reviewing the changes they're about to integrate. (See Chapter 9 for more examples.)

Keeping a Development Codeline Up to Date

As you read in Chapter 7, a development codeline is a surrogate for the codeline from which it was branched. It serves its purpose best when it's up to date—that is, when all of its parent's changes have been integrated into it.

Ann, as curator of the AGUI codeline, is in charge of keeping AGUI up to date with the MAIN codeline.

There is no Perforce mechanism that keeps codelines up to date automatically. Someone has to integrate parent codeline changes into the development codeline. Typically, that someone is you, the development codeline curator. You should plan to integrate changes regularly—the more current your development codeline is, the easier it will be to integrate *into* the parent when the project is done.

Remember that the mainline is, in theory, stable. Because changes go into the mainline only when they're complete and working, you should have no qualms about pulling them into your development codeline.

When should a development codeline be updated?

Change should flow continually to a development codeline from its parent. That is, as soon as a change occurs in the parent, the development codeline should be ready to accept it. This means you should be integrating parent codeline changes into the development codeline as they occur (see Figure 10-3).

And here's why: for smoother collaboration, you'll want to make sure that your project work isn't delivered to the parent until you've solved all the integration problems it may have caused. (Integration problems are those having to do with interfaces, compatibility, refactoring, rearchitecting, and so on.) Integration problems should be worked out in the development codeline, not in its parent codeline.

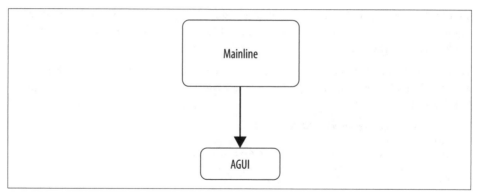

Figure 10-3. Updating the AGUI codeline

As a rule of thumb, integration problems between two codelines should be worked out in the softer of the two codelines. (See Chapter 7.) Working out integration problems always causes a bit of instability; the softer codeline can accommodate instability better than the firmer one can.

As you can imagine, the sooner you integrate parent changes into the development codeline, the sooner you and your development team will be able to flush out looming integration problems. Deferring the integration until more changes pile up only makes the problems harder to solve.

Realistically, a little bit of a lag before a change is merged from parent into development codeline doesn't hurt. So, while it's important to keep a development codeline up to date, you don't have to drop everything when the parent changes. In fact, sometimes it's even better to put off integrating for a bit. If your development codeline is currently broken—for example, parts of it can't be built, or test failures are high—you should probably get it working again before perturbing it by pulling in parent changes.

But whatever you do, don't put off the chore of updating a development codeline for too long. The whole point of using a development codeline is to enable parallel development. Unless your development codeline is up to date, you're not enabling parallel development—you're avoiding it.

Which changes need integrating?

Remember, only some of the MAIN codeline's modules were branched into the AGUI development codeline. Changes to omitted modules will have no bearing on the development codeline, obviously, and changes to virtual modules don't need integrating. But you do have to integrate *all* changes to the modules that were branched. If you don't, you'll have a miserable time trying to deliver your project work back into the parent later.

To see which changes need integrating into a development codeline, use `interchanges` with the branch view you set up. The branch view filters out the irrelevant modules. For example:

```
p4 interchanges -r -b AGUI-MAIN
Change 9325 by nina 'Fix dialog resize problem in...'
Change 9324 by ron  'DB profiling for distributed...'
Change 9321 by bill 'Preferences can now be saved...'
Change 9318 by don  'Test driver's new filter for...'
```

(The -r option makes `interchanges` use the branch view's mapping in reverse.)

The output shows that since the AGUI codeline was branched or last updated, four new changes have been submitted into MAIN. These changes will need to be integrated from MAIN into AGUI. Of these changes, some will affect the static modules and some will affect the active modules.

Changes to static modules are a snap to integrate. Because their files are not changing in the development codeline, they won't need merging, and resolving them will be trivial. Nor do you have to worry about structural changes to them—you can go ahead and let Perforce move and rename files in the target codeline to match their parent counterparts.

The tricky changes to integrate are the ones affecting the active modules. The active modules will certainly have changed in the development codeline, and they may have changed a lot. Even minor changes in the parent codeline can be nontrivial to pull in if the development codeline's files have changed significantly. You'll have to be prepared to resolve conflicts and to reconcile structural changes. (If you're unsure about what this entails, now would be a good time to review Chapter 4.)

Adjusting the development codeline's branch view

The branch view you use to branch a development codeline has another use: it can reconcile the file structure of the parent codeline with the structure of the development codeline.

For example, developers have renamed, moved, and deleted files in AGUI's active modules since the codeline was branched. MAIN's changes can easily be merged into AGUI if the AGUI-MAIN branch view maps the new file structure in AGUI to the old file structure in MAIN. So, before Ann integrates changes from MAIN into AGUI, she adjusts the branch view. In Chapter 9 you read about doing this for release codelines. The procedure is analogous for development codelines.

First, Ann inspects the changes that have occured in the AGUI codeline, looking for evidence that files have been renamed, moved, or deleted. Perfect for this example, each one of them shows such evidence:

```
p4 interchanges -l -b AGUI-MAIN
Change 9366 by ann on 2005/03/09
    Get rid of obsolete setup script.
    ...
    DELETED: gui/fx/lgen.pl
    ...
Change 9362 by bob on 2005/03/06
    The Trim object is now visible in...
    ...
    RENAMED: gui/fx/st.cpp -> gui/fx/trim.cpp
    ...
Change 9349 by ann on 2005/03/05
    Changed the structure of the...
    ...
    RENAMED: gui/lmgr/... -> gui/fx/...
    ...
Change 9345 on 2005/03/02 by bill
    New test driver for GUI applications.
    ...
    MOVED t011.pl and t015.pl from gui/spin/test to tests/gui
    ...
```

(The -l flag makes interchanges show complete change descriptions.)

P4V's Folder Diff can also help you detect structural changes. By comparing old and new versions of a codeline, you can get a visual overview of the files whose names and locations no longer match. In Figure 10-4, for example, the original AGUI (left) is compared to the current AGUI (right).

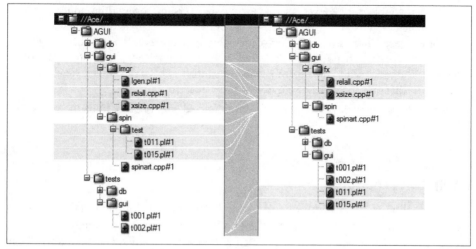

Figure 10-4. AGUI's structural changes shown in P4V

Once Ann has gathered information about structural changes, she can update the AGUI-MAIN branch view to reconcile the new file structure with the old:

```
p4 branch AGUI-MAIN

Branch          AGUI-MAIN
Description     AGUI development
                Last reconciled @9366
View            //Ace/AGUI/gui/...          //Ace/MAIN/gui/...
                //Ace/AGUI/tests/...        //Ace/MAIN/tests/...
                //Ace/AGUI/db/...           //Ace/MAIN/db/...
                //Ace/AGUI/gui/fx/...       //Ace/MAIN/gui/lmgr/...
                //Ace/AGUI/gui/fx/trim.cpp  //Ace/MAIN/gui/lmgr/st.cpp
                //Ace/AGUI/tests/gui/t011.pl //Ace/MAIN/gui/spin/test/t011.pl
                //Ace/AGUI/tests/gui/t015.pl //Ace/MAIN/gui/spin/test/t015.pl
                -//Ace/AGUI/gui/fx/lgen.pl   //Ace/MAIN/gui/lmgr/lgen.pl
```

The last three view lines are the reconcilers Ann just added. Note that Ann also put a note to herself—"Last reconciled @9366"—in the spec's description. She'll be adjusting the branch view again from time to time, and each time she does so the branch view's description will tell her which changes she's already reconciled.

Who Adjusts the Branch View?

A branch view can be updated by anyone as long as its spec is not locked. You can choose to leave a branch view's spec unlocked so that developers can adjust it themselves as they make structural changes.

But a spec is not like a file—Perforce doesn't detect conflicts in specs when users make changes to them. If two people happen to be adjusting a branch view's spec at the same time, the second person could overwrite adjustments made by the first.

As long as your Perforce Server is set up to save spec versions, overwriting adjustments to a branch view isn't a catastrophe—the overwritten spec version can always be retrieved. (See Chapter 6.) However, developers may not even *notice* when they've overwritten one another's adjustments, and that could complicate the curator's task of keeping the codeline up to date. It may just be simpler to keep the branch view's spec locked so that only the codeline curator can adjust it.

You can set the branch view's owner, and the "locked" option, by editing the its spec form.

Integrating changes

Parent codeline changes should be integrated into the development codeline incrementally, in order. This lets you test the effects of each one so that there's no question about whether or not it causes problems or perturbs results. (While it's true that these are stable changes, coming from a firmer codeline, there's no guarantee that they're compatible with changes in the development codeline.)

Before integrating parent changes into the development codeline, make sure that:

- The branch view has been adjusted to account for structural changes in the development codeline.
- You are using a workspace with a view of the development codeline.
- Your workspace is synchronized and no files are currently opened in it.

Ann lists the MAIN changes that need to be pulled into AGUI:

```
p4 interchanges -r -b AGUI-MAIN
Change 9318 by don  'Test driver's new filter for...'
Change 9321 by bill 'Preferences can now be saved...'
Change 9324 by ron  'DB profiling for distributed...'
Change 9325 by nina 'Fix dialog resize problem in...'
```

The first change to integrate is the first one in the list, 9318. Ann uses these commands to integrate it:

```
p4 integ -t -r -b AGUI-MAIN @9318
p4 resolve
p4 submit
```

After testing to make sure no problems were introduced, Ann repeats the same sequence of commands for changes 9321, 9324, and 9325.

Notice the -t flag on the integ command—this causes file type changes to be propagated from MAIN into AGUI. In general, this is a good thing—it makes type changes introduced in parallel, completed development projects visible to developers in AGUI. However, as you may remember reading in a previous chapter, changes to a file's type aren't handled by resolve. Take a look back at Chapter 3 to find out about using fstat to detect imminent file type conflicts, and reopen to reconcile type changes.

Working with Third-Party Software

Third-party software is the software that comes from other suppliers and is used in source or binary form to build your software. If you're wondering whether you should check in third-party code, ask yourself, "Are we going to modify it?" If the answer is yes, you should check it in. The vendor's source will be the common base for changes you'll make; it needs to be in your depot. (You'll see an example in a moment.)

There are other reasons to put third-party software in your depot:

- Most vendors distribute multiple versions or frequent upgrades of software. If you submit their distributions into your depot, you'll always know which versions of their software go with which versions of yours.

- You may want control over the versions your developers use. Rather than leaving it up to developers to figure out which versions to download and when, use your depot to present the correct version to codelines and workspaces.

- The Perforce depot is often the easiest place for you to store files. You don't have to get root access or set up network shares to make third-party software available to your developers. Just put it in the depot.

- It may be hard or inconvenient for your developers to download from external vendors. If you put third-party software in your depot along with other files they use, there's never any question about how developers are to get it.

 There's a lot of switching between workspaces in the scenario described in this section. If you're not clear on how to switch between workspaces, take a look at Chapter 2.

Importing third-party software

As we hinted in Chapter 8, you should designate a depot path for storing imported, third-party code. At Ace Engineering, for example, software developed externally is imported into the //Ace/IMPORT path (a.k.a. the IMPORT stream).

You can download a supplier's distribution and add it to your depot as you would any new collection of files. For example, Ann's going to download FWindo,* a toolkit she and her developers plan to use for GUI development. It's the FWindo 4.1 distribution, and it comes in a file called *FWindo41.zip*. She has downloaded this file and unzipped it into her *c:\ws\fwindo* directory. She will submit the tree of unzipped files to the //Ace/IMPORT/fwindo path in the depot.

Ann creates a workspace with a view of //Ace/IMPORT/fwindo:

```
p4 client IMPORT-fwindo-ann
```

Client	IMPORT-fwindo-ann
Root	c:\ws\fwindo
View	//Ace/IMPORT/fwindo/... //IMPORT-fwindo-ann/...

With the IMPORT-fwindo-ann workspace as her current workspace, she opens the files for adding:

```
dir /s/b/a-d c:\ws\fwindo | p4 -x- add -f
```

(See Chapter 2 if you're not sure what just happened here.)

---

* No, there is no such thing as FWindo. Or if there is, it's a coincidence.

When Ann submits the change, she uses the changelist's description to identify the origin and version of the files:

```
p4 submit
```

Change	new
Description	FWindo 4.1 unpacked from FWindo41.zip, downloaded from www.mobettawindows.com
Files	//Ace/IMPORT/fwindo/src/include/fwin.h#1
	//Ace/IMPORT/fwindo/src/sample/main.c#1
	//Ace/IMPORT/fwindo/bin/win32/libfwin.dll#1
	//Ace/IMPORT/fwindo/bin/linux/libfwin.so#1

Lastly, she removes the files from her workspace:

```
p4 sync #none
```

Branching imported code to the development codeline

Next, Ann will branch the FWindo files from the IMPORT stream into the AGUI codeline. The files will make up a new module in AGUI, called *fwindo*. She switches to the AGUI-master workspace and opens the files for branching:

```
p4 integ //Ace/IMPORT/fwindo/... //Ace/AGUI/fwindo/...
```

(This is the simple form of the integ command. It doesn't use a branch view. Instead, it lists the donor and target filespecs on the command line.)

When Ann submits the opened files, AGUI's new module is created in the depot:

```
p4 submit
//Ace/AGUI/fwindo/src/include/fwin.h#1
//Ace/AGUI/fwindo/src/sample/main.c#1
//Ace/AGUI/fwindo/bin/win32/libfwin.dll#1
//Ace/AGUI/fwindo/bin/linux/libfwin.so#1
```

Once she's submitted the files, developers working in AGUI can resynchronize their workspaces to have these files copied into them.

Updating the development codeline's branch view

The *fwindo* module is now an active module in the AGUI development codeline. It's going to track with the rest of the codeline, and when completed AGUI work is delivered into MAIN, *fwindo* will be branched into MAIN as well. In order to make sure that this happens, Ann adds a mapping line to the AGUI-MAIN branch view:

```
p4 branch AGUI-MAIN
```

Branch	AGUI-MAIN	
View	//Ace/AGUI/gui/...	//Ace/MAIN/gui/...
	//Ace/AGUI/tests/...	//Ace/MAIN/tests/...
	//Ace/AGUI/db/...	//Ace/MAIN/db/...
	//Ace/AGUI/fwindo/...	//Ace/MAIN/fwindo/...
	...	

The *fwindo* mapping line ensures that the new module will be visible to integrate commands that use the AGUI-MAIN branch view.

Importing a new distribution

When FWindo 4.2 is available, Ann imports the new distribution on top of the old one. She switches to the IMPORT-fwindo-ann workspace again and uses the following recipe:

1. As before, she unzips the *FWindo42.zip* file into her *c:\ws\fwindo* directory.

2. She uses the sync -k command to make Perforce think that her workspace is synchronized with the depot's FWindo files:

   ```
   p4 sync -k //Ace/IMPORT/fwindo/...
   ```

3. She uses the technique described in Chapter 2's "Reconciling offline changes" section to open files for adding, editing, or deleting, as needed:

   ```
   cd c:\ws\fwindo
   p4 diff -se | p4 -x- edit
   p4 diff -sd | p4 -x- delete
   dir /s/b/a-d | p4 -x- add -f
   ```

4. She submits the files, again using the changelist description to document their origin:

   ```
   p4 submit
   ```

Change	new
Description	FWindo 4.2 unpacked from FWindo42.zip, downloaded from www.mobettawindows.com
Files	//Ace/IMPORT/fwindo/src/sample/main.c#2
	//Ace/IMPORT/fwindo/bin/win32/libfwin.dll#2
	//Ace/IMPORT/fwindo/bin/linux/libfwin.so#2

The net effect of this recipe is that the files in the depot are updated per the new distribution. Files that are the same in both distributions remain unchanged in the depot.

Merging a new distribution with local changes

Having just imported a new FWindo distribution, Ann's next task is to merge the distribution with changes that Ace developers have made to the previous version. She does this by switching back to the AGUI-master workspace and pulling the new distribution into the AGUI codeline:

```
p4 integ //Ace/IMPORT/fwindo/... //Ace/AGUI/fwindo/...
p4 resolve -am
//Ace/AGUI/fwindo/src/sample/main.c#4
- merge from //Ace/IMPORT/fwindo/src/sample/main.c#2
//Ace/AGUI/fwindo/bin/win32/libfwin.dll#2
- copy from //Ace/IMPORT/fwindo/bin/win32/libfwin.dll#2
```

```
//Ace/AGUI/fwindo/bin/linux/libfwin.so#2
- copy from //Ace/IMPORT/fwindo/bin/linux/libfwin.so#2
```

p4 submit

Notice the resolve output: it shows that one of the files is being merged, not copied. Apparently during the course of project development, someone on the GUI team changed one of FWindo's source files:

```
p4 filelog //Ace/AGUI/fwindo/src/sample/main.c
//Ace/AGUI/fwindo/src/sample/main.c
... #3 change 7419 edit   by bill 'Fix fwindo sample'
... #2 change 7401 edit   by bill 'Beef up sample code'
... #1 change 6990 branch by ann  'New FWindo toolkit (4.1)'
```

The fact that an Ace developer changed a source file that came from an external source is not a problem as long as new distributions are submitted to the IMPORT stream first. This is what makes it possible to merge new distributions with parallel changes in the development codeline.

Delivering Completed Development Work

Once work on a project is completed, you'll want to deliver it from the development codeline to its parent. Likewise, if a development codeline is being used for ongoing development, you'll want to deliver work to its parent at points of completion. In either case, delivery is done by using integrate, resolve, and submit to propagate new file content *and new file structure* to the parent codeline.

Delivering completed work is typically the job of the development codeline curator. Most of the effort is in the setup, not in the integration; the actual integration is likely to be trivial because no file merging is involved.

Merge down, copy up

Delivering completed work is a matter of first bringing the development codeline up to date with the parent codeline, then copying the merged files back to the parent. In the case of the AGUI codeline, completed work will be delivered by merging MAIN into AGUI first, then copying AGUI to MAIN, as shown in Figure 10-5.

One advantage of this "merge down, copy up" approach is that when there are problems with merging, interfaces, and compatibility, the development codeline bears the brunt. The parent—the firmer codeline—remains unsullied while you sort out problems in the development codeline. Only after you've submitted fixes to the development codeline do you copy files from the development codeline to the parent.

Another advantage of merge down, copy up is that merging down gives you a preview of what the parent codeline will look like once you've delivered completed work

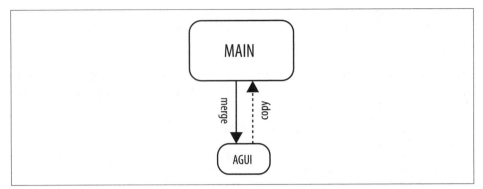

Figure 10-5. Delivering completed AGUI work to MAIN

to the parent. The development codeline *is* your preview—you can batter it with the same tests its parent codeline is subject to and you can show it to anyone who wants to know what you're about to deliver to the parent.

Is Merging Dangerous?

Some people are convinced that merging is so dangerous that parallel development can succeed only when merging is outlawed entirely. But when merging is outlawed, you're no longer doing parallel development, you're doing serial development. In parallel development, merging is unavoidable.

But is merging dangerous? No—it's no more dangerous than writing new code. But neither is merging any safer than writing new code. So the question is, where do you want developers writing new code, in soft codelines or in firm codelines? Why, in soft codelines, of course. Well, merging is just like writing new code—it should be done in soft codelines, not in firm codelines.

When should development be delivered?

Development work should be delivered to its parent codeline only at points of completion. (When it's "code-complete," as they say.) Generally speaking, a point of completion is when software in the development codeline is in good enough shape not to disrupt the parent. It must be functional, by the standards of the parent codeline. If the parent is the mainline, it should be essentially ready for release stabilization.

In particular, work can be delivered when:

- The development codeline is completely up to date with its parent. That is, there are no changes in the parent that have not already been integrated into the development codeline. (See "Keeping a Development Codeline Up to Date," earlier in this chapter.)

- Integration problems (that is, interface and compatibility problems) have been worked out in the development codeline.

- The development codeline can pass the same tests that are applied to its parent.

Identifying a point of completion

Every point of completion has a revision number, by the way. For example, the AGUI codeline is now at a point of completion, as shown in Figure 10-6. We see that it was most recently changed by changelist 9477:

```
p4 changes -m1 //Ace/AGUI/...
Change 9477 by ann on 2005/03/09 'Get rid of obsolete setup script'
```

@9477 identifies AGUI's point of completion; //Ace/AGUI/...@9477 is the version that will be delivered to MAIN.

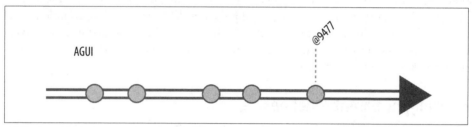

Figure 10-6. AGUI's point of completion

If you want a more memorable way to refer to a point of completion, you can also use a label. Ann, for example, prefers to use the label AGUI-complete (see Figure 10-7). She applies it to the AGUI codeline:

```
p4 tag -l AGUI-complete //Ace/AGUI/...@9477
```

Now she'll be able to refer to the label when she delivers completed work from AGUI to MAIN.

 Development codelines that are used for ongoing development can have more than one point of completion. Each point of completion marks a version of the development codeline that can be delivered to the parent.

Which changes should be integrated into the parent?

Once a point of completion is determined, all changes should be integrated into the parent lock, stock and barrel. In other words, don't cherry-pick. The simplifying

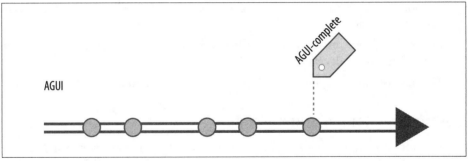

Figure 10-7. Labeling a point of completion

effect of working in a development codeline is lost if you're not treating the codeline as an absolute variant of its parent.

Integrating the entire development codeline into the parent isn't as daunting as it sounds. For one thing, only the active modules will have files that need integrating. (Files in static modules have changed, yes, but only to pull in parent codeline changes.) For another, you've been keeping the development codeline completely up to date; there's nothing in the parent that hasn't already been merged into the development codeline. Development codeline files can simply be copy-integrated into the parent—they won't need merging.

Freezing the parent codeline

The merge down, copy up method relies on being able to temporarily freeze the parent codeline for as long as it takes to complete the cycle. For example, Ann will need a way to ensure that no one submits a change to MAIN until she's finished merging from MAIN to AGUI and copy-integrating from AGUI back into MAIN.

There is no automatic way to freeze a codeline in Perforce. Depending on the size and nature of your shop, you may be able to effect a freeze with something as simple as a friendly email to your fellow developers.

If you're a Perforce superuser, you're in luck—you can use protections to freeze a codeline. (For more on protections, see Chapter 6.) Ann, it so happens, is a superuser. She can freeze the MAIN codeline by running protect and restricting access to the *//Ace/MAIN* path:

```
p4 protect

Protections     ...
                open    user  *    *  //Ace/MAIN/...
                write   user  ann  *  //Ace/MAIN/...
```

This downgrades everyone's access to MAIN; open means users can synchronize workspaces and open files, but they can't submit changes. The only user who can submit changes to MAIN now is Ann.

Make sure the development codeline is already up to date before freezing the parent codeline. (See "Keeping a Development Codeline Up to Date," earlier in the chapter.) This minimizes the amount of time you'll need to keep the freeze in effect. After you've frozen the parent codeline, check for updates again. This catches changes that may have slipped into the parent codeline between the last update and the freeze.

Note that merging late-breaking changes from the parent affects the point of completion in the development codeline. The new point of completion is the point at which the development codeline is completely up to date with its parent. If you're using a label, be sure to reapply the label to the new point of completion.

Which workspace?

To update a development codeline, you need a workspace with a view of the development codeline, of course. Ann's been using the AGUI-master workspace to update the AGUI codeline.

To integrate from a development codeline into a parent codeline, you need a workspace with a view of the parent codeline. In Ann's case, she'll need a workspace with a view of MAIN. She uses the MAIN-master workspace as a template to create a workspace for herself called MAIN-ann:

```
p4 client -t MAIN-master MAIN-ann
```

Client	MAIN-ann
Root	c:\ws\main

```
View    //Ace/MAIN/built/...    //MAIN-ann/built/...
        //Ace/MAIN/db/...       //MAIN-ann/db/...
        //Ace/MAIN/doc/...      //MAIN-ann/doc/...
        //Ace/MAIN/utils/...    //MAIN-ann/utils/...
        //Ace/MAIN/tests/...    //MAIN-ann/tests/...
        //Ace/MAIN/gui/...      //MAIN-ann/gui/...
```

Ann will be switching back and forth between her MAIN-ann and AGUI-master workspaces as she completes the delivery procedure.

Preparing a change description

When you integrate the development codeline into its parent, you'll be submitting a changelist. A very nice thing to do for downstream developers is to use the changelist to document your development codeline's structural changes. This will be useful to anyone merging bug fixes from an older release into the newly restructured parent codeline. It informs them of the structural changes *they'll* need to reconcile.

You can prepare a change description in advance, by creating a new pending changelist. (You'll have to do this in a workspace with a view of the parent codeline.) The structural changes to document are the ones currently mapped in the development codeline's branch view. For example, these are the lines in the AGUI-MAIN branch view that map the new AGUI structure to the old MAIN structure:

```
 //Ace/AGUI/gui/fx/...       //Ace/MAIN/gui/lmgr/...
 //Ace/AGUI/gui/fx/trim.cpp //Ace/MAIN/gui/lmgr/st.cpp
-//Ace/AGUI/gui/fx/lgen.pl  //Ace/MAIN/gui/lmgr/lgen.pl
```

And here Ann creates a new, empty, pending changelist and enters a description that documents these structural changes:

p4 changelist

Change	new
Description	GUI makeover is done. New look-and-feel ready to go!

```
            ...
            NEW:     fwindo/...
            MOVED:   gui/lmgr/...    -> gui/fx/...
            RENAMED: gui/lmgr/st.cpp -> gui/fx/trim.cpp
            DELETED: gui/lmgr/lgen.pl
```

Saving the changelist spec form creates the pending changelist number:

```
Change 9489 created.
```

Ann will use this pending changelist number, 9489, when she opens files in MAIN for integration, as we'll see in a moment.

Normalizing the branch view

Having documented the structural changes, you can now normalize the branch view. That is, you can remove the view mapping lines that reconcile the old and new file structures. You won't need them as you integrate into the parent codeline, because you want the new file structure copied to the parent as is. And you won't need them after you've integrated, because at that point the two file structures will be the same again.

For example, Ann updates the AGUI-MAIN branch view and removes lines that map AGUI's new structure to MAIN's old structure. This restores the branch view to a simple list of modules:

p4 branch AGUI-MAIN

Branch	AGUI-MAIN

View	`//Ace/AGUI/gui/...     //Ace/MAIN/gui/...`
	`//Ace/AGUI/tests/...   //Ace/MAIN/tests/...`
	`//Ace/AGUI/db/...      //Ace/MAIN/db/...`
	`//Ace/AGUI/fwindo/...  //Ace/MAIN/fwindo/...`

Note that the new module, *fwindo*, *is* mapped in the normalized branch view. This ensures that when Ann delivers AGUI work to MAIN, the new module will be delivered as well.

Integrating into the parent codeline

At this point, you should have:

- A completely up-to-date development codeline.
- An identifiable point of completion in the development codeline.
- A frozen parent codeline.
- A workspace with a view of the parent codeline.
- A prepared change description in an empty pending changelist.
- A normalized branch view.

With this groundwork laid, integrating the development codeline into the parent codeline is straightforward.

Ann demonstrates. First, she checks to make sure MAIN-ann is her current workspace and that no files are opened in it:

```
p4 info
...
Client name: MAIN-ann
...

p4 opened
File(s) not opened on this client.
```

Now she integrates the AGUI codeline into MAIN:

```
p4 integ -t -c 9489 -b AGUI-MAIN -d -i -v @AGUI-complete
p4 resolve -at
p4 submit -c 9489
Change 9489 renumbered 9496.
Change 9496 submitted.
```

In the preceding commands, notice that:

- Using `-c 9489` with the `integrate` command causes pending changelist 9489 to be used for this operation. (As you recall, Ann had already created this pending changelist.)
- Ann's using the AGUI-MAIN branch view with `integrate`. This limits the scope of the integration to the modules in the branch view.
- The `-t` flag makes `integrate` propagate file types. (The idea being that if a developer changed a file type in AGUI, the type change should be delivered to the parent codeline.)
- The `-i` and `-d` flags ensure that parent codeline files are added or deleted as necessary to match the development codeline.
- The `-v` flag suppresses `integrate`'s inclination to copy MAIN's files into the workspace. (The MAIN copies aren't needed because no merging is done by the subsequent `resolve` command.)

- Ann uses @*AGUI-complete* as the donor revision. As you recall, she tagged the AGUI codeline's point of completion with this label.

- On the `resolve` command, Ann uses -at to make sure AGUI's files are copied, not merged, to MAIN.

- Finally, Ann submits pending changelist 9489. (Note that Perforce renumbers the changelist; the submitted changelist is 9496.) At this point, the modules that are present in both MAIN and AGUI are identical, both in content and in structure.

Integrating neglected files

After you've integrated from the development codeline into its parent, check to make sure the codelines match. The `diff2` command, you'll recall, can be used to compare two codelines. For example:

```
p4 diff2 -q -b AGUI-MAIN
==== //Ace/AGUI/gui/screen/cap.cpp#2 -
     //Ace/MAIN/gui/screen/cap.cpp#8 ==== (content)
```

Files listed by this `diff2` command are those that don't match, but should. They were neglected during the development-to-parent integration, because as far as Perforce could tell, they had no outstanding changes.

(It's very unlikely that a file can be neglected this way. It happens as a consequence of two conditions combined. First, the file was resolved by ignoring at some point as the development codeline was being updated. Second, the same file has otherwise been completely untouched in the course of project development.)

At any rate, this `diff2` command lists the files that were neglected. If any of the neglected files happen to be in the active modules, you probably haven't made a complete delivery of the project work to the parent. You'll need to integrate neglected files by brute force to make the parent files match their development codeline counterparts.

For example, here Ann forces the *gui/screen/cap.cpp* file to be copied from the development codeline to the parent:

```
p4 integ -f -t -b AGUI-MAIN //Ace/MAIN/gui/screen/cap.cpp@AGUI-complete
p4 resolve -at
p4 submit
```

(The -f flag forces `integrate` to operate on files whether or not it thinks they need it.)

Thawing the parent codeline

Once you've completed your delivery to the parent codeline, don't forget to "thaw" it—that is, to undo whatever it was you did to freeze it. If other developers are waiting for email from you, don't forget to send it. If you used protections to freeze the codeline, don't forget to remove them.

Retiring a development codeline

If a development codeline won't be used after delivering completed development, it can be retired. There's nothing special about retiring development codelines; they can be retired in the same way as release codelines. You can use protections to deny write access or to hide them from view.

Not all development codelines reach retirement. Some, like the AGUI codeline, are used in perpetuity for ongoing development.

The Soft Codelines

In this section we look at the softest codelines of all: the ad hoc and private codelines used by individual developers.

Shelving work in progress

As a developer, you may find that from time to time you have to put work in progress aside in order to tend to a more urgent task. In Perforce there are a couple of ways to shelve work in progress so that you can pick it up again later:

- As you learned in Chapter 2, one way is to simply put open files into separate pending changelists. This approach works as long as the work you're shelving doesn't interfere with the new task you're taking on. In other words, as long as you can do both things in the same workspace, with files opened for two different purposes, you're fine.

- Another way to shelve work in progress is to check your files into an ad hoc sparse branch. You create the branch expressly for the purpose of shelving your work; the only files it contains are the ones you need to shelve. Later, when you're ready to resume your work, you can run integrate to pull the shelved files back into your workspace and carry on where you left off. If this procedure sounds vaguely familiar to you, it's much like what you read about in Chapter 9, in the section called "Task Branches and Patch Branches."

Private branches

Pending changelists and sparse branches are useful short-term solutions for shelving work in progress. As a developer, you may realize that there are situations where it would be nice to be able to isolate your work in progress for longer intervals. You may want to submit your files *before* merging other people's changes into them, in order to reduce the risk of merging, for example. Or, you may want to submit incomplete changes to files in order to have interim versions you can roll back to. You can't do these things if you're working in a shared development branch, but you can do them in a private branch.

A private branch is a fully populated, personal codeline branched from a development codeline. The relationship of a private branch to its parent is the same as the parent's relationship to the mainline. The care and feeding of a private branch—creating it, keeping it up to date, working in it, and delivering completed development—are also the same as for a development codeline.

As a developer, you have complete control over your private branch. (Or branches; there's nothing that limits you to having just one.) You can check in changes as often as you please, even when you know your work isn't done or even completely correct. In fact, the more frequent your check-ins, the safer your work is, because you can always back out your own changes. (See "Useful Recipes" in Chapter 2.)

For instance, Don is creating a private branch called DONDEV, to be branched from the AGUI codeline. It has one active module, *gui*, and three virtual modules, *tests*, *db*, and *utils*.

Don has set up a branch view called DONDEV-AGUI that maps the active module to its parent:

```
p4 branch DONDEV-AGUI

Branch       DONDEV-AGUI
View         //Ace/DONDEV/gui/...    //Ace/AGUI/gui/...
```

The branch view is not a requirement. It's a formality—it documents the active module—and it's a shorthand for two depot paths. Notice that the branch view is mapped toward the mainline, AGUI being closer to the mainline than DONDEV.

The branch doesn't exist until Don runs `integrate` to branch files. But before he can do that, he needs a workspace with a view of his private branch. He sets one up:

```
p4 client DONDEV-master

Client       DONDEV-master
Root         c:\ws\agui
View         //Ace/DONDEV/gui/...    //DONDEV-master/gui/...
             //Ace/MAIN/utils/...    //DONDEV-master/utils/...
             //Ace/AGUI/tests/...    //DONDEV-master/tests/...
             //Ace/AGUI/db/...       //DONDEV-master/db/...
```

Like the AGUI-master view (see "Creating a master workspace," earlier in the chapter), this view treats the *utils* as a virtual module inherited from MAIN. And, you'll notice, it treats *tests* and *db* as virtual modules inherited from AGUI.

Don switches to the DONDEV-master workspace and uses the DONDEV-AGUI branch view to branch the files:

```
p4 integ -r -b DONDEV-AGUI
p4 submit
```

Now he can edit and submit files in his own private branch.

Code reviews

Private branches make great foundations for code reviews. With private branches, the work of an individual can be reviewed before it hits shared codelines. Before Don's work is delivered, for example, the other AGUI developers can review it.

For instance, to see descriptions of the changes Don's about to deliver, developers can run:

```
p4 interchanges -l -b DONDEV-AGUI
```

To see detailed diffs of Don's changes, developers can use P4V's Folder Diff, or they can run:

```
p4 diff2 -b DONDEV-AGUI
```

Or, for a succinct list of the files Don has changed, developers can run:

```
p4 diff2 -q -b DONDEV-AGUI
```

Developers can also inspect Don's branch view to see a summary of the structural differences between his branch and the AGUI codeline:

```
p4 branch -o DONDEV-AGUI
Branch: DONDEV-AGUI
View:
    //Ace/DONDEV/gui/...            //Ace/AGUI/gui/...
    //Ace/DONDEV/gui/fx/NatCam.cpp  //Ace/AGUI/gui/spin/NatCam.cpp
    //Ace/DONDEV/gui/fx/NatLock.cpp //Ace/AGUI/gui/spin/NatLock.cpp
...
```

In fact, developers could even make workspaces of their own based on Don's private branch, if they wanted to, and synchronize and test its files.

Reparenting a private branch

A private branch, as informal as it may be, has an intended flow of change. For example, Don's DONDEV branch is updated with changes from AGUI, and eventually, the work he's done in it will be delivered to AGUI (see Figure 10-8).

Changing the intended flow of change is called *reparenting a branch*. In Perforce, you don't really have to do anything to reparent a branch, because as far as Perforce is concerned, branches are just depot paths. Perforce lets you integrate changes between any two depot paths. You don't need a branch view—you can put the paths right on the command line:

```
p4 integ //Ace/AGUI/gui/... //Ace/DONDEV/gui/...
```

However, Ace engineers are in the habit of using branch views to document the *intended* flow of change. They also find branch views convenient for use with the integrate, interchanges, and diff2 commands. To formalize changes in private branch parentage, Ace engineers retool their branch views.

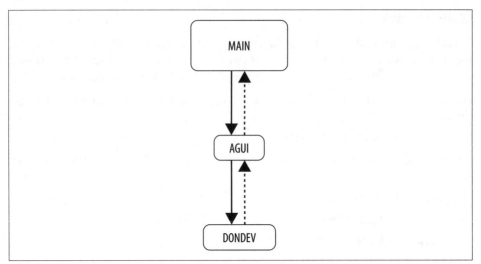

Figure 10-8. Flow of change to and from a private branch

For example, Sue also has a private branch of AGUI, called SUEDEV, as shown in Figure 10-9.

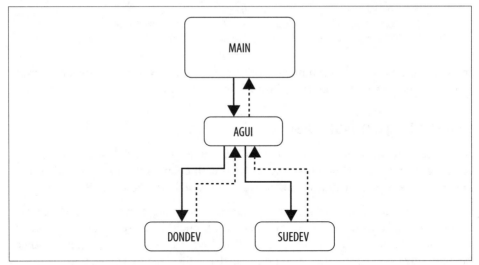

Figure 10-9. Two private branches of AGUI

The branch view that describes Sue's private branch looks very much like the one that describes Don's:

```
p4 branch SUEDEV-AGUI
```

Branch	SUEDEV-AGUI
View	//Ace/SUEDEV/gui/... //Ace/AGUI/gui/...

Sue has decided to make DONDEV the parent of her SUEDEV branch for now. (Don is coding some features she wants to experiment with in her branch.) She does this by creating a new branch view:

```
p4 branch SUEDEV-DONDEV

Branch          SUEDEV-DONDEV
View            //Ace/SUEDEV/gui/...    //Ace/DONDEV/gui/...
```

Now she can use the branch view to compare her branch to Don's and to update her private branch by pulling in Don's work. And, Don permitting, she can even use the SUEDEV-DONDEV branch view to deliver her experiments into his branch, as shown in Figure 10-10.

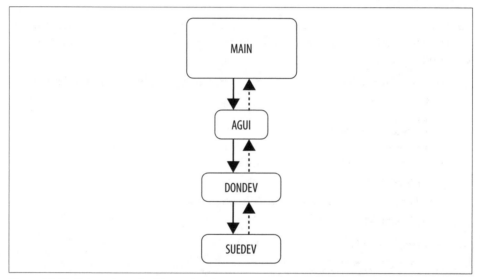

Figure 10-10. Private branch after reparenting

All of this can be done without the new branch view, of course—the branch view merely adds formality to what could otherwise be tacit intent.

A shared development codeline can be reparented as well. However, as you can imagine, reparenting shared codelines can wreak havoc with the flow of change. Because private branches are used by single users and positioned very low on the tofu scale, reparenting them isn't as risky.

Redeploying a private branch

Private branches can be redeployed. That is, a branch branched from one codeline can be recycled as a branch of another codeline. The only reason to do this, really, is to keep private branch paths from proliferating in the depot.

For instance, Don was using the DONDEV branch to do work on AGUI's *gui* module. He completed the work and delivered it from his private branch to the AGUI codeline. He now plans to do some work on MAIN's *utils* and *tests* modules. For this, he will redeploy DONDEV as a private branch of MAIN (see Figure 10-11).

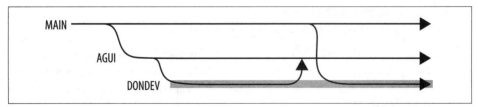

Figure 10-11. Redeploying a private branch

Before recycling a private branch, you can clear the decks, as it were, by deleting all its files. This makes a clean break in file histories and makes future integrations easier. Don demonstrates:

1. Using his DONDEV-master workspace, he deletes all the files in the DONDEV branch:

   ```
   p4 sync
   p4 delete //Ace/DONDEV/...
   p4 submit
   ```

2. He deletes the DONDEV-AGUI branch view:

   ```
   p4 branch -d DONDEV-AGUI
   ```

   ...and creates a new DONDEV-MAIN branch view:

   ```
   p4 branch DONDEV-MAIN
   ```

Branch	DONDEV-MAIN	
View	//Ace/DONDEV/tests/...	//Ace/MAIN/tests/...
	//Ace/DONDEV/utils/...	//Ace/MAIN/utils/...

3. He retools his DONDEV-master workspace spec:

   ```
   p4 client DONDEV-master
   ```

Client	DONDEV-master	
Root	c:\ws\agui	
View	//Ace/MAIN/utils/...	//DONDEV-master/utils/...
	//Ace/MAIN/tests/...	//DONDEV-master/tests/...

4. He branches files from MAIN into DONDEV:

   ```
   p4 integ -f -d -i -r -b DONDEV-MAIN
   p4 submit
   ```

   (The -d and -i flags let Perforce know it's okay to go ahead and branch files whose names are the same as those previously deleted. -f ensures that files will be branched regardless of integration history, and -r, of course, makes the branch view mapping work in reverse.)

This gives Don a fully populated DONDEV branch again. And although DONDEV is still a private development branch, its effective parent is now MAIN, as shown in Figure 10-12.

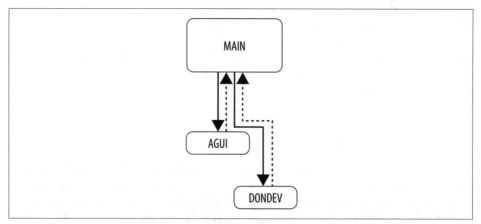

Figure 10-12. The flow of change after redeployment

You can also recycle a private branch for use with the same parent codeline. You'd typically do this if your private branch has been inactive for a long time. By deleting all its files and rebranching them, you're creating a clean break with previous history. If you're not changing a private branch's parent, you don't have to change its branch view, of course.

And yes, you can recycle shared development codelines as well. But, as with re-parenting shared codelines, it's not a good idea—it's disruptive, and it muddies the flow of change.

CHAPTER 11

Staging Streams and Web Content

In Chapter 9 you saw how Perforce is used to keep track of software that is released two or three times a year. Web-hosted software—what we're calling web content—demands that we manage codelines in an entirely different way. For one thing, we don't have to support multiple versions. The version on our web sites is the version our customers use; we don't have to keep old versions around for patches and point releases. But unlike shrinkwrapped software, which may be released several times a year, web content may have to be released several times a *week*. Given the complexity of the software that goes into a web site, we certainly don't want to be saddled with creating and managing a release codeline for each new version.

In this chapter we'll look at using staging streams to manage frequent releases. (*Stream* is another word for *codeline*. See Chapter 7.) Using web content as the context, we'll see how change moves from stage to stage, how development enters the staging pipeline, and how bug fixes are treated.

Staging Web Content

Purveyors of large and rapidly evolving web sites have learned they can reduce complexity by deploying content in stages. Each stage traps problems before subsequent stages are affected. For example, the first stage might be to test whether everything can be compiled together and started up, if nothing else. The second stage might be to evaluate appearance, and the third might be to validate behavior and performance. It's certainly beyond the scope of this book to go into detail about what happens in each stage, but it's well within the scope of Perforce to manage the staging.

The key to effective staging is to stop worrying about individual files. It's just not feasible to try and mix and match files to produce a working web site when the site is large and complex. Instead we treat web content development as a sequence of web site versions. We track each version as it moves through the staging pipeline and publish live web sites from the versions that make it all the way through. This process is what we'll focus on in this chapter.

But really, this chapter is not about web content—it's about managing the Perforce codelines in which web content evolves. In fact, it's about how to manage codelines for any kind of content staging. You'll find it useful reading even if you aren't developing web content.

With Perforce, we can manage deployment stages with staging streams. The strategy, in a nutshell, is this:

- Each staging stream has its own path in the depot.
- Each stream has its own firmness on the tofu scale. (See Chapter 7.)
- Web content versions are shunted from stage to stage in the soft-to-firm direction.
- Jobs or labels are used to mark web content versions that are ready to move to the next stage.
- Content is previewed on web sites built from staging streams.
- Automated scripts do the moving when the conditions are right.
- Integration history provides an audit trail of content in the staging pipeline.

Web content at Ace Engineering

To demonstrate the use of staging streams, we'll look again at Ace Engineering. As with all effective demonstrations, this one is simplified so that explanations and diagrams don't overpower the concepts it is intended to illustrate. However, it involves—we hope—enough real-world conditions that you can easily construe an implementation to match more complex requirements.

Ace Engineering's web site relies primarily on PHP, MySQL, and Apache. The mainline in which visual and executable content come together is a staging stream called WEBMAIN, shown in Figure 11-1. It contains two top-level modules, *app* and *www*.

Figure 11-1. Ace Engineering's web content mainline

- The *app* module contains the executable content that is used to build, manage, and validate the web site. It includes database setup and replication scripts, server configuration files, and various programs and scripts that test and validate the site. Content in the *app* module is developed by Pam's team of software engineers and web programmers.
- The *www* module contains the files that appear on the web site in situ. It contains both visual content and executable content.

The visual content in *www* includes images, text, XML, CSS, HTML, and PDF. It is developed primarily by the web design group, with input from marketing, technical, and administrative contributors. The lead web designer and overseer of visual content is Eric.

The executable content in *www* includes PHP and JavaScript developed by web programmers on Pam's team.

The release cycle

Ace Engineering's external web site is updated daily. Each update is called a "release," although the version released is usually only slightly different from its predecessor. Making a release normally involves three stages: completion, testing, and publication.

Developers integrate completed work into the WEBMAIN stream. (We'll be taking a closer look shortly at how this works.) Once a day, a web site version is copied from WEBMAIN into the WEBQA stream where it is hammered with a large battery of automated tests.

If no showstopping problems are found during testing, the WEBQA version is published by copying it into the WEBLIVE stream. The cycle usually completes within a day. Monday's WEBMAIN version, for example, will be tested and installed on the external web site by Tuesday, as illustrated in Figure 11-2.

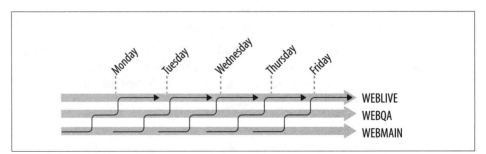

Figure 11-2. The web release cycle

The WEBMAIN stream is the softest of the three staging streams. Developers can integrate completed work into it at any time. The WEBQA stream is firmer; it is normally changed only by Brian, the lead test engineer. Other developers may submit changes to WEBQA by Brian's invitation only. The WEBLIVE stream is the firmest; the external web site is built from its files. It is also under Brian's control and normally changes only when he copies a new WEBQA release into it. Figure 11-3 shows how the staging streams stack up on the tofu scale.

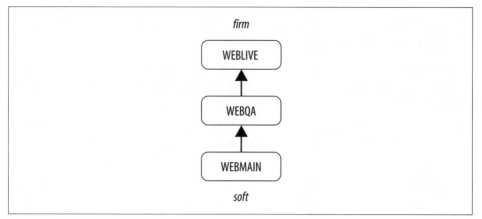

Figure 11-3. Staging streams and the tofu scale

Brian, as the curator of the web staging streams, has set up a master workspace for each stream. The WEBMAIN-master workspace, for example, looks like this:

```
p4 client WEBMAIN-master

Client      WEBMAIN-master
Root        /qa1/master/WEBMAIN
View        //Ace/WEBMAIN/...    //WEBMAIN-master/...
```

How web sites are updated

Internal web sites at Ace Engineering allow developers to view content in the staging streams (see Table 11-1).

Table 11-1. Staging streams and preview sites at Ace Engineering

Stage	Stream	Depot path	Web site
Completion	WEBMAIN	//Ace/WEBMAIN/...	http://webmain.ace.com
Testing	WEBQA	//Ace/WEBQA/...	http://webqa.ace.com
Publication	WEBLIVE	//Ace/WEBLIVE/...	http://www.ace.com

The WEBLIVE stream, as we just mentioned, contains content visible on the external web site. The internal web sites mimic the external, production web site. Each has its own Apache server and its own MySQL database.

On each web site machine, an automated script synchronizes files with changes in the Perforce depot. If files in the *app* module are affected, the script may rebuild the database and restart the web server. When a new version affects only the *www* module, the site is updated "hot," without interrupting the database or web server.

For example, the WEBQA stream's preview site is at *http://webqa.ace.com*; webqa is a Unix machine. The Apache server running on this machine is configured to find files in the */qa1/prev/webqa* directory.

A script running on the webqa machine updates this web site when changes are submitted to the *//Ace/WEBQA* path. Let's take a look at the P4 commands run by the update script:

1. The script reinitializes WEBQA-preview, the client workspace it's going to use. It uses the WEBQA-master workspace as a template. The resulting spec is:

   ```
   Client    WEBQA-preview
   Root      /qa1/prev/webqa
   View      //Ace/WEBQA/...    //WEBQA-preview/...
   ```

2. The updating script checks to see whether it's going to have to bounce the servers:

   ```
   p4 -c WEBQA-preview sync -n //Ace/WEBQA/app/...
   ```

   (Here the script uses -c to set the current workspace to WEBQA-preview for this p4 command invocation.) If this sync -n command lists files, the script proceeds to shut down the Apache and MySQL servers.

3. The script resynchronizes the entire workspace:

   ```
   p4 -c WEBQA-preview sync
   ```

   The update script restarts the web and database servers, if necessary. It does this by running initialization scripts located in the */qa1/prev/webqa/app* directory. This directory has just been resynchronized, of course, so any changes to schema or configuration will be reflected in the restarted servers.

The net effect of any change to the *//Ace/WEBQA* path is that the web site is updated according to the extent of the change. It's the same for all the preview web sites.

Pulling a release into testing

Changes are delivered to the WEBMAIN stream by developers. Content in the WEBMAIN stream is assumed to be fit for release. (In other words, a developer doesn't integrate a change into WEBMAIN unless it's ready to go.) Once a day, Brian, the lead test engineer, pulls a release from WEBMAIN into WEBQA:

```
p4 integ -i -d -t //Ace/WEBMAIN/... //Ace/WEBQA/...
p4 resolve -at
p4 submit
```

This sequence of commands shunts the WEBMAIN version into the WEBQA stream, kicking off an update of the WEBQA preview site. Note that:

- Brian runs these commands with his current workspace set to WEBQA-master. Before running them he makes sure there are no opened files in the workspace.

(Actually, Brian uses a script to run these commands. And he doesn't actually invoke the script himself; it's invoked automatically as a `cron` job.[*] But these are the commands Brian would run if he were to do this manually.)

- If the WEBQA stream doesn't exist yet, these commands will create it. In other words, these commands can be used both to create the WEBQA stream for the first release and to pull subsequent releases into it.
- The `integrate` command operates only on the files that have changed. This means that the size of the operation is no larger than the number of WEBMAIN files updated since the last release.
- The combination of flags on the `integrate` and `resolve` commands makes integration behave like a `copy` command. Files that have been added, modified, or renamed in WEBMAIN will be copied to WEBQA; files that have been deleted in WEBMAIN will be deleted in WEBQA; files in WEBQA will have the same file types as their donors in WEBMAIN.

Publishing a tested release

Brian is also in charge of publishing tested releases. He does this by copy-integrating content from WEBQA into WEBLIVE:

```
p4 integ -i -d -t //Ace/WEBQA/... //Ace/WEBLIVE/...
p4 resolve -at
p4 submit
```

These are the same commands used to pull a release from WEBMAIN into WEBQA. The operation is essentially the same, with one distinction: it is done using WEBLIVE-master as the current workspace.

The web site built from the WEBLIVE stream is the live, external web site, configured to use the production database.

Release timing is flexible

Brian controls the release testing cycle. He pulls a version from WEBMAIN to WEBQA only when a new cycle begins. No changes move from WEBMAIN to WEBQA *during* a test cycle.

If the WEBQA test cycle gets long, new changes can pile up in WEBMAIN. This is not a problem. Developers can continue delivering their changes to WEBMAIN while WEBMAIN awaits the next test cycle.

---

[*] cron is a Unix utility that runs background programs at scheduled intervals. Scheduled Tasks is its rough equivalent on Windows.

If the test cycle is short, on the other hand, the WEBMAIN stream may not have received new changes in time for the next test cycle. This is not a problem either. When Brian tries to pull a new release, Perforce simply reports that there is nothing to integrate:

```
p4 integ -i -d -t //Ace/WEBMAIN/... //Ace/WEBQA/...
//Ace/WEBMAIN/... - all revision(s) already integrated.
```

When there is nothing to integrate from WEBMAIN to WEBQA, there's nothing new to test.

The web content audit trail

Having a depot path for each deployment stage makes it easy to find out what's going on at a particular stage. For example, we can see what's hot off the press in web development by looking at the recent history of WEBMAIN:

```
p4 changes -m30 //Ace/WEBMAIN/...
```

To see the difference between the current WEBMAN and WEBQA streams, we can use:

```
p4 diff2 -q //Ace/WEBMAIN/... //Ace/WEBQA/...
```

To see what's completed but not yet tested, we can use:

```
p4 interchanges //Ace/WEBMAIN/... //Ace/WEBQA/...
```

To find out exactly what was on our web site at noon on May 23, 2005, we can use:

```
p4 files //Ace/WEBMAIN/www/...@2005/05/23:12:00:00
```

Visual Content Development

In order for web content to enter the staging pipeline, it must be ready to release. Scripts and other executable content, for example, have to be working correctly. Visual content has to be contextually appropriate and aesthetically pleasing. What this means is that developers need a place to check in their changes that is softer than WEBMAIN. They need a place where they can submit and preview their work in progress in order to know whether it's worthy of release.

At Ace Engineering, there are two codelines where developers may submit their work in progress: WEBENG and WEBVIS (see Figure 11-4). Both are branched from WEBMAIN.

WEBENG and WEBVIS are both used for ongoing web development, and both are soft enough for developers to make refinements before their work is released. Having two development codelines instead of one separates executable content

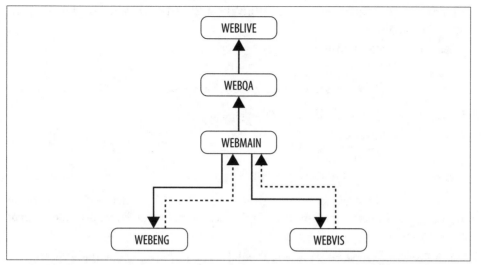

Figure 11-4. *Web development codelines*

development from visual content development. The two content types are separated because each has its own flow of change:

- Executable web content at Ace consists primarily of scripts and programs. The flow of change we explored in Chapter 10 works very well for developing executable web content. As a matter of fact, Pam manages the WEBENG codeline very much the same way Ann manages the AGUI codeline: the WEBENG codeline, in which both *app* and *www* are active modules, is kept up to date with WEB-MAIN. At points of completion, work is delivered from WEBENG to WEB-MAIN.

- Ace's visual web content is a different animal entirely. For one thing, developers tend to work piecemeal and independently. For another, the files they work on are difficult or impossible to merge. The merge down, copy up protocol simply doesn't apply to this kind of development.

In this section we'll focus on shepherding visual web content from development to release.

The visual content codeline

The WEBVIS codeline is dedicated to visual content development. Eric, the lead web designer, is in charge of it. Of the two top-level modules in WEBMAIN, only *www* is branched to WEBVIS. (The *app* module contains nothing that needs to be on local disk to work on visual content.)

Eric has set up a branch view called WEBVIS-WEBMAIN that he uses for comparison and integration:

```
p4 branch WEBVIS-WEBMAIN

Branch          WEBVIS-WEBMAIN
View            //Ace/WEBVIS/www/... //Ace/WEBMAIN/www/...
```

He has also set up a WEBVIS-master workspace:

```
p4 client WEBVIS-master

Client          WEBVIS-master
View            //Ace/WEBVIS/... //WEBVIS-master/...
```

Web designers, artists, and authors work in the WEBVIS codeline. They work on images (*.gif* and *.png*), text templates (*.tpl*), style sheets (*.css*), static documents (*.pdf* and *.html*), and so forth.

The WEBVIS codeline contains PHP and JavaScript as well, but these files aren't touched by visual content developers. Only Eric touches them, and when he does, it's only to update WEBVIS with the latest executable content from WEEBMAIN. Thus, as Pam's group delivers completed features and enhancements from WEBENG to WEBMAIN, the WEBVIS codeline stays current with them.

Like the staging streams, WEBVIS has its own preview web site, online at *http://webvis.ace.com*. As developers submit changes, they can browse this site and see how PHP renders their files.

Delivering completed work from WEBVIS to WEBMAIN is Eric's responsibility. This means Eric has to know who's working on what, and he needs to know when their work is done.

As it turns out, Perforce jobs are just the semaphores he needs. If you're going to submit changes to the WEBVIS codeline, Eric requires you to open a job first to describe the work you plan to do. And when you're done, you must close the job so Eric knows your work is ready to release. In "Enforcing the use of jobs," later in this chapter, we'll see how Eric enforces these requirements, but first, let's look at what a developer does to meet them.

Working on visual content

Linda is going to update course descriptions in Ace Engineering's online training catalog. She launches P4V and creates a workpace called WEBVIS-linda, using the WEBVIS-master workspace as a template. Before she starts working on files, however, she creates a new job. She does this with File → New → Job. In the job form, shown in Figure 11-5, she enters a brief description of her task at hand.

Linda now navigates the depot file tree (see Figure 11-6), synchronizes files and folders (that's File → Get Latest Revisions in P4V), and points and clicks her way to

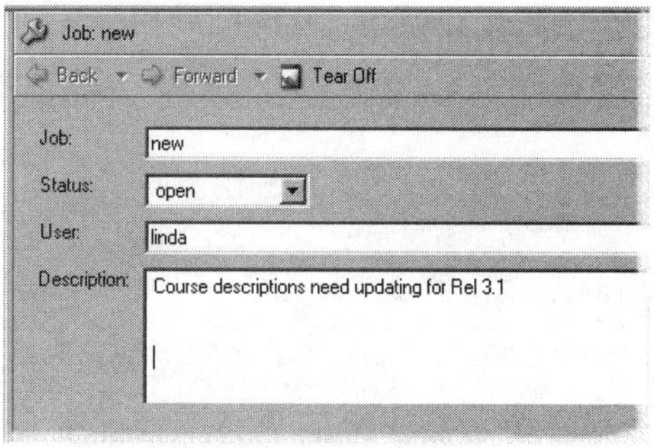

Figure 11-5. Creating a new job

checking out and editing files. She can use her web browser to see the local files she's editing, but she won't be able to see how they're rendered by PHP until checks them in.

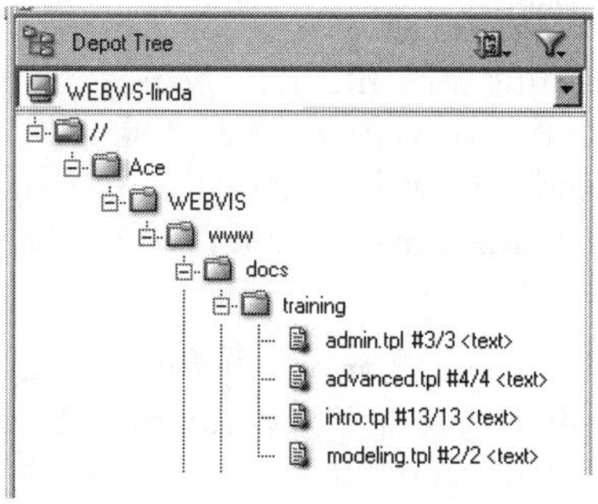

Figure 11-6. Navigating the depot file tree

When Linda is ready to check files in, she uses P4V's File → Submit command, as you see in Figure 11-7.

In P4V's Submit Changelist dialog, Linda does the following:

1. She enters a description of her change.
2. She checks her job in the "Link jobs to changelist" list.
3. She picks "open" from the Job status upon submit menu.
4. She clicks Submit.

(And why does she specify "open" as the job status? Because if she doesn't, Perforce will set it to "closed" when she submits her change. By leaving it open, she's signaling that her changes should not be released yet.)

As soon as Linda has submitted files, she can point her browser to *http://webvis.ace. com* to see how her changes look on the preview site. It's no problem if she finds

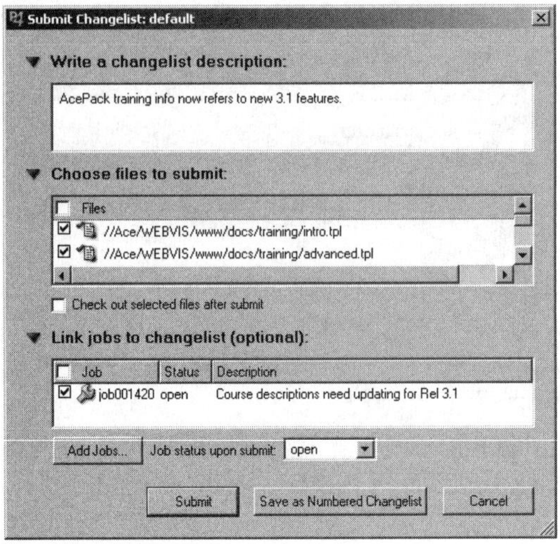

Figure 11-7. Linking a job to a changelist

something that needs correcting, or a file that she missed. She can continue to check out, change, and submit files to complete her task. She can ask other people to browse the preview site and review her changes. As long as the status of the job linked to her changelists remains open, Eric knows that her changes aren't ready to be released.

When Linda is confident her changes are ready for release, she closes her job. As we see in Figure 11-8, she finds the job by running View → Jobs and entering "user=linda status=open" in the search field.

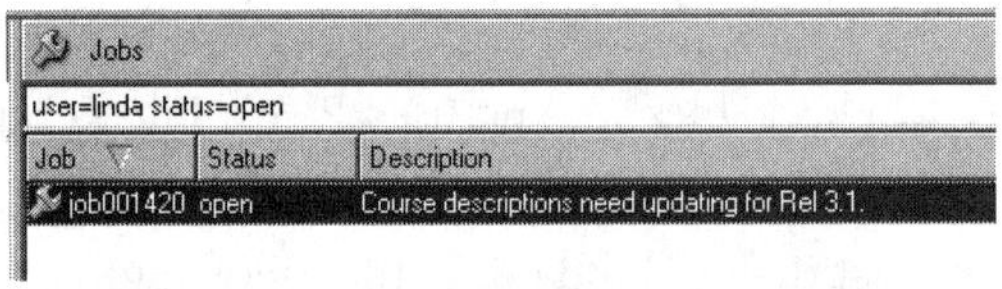

Figure 11-8. Finding a job

With her job selected, Linda uses the Edit → Edit job menu to get to the job form. There she sets the job's Status field to closed and saves the form, as shown in Figure 11-9.

What's ready to be released?

Eric maintains the continuous integration of WEBVIS into WEBMAIN with a script. The script keeps an eye on the changes submitted to WEBVIS and looks for completed work. When it finds changes that qualify, it integrates them from WEBVIS

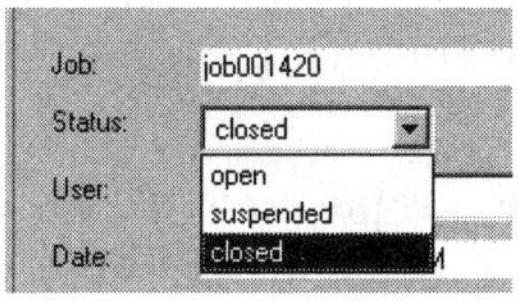

Figure 11-9. Closing a job

into WEBMAIN. The script uses a few simple P4 commands to figure out which changes can be released. Before looking at these commands, however, let's take a look at the logic behind them.

Table 11-2 shows seven unreleased changes, numbered 54 through 60. Changelist 54 contains file revisions *a#4*, *c#2*, and *d#9*, changelist 55 contains revision *b#6*, and so forth. There are four jobs—A, B, C, and D—associated with these changes. Job A is linked to changes 54, 56, and 59; job B is linked to changes 55 and 57; and so on. Jobs A, C, and D are closed. Only job B is still open.

Table 11-2. Release dependencies

Job	A	(B)	A	(B)	C	A	D
Change	54	55	56	57	58	59	60
File *a*	#4						
File *b*		#6					
File *c*	#2		#3			#4	
File *d*	#9		#10				#11
File *e*				#2		#3	
File *f*					#7		

Given that closed jobs mean work is done and open jobs mean it's not, which of these changes can be integrated into another codeline without bringing along incomplete work? In other words, which of these changes can we release?

- Clearly we can't release changes 55 and 57 yet. We know this because they're linked to job B, and job B is still open.

- Change 58 can be released. It's linked to a closed job, and its one file revision, *f#7*, has no prior, unreleased revisions. Change 58 is a completed change that is independent of all the other changes.

- Can change 59 be released? No. Although it's linked to a closed job, it contains a revision, *e#3*, that builds on *e#2*, and *e#2* can't be released. Why not? Because *e#2*'s change is linked to open job B. We can't release change 59 because it is tainted with the incomplete work of change 57.

- Moreover, since we can't release change 59, we know we can't make a complete delivery of the work associated with job A. That means that we can't release changes 54 or 56 either.

- How about change 60? It too is linked to a closed job. But the one revision in its changelist, *d#11*, builds on revisions in changes 54 and 56. And because we can't release 54 or 56, we can't release 60.

Automating continuous integration

Now that you've seen the logic behind choosing changes to release, let's look at the P4 commands used by Eric's continuous-integration script. It's important to note that Eric's script runs with a current workspace that has a view of the WEBMAIN stream. (Because the files it's going to change are in WEBMAIN, WEBMAIN must be mapped in the current workspace view.) The workspace is pristine at the outset—no opened files, no pending changelists.

1. The script lists the changes in WEBVIS that are not yet integrated to WEBMAIN:

   ```
   p4 interchanges -b WEBVIS-WEBMAIN
   Change 10029 by linda 'AcePack training...'
   Change 10030 by hamid 'Link to download...'
   Change 10033 by linda 'Fix typo...'
   Change 10034 by bruce 'Swell new icons...'
   Change 10035 by hamid 'CSS changes for...'
   ```

   (Recall that the WEBVIS-WEBMAIN branch view defines *//Ace/WEBVIS/www/* ... as the source and *//Ace/WEBMAIN/www/*... as the target.)

   If there are no unintegrated changes, the script exits.

2. The script tags the revisions in each changelist with a temporary label:

   ```
   p4 tag -l temp10029 @=10029
   p4 tag -l temp10030 @=10030
   p4 tag -l temp10033 @=10033
   p4 tag -l temp10034 @=10034
   p4 tag -l temp10035 @=10035
   ```

   (You may recall reading in earlier examples that the undocumented but succinct @= revision syntax selects files identified with a particular changelist. Run help undoc to find out more about undocumented revision syntax.)

3. The script uses the temporary labels it just created to list the jobs involved with each changelist:

   ```
   p4 jobs @temp10029
   job001420 on 2005/04/19 by linda *closed* 'Course descriptions...'

   p4 jobs @temp10030
   job001411 on 2005/04/17 by hamid *closed* 'Need download link...'

   p4 jobs @temp10033
   job001401 on 2005/04/15 by hamid *closed* 'New font scheme...'
   job001420 on 2005/04/19 by linda *closed* 'Course descriptions...'
   ```

```
p4 jobs @temp10034
job001420 on 2005/04/19 by linda *closed* 'Course descriptions...'
job001426 on 2005/04/22 by bruce *open*   'Ron wants icons for...'
```

```
p4 jobs @temp10035
job001378 on 2005/04/02 by hamid *closed* 'Promo pages ready...'
```

The script analyzes output like this to determine which changes qualify for release. In this case, changes 10030 and 10035 can be released. (10034 can't be released because it's linked to an open job. 10033 and 10029 can't be released because they're tainted by 10034.)

4. Having determined which changes to release, the script deletes the temporary labels:

```
p4 label -d temp10029
p4 label -d temp10030
p4 label -d temp10033
p4 label -d temp10034
p4 label -d temp10035
```

5. The script goes through the releasable changes in order and uses them to open files for integration:

```
p4 integ -b WEBVIS-WEBMAIN @=10030
p4 integ -b WEBVIS-WEBMAIN @=10035
```

6. The script attempts to resolve the opened files:

```
p4 resolve -as
p4 resolve -n
```

(For more about how this works, take a look back at Chapter 3.)

If resolve -n shows that files couldn't be auto-resolved safely, the script reverts the opened files and sends Eric email. (This is a rare occurrence, usually a symptom of a bug fix in WEBMAIN that hasn't been pulled into WEBVIS. Whatever the cause, it's going to need Eric's attention.)

7. If it gets this far, the script submits a change:

```
p4 submit
```

(A script can't run a plain old submit command, of course—it has to create a changelist form, insert a description, and pass the form to submit -i. See Chapter 6.)

Using jobs as ready-to-release indicators isn't an iron-clad system. Users can still get sloppy and forget to close jobs, and there's nothing to keep them from closing jobs even when their work isn't really ready for prime time. But as an informal mechanism, it works quite well to automate the continuous integration of visual content.

Enforcing the use of jobs

As a Perforce superuser, Eric has a few tricks up his sleeve to make developers remember to use jobs:

- He has installed a presubmit trigger that fires when changes are submitted to the *//Ace/WEBVIS* path. The trigger is simply a script that runs the change command to check the user's changelist. If it doesn't find at least one opened job listed, it rejects the change and the user gets an error message saying You may not submit a change without linking an open job to it.

  Eric has also installed spec triggers to keep users from deleting jobs and from reopening jobs after completed work has been released:

  p4 triggers

  ```
  Trig-    MustHaveJob  submit  //Ace/WEBVIS/...  "webvis-checkchange.rb %changelist%"
  gers     NoJobReopen  in      job   "webvis-nojobreopen.rb %user% %formfile%"
           NoJobDelete  delete  job   "webvis-nojobdelete.rb %user% %formfile%"
  ```

- He has configured depot protections to restrict access to the WEBVIS codeline.

  p4 protect

  ```
  Protections     ...
                  read   user   *             *    //Ace/WEBVIS/...
                  write  group  WEBVIS-write  *    //Ace/WEBVIS/...
                  ...
  ```

  Only members of the WEBVIS-write group can submit changes to files in the *//Ace/WEBVIS* path. Eric controls WEBVIS-write membership with the group command:

  p4 group WEBVIS-write

  ```
  Group      WEBVIS-write

  Users      ...
             hamid
             linda
             liz
             ...
  ```

- As Eric adds users to the WEBVIS-write group, he also updates their user specs so that their open jobs show up in the changelists they submit. When he added Linda to the group, for example, he also updated her user spec:

  p4 user linda

  ```
  User       linda

  Jobview    user=linda status=open
  ```

  The Jobview field in Linda's user spec is what makes jobs appear in P4V's Submit Changelist dialog when Linda checks in files.

Preventing merging

For the most part, Ace's visual web content developers work on files serially. Linda, for example, isn't likely to start changing a file someone else is already working on. And when she checks files in, it's not likely she'll find she has to merge someone else's concurrent changes into them first. Again, this is partly because ownership of visual content files tends to be fairly well partitioned. But it's also because these files can't easily be merged. We don't merge image files, for example—or if we do, we do it by hand. Even text files aren't usually merged in visual content development, mainly because the WYSIWYG editing tools we use don't lend themselves very well to automated merges.

With visual content files, it's better to prevent situations that would require merging files. Developers can do this individually, by locking files as they open them. If Linda is worried about the possibility of having to merge files, for example, she can use P4V's File → Lock command.

But there's another way to prevent inadvertent merging, and that is with the *exclusive locking* file type. Exclusive locking files can be opened by only one user at a time.

Eric has done this for the WEBVIS codeline. First, using the WEBVIS-master workspace, he changed the file type of all the files in the codeline:

```
p4 sync
p4 edit -t +l //...
p4 submit
```

(You may remember reading in Chapter 1 that the +l file type modifier means exclusive locking, and that you can change a file's type as you open it for editing.)

The other precaution Eric took was to make exclusive locking the default for new files. He did this with a Perforce *typemap*. As a superuser, Eric can run the typemap command and set default file types by filespec:

```
p4 typemap

Typemap        +l //Ace/WEBVIS/...
```

With this typemap in effect, new files in WEBVIS codeline will take on the +l file type by default.

Bug Fixes and Staging Streams

So, what happens if a bug is found in testing? Or worse, what if a bug is found in the published release? The answer depends on the severity of the bug, what it takes to fix it, and the state of current development. We'll see how these play out in three different scenarios.

Noncritical bugs

Many noncritical bugs are found during the release cycle and after a release is published. They are not fixed in the staging streams, however. They're fixed in a development codeline, either WEBVIS or WEBENG. Noncritical bug fixes enter WEBMAIN and migrate through WEBQA to WEBLIVE according to the normal release cycle.

This is quite different, you'll notice, from how we treat release codelines. We branch release codelines specifically to fix bugs. We have time in the schedule to rerun tests as we make changes in release codelines; this ensures that our bug fixes haven't broken anything else.

But with extremely frequent releases, we have to keep content moving through the cycle. If we were to make changes in WEBQA, we'd have to retest the code in WEBQA. And if were to retest the code in WEBQA, we'd have to delay testing the *next* release from WEBMAIN. Since it takes only a day or so to get WEBMAIN fixes into WEBLIVE in any case, we're better off keeping releases moving than holding them up for noncritical bugs.

Showstoppers in WEBQA

Now let's consider what happens when testing uncovers a showstopper bug in the WEBQA stage. Remember, the WEBQA stream was copied from a recent version of WEBMAIN. The first thing to do is to check the *http://webmain.ace.vis* site for evidence of the bug—or lack of it—in WEBMAIN. If we're lucky, the bug will have already been found, fixed, and released to WEBMAIN. In this case all we have to do is abort testing in WEBQA and restart it with a new version pulled in from WEBMAIN.

If the bug is not fixed in WEBMAIN we have a choice. We can fix it in WEBQA or we can fix it in a development codeline—either WEBVIS or WEBENG. Fixing it in a development codeline is easiest, because it's how developers normally work. It does mean, however, that the version currently in WEBQA will have to be abandoned. We'll have to wait until the next WEBMAIN version is ready before we can start testing again, as shown in Figure 11-10.

Or we can fix the bug in the WEBQA stream. If we do this, we may be able to expedite the release by resuming testing where we left off once the bug is fixed. Whether this is feasible depends on the nature of the bug. If the fix was messy, we'd probably want to restart testing from the beginning, in which case we may as well have fixed the bug in a development codeline anyway.

Fixing a bug in WEBQA also means that a developer has to set up a workspace mapped to the WEBQA stream. This isn't a huge problem, but it's a little bit outside of developers' normal work habits. Moreover, we'll have to integrate the bug fix

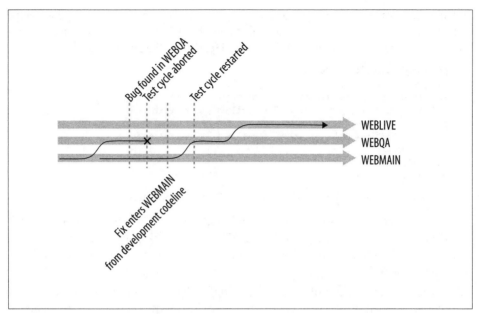

Figure 11-10. Abandoning the current test cycle

from WEBQA into WEBMAIN, and from WEBMAIN into development codelines. This is yet another reason it might have made more sense to fix the bug in a development codeline.

Rolling back the published web site

The worst-case scenario is that web content makes it all the way to the published web site—into the WEBLIVE stream, that is—and *then* we discover a showstopper. Because our live, production web servers are getting their files from the WEBLIVE stream, either we have to fix WEBLIVE fast or we have to roll it back to the last good version.

Luckily every version of the published web site is stored in the WEBLIVE stream. If we know that there was a good version online at noon on May 24, 2005, for example, we—we being Brian, in particular—can roll the stream back to that version.

Brain uses the WEBLIVE-master workspace to do this:

```
p4 client WEBLIVE-master

Client      WEBLIVE-master
Root        /qa2/master/WEBLIVE
View        //Ace/WEBLIVE/...    //WEBLIVE-master/...
```

(As you can see from the Root field, this happens to be a Unix workspace.)

In Chapter 2 you saw the recipe for backing out a change. Brian uses a similar recipe to roll back a web site. He's going to roll the WEBLIVE stream back to a dated snapshot of its content at noon on May 24, 2005. Here's how he applies the recipe:

```
p4 sync @2005/05/24:12:00:00
p4 sync -n > tempfile
sed -n -e "s/#.* - deleted as .*//p" tempfile | p4 -x- add
sed -n -e "s/#.* - updating .*//p" tempfile | p4 -x- edit
p4 sync
sed -n -e "s/#.* - added as .*//p" tempfile | p4 -x- delete
p4 resolve -ay
p4 submit
rm tempfile
```

And here's a play-by-play breakdown of how Brian's recipe works:

1. It starts out by synchronizing the workspace to version *@2005/05/24:12:00:00*. (Remember, Brian's using the WEBLIVE-master workspace to do this. It has a view of the *//Ace/WEBLIVE* path.) The workspace now contains the good version of the web site.

2. It captures the output of sync -n in *tempfile*. The output is a preview of what would happen if the workspace were to be resynchronized to the current WEBLIVE version now. It is also the list of files that need to be rolled back. Here's a sample of the sync -n output:

    ```
    ...
    //Ace/WEBLIVE/www/docs/search/advanced.php#3 - added as ...
    //Ace/WEBLIVE/www/docs/auth/passwd.php#9 - updating ...
    //Ace/WEBLIVE/www/docs/includes/auth.inc#4 - deleted as ...
    ...
    ```

3. It uses the Unix sed command to filter *tempfile* for lines containing deleted as and updating, and passes the filtered output to the P4 add and edit commands, respectively. This opens files for adding and editing, as necessary, to match the good version.

4. The workspace is resynchronized, this time with the current version. This doesn't alter the opened files, of course.

5. Lines in *tempfile* that contain the string added as are filtered and passed to the delete command. This opens files for deleting, as necessary, to match the good version.

6. The opened files are resolved. The -ay flag makes resolve accept the workspace files.

7. The opened files are submitted and *tempfile* is removed.

The net effect of this sequence of commands is to restore the WEBLIVE stream to its contents as of noon on May 24, 2005. Now it's up to the tools that automatically rebuild and reinstall the web site to do their thing.

Rolling back WEBLIVE to a previous version is trivial, as far as Perforce is concerned. Admittedly, it might not be trivial as far as regenerating the web site goes—databases have to match applications, and so forth.

Why Not Use a Label?

The tools that build Ace's live web sites get files by synchronizing with the WEBLIVE stream. Why not have the tools synchronize with labeled revisions rather than with the head revisions? If they did, Brian could effectively roll back Ace's published web site simply by reapplying the label to an earlier WEBLIVE version.

But here's the deal: applying a label doesn't create an event in the history of the WEBLIVE stream. Rolling back the WEBLIVE stream by submitting a change, on the other hand, *does* create such an event. It's an event that's recorded permanently in the stream's history:

```
p4 changes //Ace/WEBLIVE/...
Change 11283 on 2005/05/25 by brian "Roll back to 2005/05/24:12:00:00"
Change 11272 on 2005/05/25 by brian "Copy from WEBQA to WEBLIVE"
Change 11263 on 2005/05/24 by brian "Copy from WEBQA to WEBLIVE"
Change 11200 on 2005/05/23 by brian "Copy from WEBQA to WEBLIVE"
...
```

Brian builds Ace's live web sites from WEBLIVE's head revisions so that he can point to the history of WEBLIVE as the irrefutable record of what was on the web at any point in time.

Forcing integration after a rollback

Once we've rolled back WEBLIVE, we can fix the showstopper bug in a development codeline and let the usual release cycle propel the fix through testing to the live web site. There is one thing Brian will have to do differently, however. The next release he publishes is going to have to be force-integrated from WEBQA, to WEBLIVE:

```
p4 integ -f -i -d -t //Ace/WEBQA/... //Ace/WEBLIVE/...
p4 resolve -at
p4 submit
```

(The -f flag makes integ integrate files even when integration history shows all changes are accounted for.) This is a bit heavy-handed, in that all files will be opened and recopied, even if they haven't changed at all. But it's the best way to ensure that rolled-back files in WEBLIVE don't take precedence over previously published versions in WEBQA. It guarantees that what's going live in WEBLIVE is exactly what was tested in WEBQA.

Major Web Development

The staging streams and development codelines described in the previous examples are suitable for ongoing, iterative web content development. They don't really work for major web development projects. If we have a new development project afoot—a project that will take several months to complete, for example—we're going to have to isolate it to keep it from disrupting ongoing development. On the other hand, we don't want the project living under a rock, either—we need a way to get it into the QA cycle and onto beta test sites well in advance of introducing it into our production web content pipeline.

Our solution is to set up a parallel pipeline, as shown in the example in Figure 11-11. The Perforce commands for creating and using a parallel pipeline have already been covered, in this chapter and in previous chapters. Instead of demonstrating with examples here, let's just take a look at the big picture.

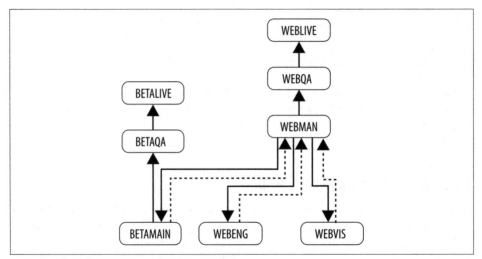

Figure 11-11. Parallel pipeline for major new development

To launch our major new development project, we branched WEBMAIN into a development codeline called BETAMAIN. BETAMAIN is a shared development codeline; our developers will use it for the new project. As bug fixes and minor enhancements flow into WEBMAIN, they are merged into BETAMAIN. However, until the project is complete, no change will flow from BETAMAIN to WEBMAIN. This ensures that content leading to the WEBLIVE steam remains undisturbed by the groundbreaking changes in BETAMAIN.

Meanwhile, we've branched BETAMAIN into a staging stream called BETAQA. BETAQA serves the same purpose as WEBQA—it's used to subject web content to testing. Change flows between BETAMAIN and BETAQA as the project evolves. The test cycle in BETAQA is necessarily irregular—even infrequent at first—but as the project matures, tests become more extensive and the cycle becomes more frequent. All the while change is flowing from WEBMAIN into BETAMAIN, keeping BETA-MAIN completely up to date with our current web content.

Eventually, when BETAMAIN matures to a point that it's ready to see the light of day, we branch BETAQA into BETALIVE. External beta web sites are built from BETALIVE, selected customers come to the beta web sites, and bugs are reported. Bugs are fixed in BETAMAIN; they flow through BETAQA to BETALIVE. The flow of change from BETAMAIN to BETALIVE now matches the flow of change from WEBMAIN to WEBLIVE. This parallel pipeline allows us to stabilize the development project without affecting our production web sites.

When the content in the beta pipeline meets quality expectations, we deliver our completed development work from BETAMAIN to WEBMAIN. (See "Delivering Completed Development Work" in Chapter 10.) The fruits of our major development project, now in the production web content stream, begin flowing through WEBQA to WEBLIVE. Our ongoing development codelines, WEBENG and WEB-VIS, are updated with the new content in WEBMAIN. And, finally, we mothball the BETAMAIN, BETAQA, and BETALIVE codelines.

Setting Up a Perforce Test Environment

This book is not a tutorial—there are no exercises to follow, no drills to complete, and no working sample programs to run. But if your interest is piqued as you read along, you may want to try a few things yourself. You'll be happy to know that it takes about 10 minutes to set up a Perforce test environment, complete with server.

There are caveats, however:

- Although you don't need a Perforce license to run a Perforce Server, an unlicensed server will support only two users and five workspaces.

- The quick setup steps described here are no substitute for a well-informed Perforce installation procedure. If you want to set up a Perforce Server for production use, please follow the instructions in the *Perforce System Administrator's Guide*.

- Perforce installation procedures vary slightly from release to release. The procedures described here are based on Perforce Release 2005.1.

Setup

You should plan to download and install, at a minimum, P4, the Perforce Command-Line Client, and P4D, the Perforce Server. You should also install P4V, the Perforce Visual Client, and P4Web, the Perforce Web Client, as both come up occasionally in examples in this book.

You can run the Perforce Server on the same machine you'll be using to run your client programs. Or, if you prefer, you can use the client programs on one machine while running the server on another. In either case, make sure you download and install the software that matches the machines on which you plan to run it.

Perforce offers two graphical clients for Windows, P4V and P4Win. P4V is newer and is available for non-Windows platforms as well as for Windows. As of Release 2005.1, P4V comes bundled in Perforce's core product installer for Windows. (The core installer also includes P4, P4D, and P4Web.)

P4Win is Perforce's classic Windows client. It can be downloaded separately in its own installer.

There are also two graphical merge tools available on Windows. The newer one is P4Merge; it's available both as a stand-alone program and as an embedded feature of P4V. P4Merge comes with the core installer. The classic merge tool for Windows, P4WinMerge, comes with the P4Win installer.

Installing Perforce on Windows

You don't have to be a Windows administrator to install Perforce for your own use. However, the steps that follow match the Perforce installer's behavior when *are* an administrator. If you're not an administrator you'll see different dialogs and defaults, and programs that are normally installed as services will be installed as command executables.

1. Go to *www.perforce.com* and follow the Download links to the Windows page. Download the core installer for Windows and run it. In the first configuration dialog, select Administrator → Typical. Now follow the dialogs to the end, accepting the default values.

2. In a Command Prompt window, run these commands to create your Perforce workspace:

   ```
   mkdir c:\p4workspace
   pushd c:\p4workspace
   p4 set P4CLIENT=testws
   p4 client -o | p4 client -i
   ```

   This sets up a Perforce workspace called "testws," rooted in *c:\p4workspace*.

3. You can launch P4V from the Windows toolbar with Start → Programs → Perforce → P4V. Enter "testws" as the workspace name in P4V's Open Connection dialog.

4. The installer will have started a P4Web service for you. To use it, point your browser to:

   ```
   http://localhost:8080/
   ```

Installing Perforce on Linux and other Unix systems

1. Make three directories, one for the Perforce executables, one for the Perforce Server to use for its depot and database, and one for you to use as your workspace:

   ```
   mkdir $HOME/p4bin
   mkdir $HOME/p4server
   mkdir $HOME/p4workspace
   ```

   Put the *$HOME/p4bin* directory in your executable path.

2. Go to *http://www.perforce.com* and follow the Download links to the software for your operating system. Download the P4, P4D, P4V, and P4Web components to your *$HOME/p4bin* directory.

3. Unpack the P4V archive:

   ```
   cd $HOME/p4bin
   gunzip p4v.tgz
   tar xvf p4v.tar
   ```

4. Make the program files executable:

   ```
   cd $HOME/p4bin
   chmod a+x p4 p4d p4v p4web
   ```

5. Start the Perforce Server program, p4d, using the parameters shown here:

   ```
   p4d -d -p 1666 -r $HOME/p4server &
   ```

6. Set environment variables P4PORT and P4CLIENT to 1666 and testws, respectively. For example:

   ```
   export P4PORT=1666
   export P4CLIENT=testws
   ```

   (The actual commands you use will depend on your shell, of course.) You can add these settings to your session startup scripts.

7. Run these commands to create your client workspace:

   ```
   cd $HOME/p4workspace
   p4 client -o | p4 client -i
   ```

   You now have a Perforce workspace called testws, rooted in *$HOME/p4workspace*.

8. You can launch P4V with:

   ```
   p4v &
   ```

9. You can start the daemon for a P4Web viewer with:

   ```
   p4web -b -w 8080 &
   ```

   To use P4Web, point your browser to:

   ```
   http://localhost:8080/
   ```

Installing Perforce on Mac OS X

Installing Perforce on Mac OS X is essentially the same as on Linux, with two differences:

1. There's no P4D for Mac OS X proper. Instead, you'll need to download the P4D built for Darwin. (The Perforce Software download pages will guide you to it.)

2. P4V comes as a disk image file for Mac OS X. After downloading the *P4V.dmg* file, select it in the Finder and double-click it to start P4V.

Your test environment

You now have at your disposal:

- A running Perforce Server whose address is localhost:1666.

- A client workspace known to your Perforce Server by the name testws. On Unix, your workspace is rooted in *$HOME/p4workspace*. On Windows, it's rooted in *c:\p4workspace*.

- The P4 client program—that is, the p4 command. You can use P4 from any command shell. (Note that you have to cd to a directory within your workspace for P4 to operate on files. You'll be reading more about this in Chapter 2.)

- The P4V application. You can quit and restart this application whenever you want.

- A "viewer" mode P4Web HTTP daemon listening at localhost:8080. (P4Web also has a "standard" mode, but it doesn't come up in this book.) You can kill this daemon and restart it whenever you want. It needs to be up only when you're using your web browser with Perforce.

In this test environment, the Perforce server and the client programs are running on the same machine. The server knows you by the login name you use for your local machine. You don't need a password to connect to it. It's an unlicensed server, and supports at most two users and five workspaces. It's fully functional, however, and can do everything a licensed server can do.

Your test depot is currently empty. In Chapter 2 you'll see how to add files to it. Until then you'll probably find P4V and P4Web to be somewhat unsatisfying to use, as their main thrust is to explore the contents of a depot.

Eventually you'll want to discard your test environment and set up a real Perforce environment. But first, play around a bit and get familiar with Perforce.

Connecting to Other Servers

Your Perforce environment is set up to connect you to your test server. Once you've downloaded and installed the Perforce client programs, however, you can use them to access any Perforce Server available to you.

First, find out the address of the Perforce Server you'd like to connect to. The address will be of the form *hostname:port*, where *hostname* is the network-visible name (or the IP address) of the machine on which the server is running, and *port* is a TCP/IP port number.

 One Perforce Server that is available to everyone is the Perforce Public Depot. Its address is `public.perforce.com:1666`.

You can configure your Perforce Server address by setting `P4PORT`:

- On Unix and Mac OS X, you can set `P4PORT` as an environment variable. For example:

    ```
    export P4PORT=public.perforce.com:1666
    ```
- On Windows, you can use P4 to set `P4PORT` in the Windows registry:

    ```
    p4 set P4PORT=public.perforce.com:1666
    ```

Both P4 and P4Web will respect your environment's `P4PORT` setting. The P4Web daemon, however, will have to be stopped and restarted after `P4PORT` is changed.

P4V, on the other hand, keeps its own registry of server addresses. It remembers the ones you've connected to, and other than the first time you start it up, it won't refer to your machine's `P4PORT` setting at all. To change to a different server, use P4V's **Connection** → Open Connection dialog.

Which server am I connected to?

The Perforce Server you're connected to tells you a little about itself when you run P4's info command:

```
p4 info
Server address: public.perforce.com:1666
Server root: /usr/depot/public
Server date: 2005/07/31 09:58:21 -0700 PDT
Server version: P4D/FREEBSD4/2005.1/80277 (2005/05/25)
Server license: Perforce Public Depot 1000 users (expires 2007/07/31)
```

P4V and P4Web display your Perforce Server address in the top of the main window or page.

Getting Help

While you're learning about Perforce you can get help from any of these sources:

- The Perforce manuals online at *http://www.perforce.com/perforce/technical.html*.
- The Help button in any of the Perforce graphical interfaces (P4V, P4Win, and P4Web).
- The P4 help command:

      p4 help

- The Perforce user discussion list and email archive at *http://maillist.perforce.com/mailman/listinfo/perforce-user*.
- The Perforce Software technical support staff at support@perforce.com.

Perforce Terminology and P4 Commands

Perforce has been a player in the software development world for 10 years now. Its first user interface was P4, the Perforce Command-Line Client. To this day, P4 remains the canonical interface to the Perforce Server. Some P4 command terminology is anchored deep in the server and dates back to the earliest versions of Perforce. Some has been updated to reflect new environments and tools with which Perforce is used. The total effect is not always consistent; Perforce terminology and P4 commands are, admittedly, a bit confusing.

This appendix explains the terms that seem to be the most confusing, and within each explanation, lists the P4 commands that are related to them.

"Submit" and "check in"
> In Perforce, *submit* and *check in* mean the same thing. We usually say *submit* because the P4 submit command checks files in to the repository.

"Changelist" and "change"
> A *changelist*, in Perforce, is a collection of files submitted together. In the earliest versions of Perforce, the term *changelist* didn't exist. The concept did exist, however, and its corresponding database object was called a *change*. When that proved difficult to document in clear English, the term *changelist* was introduced, although the early terminology persists in the Perforce Server. In this book, *change* and *changelist* are often used interchangeably.
>
> - The P4 change command doesn't change files. It allows you to define a changelist.
> - The submit command submits a changelist.
> - The changes command shows pending and submitted changelists.
> - The changelist and changelists commands are aliases for change and changes.
> - The filelog command shows *when* files were changed, and by whom.

- The P4 commands that show *how* files have changed are annotate, diff, and diff2.

"Client" and "workspace"

Perforce workspaces were originally called *clients*. By popular demand, that terminology is changing; Perforce tools and documentation now refer to *workspaces*. As you'll see in command logs and error messages, however, the Perforce Server still thinks of them as *clients*.

- The P4 client command defines a workspace.

- The clients command lists workspaces.

- The workspace and workspaces commands are aliases for the client and clients commands.

"View"

In the lexicon of the Perforce Server, a *view* is the scope of files that can be affected by an operation. Some P4 commands have names that look like they operate on files when, in fact, what they really do is allow you to define views. In particular:

- The P4 branch command lets you define a view that can be used for branching or comparison operations.

- The P4 label command lets you define a view that can limit the files to which a label may be applied.

- The P4 protect command lets you define views that limit access to the Perforce repository.

Note that in most GUI applications, including the Perforce GUIs, View is a menu choice that controls the application's windows. Thus, in the context of a Perforce GUI, the word *view* can mean either a window control or a file view.

"Open," "check out," "mark," "get," and "synchronize"

In most desktop environments, opening a file means launching an application to display and modify it. But to the Perforce Server, opening a file means marking it as a file you plan to modify and submit to the depot. It's no surprise that Perforce GUI menu choices labeled Open are confusing. Some Perforce GUIs (notably P4V) now use *check out* or *mark* instead of *open*.

But if you're familiar with other SCM systems, you may expect *check out* to mean getting copies of files to work on. Perforce's word for that is *synchronize*. Unless you're using P4V, that is, in which case it's *get*.

- The P4 sync command gets local copies of files from the depot and puts them in your workspace. (It *synchronizes* your workspace.)

- The P4 get command is an undocumented alias for sync.

- The P4 have command lists synchronized files.

- Synchronized files can be opened—that is, marked as files you're going to submit—with various P4 commands, including add, edit, and delete.

- The P4 opened command lists opened files.

"Spec"

The Perforce database contains objects that define things like users, workspaces, and so forth. In Perforce, *spec* is short for "specification of a database object." Many database objects can be created or modified by filling in Perforce-supplied *spec forms*. Sometimes a *spec form* is simply called a *spec*. Thus you'll often see expressions like "open up a spec" and "edit the spec" in Perforce documentation.

"Branch"

In the context of SCM, the word *branch* usually refers to either a single branched file or a set of branched files. In Perforce, however, there is a database object called a *branch* that is neither of those things. It is instead a view that may or may not be used in branching operations. Not surprisingly, this is extremely confusing to users. In this book, we have tried to be consistent about using *branch* as a noun only when referring to a set of branched files. We refer to the database object as a *branch view*.

- The P4 branch command does not branch files. Instead, it creates or updates a spec in which a branch view is defined.

- The P4 command that branches files is integrate.

- The P4 branches command does not list branched files. Instead, it lists branch views.

- The commands that list branched files are filelog and integrated.

"Label"

Similarly, the P4 label command does not label files. Instead, it creates or updates a Perforce database object called a *label* that defines a label name and a set of files to which the label *may* be applied.

If that's not confusing enough, the vestigial labelsync command is. In early versions of Perforce, there was no command that could simply apply a label to an arbitrary configuration of file revisions. The only configuration that could be labeled was the collection of files synchronized in a workspace. Hence the name labelsync was used for the command that did the labeling.

- Today, the P4 commands that label files are tag and labelsync.

- The command that synchronizes a workspace with a labeled file configuration is sync.

- The command that lists labeled files is files.

- Happily, the P4 labels command *does* list label names.

"Depot"

The master file repository maintained by the Perforce Server is referred to as the *depot*. At the option of a Perforce administrator, the repository can be subdivided into separate, named locations; these are also known as *depots*. In contexts where the distinction is important, this book refers to the latter as *named depots*.

- The P4 depot command defines a named depot.
- The depots command lists named depots.

"Integrate"

In Perforce, to *integrate* is to propagate changes from one collection of files into another. Changes can be *integrated* by copying or merging, or by simply recording the fact that they were intentionally ignored.

- The integrate command opens files in the workspace to prepare them for integrating.
- The resolve command merges or copies content into files opened for integrating.
- The integrated command lists integrated files that have been submitted.
- The integ and integed commands are aliases for integrate and integrated.

Outside of Perforce, the meaning of *integrate* is oh-so-subtly different, just different enough to be confusing. *To integrate* can mean to combine the work of individual development teams, or to absorb a development project into a production version of software. And *integrated* is often used to mean that separate software products can work together. Thus the meaning of a phrase like "integrated with Perforce" is entirely a matter of context.

Bibliography

Appleton, Brad, Stephen Berczuk, Ralph Cabrera, and Robert Orenstein. "Streamed Lines: Branching Patterns for Parallel Software Development." Paper presented at the PLoP '98 Conference Proceedings. *http://www.cmcrossroads.com/bradapp/acme/branching/*.

Appleton, Brad, Steve Konieczka, and Steve Berczuk. "Codeline Merging and Locking: Continuous Updates and Two-Phased Commits." *CM Crossroads* (November 2003). *http://www.cmcrossroads.com/articles/agilenov03.pdf*.

Berczuk, Steve. "Pragmatic Software Configuration Management." *IEEE Software Magazine* (March/April 2003). *http://www.berczuk.com/pubs/IEEESW_2003-03.pdf*.

Berczuk, Steve, and Brad Appleton. *Software Configuration Management Patterns: Effective Teamwork, Practical Integration*. Reading, MA: Addison Wesley, 2002.

Berczuk, Steve, Steve Konieczka, and Brad Appleton. "Patterns and Software Configuration Management." *CM Crossroads* (April 2004). *http://www.cmcrossroads.com/newsletter/articles/agileapr04.pdf*.

Bret, Tom. "Parallel Development Strategies for Software Configuration Management." *Methods & Tools* (Summer 2004). *http://www.methodsandtools.com/PDF/mt200402.pdf*.

Dart, Susan. *Configuration Management: The Missing Link in Web Engineering*. Norwood, MA: Artech House Publishers, 2000.

de Jonge, Merijn. "To Use or Be Reused; Techniques for Component Composition and Construction." *http://www.cs.uu.nl/~mdejonge/papers/ToReuseOrToBeReused.pdf*. Also "Package-based Software Development," by the same author.

Fogel, Karl, and Moshe Bar. *Open Source Development with CVS*. Phoenix, AZ: Paraglyph, 2003.

Hunt, Andrew, and David Thomas. *The Pragmatic Programmer: From Journeyman to Master*. Reading, MA: Addison Wesley, 1999.

Kenefick, Sean. *Real World Software Configuration Management*. Berkeley, CA: Apress, 2003.

Moreira, Mario. "ABCs of a Branching and Merging Strategy." *CM Crossroads* (November 2003). *http://www.cmcrossroads.com/newsletter/articles/mmnov03.pdf*.

Nakano, Russell. *Web Content Management: A Collaborative Approach*. Reading, MA: Addison Wesley, 2002.

RetroLogic Systems. "The Online Jargon File v 4.4.7." 2005. *http://www.retrologic. com/jargon-file.html*.

Sayko, Michael. "Merging Defect Fixes into the Development Codeline." *CM Crossroads* (November 2003). *http://www.cmcrossroads.com/articles/msnov03.pdf*.

Seiwald, Christopher. "Inter-File Branching: A Practical Method for Representing Variants." Paper presented at the Sixth International Workshop on Software Configuration Management (I-SCM6), Berlin, Germany, March 1996; in *Software Configuration Management: Selected Papers of the ICSE SCM-6 Workshop*. Edited by Ian Somerville. Berlin: Springer-Verlag, 1996: 67–75.

Smith, Tony. "P4Ruby—Programmers Guide." The Perforce Public Depot. *http:// public.perforce.com/guest/tony_smith/perforce/API/Ruby/main/doc/index.html*.

Thomas, David, and Andrew Hunt. *Programming Ruby: The Pragmatic Programmers' Guide*. Reading, MA: Addison Wesley Longman, 2001. *http://www. rubycentral.com/book/*.

———. *Pragmatic Version Control Using CVS*. The Pragmatic Bookshelf, 2004.

White, Brian A. *Software Configuration Management Strategies and Rational ClearCase: A Practical Introduction*. Reading, MA: Addison Wesley, 2000.

Williams, Hugh E., and David Lane. *Web Database Applications with PHP and MySQL*. Sebastopol, CA: O'Reilly Media, 2004.

Glossary

This glossary lists terms used in this book, and their meanings, as used in this book. Many of these terms have subtly different meanings elsewhere; that is the nature of the abstract and subjective language of software configuration management.

auto-resolve

Automatically resolving files in a batch. (As opposed to resolving them interactively, one by one.)

body of code

A mainline and all the codelines branched from it.

branch

A set of files evolving as a variant of another set of files. *To branch* is to clone a set of files so that it can be modified independently of its original.

branch view

An object in the Perforce database that can be used to store donor and target filespecs used in branching and other operations.

build

In SCM jargon, the result of building software from source files.

build tool

A program that converts source files into usable software.

changelist

In Perforce, a collection of files checked in together.

changelist number

The unique indentifier of a changelist. It is also a revision number that refers to a snapshot of the entire depot at the time the changelist was submitted.

cherry-picking

Integrating changes from one codeline into another in a way that skips over some of the changes in the donor codeline.

client spec

Perforce-speak for *client workspace specification*, the parameters that define your workspace.

client workspace

See *workspace*.

clone

Occasionally used in this book to mean copying one set of depot files to another.

codeline

A branch, but more particularly, a branch designated for a specific phase of software development or release. E.g., "the Release 1.0 codeline" is a collection of files branched in order to fix bugs and stabilize code for Release 1.0.

component

A part of a software product that can be built or used independently. A software product typically consists of one or more components.

configuration
In the context of labeling files, short for a configuration of files.

conflict
In the context of merging files, the case where files can't be combined automatically—someone has to intervene to edit or choose the usable result.

copy-integrate
To use the Perforce integrate and resolve commands to propagate changes by copying files instead of merging them.

delta
The part of a file that changed between versions.

depot
Generally, the Perforce repository where files are stored. However, the depot can be divided into named locations, each of which is also called a *depot*.

developer
(Or *software developer*.) Anyone whose work involves creating computer files from intellectual thought.

diff
Comparison of two text files showing the lines that are different. *To diff* files is to compare files. (This probably dates back to the first Unix diff tool.)

domain
Used in this book to mean a Perforce database, its associated repository, and the Perforce Servers configured to access them, collectively.

donor
Can be any collection of files—a codeline, a module within a codeline, a directory, or simply a file. The Perforce integrate command propagates change from the donor (also known as the *source* or *origin*) to a set of files called the *target*.

filespec
A Perforce syntax for referring to collections of directories, files, and revisions.

fix
Generally speaking, a change that corrects a defect. In the Perforce database

schema, a record that associates a job with a changelist.

GUI
Graphical user interface.

have list
Perforce jargon for the list of file revisions known to have been copied from the depot to a workspace.

head revision
The most recent revision—that is, the latest, newest, or tip revision.

hub
The machine on which the Perforce Server runs in a Perforce domain.

incremental integration
Integrating changes one changelist at a time, in order, from one codeline to another.

installer
A program that takes files from a release image and installs it on a machine for use. Usually one of the components of a software product.

integrate
In the context of Perforce operations, to propagate changes from one set of files into another.

integration records
Database records kept by Perforce that show the history of revisions integrated between files.

job
A type of database object in Perforce, used primarily to associate external information (like bug reports and change requests) with changelists.

label
A symbolic name applied to a set of files at specific revisions.

mainline
The main codeline.

mainline model
A model of software evolution where all branches can trace their lineage to a single, main codeline, and all changes are eventually merged into the main codeline.

merge

To merge files is to combine their content and produce a usable result file. To merge branches is to merge each of the files in one branch with its counterpart in the other. (With respect to branches, *merge* and *integrate* are used somewhat interchangeably in this book.)

metadata

Data describing data. In the context of SCM, data about files, users, workspaces, and other SCM objects.

module

A collection of directories and files that go together because all are needed on disk in order to do work on any one of them.

nightly build

An automated, regularly ocurring build of software in a particular codeline.

open files

In Perforce, the files you are working on and plan to submit to the depot.

overlay

In Perforce, to use a client view to map more than one depot file (or set of files) into a single workspace location. For example, a workspace can have a view of a codeline overlaid by a sparse branch.

parallel changes

Changes made in more than one branch, or one codeline, involving variants of the same set of files.

parent

The codeline from which a codeline was branched.

pending changelist

A collection of files you intend to submit together to the depot.

platform

In this book, synonymous with *operating system*.

point release

A re-release intended to fix bugs and add minor improvements to software previously released.

private branch

A codeline owned, used, and controlled by a single developer.

product

In the context of this book, a *software product*—the thing you are striving to develop and release.

protections

In Perforce, the mechanism that controls the files that users can access and the commands that they can run.

refactoring

Improving the logic of a software system, ideally without (but too often while) changing the outward behavior of the system.

release

A version of a product available for distribution.

release codeline

A codeline that contains code from which releases are built.

release image

The form a software product takes when it is released. Consists of directories and files organized in a certain way.

repository

Where the master copies of versioned files are stored. (See *depot*.)

resolve

To decide what to do with parallel changes to a file.

revision

An identifiable instance of a file or a collection of files that is unique in its evolution. In other words, each modification to a given file produces a new revision of the file. Each modification to any of the files in a collection of files produces a new revision of the file collection.

rolling label

A label that is reused (or rolled forward) as files change. For example, a label that is reapplied every week to tag the latest build configuration is a rolling build label.

safe auto-resolve

Automatically resolving files that don't require merging.

SCM

Software configuration management is the business of keeping track of files and procedures you use to build software so that you can (a) trace the origins of bugs in your software, (b) build better software faster, (c) build as many software versions as you need, and (d) tell what features and bugs are in each version.

scratch build

Building software from scratch; that is, building in a workspace newly populated with source files and nothing else.

shared codeline

A codeline to which more than one user may submit changes.

shrink-wrapped software

A software product that is released periodically in identifiable versions, often concurrently with previous releases of the product.

snapshot

The state of a collection of files at a particular point in time.

source files

The files created and updated by software developers, as opposed to the files generated and regenerated by build tools. (The difference can be subtle.)

sparse branch

A codeline that contains a small subset of its parent codeline's files.

spec

In Perforce, the user interface to many non-file objects in the database; also called a *spec form*.

staging codeline

A codeline that is reused for a specific stage of release testing.

stream

Another word for *codeline*.

structural changes

Changes that involve renaming, moving, or deleting files.

submit

Perforce's word for checking files in to the repository.

superuser

A user who can run privileged Perforce commands.

sync daemon

A background program or service that keeps a workspace synchronized.

synchronize

In Perforce, to bring a workspace up to date with a particular version of files in the depot; abbreviated as *sync*.

tag

To apply a label to a file.

target

The set of files created or updated in branching, renaming, or integration operations. (See also *donor*.)

task branch

A codeline used to temporarily isolate work on a single task.

third-party code

Files you get from a third party to use in developing your own software.

tofu scale

An informal assessment (soft, medium, or firm) of codeline stability and quality.

unresolved

Opened files that can't be submitted because they haven't been resolved yet. (See *resolve*.)

vendor drop

A version of third-party code placed in your repository.

version

In the context of a file or a collection of files, a *revision*. In the context of a release, the identifer of the release.

virtual modules

A module that appears to exist in a codeline by dint of a workspace view.

workspace

The area on your own computer where you work on Perforce-managed files.

Index

A

accept edited (ae) command, 60
accept merged (am) command, 60
accept theirs (at), 60
accept yours (ay) command, 60
access
    codelines, 204
    depots, 144–146
    domains, xv
    files, 144–146
        in other domains, 146–150
accuracy of merge detection, 214
active development streams, 178
active modules, 252
ad hoc branches, 179
ad hoc codelines, 275–281
add command, 33
adding files, 18
    to depots, 32
    detecting, 67
    preventing propagation, 116
addresses, 146
    servers, configuring, 309
ae (accept edited) command, 60
allocating disk space, 199
alternate merge tools, configuring, 83
am (accept merged) command, 60
annotate command, 12
annotations, release codelines, 241
Apache, 163
applications
    comm, 111
    distributed software, 149
    sort, 111

triggers, 161
version control, 163–166
Windows, version control, 165
applying
    branch views, 113
    jobs, 137–142
    labels, 129–136
    local files, 31–39
    P4FTP as sync daemons, 236
    third-party software, development
        codelines, 263–267
archiving rolling labels, 134
at (accept theirs) command, 60
auditing web content, 288
automatically resolving files, 53
automating continuous integration, 294
auto-resolve, 102
ay (accept yours) command, 60

B

backing out
    changes, 81
    recent changes, 47
Back-in-Time Browsing, 157
backporting bug fixes, 237
base
    integrating, 101
    unresolved files, 54
behind-the-scenes version control, 163–166
BETAMAIN codelines, 302
binary files, merging, 61
bits and pieces, synchronizing in, 27
bodies of code, 188
bookmarks, monitoring changes, 154

We'd like to hear your suggestions for improving our indexes. Send email to *index@oreilly.com*.

branch command, 113, 312
branch points
    label views for, 220
    labeling, 221
branch views, 87, 113, 313
    annotations, 241
    development codelines, 254
        updating, 265
    normalizing, 272
    release codelines, 219
    reversing, 115
    searching, 114
    updating, 225
branches command, 313
branching, x, 87, 313
    ad hoc branches, 179
    codelines, 201
    custom-code branches, 180
    development codelines, 171, 175, 251,
        255
        imported code to, 265
    files, 88
        comparing, 96
        creating, 89–96
        deleting, 92
        integrating changes, 96–112
        previewing, 92
        redoing, 93
        resolving, 100
        reverting, 92
        submitting, 93
        undoing, 93
        viewing, 94
        viewing histories, 95
    patch branches, creating, 246–248
    posting branches, 180
    private branches, 179, 275
        redeploying, 279–281
        reparenting, 277
    release codelines, 170, 174, 217
        branching, 218
        previewing, 220
    sparse branches, 179
    static modules, 253
    task branches, 178
        creating, 242–246
breaking up changelists, 112
browsing
    Back-in-Time Browsing, 157
    bookmarks, monitoring changes, 154
    depot files, 7–14
    (see also navigating file trees)

budgets, planning, xvi
bug fixes, 170
    backporting, 237
    codelines, 208–215
    and staging streams, 297–301
    task branches, 244
    tracking, 224
    (see also troubleshooting)
building release codelines, 231
built modules, 218, 253

C
case sensitivity, naming depots, 196
centralized repositories, xiii
changelist command, 311
changelists, x, 5–6
    additional, creating, 40
    breaking up, 112
    configurations, saving, 127
    content, 42
    descriptions, writing, 257
    integrating, 98
    jobs
        linking, 139
        marking as, 142
        searching numbers by, 142
    pending, 39–44
    resolving, 74
    submitting, 20, 76
    synchronizing, 74
    viewing, 9
changelists command, 311
changes, 5–6, 311
    backing out, 81
    branch to branch, integrating, 96–112
    checking, 225
    dependencies, hidden, 229
    descriptions, preparing, 271
    development codelines, integrating, 259,
        262
    documenting, 224
    flow of, 172
        task branches, 243
    local, merging new distributions, 266
    to the mainline model, 230
    monitoring, 152–157
    notification, 152–157
    out of order, integrating, 229
    parent codelines, integrating, 269
    preventing, 240
    propagation, 178
    resolving, 76

review daemons, 152
structural, reconciling, 112–117
task branches, integrating, 246
tracking, xi, 5–6
unintegrated, searching, 228
viewing, 111
changes command, 8, 27
changes -s pending command, 41
characters
    comparing, 65
    matching, 2
    special, 29–31
check in command, 311
check out command, 312
checking changes, 225
cherry-picking integration, 109
chunks, 62
client command, 202
clients, xi
    programmable, xiii
    specs, editing, 21
    workspaces, defining, 17
clients command, 24, 312
cloning directories, 34, 90
code
    bodies of, 188
    reviews, 277
Codeline.html files, 203
codelines, 87
    access, 204
    ad hoc, 275–281
    BETAMAIN, 302
    branching, 201
    containerizing, 188
    curators, 199
    defining, 23
    development
        applying third-party
            software, 263–267
        branch views, 254
        branching, 251, 255
        branching imported code to, 265
        creating, 249–255
        delivering, 267–275
        modifying branch views, 260
        naming, 251
        noncritical bugs, 298
        ownership, 251
        retiring, 275
        soft, 275–281
        updating, 258–263
        updating branch views, 265

updating workspaces, 271
    working in, 255–258
diagrams, 180
flow of change, 172
grouping, 192
mainline model, 169–181
    applying, 183–185
management
    bug fixes, 208–215
    maintenance, 199–205
    nightly builds, 205–208
    organizing depots, 189–199
modules, selecting, 200
naming, 200
one-way, 179
parent
    freezing, 270
    integrating changes, 269
    integrating development codelines
        into, 273
    thawing, 274
private, 275–281
proliferation, 196
relationships, 193
release
    annotations, 241
    backporting bug fixes, 237
    branch views, 219
    branching, 217
    branching modules, 218
    building, 231
    creating, 216–222, 231–234
    creating patch branches, 246–248
    creating task branches, 242–246
    distributing, 235–237
    generating note information, 234
    integrating into the mainline, 227–231
    labels, 232
    naming, 217
    ownership, 217
    previewing branching, 220
    pulling late-breaking developments
        into, 238
    releasing wrong builds, 236
    retiring, 240–242
    working in, 222–227
remote depot, 179
retiring, 205
third-party, 179
tracking, 203
types, 178
WEBENG, 288

codelines (*continued*)
   WEBVIS, 288, 289
   working in, 202
collaboration, customizing, 74–78
collections (files), 2
combining
   files
      detecting, 70
      reconciling, 118
   mappings, 23
comm program, 111
commands
   accept edited (ae), 60
   add, 33
   am (accept merged), 60
   annotate, 12
   at (accept theirs), 60
   ay (accept yours), 60
   branch, 113, 312
   branches, 313
   bug fixes, detecting merged, 211
   changelist, 311
   changelists, 311
   changes, 8, 27
   changes -s pending, 41
   check in, 311
   check out, 312
   client, 202
   clients, 24, 312
   counter, 153
   d (diff), 60
   delete, 33
   depots, 148, 314
   describe, 9, 154
   diff2, 231, 274
   dir, 33
   dirs, 8
   dt (diff theirs), 60
   dy (diff yours), 60
   edit (e), 60
   filelog, 104, 311
   files, 10
   find, 33
   fixes -i, 214
   Folder History, 96
   fstat, 157
   get, 312
   group, 197
   have, 312
   info, 24
   integ, 314
   integed, 314
   integrate, 35, 125, 314
      branching files, 90
   integrated, 314
   interchanges, 230
   job, 138
   jobs -i, 214
   jobspec, 137
   label, 312, 313
   labels, 233
   labelsync, 132
   mark, 312
   open, 312
   opened, 32, 312
   P4, 311–314
   print, 12
   protect, 312
   resolve, 43, 314
   resolved, 61
   revert, 39
   review, 153
   reviews, 154
   s (skip), 60
   submit, 42, 140, 311
      troubleshooting, 42
   sync, 26
   synchronize, 312
   tag, 132
   triggers, 161
   user, 153
comparing
   depots
      directories, 14
      files, 13
   files, branching, 96
   labels, 133
   snapshots, 128
   whitespace, 65
configuration
   additional changelists, 40
   alternate merge tools, 83
   branching, 89–96
   depots, 144
   development codelines, 249–255
   files, 17–20
   installation, xv
   jobs, 138
   master workspaces, 254
   P4, 82
   P4MERGE, 85
   patch branches, 246–248
   Perforce Server addresses, 309
   point releases, 232

release codelines, 216–222, 231–234
saving, 127–129
SCM, ix
spec depots, 150
task branches, 242–246
text environments, 305–310
workspaces, 17, 20–25
conflicts, 50, 62
connecting servers, 309
containerizing, 186–188
containers, filespecs as, 189
content
    changelists, 42
    files
        replacing and swapping, 36
        viewing, 12
    web
        auditing, 288
        executable, 289
        major web development projects, 302
        staging, 282–288
        visual content development, 288–297
continuous integration, automating, 294
controlling
    access to codelines, 204
    versions, 163–166
conventions, depot path naming, 194
copying
    depot files, 34
    donor files, 104
    files
        ignoring (theirs), 57
        resolving (theirs into yours), 55
    lazy, 93
    workspaces, skipping, 94
cost, xvi
counter command, 153
curators (codelines), 199
current workspaces
    configuring, 25
    labeling, 132
    naming, 24
    (see also workspaces)
custom-code branches, 180
customization
    collaboration, 74–78
    jobs, 138
    merging, 78–86
    P4Web URL syntax, 156
    triggers, 161
    workspace views, 22

D

d (diff) command, 60
daemons
    change review, 152
    sync, applying P4FTP as, 236
dates
    configurations, saving, 127
    filespecs, 5
    scripting, 159
db module, 253
decoding integration histories, 124
defining
    client workspaces, 17
    codelines, 23
    depots, 148
    modules, 23
delete command, 33
deleting
    depot files, 33
    empty pending changelists, 42
    files, 44–45
        branching, 92
        detecting, 68
        editing, 71
        preventing target files from being, 116
    jobs, 141
    labels, 135
delivering development codelines, 267–275
dependencies, hidden, 229
depot command, 314
depots, x
    access, 144–146
    creating, 144
    defining, 148
    directories, comparing, 14
    evolution, 92
    files
        adding, 18, 32
        browsing, 7–14
        cloning, 34
        comparing, 13
        deleting, 33, 44
        detecting that didn't come from, 29
        editing, 18
        modifying, 35
        renaming, 35
        submitting changes to, 19
        synchronizing, 18
        viewing previous changes, 27
    filespec syntax, 1–6
    hierarchies, 2, 191
    mirroring, 192

depots *(continued)*
  naming, 191
  organizing, 189–199
  paths
    naming conventions, 194
    subscribing as reviewers, 153
  remote, 148
  reorganizing, 198
  scope of, 191
  security, 145
  specs, restoring and saving, 150
  structures, reconciling changes, 66–74
depots command, 148
describe command, 9, 154
descriptions, writing changelist, 257
designating file types, 36
detection
  added files, 67
  combined files, 70
  deleted files, 68
  files
    depots, not from, 29
    missing, 28
  merged bug fixes, 211
  moved files, 70
  renamed files, 68
developer workspaces, 223
development
  active streams, 178
  distributed, 150
  software
    applying mainline model, 183–185
    mainline model, 169–181
    overview of, 167–169
  visual content, 288–297
development codelines, 251
  branch views, 254
    modifying, 260
    updating, 265
  branching, 171, 175, 251, 255
    imported codes to, 265
  creating, 249–255
  delivering, 267–275
  flow of change, 173
  noncritical bugs, 298
  ownership, 251
  parent codelines, integrating into, 273
  retiring, 275
  soft, 275–281
  sub-branches, 176
  third-party software, applying, 263–267
  updating, 258–263

working in, 255–258
  workspaces, updating, 271
diagrams
  codelines, 180
  flow, 183
diff (d) command, 60
diff theirs (dt) command, 60
diff yours (dy) command, 60
diff2 command, 231, 274
dir command, 33
directories
  cloning, 34, 90
  depots, 2
    comparing, 14
  files, 3
  listing, 8, 10
  mapping, 115
  moving, 35
  renaming, 35
  trees, adding, 33
dirs command, 8
disk space, allocating, 199
distributed development, 150
distributed software, 149
distribution
  FTP, 236
  importing, 266
  merging, 266
  release codelines, 235–237
  streams, 179
DIST-update workspace, 235
doc module, 253
documentation
  changes, 224
  web content, ix
domains
  access, xv
  depots, mirroring, 192
  extending, 151
  file access in other, 146–150
  switching, 147
donor files
  changes, ignoring, 107
  copying, 104
  merging, 103
drawing timelines, 180
dt (diff theirs) command, 60
dy (diff yours) command, 60

E

e (edit) command, 60

editing
  client specs, 21
  files, 18
    branching, 91
    deleting, 71
    integrating, 108
    moving, 70
    opening for, 31
    renaming, 72
    resolving parallel changes, 19
  overview of, 124
  synchronization, 28
empty pending changelists, deleting, 42
enforcing use of jobs, 296
evolution (of depots), 92
exclusive locking files, 297
executable web content, 289
existing files, modifying type of, 37
extensions
  domains, 151
  scripting languages, 160
external databases, xiv

F

false positives (bug fixes), 213
features of Perforce, xiii
fields
  jobs, 138
  Protections, tokens, 145
File menus, 59
File Transfer Protocol (FTP), 164
  distribution streams, 236
filelog command, 104, 311
filenames, wildcards, 2
files
  access, 144–146
    in other domains, 146–150
  adding, 18
    detecting, 67
    preventing propagation, 116
  branching, 88
    creating, 89–96
    integrating changes, 96–112
    previewing, 92
  changelists, moving, 41
  Codeline.html, 203
  collections, 2
  combining
    detecting, 70
    reconciling, 118

comparing, branching, 96
configuring, 17–20
content
  replacing and swapping, 36
  viewing, 12
deleting, 44–45
  branching, 92
  detecting, 68
depots, 2
  adding, 32
  browsing, 7–14
  cloning, 34
  comparing, 13
  deleting, 33, 44
  detecting that didn't come from, 29
  modifying, 35
  renaming, 35
  viewing previous changes, 27
  (see also depots)
directory trees, adding, 33
donor
  copying, 104
  ignoring, 107
  merging, 103
editing
  deleting, 71
  integrating, 108
  opening for, 31
  renaming, 72
  submitting changes to depots, 19
exclusive locking, 297
generated
  opening, 207
  storing, 195
  submitting, 207
histories, viewing, 10
hyperlinks, 155
labels, applying to, 129
listing, 10
local, applying, 31–39
locking, 36
merging
  forcing, 78
  troubleshooting, 76
  undoing, 80
moving, 35
  detecting, 70
neglected, integrating, 274
non-text, merging, 85
obliterating, 45

files *(continued)*
  opening, 38
    for branching, 89
    submitting, 42
  parallel changes, resolving, 19
  redoing branching, 93
  renaming, detecting, 68
  resolving, 43, 49–62
    automating, 53
    branching, 100
    copying, 55
    ignoring, 57
    interactively, 58–60
    merging, 58
    merging binary, 61
    redoing/undoing, 79
    synchronizing, 50–52
    variants, 54
    viewing, 61
    viewing unresolved files, 53
  restoring, 44–45
  reverting, 39, 81
    branching, 92
  rolling labels, archiving, 134
  saving, 13
  searching, 10
  split, reconciling, 118
  submitting, 39–44
    branching, 93
  targets, preventing deletion, 116
  text, merging, 62–66
  trees, navigating, 8
  triggers, 161
  types, xv, 15–16
    designating, 36
    modifying, 37
    reconciling changes, 73
  undoing branching, 93
  unresolved, listing, 44
  unsynchronized, listing, 26
  versions, 3
  viewing
    branching, 94
    histories (branching), 95
  workspaces
    detecting missing, 28
    filters, 256
    listing, 28
    replacing, 29
files command, 10
filespecs, x
  as containers, 189
  syntax, 1–6

filters, workspace files, 256
find command, 33
firewalls, xv
fixes
  bug fixes (see bug fixes)
  jobs, searching, 141
fixes -i command, 214
flow diagrams, 183
flow of change, 172
  task branches, 243
Folder History, 9, 96
forced merging, 78
forcing integration after a rollback, 301
formatting workspaces, 29–31
forms
  client specs, editing, 21
  spec, 20
    scripting, 159
free licenses, xvi
freezing parent codelines, 270
fstat command, 157
FTP (File Transfer Protocol), 164
  distribution streams, 236

G

generated files
  opening, 207
  storing, 195
  submitting, 207
generating release note information, 234
get command, 312
GoodBuild label, 133
graphical user interfaces (see GUIs)
group command, 197
groups, 146
  codelines, 192
gui module, 253
GUIs (graphical user interfaces), xi

H

have command, 312
help, 310
hidden dependencies, 229
hiding retired codelines, 241
hierarchies, depots, 2, 191
histories
  directories, listing, 8
  filelog command, 104
  files
    viewing, 10
    viewing branching, 95

Folder History, 9, 96
integration, 89
    decoding, 124
    undoing, 119
    viewing, 105
synchronization, 27
hyperlinks
    files, 155
    objects, 155

I

identifying points of completion, 269
ignoring donor file changes, 107
importing
    distributions, 266
    third-party software, 264
incrementally integrating changes, 97
info command, 24
installation, xv
    Perforce on Linux/Unix systems, 307
    Perforce on Mac OS X, 308
    Perforce on Windows, 306
integ command, 314
integed command, 314
integrate command, 35, 314
    branching files, 90
    syntax, 125
integrated command, 314
integration, 50, 87
    changelists, 98
    changes (see changes)
    cherry-picking, 109
    codeline changes in the
        mainline, 227–231
    continuous, automating, 294
    development codeline changes, 259, 262
    files, editing, 108
    histories, 89
        decoding, 124
        undoing, 119
        viewing, 105
    history, xi
    neglected files, 274
    overview of, 120–123
    parent codelines
        changes, 269
        development codelines, 273
    records, 213
    redoing, 119
    repeating, 99
    rollback, forcing after a, 301

subdirectories, 108
    task branch changes, 246
interactively resolving files, 58–60
interchangers, 123
interchanges command, 230
interfaces
    Back-in-Time Browsing, 157
    bookmarks, monitoring changes, 154
    GUIs, xi
    programmable, xiii

J

job command, 138
jobs, x
    applying, 137–142
    changelists, marking as, 142
    configurations, saving, 127–129
    creating, 138
    deleting, 141
    enforcing use of, 296
    linking, 139
    locking, 142
    overview of, 137
    pre-selecting, 140
    release codelines, generating note
        information, 234
    restoring, 141
    searching, 139
        changelists number by, 142
        fixes, 141
jobs -i command, 214
jobspec command, 137

L

label command, 312, 313
labels
    annotations, 241
    applying, 129–136
    branch points, 221
    comparing, 133
    configuration, saving, 127–129
    deleting, 135
    files, applying to, 129
    GoodBuild, 133
    need for, 131
    nightly builds (codelines), 208
    release codelines, 232
    rolling, 133
        archiving, 134
    searching, 133
    views, 135

labels (continued)
    views for branch points, 220
    web sites, rolling back published, 301
    workspaces, naming, 136
labels command, 233
labelsync command, 132
languages, scripting extensions, 160
lazy copying, 93
level of file access, configuring, 145
linage of codelines, 193
lines, merging moved, 64
linking
    files and objects, 155
    jobs, 139
Linux, installing Perforce on, 307
listing
    branch views, 114
    directories, 8, 10
    files, 10
        in workspaces, 28
    labels, 130
    unresolved files, 44
    unsynchronized files, 26
    workspaces, 24
local changes, merging new
            distributions, 266
local files, applying, 31–39
local syntax, 29–31
location of codelines, 193
locking
    files, 36, 297
    jobs, 142
    labels, 131
logical changelists, submitting, 76
lowercase, naming depots, 196

M

Mac OS X, installing Perforce on, 308
MAIN
    merging, 267
    workspaces, integrating changes, 228
mainline model, 169–181
    applying, 183–185
    changes to, 230
    codeline changes, integrating
            into, 227–231
    flow of change, 172
maintenance
    codelines, 199–205
    (see also bug fixes)
    (see also troubleshooting)

major web development projects, 302
management
    codelines
        bug fixes, 208–215
        maintenance, 199–205
        nightly builds, 205–208
        organizing depots, 189–199
    SCM, ix
mappings, 3
    combining, 23
    directories, 115
mark command, 312
marking
    changelists, jobs as, 142
    configurations, 127–129
marshalled output, 158
master workspaces, 201, 219
    creating, 254
    (see also workspaces)
matching wildcards, 2
menus, File, 59
merged bug fixes, detecting, 211
merging, 50
    alternate merge tools, configuring, 83
    customizing, 78–86
    distributions, 266
    donor files, 103
    files
        binary, 61
        non-text, 85
        resolving (theirs into yours), 58
        text, 62–66
        troubleshooting, 76
        undoing, 80
    forced, 78
    MAIN, 267
    moved lines, 64
    P4MERGE, configuring, 85
    preventing, 297
    text, 103
mirroring depots, 192
missing workspace files, detecting, 28
mixed case, naming depots, 196
models (mainline), 169–181
    applying, 183–185
    flow of change, 172
modifiers, types, 16
modifying
    backing out changes, 81
    branch views, development
            codelines, 260
    depots, reconciling changes, 66–74

files, 35
    reconciling type changes, 73
    types, 37
monitoring, 152–157
notification, 152–157
offline changes, reconciling, 46
recent changes, backing out, 47
modules
    active, 252
    built, 218, 253
    codelines, selecting, 200
    containerizing, 186
    db, 253
    defining, 23
    doc, 253
    gui, 253
    private, 252
    release codelines, branching, 218
    reshaping, 198
    static, 252
        branching, 253
    sub-modules, 188
    test, 253
    top-level, 187
    unneeded, 252
    utils, 253
    virtual, 252
    WebKeeper, 163
monitoring changes, 152–157
moved lines, merging, 64
moving files, 35
    from changelists, 41
    detecting, 70
multiple pending changelists, 41

N

naming, 146
    codelines, 200
    depots, 191
        path naming conventions, 194
    development codelines, 251
    files, renaming, 35
    release codelines, 217
    workspaces, 24, 136
navigating file trees, 8
neglected files, integrating, 274
NFS (networked file sharing), xiv
nightly builds (codelines), 205–208
noncritical bugs, 298
non-text files, merging, 85
normalizing branch views, 272

notification of changes, 152–157
numbers
    changelists, marking, 142
    pending changelists, submitting, 42

O

Object Database Connectivity (ODBC), 165
objects, hyperlinks, 155
obliterating files, 45
ODBC (Object Database Connectivity), 165
offline changes, reconciling, 46
one-way codelines, 179
open command, 312
opened command, 32, 312
opening
    exclusive locking files, 297
    files, 38
        for branching, 89
        editing, 31
        locking, 36
        submitting, 42
    generated files, 207
operating systems, xvi
order, integrating changes out of, 229
organizing depots, 189–199
out-of-sync workspaces, 52
output
    marshalled, 158
    tagged, 158
ownership
    depots, organizing, 197
    development codelines, 251
    release codelines, 217

P

P4
    changes, monitoring, 154
    commands, 311–314
    configuring, 82
P4FTP, applying as sync daemon, 236
P4MERGE, configuring, 82, 85
P4Web
    URL syntax, customizing, 156
    version control, 163
packaging streams, 179
parent codelines
    changes, integrating, 269
    development codelines, integrating
        into, 273
    flow of change between task branches
        and, 243

parent codelines (*continued*)
   freezing, 270
   thawing, 274
patch branches, 175
   creating, 246–248
paths, 146
   depot reviewer, subscribing as, 153
pending changelists, 19, 39–44
   numbered, submitting, 42
Perforce Proxy, 151
planning budgets, xvi
platforms, xvi
plug-ins, xiii, 165
point of completion, identifying, 269
point releases, creating, 232
points in time, branching from, 91
posting branches, 180
preparing change descriptions, 271
pre-selecting jobs, 140
preventing
   added files from propagating, 116
   changes, 240
   merging, 297
   target files from being deleted, 116
   unchanged files from being submitted, 40
   warnings, 117
previewing
   branching, release codelines, 220
   files, branching, 92
pricing, xvi
print command, 12
private branches, 179, 275
   redeploying, 279–281
   reparenting, 277
private codelines, 275–281
private modules, 252
process rules, xv
product distribution, xv
programmable interfaces, xiii
programs
   triggers, 161
   (see also applications)
proliferation, codeline, 196
propagation
   added files, preventing from, 116
   changes, 178
protect command, 312
protections
   codeline clutter, reducing, 197
   depots, 145
   retired codelines, hiding, 241

Protections field, tokens, 145
protocols (FTP), distribution streams, 236
publishing web sites
   rolling back, 299
   updates, 287

R

recent changes, backing out, 47
reconciling
   combined files, 118
   file type changes, 73
   offline changes, 46
   split files, 118
   structural changes, 66–74, 112–117
record integration, 213
redeploying private branches, 279–281
redoing
   files
     branching, 93
     resolved, 79
   integration, 119
reducing codeline clutter, 197
references (labels), need for, 131
relationships, codelines, 193
release codelines
   annotations, 241
   branch views, 219
   branching, 170, 174, 217
     previewing, 220
   bug fixes, backporting, 237
   building, 231
   changes, integrating into the
     mainline, 227–231
   creating, 216–222, 231–234
   distributing, 235–237
   flow of change, 172
   labels, 232
   late-breaking developments, pulling
     into, 238
   modules, branching, 218
   naming, 217
   ownership, 217
   patch branches, creating, 246–248
   retiring, 240–242
   task branches, creating, 242–246
   working in, 222–227
   wrong builds, releasing, 236
release cycles (web sites), 284
remote depots, 148, 179
removing (see deleting)

renaming
    directories, 35
    files
        detecting, 68
        editing, 72
reorganizing depots, 198
reparenting private branches, 277
repeating integrations, 99
replacing
    content, 36
    files, 29
repositories
    centralized, xiii
    (see also depots)
reshaping modules, 198
resolve command, 43, 314
resolved command, 61
resolving
    auto-resolve, 102
    changelists, 74
    changes, 76
    files, 43, 49–62
        automating, 53
        branching, 100
        copying, 55
        ignoring, 57
        interactively, 58–60
        merging, 58
        merging binary, 61
        redoing/undoing, 79
        synchronizing, 50–52
        variants, 54
        viewing, 61
        viewing unresolved files, 53
    parallel changes, 19
restoring
    configurations, 127–129
    files, 44–45
    jobs, 141
    specs, 150
retiring
    codelines, 205
    development codelines, 275
    release codelines, 240–242
reusing labels, 133
reversing branch views, 115
revert command, 39
reverting files, 39, 81
    branching, 92
review command, 153
reviewing
    change review daemons, 152
    code, 277

depot paths, subscribing to, 153
    task branch changes, 246
reviews command, 154
Revision Graph, 104
revisions, 28
    changelists, 5
    client specs, 21
    files, 3, 18
        branching, 91
        integrating, 108
        moving, 70
        opening fro editing, 31
        resolving parallel changes, 19
    overview of, 124
rolling back published web sites, 299
rolling labels, 133
    archiving, 134

S

s (skip) command, 60
saving
    configuration, 127–129
    files, 13
    specs, 150
scales, tofu, 176
scheduling files, resolving, 52
SCM (software configuration
            management), ix
scope of depots, 191
scripting, 157–163
searching
    branch views, 114
    files, 10
    jobs, 139
        changelist numbers by, 142
        fixes, 141
    labels, 130, 133
    unintegrated changes, 228
Secure Shell (SSH), xv
security
    depots, 145
    firewalls, xv
selecting modules in codelines, 200
servers, xi
    addresses, configuring, 309
    connecting, 309
    requirements, xiv
    scripts, troubleshooting, 160
    test environments, setting up, 305–310
shelving works in progress, 275
skip (s) command, 60
skipping workspace copying, 94

snapshots
  comparing, 128
  release codelines, 231
  workspaces, naming, 136
soft codelines, 275–281
software
  developers, ix
  development
    mainline model, 169–181, 183–185
    overview of, 167–169
  distributed, 149
  version control, 163–166
  (see also applications)
software configuration management (see
    SCM)
sort program, 111
spaces, comparing, 65
sparse branches, 179
spec forms, 20
  scripting, 159
special characters, 29–31
specs, 20, 313
  restoring, 150
  saving, 150
  scripting, 159
  triggers, 161
speed, xiii
split files, reconciling, 118
SSH (Secure Shell), xv
stabilization, 170
staging, 179
  streams (bug fixes and), 297–301
  web content, 282–288
static modules, 252
  branching, 253
storing generated files, 195
streams, 87
  active development, 178
  distribution, 179
    release codelines, 235
  FTP, 236
  packaging, 179
  staging, 179
    bug fixes and, 297–301
  WEBLIVE, 285
    rolling back, 301
  WEBMAIN, 284, 294
  WEBQA, 286
    bug fixes, 298
structural changes, reconciling, 112–117
structures, reconciling depot changes, 66–74
sub-branches, development codelines, 176

subdirectories, integrating, 108
submit command, 42, 140, 311
  troubleshooting, 42
submitting
  changelists, 20, 76
  files, 39–44
    branching, 93
  generated files, 207
  pending changelists, 39
    numbered, 42
sub-modules, 188
subscribing as depot path reviewers, 153
swapping file content, 36
switching
  domains, 147
  between workspaces, 25
sync command, 26
sync daemons, applying P4FTP as, 236
synchronization, 28
  changelists, 74
  files, resolving, 50–52
  histories, 27
  nightly builds, 206
  revisions, 28
  workspaces, 18, 26–29, 74
synchronize command, 312
syntax
  filespecs, 1–6
  integrate command, 125
  local, 29–31
  P4Web URL, customizing, 156
  scripting, 157–163

T

tabs, comparing, 65
tag command, 132
tagged output, 158
targets
  donor files
    copying, 104
    merging, 103
  files, preventing deletion of, 116
task branches, 178
  creating, 242–246
templates, customizing jobs, 138
terminology, 311–314
test environments, setting up, 305–310
testing web site updates, 286
tests module, 253
text
  files, 62–66
  merging, 103

thawing parent codelines, 274
theirs
  integrating, 101
  unresolved files, 54
third-party codelines, 179
third-party software
  development codelines, applying
    to, 263–267
  importing, 264
three-way merges, 62
tidy views, 190
Time-lapse View, 12
timelines
  drawing, 180
  task branches, 242
times
  filespecs, 5
  scripting, 159
timing web site updates, 287
tofu scale, 176
tokens, Protection field, 145
top-level modules, 187
tracking, 5–6
  bugs, 224
  changes, xi
  codelines, 203
trees
  branching, 88
    creating, 89–96
    integrating changes, 96–112
  directories, adding, 33
  files, navigating, 8
triggers command, 161
troubleshooting
  help, 310
  jobs, 141
  merged files, 76
  out-of-sync workspaces, 52
  scripts, 160
  submit command, 42
  versions, 170
  views, 221
tunnels, xv
types, 146
  codelines, 178
  files, xv, 15–16
    designating, 36
    modifying, 37
    reconciling changes, 73
  modifiers, 16

U

unchanged files, preventing from being
    submitted, 40
undoing
  files
    branching, 93
    merging, 80
    resolving, 79
  integration histories, 119
unintegrated changes, searching, 228
unique labels, archiving rolling labels
    with, 134
Unix, installing Perforce on, 307
unneeded modules, 252
unresolved files
  listing, 44
  viewing, 53
unsynchronized files, listing, 26
updating, 245
  branch views, 225
  development codelines, 258–263
    workspaces, 271
  task branches, 245
  web sites, 285
    publishing, 287
    release cycles, 284
    testing, 286
    timing, 287
  workspaces, 245
upgrading release codelines, branching
    from, 174
uppercase, naming depots, 196
user command, 153
utils module, 253

V

variants, unresolved files, 54
vendor drops, xv
versions
  control, 163–166
  files, 3
  release codelines, branching from, 174
  sync command, 26
  troubleshooting, 170
viewing
  changelists, 9, 42
  changes, 111
  depot files, 7–14

viewing *(continued)*
   files
      branching, 94
      content, 12
      histories, 10, 95
      resolving, 61
   integration histories, 105
   labels, 130
   previous file changes, 27
   unresolved files, 53
views, x, 3, 198
   branch, 87, 113, 313
      annotations, 241
      development codelines, 254
      modifying development codelines, 260
      normalizing, 272
      release codelines, 219
      reversing, 115
      searching, 114
      updating, 225
      updating development codelines, 265
   labels, 135, 220
   tidy, 190
   Time-lapse View, 12
   troubleshooting, 221
   workspaces, customizing, 22
virtual modules, 252
Virtual Private Network (see VPN)
visual content development, 288–297
VPN (Virtual Private Network), xv

W

warnings, preventing, 117
web content
   auditing, 288
   documentation, ix
   executable, 289
   major web development projects, 302
   staging, 282–288
   visual content development, 288–297
web sites
   release cycles, 284
   rolling back, 299
   updating, 285
      publishing, 287
      testing, 286
      timing, 287
WEBENG codeline, 288
WebKeeper module, 163
WEBLIVE stream, 285
   rolling back, 301
WEBMAIN stream, 284, 294

WEBQA stream, 286
   bug fixes, 298
WebReview, 162
WEBVIS codeline, 288, 289
whitespace, comparing, 65
wildcards, 2
   expansion, 29–31
Windows
   applications, version control, 165
   Perforce, installing on, 306
working in
   codelines, 202
   development codelines, 255–258
   release codelines, 222–227
works in progress, shelving, 275
WorkspaceCheck, 162
workspaces, x, 245
   configuring, 17, 20–25
      labeling, 132
   copying, skipping, 94
   developer's, 223
   development codelines, updating, 271
   DIST-update, 235
   files
      deleting, 44
      detecting missing, 28
      filters, 256
      listing, 28
      replacing, 29
      reverting, 81
   filespec syntax, 1–6
   formatting, 29–31
   listing, 24
   local files, applying, 31–39
   MAIN, integrating changes, 228
   master, 201, 219
      creating, 254
   naming, 24, 136
   nightly build, 205
   out-of-sync, 52
   reshaping modules, 198
   switching between, 25
   synchronizing, 18, 26–29, 74
   views
      customizing, 22
      reshaping modules, 198
writing changelist descriptions, 257

Y

yours
   integrating, 101
   unresolved files, 54

About the Author

Laura Wingerd is the vice president of product technology at Perforce Software. She divides her time between promoting sound software configuration management to Perforce's technical staff and promoting Perforce to the software development industry. She joined Perforce in 1997, just as the company moved out of the garage of its founder, Christopher Seiwald. She and Seiwald wrote "High-Level Best Practices in Software Configuration Management," a white paper widely referenced in books and articles. Prior to joining Perforce, Laura worked at Sybase, first developing a software build system for a skunk-works development project, and then orchestrating a massive conversion of a build system for core database and networking products.

Colophon

Our look is the result of reader comments, our own experimentation, and feedback from distribution channels. Distinctive covers complement our distinctive approach to technical topics, breathing personality and life into potentially dry subjects.

The animals on the cover of *Practical Perforce* are herring, of which there are over 200 species. In particular, the Atlantic herring (*Clupea harengus*) lives in the coastal waters off New England and can be found from Nova Scotia to Cape Cod.

Atlantic herring begin their lives as larvae measuring five to seven millimeters long. They emerge from an egg bed that can contain as many as seven million eggs. Tiny, scaleless, and transparent, they are weak swimmers and rely on a yolk sack for nourishment after hatching. Soon after the yolk is used up, they develop mouth parts that enable them to eat such prey as tiny plankton and the eggs and larvae of clams, shrimp, and barnacles.

The larval stage can last from 3 to 11 months (usually 6 months) depending on environmental factors such as water temperature and scarcity of food. Of the millions of eggs deposited by herring each year, it is estimated that only one percent will survive to be juvenile herring or "brits."

Usually around spring, the larvae grow into brits that look like smaller herring. Silvery blue-green scales begin to form, and their bodies grow thicker and flatter, measuring about 40 millimeters in length. At this time, the brits begin to form schools that migrate shoreward and toward the surface. The growth rates of brits are determined by the size of the school—a smaller population means the brits will grow bigger, while a crowded school means the fish will stay smaller. The brits feed on plankton at night near surface waters. They are also a virtual swimming buffet for such predators as mackerel, striped bass, puffins, and gulls. Brit schools often hide under docks and piers to escape predators.

At 3 to 4 years, brits grow into fully mature herring and measure 23 to 26 centimeters long. Some distinguishing features are a dorsal fin midway along the body and a saw-toothed keel located along the belly. Herring can live for 12 years and weigh up to 1.5 pounds. Adults migrate in schools, and in late summer and early fall they move toward the coastal waters of Maine to spawn. The spawning pattern moves from north to south, starting in the Bay of Fundy and moving to eastern Maine waters in late July and early August, or sometimes as late as November or even December.

Herring fertilize their eggs externally, with the female laying as many as 20,000 to 50,000 eggs (larger females can lay up to 200,000) that are then fertilized by the male with a substance called milt. Herring do not die after spawning but can continue to spawn for several years. Their sticky eggs sink to the ocean floor and collect in thick mats that will begin to hatch in 7 to 10 days.

Humans have fished herrings since as early as 240 A.D. and have used them both as a food source and as bait in lobster traps.

Adam Witwer was the production editor for *Practical Perforce*. Argosy Publishing provided production services. Sanders Kleinfeld and Claire Cloutier provided quality control.

Karen Montgomery designed the cover of this book, based on a series design by Edie Freedman, and produced the layout with Adobe InDesign CS using Adobe's ITC Garamond font. The cover image is from *Cassell's Natural History*.

David Futato designed the interior layout. This book was converted by Keith Fahlgren to FrameMaker 5.5.6 with a format conversion tool created by Erik Ray, Jason McIntosh, Neil Walls, and Mike Sierra that uses Perl and XML technologies. The text font is Linotype Birka; the heading font is Adobe Myriad Condensed; and the code font is LucasFont's TheSans Mono Condensed. The illustrations that appear in the book were produced by Robert Romano, Jessamyn Read, and Lesley Borash using Macromedia FreeHand MX and Adobe Photoshop CS. The tip and warning icons were drawn by Christopher Bing. This colophon was written by Jansen Fernald.

Better than e-books

Buy *Practical Perforce* and access the
digital edition FREE on Safari for 45 days.

Go to www.oreilly.com/go/safarienabled
and type in coupon code VFLK-WMZJ-XRLL-TBJJ-RBWM

Search
thousands of
top tech books

Download
whole chapters

Cut and Paste
code examples

Find
answers fast

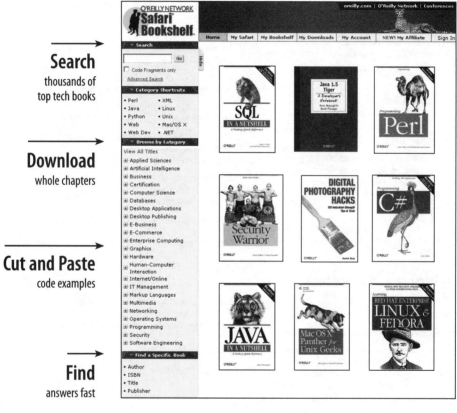

Search Safari! The premier electronic reference
library for programmers and IT professionals.

Keep in touch with O'Reilly

Download examples from our books

To find example files from a book, go to: *www.oreilly.com/catalog* select the book, and follow the "Examples" link.

Register your O'Reilly books

Register your book at *register.oreilly.com* Why register your books? Once you've registered your O'Reilly books you can:

- Win O'Reilly books, T-shirts or discount coupons in our monthly drawing.
- Get special offers available only to registered O'Reilly customers.
- Get catalogs announcing new books (US and UK only).
- Get email notification of new editions of the O'Reilly books you own.

Join our email lists

Sign up to get topic-specific email announcements of new books and conferences, special offers, and O'Reilly Network technology newsletters at:

elists.oreilly.com

It's easy to customize your free elists subscription so you'll get exactly the O'Reilly news you want.

Get the latest news, tips, and tools

www.oreilly.com

- "Top 100 Sites on the Web"—PC Magazine
- CIO Magazine's Web Business 50 Awards

Our web site contains a library of comprehensive product information (including book excerpts and tables of contents), downloadable software, background articles, interviews with technology leaders, links to relevant sites, book cover art, and more.

Work for O'Reilly

Check out our web site for current employment opportunities:

jobs.oreilly.com

Contact us

O'Reilly Media, Inc.
1005 Gravenstein Hwy North
Sebastopol, CA 95472 USA
Tel: 707-827-7000 or 800-998-9938
    (6am to 5pm PST)
Fax: 707-829-0104

Contact us by email

For answers to problems regarding your order or our products:
order@oreilly.com

To request a copy of our latest catalog:
catalog@oreilly.com

For book content technical questions or corrections: **booktech@oreilly.com**

For educational, library, government, and corporate sales: **corporate@oreilly.com**

To submit new book proposals to our editors and product managers:
proposals@oreilly.com

For information about our international distributors or translation queries:
international@oreilly.com

For information about academic use of O'Reilly books:
adoption@oreilly.com
or visit:
academic.oreilly.com

For a list of our distributors outside of North America check out:
international.oreilly.com/distributors.html

Order a book online

www.oreilly.com/order_new

Our books are available at most retail and online bookstores.
To order direct: 1-800-998-9938 • *order@oreilly.com* • *www.oreilly.com*
Online editions of most O'Reilly titles are available by subscription at *safari.oreilly.com*